Praise for the First Edition of *Babysense*

"I am a family practitioner who has used your book both as a resource for my own two children and in my patient-education library. I would like to express my appreciation and gratitude for your effort in putting together a book which I have found to be the most comprehensive and practical of its type."

—Kathleen McAuliffe, M.D., Portland, OR

"Babysense has been a baby bible for us."

—Gail and Mike Hill, Calgary, Alberta, Canada

"It has been below zero for the last three days, and I have not set foot outside of this house. . . . We have no bread, milk, or butter. I can't get to the store because it is too cold to take the baby out, and I can't get a sitter to come here. As you can imagine, I am feeling housebound and frustrated. I opened *Babysense* and by chance read "Getting Control of Your Time and Your Life" and "The Transition into Motherhood." I laughed and cried. I identified with every woman's comments. I feel sane again. I have regained my sense of humor and perspective. In reading *Babysense,* I no longer feel isolated and alone. In fact, I feel very much as if someone has put her arms around me and given me a great big, warm, supportive hug. Thank you!"

—Mary Summerbell, Janesville, WI

"I am an obstetrical nurse with a ten-month-old of my own. *Babysense* is one of the best childcare, family-care books I've read. It's a real source of comfort to me personally. I've begun recommending it to postpartum ladies because it is so full of warmth and good ideas."

—Susan Mitchell, Asheville, NC

"I have indeed found *Babysense* to be a useful and supportive book. [It] serves as a grandmother, with the very important difference that this grandmother gives you a whole panorama of advice, instead of looking disapprovingly when you don't follow her."

—Hephzibah Berman, Haifa, Israel

"A move across country following the birth pulled my support system out from under me. No family, no friends, no doctor! *Babysense* and its many contributors became my new support system. I took comfort knowing many of my feelings were shared by others."

—Kari Burke, Whitby, Ontario, Canada

"Just last night I had my husband read the chapter 'The Transition into Motherhood' to help explain to him how I've been feeling lately. What you wrote described my feelings, and the comments of the parents were right on the mark. Unlike many other baby-care books, yours truly is supportive."

—Lucy Becker, Aimes, IA

"I have an eleven-month-old baby boy and am a pediatric clinical nurse specialist. When Eric was born, however, everything I had learned from years of school and experience seemed to fly out the window. *Babysense* has been an invaluable source of comfort, reassurance, support, and information. I have recommended it to all my friends who are expecting or are new mothers, and have given it as a gift."

—Nancy Ilgenfritz, Atlanta, GA

"I want to thank you for such an informative book. I've turned to it many times for reassurance and have recommended it to all my friends. My husband thanks you; my mother-in-law thanks you; and my friends thank you. You have helped many mothers with this book."

—Suzanne Welhouse, Appleton, WI

"Babysense gives down-to-earth suggestions and answered most of the questions that I have encountered."

—Doris Tallyn, Windber, PA

"Let's face it, we all need and want help, guidance, and understanding, and where better to get it than from other mothers?"

—Katie and Bob Lewicki, Reynoldsburg, OH

"The practical information was terrific, but the real value to me was the emotional support. Knowing that other parents feel uncertain, confused, and have even sometimes felt that they have made a terrible mistake to have a baby is so comforting. My friend is pregnant, and I bought her *Babysense.* She loves it, but reads it and laughs. I told her 'Just you wait!'"

—Kathy Waterbury, Cupertino, CA

"Our staff at Oceanside Public Library reviewed *Babysense* and think it is excellent. It answers the questions that we are constantly asked by young mothers."

—Helen Nelson, Oceanside, CA

"I've found other books, but none of them has been so helpful or has given me the feeling of having someone there to answer questions."

—Claudia Roedl, U.S. Army, Germany

"I do want you to know how much *Babysense* touched me. It got me started examining my experiences and my feelings."

—Beverly Lecroy, Benton, AR

"In my opinion *Babysense* has replaced Dr. Spock tenfold, and from now on it's the only baby gift I'm giving. You have taken the emotions of new parenthood and combined them with the information we need."

—Jackie Greenfield, Harcourt, IN

"After reading *Babysense*, I can now see I was trying to keep up the pretense of my prebaby style. And I feel I never had time to start being Mom. After reading your chapter 'The Transition into Motherhood,' I don't feel so alone or hurt anymore."

—Linda Frommer, San Pablo, CA

"The most significant reaction I had was one of relief that I was normal. Parenthood includes pain with joy, and many other people have felt the very same feelings I have."

—Ann Barraclough, South Laguna, CA

"*Babysense* gave me a sense of 'unity' instead of feeling like a lone survivor on a deserted island!"

—Karen Reidinger, Shamokin, PA

"It's a marvelous guide for the nuts and bolts of parenting."

—Barbara Posner, Pound Ridge, NY

"You have a gift for reaching other mothers' hearts."

—Jan McManus, Cincinnati, OH

"When I was pregnant I looked at your book and thought, 'How funny!' Now that I have an eight-month-old, I literally take refuge in it."

—Isabel Beisterfeld, St. Louis, MO

"Enclosed you will find my voluminous response to your questionnaire. I hope you get as much out of reading it as I did writing it!"

—Nelda Summers Richards, Indianapolis, IN

"*Babysense* is a welcome change from the basic child-care book, which is rather dry and dictatorial. It's interesting. I received your book as a gift from my former boss, who is not only a confirmed bachelor but panics when he gets near a baby. He simply picked it off a shelf. I am eternally grateful to him."

—Dabney J. Bankert, Ferndale, MI

"*Babysense* makes the perfect baby-shower gift."

—Arlene Slingerland, Cranford, NJ

"The section on parent-support groups has helped me crystallize my intentions to design similar workshops. I am a clinical psychologist and want to incorporate my interests in child development, psychology, and teaching as I raise my own son. This is an ideal way for me to do so."

—Diane Roscioli, Souderton, PA

"So many books only concern themselves with the baby's achievements from month to month, but *Babysense* cares about parents as well."

—Randi Kulik, East Windsor, NY

"I have thanked my mother time and again because she borrowed a copy of *Babysense* from a co-worker while I was pregnant. I found it so helpful that I immediately went out and reserved two copies at the local bookstore for myself and a friend who was expecting six weeks after me. We spent many lunch periods talking about different chapters. How often we commented, 'I'm so glad she wrote about this!' and 'I never would have thought about that!'"

—Paula J. Campbell, Erasmus, PA

"Although I have purchased and read several books relating to baby care, pregnancy, etc., this is the first time I have been compelled to write to an author. I must give you greatest thanks for the chapter on postpartum. We're also using your book to select a baby backpack carrier and a high chair as well. With supergrandma back at work and Daddy leaving each morning, I must give you my greatest thanks. You have, in my mind, surpassed your goal of providing a 'practical and supportive guide to baby care.'"

—Muriel Morse, Pasadena, CA

"My son is almost five months old now, but for the first month he slept at the foot of my bed, and *Babysense* stayed open on my night table. I use the book all the time."

—Laura Smith, Honolulu, HI

·Babysense·

ALSO BY FRANCES WELLS BURCK

Mothers Talking: Sharing the Secret

·Babysense·

A Practical and Supportive Guide to Baby Care

Written by Frances Wells Burck
with the help of more than 500 parents

Illustrations by Diana Thewlis

ST. MARTIN'S PRESS · NEW YORK

Grateful acknowledgment is made by the publisher for permission to reprint the following materials:

"About Men: A Case of Colic," by Joel Berman. Copyright © 1987 by The New York Times Company. Reprinted by permission.

(Credits are continued on page 306)

Design by Janet Tingey

Library of Congress Cataloging-in-Publication Data

Burck, Frances Wells.
     Babysense: a practical and supportive guide to baby care/Frances Wells Burck.—[New rev. ed.]
        p. cm.
     Rev. ed. of: Baby sense, c1979.
     Includes index.
     ISBN 0–312–05055–0 ISBN 0–312–05056–9 (pbk.)
     1. Infants—Care. I. Burck, Frances Wells. Baby sense.
II. Title.
RJ61.B948 1991
649'.122—dc20   90–19119
                                       CIP

Second Edition: March 1991

10 9 8 7 6 5 4 3 2 1

For Caitlin, My First

• CONTENTS •

• ACKNOWLEDGMENTS •

Everyone who has contributed ideas, information, experiences, and feelings is thanked in the back of this book, but the following people have offered a special kind of help. I thank David Outerbridge for his vision and his love of books, and for helping me in myriad ways to organize and translate a foggy idea into a reality. My agents, Susan and Bob Lescher, have shared their high standards, fine judgment, and encouragement. Barbara Anderson at St. Martin's has patiently guided me with meticulous editing, tact, and good cheer through both editions. Her assistant, Marian Lizzi, deserves a word of thanks as well. Phyllis Silverman and Lorraine Roccissano have welcomed me to tape their mother/infant discussion groups, which provided many of the voices in this book. Drs. Irwin Rappaport, Harriet Hudson, and Doug Puder, the pediatricians in my life, have answered many questions on baby care. Eugene Schwartz, Nancy Hentila, Diane Sirois, Lynn Holsapple, Lisa Reitnaur Morris, Sarah Ratcliff, Zadie Lawler, and Arthur Cunningham have brought special gifts in their teaching and nurturing of my daughters when I was writing. The following friends, all mothers whom I admire and wonderful listeners, have been available when I needed them: Martha Krance, Katherine Stoessel, Anita Shreve, Stephanie Ratcliff, Julie Palmer, Diane Churchill, Lisa McMullin, and Meredith Hughes. My loving and patient husband, Charlie, besides sharing his deftness as a fair but critical reader and editor, has been nothing short of heroic in his support. Without my daughters, Caitlin, Abigail, and Georgianna, the lights of my life, there would be no book. Besides providing me with the richest of subjects, they continue to teach me daily about the joys and challenges of motherhood.

· PREFACE ·

This edition of *Babysense* has far fewer quotes from established baby-care authors than the original edition and many more from parents. In the two years it has taken to revise the book, I have seen so much more clearly than ever before that parents, because of their concern and commitment, and because of the sheer number of hours they spend with their babies, are the true experts. This is a parent-to-parent book. It is a celebration of what parents know. That is the most important message *Babysense* has to offer.

• • •

As soon as I delivered the manuscript for the first edition of *Babysense* in 1978, I knew that I wanted to add more. By the time it was published nine months later, I'd already collected several more questionnaires and a folder full of new information. I envisioned a revised edition in two or three years. Instead, more than a decade has passed. The baby who inspired the book is now an adolescent and is baby-sitting for other people's children. What happened?

I had two more babies and kept saying to myself, "Just let me get out from under, and then I'll return to *Babysense.*" Having three children in six years was challenging, however. I was swamped. Dealing with night waking, sibling rivalry, toilet training, ear infections, and chicken pox; starting a cooperative nursery school; finding child care; helping with homework; participating in car pools and PTA meetings; getting ready for summer camp; not to mention orchestrating the intricacies of my children's social lives—all took their toll of time and emotional energy. Because I had moved from the city to the suburbs and left my support network behind, I was also busy making new friends.

While I was indeed waylaid by the genuine busyness of my life, I would not be honest if I didn't admit to procrastination as well when it came to revising the book. When I finally had time to write again, I was out of the baby stage and could not help looking back wistfully at the first year of my first child, Caitlin's, life and remembering it as one of relative peace and tranquility. At that point, Caitlin was just heading toward puberty, and I asked myself, "What was so pressing about her infancy that compelled me to write a book? That was duck soup compared to this. I need help *now!*" Instead of returning to *Babysense*, I found a new network through *Mothers Talking*, a book of interviews with women about the challenges and rewards of motherhood.

And so a decade passed.

In retrospect, I think the passage of these years has been good for me and for the book. I've had three babies, who have taught me to be more sensitive to their individual differences in temperament and to see how strongly such differences can influence one's perception of infancy. Besides having more experience and confidence in myself as a mother, I have also had the benefit of interviewing hundreds of new parents and have heard from many more who have taken the time to fill out the questionnaire in the back of the book.

It is to these parents that I owe the most. I may have been out of the baby stage myself, but they weren't, and they wanted to talk. When I finally immersed myself in the revision and began to listen to their taped interviews, to read their questionnaires, and to go over my own journals, I was right back there, too.

I see myself, a dazed young woman, still tender

from childbirth, getting out of the car with my brand-new baby. She is wrapped in a white blanket, with one fist up against her cheek. She has little beads of sweat like dew on her brow and is sleeping on that sultry August morning in New York. A few neighbors have gathered on my steps to meet her. They are smiling and excited. Annie, from across the street, has brought a piece of linen handwork that she has cross-stitched for the baby's dresser. Pete, the foreman of the glass business next door, bends over Caitlin and strokes her tiny, clenched fingers. "The hands are yours," he tells me as he carries my suitcase up the steps. Charlie, wearing a red polka-dot bow tie, is laden with flowers and a shopping bag of gifts. He follows to unlock the door. Before I climb the steps, I catch a fleeting glimpse of myself in the car window and am stunned by the image of myself holding a baby. Then I turn and climb the stairs. Smiling and trembling, I cross the threshold of what I sensed even then was the beginning of the rest of my life.

Everyone who has a baby has shared that moment. It takes time for all of us to catch up with what it means. New parents have told me, "Giving birth turned who I was inside out and upside down." "I've changed species." And, most often, "Is there something wrong with me because I find being the mother of this baby so hard?"

What do we do when we feel this way? We buy books, convinced that what we need to quell the anxiety, and feel more in control, is to have an authority tell us what to do. But that isn't the only solution.

As I became more mobile, I began to meet other new parents in the park. They willingly shared a wealth of information and advice. As we talked, I realized that I was starting to feel differently about motherhood. It wasn't only the sheer practical help that they offered, but also their humanness, that made me feel better. It takes time to see this because each of us is afraid to reveal our vulnerability to the other. At first, we want to show only our competence: Everything is fine. Things are running smoothly. Having a baby is no big deal. But we know better.

With time and trust, I began to see these other women as multidimensional, real people. They too were burdened by the sheer logistics of baby care. It had taken them an hour to get out the door to come to the park. Their laundry wasn't folded, and they weren't making gourmet dinners for spouses and friends. Some of them weren't even speaking to their spouses (which in the late 1970s usually meant "husbands"). They too were experiencing the roller coaster of emotions: the excitement, love, joy, fear, anger, and confusion that accompany the biggest transition we will ever make in our lives. As we nursed and rocked our babies, we bemoaned our fate. We asked ourselves, "What have we done?" The responsibility and the commitment of having a baby had shaken us to the core.

On our park benches we confirmed for each other the simplest, but most basic, lesson: Just because everyone has children and has been having them for millennia doesn't mean it's not a big deal. HAVING A BABY IS A BIG DEAL! And the amount of support (and respect) that we need and deserve is commensurate with the magnitude of that deal. Where can we get that support?

The best source is each other. When we know that others have been through it before us, and are moving along through it right at this moment, then we are not alone. This makes all the difference. It isn't simply that other new parents can help us feel better about our doubts and our mistakes. They can also help confirm our expertise, a reassurance we need in this time of fundamental change.

I want to thank all of the parents who contributed to this book. Writing about parenting is a major responsibility, and I take it very seriously. I worry. Can I give shape and voice to the wealth of material that has come my way? As the manuscript deadline approached, I barely noticed that spring had come and gone. I was not truly present as a mother, and the irony of my absence did not escape me. There was rarely clean laundry, and two birthday celebrations were postponed. My daughters, who microwaved TV dinners and frozen pizza, were bringing *me* sandwiches and cups of tea. They made their own brownies for the PTA bake sale. Caitlin, to whom this book is dedicated, helped the younger two with their homework.

The very last thing I did for this revised edition was to type up the list of new contributors, readers who have written to me over the years. As I did so, I was overcome with emotion. In offering their experiences, each one was not only giving back by sharing a part of herself, but also saying "thank you" for making this book, so that she could find herself within it. I knew my work was worthwhile.

Having children has changed me and so has writing *Babysense.* Just as one forgets about the pain of childbirth when it is over, I have already forgotten about the most burdensome aspects of this project and see it as the privilege that it truly has been. Writing is solitary work. So it is a wonderful and rare experience to know your readership as intimately as I feel I know mine and to have benefited so directly from their help and appreciation. Thank you, all.

• INTRODUCTION •

I hope *Babysense* is the book I needed when our first child was born—a book that is practical as well as supportive. I say "hope" rather tentatively because I will never again be a first-time parent. I have tried very hard not to forget how that felt, but those early weeks and months are only a memory now, a vivid pastiche of highs and lows, joys, discoveries, great tenderness—and some horrors. Though I am no longer a brand-new parent, it's more than likely that you are, with a baby who is either in your arms or in your thoughts during most of your waking hours. Each baby brings his or her joys and challenges, but never again will one be quite so consuming, so nerve-racking, or so memorable as the first—because you are so "new" together.

When I look back over the first year of my first daughter's life, I realize there is a great deal I know now that I wish I'd known then. This is true for all of us. Much of parenting in our complex world is an art that can be learned only through experience. We do not know how to be parents from instinct.

Some mastery of the practical and the logistical—learning how to bathe a newborn, prepare a day's supply of formula, find and assess good medical care, and so on—is essential both to the baby and the parent on the most basic physical level. Knowing that you are not alone in your feelings can truly make a difference in terms of psychological survival. It is both these types of knowledge—about our babies' needs and our own—that frees us to know them, love them, and above all enjoy them without the distortions fostered by feelings of inadequacy.

My husband and I spent a lot of time reinventing the wheel—working out solutions to problems that had been worked out before by countless other parents. We were just too isolated to know any better. This is the biggest problem most new parents face. A lucky few will have a friend with a slightly older baby who has already lived through a particular growth stage and has some suggestions. More frequently we found that when our first daughter was an infant, our friends had children already walking and talking or they had no children at all. The few parents we knew had forgotten the moment of getting their newborn to burp, or keeping an eight-month-old from climbing out of the high chair. They had forgotten the nerve-fraying bone weariness of coping with months of night waking and the terror of the first high fever. So instead of turning to friends for advice and support, we had to rely on books and on our busy pediatrician.

A generation or two ago a new parent was not quite so alone as we were in the beginning. Many women—sisters, aunts, cousins, grandmothers, former schoolmates, the large family living next door—and perhaps a general practitioner who knew the whole family well, made up a kind of extended family or network. They supplied the information and expertise and the much-needed extra pair of hands to give direction and help to a new mother. Most of us today have moved from the places we grew up in and can't rely on this informal grapevine to tell us whether the baby is too hot, too cold, or suffering from prickly heat and not roseola. Many of us have also had to adjust to smaller budgets after we had a baby and to living in cramped spaces. We can afford to buy and store only a few of the most essential pieces of equipment, and to make matters more complicated, there is more "stuff" (and aggressive marketing of it) available than ever before.

We have new concerns, too—ones that did not exist in the past. Many of us are older than our mothers were when they gave birth to their first child. We may have worked for several years or have established ourselves in jobs or careers that we must now balance with motherhood. Roles within marriages have changed, too. We feel we must structure our time and share the work of family life without being swallowed up by it. Equally intimidating is the sophisticated body of knowledge on infancy, the myriad theories, and the "expert" opinions, which often complicate our lives by forcing us to make even more choices.

The more we know, the more responsibility we feel we must assume for the well-being of our children. While my grandmother dealt with the cruel reality of infant mortality, for example, she did not have to worry about the quantity of additives in the food she fed her children or fret about the best car safety restraint and how to install it. She certainly never considered the logistics of taking a baby on a business trip, nor did she regard my grandfather as competent and able to enjoy taking care of any of their babies' physical needs. She didn't know (though she may well have intuited) that within hours after birth, the newborn begins to show a preference for increasingly complex visual stimuli.

Babysense explores these concerns. Above all, it is a practical book. The practical side of baby care is presented as simply as possible. Our babies must be well nourished, healthy, and comfortable. The book covers feeding, from making the decision to breast- or bottle-feed and the basics of nutrition, to helping the baby toward independence through self-feeding. This is not a medical manual, but it does describe how to find good health care and some of the basics, such as

how to take a baby's temperature, administer medicine, and know when to call the doctor. The book covers how to make your baby's environment safe. It also contains information on making the baby comfortable: how to deal with crying, sleep, and mealtimes as well as how to bathe and dress the baby in easy-to-care-for clothing. *Babysense* has a comprehensive section on mobility—from simply getting out the door to traveling around the world on airplanes. Any parent with a baby has to evaluate the vast amount of equipment on the market. *Babysense* will help readers to make time-, money-, and space-saving choices and to meet both the baby's and the parents' needs.

Beyond the purely practical, *Babysense* is about how babies grow and learn. As the baby progresses from reaching, turning over, creeping, and sitting to crawling, standing, and finally walking, there are many challenges and rewards as well as frustrations for the infant and the parents along the way. *Babysense* offers parents worried about "understimulating" their babies information about development and appropriate toys and games. It also reassures parents that despite our own inexperience, our babies flourish simply by being cared for by loving and interested parents.

When Caitlin, my first daughter, was an infant, I bought several baby-care books but had little time to read them all. Many of them were very authoritative and prescriptive. What I really needed and wanted was *one* book that was practical and supportive—that would make me feel less alone. I wanted to read about parents who were *real* people rather than the shadowy composites that hover in the background of much of the literature on infancy.

Unlike most baby-care books, *Babysense* is about new parents as well as their babies. Living with a baby involves so many adjustments. Most

of us start with misconceptions—or no conception—about what these changes will entail. Caring for a baby makes tremendous demands on our time, our relationships, our work, and our interests. This book recognizes and identifies these changes and provides support and practical suggestions whenever possible. There are just as many how-tos for parents as there are for babies.

The most important aspect of *Babysense* is that it is largely the product of people who live with babies. When I did begin to meet other parents, mainly mothers with whom I could share my experiences, discoveries, questions, and, above all, my feelings, my life became much easier. Other parents are an invaluable source of information and support. Knowing them has been a tremendously reassuring and enriching experience for me, and it is what made me decide to write this book. I have tried to convey much of this "grapevine" information as well as the generous and honest spirit with which it was given. Though we couldn't be without the experts, and I certainly rely on them—the pediatricians, infant researchers and psychologists, nutritionists, manufacturers of baby-care products, and the consumer advocates—parents are the ultimate experts. They are the ones who are truly responsible for and make the tremendous emotional investment in their babies. There is clearly no more knowledgeable a group when it comes to the day-in, day-out care of a baby. And who is better equipped than parent experts at providing a realistic picture of what life with a baby is like? We know, and we speak the truth.

To reach many of my parent contributors, I developed a questionnaire. The last question was, "Do you know any new parents who might be willing to fill out this questionnaire?" The answers led me to many, many more parents. These completed questionnaires, as well as the many mother-infant discussion groups I participated in over the last decade, form the backbone of my material. Many of the quotes in the book come from these taped sessions. I have also conducted hundreds of informal interviews with just about every woman I met with a baby in supermarkets, department stores, parks, restaurants, airports, and doctors' offices. There isn't anyone I talked to who didn't share some "babysense" and make a contribution to this book. I should add that I interviewed and quoted myself and my husband as well. I did not change our names.

Though I have not devoted specific chapters to single parenthood, adoption, twins, and premature babies, you will hear voices concerned with these topics scattered throughout the book. There are mothers from their teens to their mid-forties, married and single, from all over the United States and Canada and some foreign countries. There are mothers who stay at home full-time and those with jobs and careers. Most of the mothers in this book are first-time mothers, but not all of them.

There are fathers in *Babysense*, but not many. With few exceptions, fathers did not answer my questionnaire even though they were invited to. It is not that fathers don't care passionately for their children and take care of them more and more. They do. I celebrate this phenomenon. Everyone benefits when the joy as well as the work is shared. Why? Because care begets love, attachment, and intimacy, which are the foundations of self-esteem. Fathers, however, don't seem to be communicators—yet—about baby care the way mothers are.

I must also confess that when I originally wrote *Babysense* more than a decade ago, I asked my husband to write a chapter on fathers. He did. I lost it. He wasn't annoyed as much as perplexed. Then he generously offered to rewrite the chapter from his notes. I lost that, too. I've since puzzled over it. Did I not like what he wrote? As I recall, the chapter was well written and straightforward, though brief. There was no angst in it, however, whereas the rest of the book somehow reflected struggle, not only on my part but also on the parts of the women contributors.

Now that I have some perspective, I understand that having a child had changed me so profoundly that I had to write a book about it in order to understand the complexity of the experience. It was *women* who helped me to do this, who shared their feelings and their hard-won information, and offered their support. What can I say? My husband's chapter just didn't fit into the book. *Babysense* is a book by women on baby care. As fathers take an increasingly greater part in their children's infancy, they, too, will pen books. In fact, there already are some very good ones by fathers, and I refer you to them on page 148.

If you wish, you can make *Babysense* a more personal and fun book to read by using the baby record-keeping section that begins on page 271. It seems appropriate, in a book written largely by parents, that there should be a place for you to make notes about your baby's early life as well as your feelings. I urge you to do this. Your child's babyhood is so fleeting, and I know from my own experience that s/he *will* ask you what s/he was like as a baby. What did s/he do that was funny, and what were her/his first words? Where was s/he when s/he took her first step? And did she really spit her peas all over Aunt Martha?

Dear Reader,

    There is one other thing you can do if you like. Babies have a way of inspiring us to pass along what has been of use to us. Keep a running list of your own tips and suggestions for baby care on page 302. Include that along with the answers to the questionnaire in the back, and send it to me care of St. Martin's Press. (Be sure to keep a copy for yourself!) Share your hard-won expertise and help me to keep *Babysense* alive and up-to-date. I want it to be in print for your children and mine when they take on the most difficult and rewarding job there is. Surely they will need all the "babysense" they can get. Don't we all?

Best wishes, Frances

Frances Wells Burck
c/o St. Martin's Press
175 Fifth Avenue
New York, N.Y. 10010

PART ONE

Waiting and Getting Acquainted with Your Newborn

• CHAPTER 1 •

Waiting

You're in your last month of pregnancy and weigh more than you ever have in your entire life. From your amplitude, it's apparent to everyone that you are on the verge of becoming someone's mother. You may notice other women looking at you and smiling warmly. You sense that they want to talk to you, and sometimes they do. They want to know, "Is this your first baby?" They wish you luck. They remember. Even though they are strangers, they know something significant about you and share your excitement. They haven't forgotten what a luxurious abstraction that yet-to-be-born baby is, or the miracle she or he will soon become. Maybe that is why they smile so knowingly.

People who have children have asked, "Are you ready?" They may also have tactfully (or not so tactfully) hinted that your life will change dramatically. They make what sound to you like ridiculous, bizarre suggestions: "Have dinner at all the best restaurants." "Go to every movie you have ever wanted to see." "Waste an entire afternoon window shopping." "Take a joyride at midnight." "Ride the Orient Express." "Read novels." "Stay in bed until noon." "Take a two-hour bub-

ble bath." "Daydream." "Love each other." "Do nothing." "Do everything." And "Get your husband to sign a child-care-household division-of-responsibilities contract!"

But there's hardly room in your stomach for an expensive dinner, and you're not up for snails in garlic sauce. Can you sit through a two-and-a-half hour movie without making six trips to the ladies' room? Window-shopping might be fun, but your back and feet hurt. As for staying in bed until noon or taking a two-hour bubble bath—these things are just too self-indulgent and boring. Reading novels is a possibility, but the house is so dirty. You suddenly can't tolerate dirt, disorder, or anything that suggests incompletion. And you wouldn't consider asking your husband what his intentions are regarding child care. You are two mature people who love and respect each other. Together you made this decision to have a child, and together you will stand by it.

The one thing you are able to do is daydream—about the birth itself, once months away, now only weeks, or perhaps days that can be counted. Maybe you have even reached the point where you are mumbling under your breath, "I've had

enough! Just get this baby out!" Yet another part of you is frightened and wishes to keep that baby inside of you forever. What will they do to me in the hospital? What will childbirth be like? Will I be able to handle the pain? Will I make a fool of myself, and so what if I do! And of course, uppermost in your mind is the question: Will the baby be okay?

You try to imagine what it will be like to hold your baby in your arms, to care for it, and to be connected—forever—but you can't. The birth is what is important now, and you return to that event, which seems so much more concrete and immediate than what comes next—the reality of a living, breathing infant of your own.

But those parents giving all that strange-sounding advice are trying to tell you something: Having a baby is going to change your life like nothing else ever has before. The most immediate and direct effect will be on your time. To put it bluntly, there won't be much of it, at least not during the early weeks and months. The people who say "indulge yourself now" are only remembering what it was like once they had a baby. An entire day could pass where they hardly had time

Childbirth Education

If you are interested in childbirth preparation, the following organization can put you in touch with classes in your area:

International Childbirth Education
    Association (ICEA)
Post Office Box 20048
Minneapolis, MN 55420
(612) 854-8660

This volunteer organization brings together persons interested in family-centered maternity and infant care.

All Parents Should Know About . . .

Parent Action (A Division of The Family
    Resource Coalition)
230 North Michigan
Suite 1625
Chicago, IL 50601

For $5, parents can join this group, whose goal is to fight for laws and policies that will help families.

to go to the bathroom, much less take a shower, make a bed, or wash a single dish. Within a week or two of your baby's birth, you'll realize that sleeping late is not an indulgence, but rather a luxury that ranks right up there with drifting through the Vale of Kashmir on a houseboat.

So put yourself on the top of the list of special people to be cared for NOW. Pursue the luxuries, and savor this time, the last "before children" (or B.C.) moments—as they will never come to you again. At the same time, you can start to deal with the necessities of the near future. One of the reasons that you will not have much time is that the logistics of child care impinge more broadly on your life than you'd ever think possible. The difficulty of the early weeks in particular can mount in inverse proportion to parents' preparedness. You may not need a written contract with your husband, but you surely need to discuss the demands that will be made on his time, because you are both going to need all the support you can get.

In myriad other ways you need to organize yourself. You must get supplies as well as services for the baby. If you have felt superstitious about having baby items in your house before you give birth, rise above that. It's time to prepare for the possibility that there *may* indeed be a baby.

Goods and Services to Obtain and Arrange Before You Give Birth

What You Need for the Baby
- ❏ First and foremost, a pediatrician, family practitioner, nurse practitioner, or a clinic before the baby is born! (See pages 223–26 for suggestions.)
- ❏ Don't wait until you hear "it's a boy!" to decide about circumcision. (See page 226.)
- ❏ A car seat if you drive. (See pages 198–201.)

The first time you will use this is on your trip home from the hospital.
- ❏ Enough baby clothing so that you need do the laundry only every other day. (See pages 120–122 for suggestions.)
- ❏ A system for doing the laundry. If you don't have your own washer and dryer and will be using coin-operated machines, you should have a full week's worth of baby clothes, since leaving the house to wash clothes can be a mind-boggling task at first. If you are considering a washing machine and don't own one yet, buy it immediately!
- ❏ Regarding diapers, you should have four to six dozen on hand, plus a diaper pail, if you plan to use your own cloth diapers. (See pages 124–27 for suggestions on diapers and supplies.)
- ❏ If you will be using a diaper service, contact those in your area for the best prices and choose one. You might want to have the first week's supply delivered in advance, so that you don't have to think about making contact again.
- ❏ One or two boxes of newborn-size disposable diapers, whether or not you use cloth.
- ❏ A place to store clothing, and a changing table. (See page 123 for suggestions.)
- ❏ A place for the baby to sleep and some bedding.
- ❏ Bottle-feeding equipment if you will bottle-feed. (See page 56.)
- ❏ Toiletries for the baby: powder or cornstarch, lotion, diaper-rash medication, and nail scissors.
- ❏ Two pacifiers. (See page 93.)
- ❏ A well-stocked medicine cabinet. (See page 235.)
- ❏ Optional: A rocking chair or hammock are useful options for soothing the baby and relaxing a parent, and so is a sling, front pack car-

rier (page 194), infant swing (page 97), and infant seat (page 193).

❏ Optional: an intercom.

What You Need to Do for Yourself

❏ Preregister at the hospital to shorten your admission time. It can also be reassuring and comforting to have had a tour of the hospital where you will give birth, to see a labor, birthing, and/or delivery room, and to know what private and semiprivate rooms look like. You might also inquire about rooming-in, an arrangement in which the baby spends a good deal of time with you, rather than in the nursery. (See Rooming-In, an Option To Keep in Perspective, page 8.)

❏ If you are interested in learning infant CPR, first aid, how to bathe a baby, breast-feeding basics, etc., late pregnancy is a good time to begin. Find out about such programs through your doctor, childbirth-preparation instructor, local hospital, community college, or Red Cross. The La Leche League welcomes pregnant women in their discussion groups. (See page 23 for information on how to get in touch with them.) All of these group activities are good ways to meet other new parents.

❏ Most of the preparations we make before the baby is born have to do with goods and services. If you have never stayed at home before, scout your community for other mothers. Friends are a mother's mainstay. Once you have a baby, it may be weeks or months before you will have time to be "outgoing," but these early weeks and months are the time when contacts can be the most reassuring. See if your community has a mothers' center or other kinds of parent support programs. You may not want to attend such a group immediately, but it is reassuring to know what resources are available. (See page 154.)

❏ Arrange for help. Have ready either a husband, relative, friend, or paid worker to help at home so that you can concentrate on taking care of your baby. Some people prefer to have this kind of help a few days or even weeks *after* they arrive home from the hospital. (It is then that the house begins to show signs of neglect.) This way they've had a chance to settle in alone without having to think about anyone but the baby. (See Planning for Your Arrival Home from the Hospital on page 6.)

❏ Have enough staples in the house to last for at least two weeks. If you are really organized, you can prepare meals in advance and freeze them. (Even if your husband cooks, he'll be tired and busy too.) Have plenty of high-protein convenience foods, healthy snacks, and juice on hand. Consider using paper goods to cut down on dish washing.

❏ If you plan to breast-feed, you'll need two or three comfortable nursing bras, plus a box of nursing pads. Be sure to look over the breast-feeding section of this book for suggestions on buying bras and preparing your nipples in advance. (See Chapter 3.)

❏ Think about the services in your community that can be helpful, such as grocery stores, drugstores, or restaurants that deliver, as well as household cleaning services or an older baby-sitter with a car.

❏ Firm up plans for your maternity leave if you are working. (Read the chapter on working and child care, page 181.)

❏ Pack your suitcase. (See below.)

❏ Prepare your pet. (See page 216.)

Packing Your Suitcase for the Hospital

Take a larger suitcase than you think you will need. You'll want extra room to bring home gifts as well as to pack the following:

❏ *Babysense: A Practical and Supportive Guide to Baby Care.*

❏ Two or three short nightgowns, with long front openings if you plan to nurse. Don't take anything fancy, because it will probably get bloodstained.

❏ A robe.

❏ Slippers.

❏ At least six pairs of underpants.

❏ Two or three nursing bras if you plan to nurse. (See page 26 for how to select one.)

❏ Toothbrush, toothpaste, shampoo, lotion, your own soap and soap box, hand mirror, makeup, and other toiletries.

❏ Address/phone book.

❏ Stationery, stamps, birth announcements, envelopes.

❏ Something to wear home in which you feel thin and elegant.

❏ Something for the baby to wear home.

❏ A receiving blanket.

❏ Your favorite magazine or book to read.

❏ One pacifier. (See page 93).

❏ Lamaze Bag. If you have taken a class, your instructor may have suggested that you bring along a special bag containing such things as Chapstick, lollipops, tennis balls, ice packs, and a washcloth as well as a watch or digital clock with second hand to time contractions. In a separate brown bag, include a high-protein, high-energy snack for Dad, who will probably get hungry during your labor. These items should not go in your suitcase, which will be put away in a locker or in your room.

❏ Lots of change for the pay phone, coffee machine, etc.

❏ Your insurance card or number.

❏ *Note:* On page 296 is a space to make a master list of all the things you need to do and buy before the birth of your baby.

Your Rights As a Patient

In recent years hospitals have become more and more supportive of the needs of the new mother, the new father, and the baby. It never hurts, however, to know in advance that as an obstetric patient, you do have certain rights. The following guidelines have been drawn up by the American Hospital Association. They may not be posted in your hospital, so keep this handy.

The pregnant patient has the right to participate in decisions involving her well-being and that of her unborn child, unless there is a clear-cut medical emergency that prevents her participation. The pregnant patient, because she represents *two* patients rather than one, should be recognized as having the additional rights below.

1. The pregnant patient has the right, prior to the administration of any drug or procedure, to be informed by the health professional caring for her of any potential direct or indirect effects, risks, or hazards to herself or her unborn or newborn infant that may result from the use of a drug or procedure prescribed for or administered to her during pregnancy, labor, birth, or lactation.

2. The pregnant patient has the right, prior to the administration of any drug, to be informed of the brand name and generic name of the drug in order that she may advise the health professional of any past adverse reaction to the drug.

3. The pregnant patient has the right to determine for herself, without pressure from her attendant, whether she will accept the risks inherent in the proposed therapy or refuse a drug or procedure.

4. She has the right to know the name and qualifications of the individual administering any medication or procedure to her during labor or birth.

5. She has the right to be informed, prior to the administration of any procedure, whether that procedure is being administered to her for her or her baby's benefit (medically indicated) or as an elective procedure (for convenience, teaching purposes, or research).

6. She has the right to be accompanied during the stress of labor and birth by someone she cares for and to whom she looks for emotional comfort and encouragement.

7. She has the right to have her baby cared for by her bedside if her baby is normal and to feed her baby according to her baby's needs rather than according to the hospital's regimen.

8. She has the right to be informed if there is any known or indicated aspect of her or her baby's care or condition that may cause her or her baby later difficulty or problems.

9. She has the right to have her baby's hospital medical records be complete, accurate, and legible and to have these records, including nurses' notes, and to receive a copy upon payment of a reasonable fee and without incurring the expense of retaining an attorney.

P.S. The following advice may be hard to follow, but at least consider it: It's very tempting to use your entire hospital stay to whoop it up and celebrate your baby's birth. After all, you are relieved, proud, and excited. But try to keep the phone calls and visitors within reasonable limits, or you will run the risk of becoming overly tired—and miss the opportunity to take advantage of the education and support that the postpartum care staff has to offer. The first days of your baby's life are a special time to become acquainted in an environment where both of your needs can be attended. This kind of rest and care is like money in the bank toward the days and nights that are to come. Don't squander it.

Planning for Your Arrival Home from the Hospital

Whether you hire a baby nurse or a *doula,* who takes care of you (see page 9), or have a friend, sister, or mother come to help out is an individual matter. Just make sure that this is the right person in the sense that she or he is neither obtrusive nor domineering—or, just the opposite, someone who needs a lot of direction and would demand too much of your precious time and thought, which would be better spent on your new family. One of the best arrangements can be having a person who comes in every day for a couple of hours and takes care of whatever needs to be done—practically without you telling them.

If you are relying on a stranger for help, it's best to interview in advance and go over—to the letter—what the person's responsibilities will be. Mothers elaborate on what worked—and didn't work—for them:

It was very important to me to have a little time at home with just my baby and my husband before my mother came to help. I suppose I felt I wanted to work things out my way so that my mother wouldn't take over. I also wanted it to be a special private time for the three of us. When my mother did come, four or five days later, I enjoyed it very much. She was tremendously helpful.

• • •

My baby was born early, and I had a long hospital stay. It was a very tense time for my husband and me. I wanted to get home with Annie but dreaded what I would find there in terms of the chaos and dirt. As a surprise, three wonderful neighbors had come in and cleaned. It was May. I can remember walking up the front steps, my arms full of Annie in a pink checked blanket, and waiting for Jim to come with the suitcase and unlock the door. When we went in, I was hit by the scent of lilacs. Besides leaving my house in perfect order, they'd left vases and vases full of lilacs.

• • •

I took my sister's advice and tried to spread my visitors out over the first couple of weeks. After Kim went back to work, I really enjoyed some adult company for a little while every day. My sister had said that after the first week of visitors, she was totally alone, and this is when she began to get depressed.

• • •

I had too much help. My mother as well as my mother-in-law. Too many houseguests at the same time. Too many cooks!

• • •

I hired a woman to come in three hours a day to cook dinner, buy groceries, keep the house in order, and do the laundry. This was the perfect solution. I didn't want someone there all day because I wanted to be alone with the baby, but I was happy to have her company and help for part of the day.

• • •

My parents gave us a present of a baby nurse for two weeks, but we ended up letting her go after a week, mainly because I felt she was irritating. Having to deal with her was causing me tension, which I didn't need. I really wanted to be taking care of Birch myself. She was not helpful as far as the cooking and the laundry went. She ate dinner with us, which made dinners unpleasant because she was a nonstop talker and had opinions on everything from the price of beans to the Common Market.

Ostensibly she supported breast-feeding, but she kept pushing a schedule. Kim also overheard her talking to the baby about the relief bottle of formula as "the good stuff." I will say, though, that it was helpful having someone around who knew what to do. She did show me how to put on a double diaper and seemed to know about dressing him so that he was neither too warm nor too cold. But all in all, I would rather have had a book for this information and a little help with the housework on a daily basis.

• • •

Peter stayed home for a week. The three of us spent most of the time lying in our king-sized bed, cuddling, snoozing, and dreaming. Peter did the cooking, cleaning, and shopping, which I think eventually wore him out. By the end of the week, he admitted that he was feeling a little as if I was the queen and he the servant. He was happy to get back to work in that sense. His life had changed just as dramatically as mine. In retrospect, I think he too needed some attention and care.

• • •

I had a two-year-old and needed help with her more than anything else, so that I could rest and attach to the new baby. I couldn't find anyone to help and ended up hiring two young teenage girls who were cousins, Jackie and Monique. They were absolutely great! They worked as a team.

Building a Parenting Library

Most of the books recommended in *Babysense*'s resource sections deal either with babies or specific subjects. The following are books you can turn to for support, inspiration, and guidance throughout your baby's childhood.

Briggs, Dorothy Corkille, *Your Child's Self-Esteem: The Key to His Life* (New York: Doubleday, 1970)

Burck, Frances Wells, *Mothers Talking: Sharing the Secret* (New York: St. Martin's Press, Inc., 1987)

Fraiberg, Selma, *The Magic Years: Understanding and Handling the Problems of Early Childhood* (New York: Scribner's, 1984)

Galinsky, Ellen, *Between Generations: The Six Stages of Parenthood* (New York: Times Books, 1981)

Kelly, Marguerite, and Parsons, Ella S., *The Mother's Almanac* (New York: Doubleday, 1975)

Pearce, Joseph Chilton, *The Magical Child* (New York: Bantam Books, 1980)

Theroux, Phyllis, *Night Lights: Bedtime Stories for Parents in the Dark* (New York: Viking, 1987)

Rooming-In: An Option to Keep in Perspective

Rooming-in used to mean that mother and baby could spend the daytime, other than visiting hours, together in the mother's hospital room. At night the baby slept in the nursery. Mothers had the option of deciding whether they wanted the baby brought for feedings at regular "hospital intervals" or on demand. This arrangement, besides fostering closeness and contact between mother and infant, has proved particularly good for new nursing mothers who need to feed on demand in order to establish their milk supply.

Now many hospitals offer "full-time rooming-in," which means that the baby can stay with the mother all day, with the exception of visiting hours, and all night. This kind of arrangement can give you a taste of what life with a baby is really like. But don't be a martyr if you really need to sleep, a mother of four advises:

Remember that when you sign up for full rooming-in, this is not written in stone. You can change your mind! You don't have to be a purist and a martyr. If you are too tired, day or night, and the baby is screaming, you can send her back to the nursery and get some sleep. If one night you ask that the baby be brought on demand for feeding, you can change your mind the next night, and that's fine, too. Play it by ear. Be flexible.

My roommate delivered a 9-pound boy after a twenty-six-hour labor and was so sore and exhausted that she was crying with fatigue. Yet she wouldn't let herself off the hook because she had made a commitment to full-time rooming-in. What if her milk supply wasn't large enough? What if she didn't bond fully with the baby? What about the woman across the hall who had twins in her room twenty-four hours a day? What if the nursery staff thought she was a bad mother? I said to her, "Playing the marytr is bound to cause resentment toward your baby, maybe not consciously, but subconsciously. Give yourself a break. Take what you need now for yourself because those nice nurses aren't going to be standing outside your bedroom door at 3:30 A.M. next week to offer you relief."

Age-Old Helpers

Husbands, mothers, mothers-in-law, sisters, friends, neighbors, or even an official registered baby nurse aren't always available. Nor are they necessarily the most suitable helpers for a new mother. Consider the following:

The Visiting Nurse Association

This worthy organization started in 1885 with a mission to ensure the survival of infants and children by providing mothers with milk and health-care information. The VNA is still eager to share its expertise. Call toll-free (1-800-426-2547) for referrals to the Visiting Nurse Association in your community.

They took turns watching Abigail and doing the household chores such as making the beds, washing the dishes, emptying the garbage, washing the clothes and putting them away, and even some light cooking. This was perfect. They were thrilled to earn the money and have the responsibility. They had each other for company, my child was well taken care of, and I could devote myself to the baby.

• • •

I had an idealized picture of sharing this very special time after childbirth with my own mother, but the fact is that we have never gotten along. Whatever made me think this would be a good time to have her visit? When we brought Phillip home, I longed for nurturing for myself. But all she could do was show me what poor mothering I had had, which was infuriating.

• • •

I had a doula, a woman who is trained specifically to care for new mothers. I found Louise through an ad in a community newspaper for parents. She came every day for three hours and was wonderful. She was able to counsel me on breast-feeding, nutrition, and on how to take care of the baby. She showed me how to bathe and burp him. My nipples were sore and engorged, and she did useful things like bring me hot compresses and pillows to help position him properly. I was very teary, and she was so compassionate. Jeremy is four months old now. I think of Louise often and the worthwhile service she performs.

• • •

With twins you must have help, help, and then more help! You need an extra pair of arms to hold and to comfort, or to feed during fussy times. You need moral support, and someone to help you get organized and keep track of who ate when or had a bath or a bowel movement—and to keep track of when you eat, too! You need another human being to remind you that your whole life isn't babies, babies, babies, even though it seems that way. I also needed help taking them to see the pediatrician. My husband wasn't available because he is in the merchant marine and had to ship out when Emily and Martha were only four days old. Fortunately my mother lives nearby, and so does my younger sister, who is in nursing school. They took shifts helping with the babies, the house, and the shopping for the first two weeks, and that really got me through. Later I hired a high-school girl to come in every afternoon for an hour or two.

• CHAPTER 2 •

Getting Acquainted with Your Newborn

What Happens Once the Baby Is Born

No book, movie, doctor, or other parent can truly prepare you for the actual moment of your child's birth. It is a deeply personal experience, and every birth is different. For some it is the highest and most joyful moment in their lives. For others childbirth is a quiet and peaceful experience, where the baby slips rather than bursts forth into life. Or the overriding feelings may be ones of sheer relief and exhaustion. For some parents the birth feels anticlimactic, confusing, disappointing, or frightening if there are complications. But in the midst of the action and the jumble of feelings, it is reassuring to know what to expect and to be familiar with the events and procedures taking place.

The second your baby is born, he will make the miraculous transition from total dependency on the life-sustaining forces of your body to living on his own. Prior to birth, the rich placenta has supplied him with nutrients and oxygen. Once he is out of the womb's warm and nourishing environment, the first priority will be to help him breathe. The doctor or a nurse will suction mucus from his nose and mouth. Within seconds his overall condition will be observed. (See Newborn Tests and Exams, pages 12–13.) Then he will be wrapped in a blanket for warmth. Some doctors place the baby on the mother's abdomen before clamping and cutting the umbilical cord. Before you and the baby leave the delivery room, you will each receive matching identification bracelets with your name on them. The baby's footprint may also be recorded.

Immediately after birth is a good time to hold the baby, not only to confirm his existence, but also to begin the process of "bonding" or attaching. During the first hour after birth the baby is more likely to be in what researchers call a "quiet alert" phase than later, when he will sleep deeply and be difficult to rouse. Some women also nurse the baby for the first time on the delivery table.

The term *bonding* came into wide usage in the mid-1970s when Drs. Marshall Klaus and John Kennel published *Maternal-Infant Bonding.* The doctors cited many studies that appeared to show long-term benefits from early maternal-infant contact so long as the contact took place during a critical period, the hour right after birth.

Though the legitimacy of some of their research has been questioned, the overall impact of their work has been beneficial. Birthing and hospital procedures are more flexible and family centered as a result.

We may wish for the ideal of bonding on the delivery table, but its significance has grown out of proportion. Many women unable to share this intimate moment have felt a powerful sense of loss and guilt that eroded their self-image as mothers. If you are not able to make immediate eye-to-eye, skin-to-skin contact with your baby—if you are too exhausted or in too much pain, if you've had a cesarean, or the baby has to go directly to a neonatal intensive care unit—you may feel a legitimate sense of disappointment. Let yourself feel it clearly, but without guilt. Then don't dwell on it. Any experienced mother will agree that the way we attach to our babies is a long, complex, and mysterious process. Attachment occurs moment by moment with each of the small yet significant thoughts and gestures that go into a baby's love and care. Infancy is only the beginning of a rich relationship that extends for a lifetime.

Newborn Tests and Exams

Before your baby has left the hospital, he will probably have received three physical exams and a number of routine tests designed to assess his health and well-being.

Apgar Test. Named after its originator, Dr. Virginia Apgar, the Apgar test is designed to measure five specific indicators of how the baby is adjusting to life outside the womb: heart rate, respiratory effort, muscle tone, response to stimuli, and skin color. Once the baby is delivered and breathing properly, a delivery-room nurse usually makes this evaluation twice, once at one minute after birth and then again at five minutes. Sometimes a third evaluation is made at fifteen minutes. The nurse assigns a rating of 0, 1, or 2 to each of the five categories. The highest possible score is 10, generally very rare at the one-minute test, where 8 is the most common score. By five minutes, the baby's score is generally up to 9 or 10. A lower score does not necessarily mean that there is a significant problem.

PKU Screening. This is a routine test in which a small amount of blood is taken from the baby's heel to screen for phenylketonuria, a rare abnormality of protein metabolism that if left untreated causes brain damage and retardation. A change in diet, if begun immediately after birth, allows a PKU victim to lead a normal life.

Thyroid Function. A small amount of blood is taken from the baby's heel to detect hypothyroidism (which used to be called "cretinism"), or the underproduction of certain hormones essential for normal mental and physical development. If the condition exists, doctors begin hormone treatment immediately to prevent physical stunting and mental retardation. This test is now required in many states.

Additional Blood Tests. The baby may also be tested for galactosemia, an abnormality in blood-sugar metabolism, and sickle cell disease. If the mother has type O and/or Rh-negative blood and her baby has a different blood type, the baby will get a Coombs test in which a small amount of blood is taken from the umbilical cord to determine whether the hemolytic antibody, which destroys red blood cells, is present. A positive result alerts doctors that Rh sensitization has occurred.

Hearing Test. A hearing test may be administered for several reasons: 1) if the baby weighs less than 3½ pounds; 2) if there is a family history of hearing loss; 3) if the baby is severely jaundiced; 4) if there is a malformation of the head or neck; and 5) if there was a lack of oxygen before, during, or after delivery.

General Evaluation. Within half an hour of birth, the baby will be weighed and measured. Later, after she has been put under a warmer (newborns are prone to getting cold), bathed, given a vitamin K shot in the leg and erythromycin (which has replaced the potentially irritating silver nitrate drop) in the eyes to guard against infections, a pediatric nurse or pediatrician will usually perform a more detailed examination in which the infant's pulse, blood pressure, and temperature will be taken. He will check the size and proportion of the head in relation to the rest of the body and determine whether the fontanels, the soft spots that allow room for brain growth, are open. The doctor will listen to the baby's heart, lungs, and nasal breathing to make sure there are no obstructions in the nose. He will also inspect the eyes for any infection that may have been picked up in the birth canal, and for cataracts and glaucoma. He will check the genitals and all joints. He will elicit such reflexes as the Moro reflex, or startle response to an unexpected, sudden stimulus. An abnormal response may indicate an injury to a joint or limb, which can occur during a difficult birth. Hospital staff will also watch the baby closely for signs of jaundice and listen to the heartbeat often.

Bilirubin Check. Most newborns develop some degree of jaundice, a yellowing of the skin and eyeballs. This is caused by the buildup of the yellow pigment called *bilirubin,* a waste product formed by the breakdown of the hemoglobin necessary to transport oxygen to the baby via the placenta. Once the baby is breathing and receiving oxygen from the air, these "old" red blood cells are no longer necessary and must be processed out by the liver. If the bilirubin level rises too far, generally because of a temporary immaturity or inefficiency of the liver, the pigment can cause mental retardation. That is why bilirubin level is so carefully monitored. If it is high, the baby may be placed under special lights that convert the pigment to a harmless substance that is excreted.

The Brazelton Neonatal Behavioral Assessment Scale (NBAS). T. Berry Brazelton, the well-known infant researcher, pediatrician, and author, has developed a half-hour test to help tell doctors and parents what kind of temperament the newborn has. The twenty-eight item exam includes the use of a variety of stimuli—lights, bells, rattles, colors, and shapes—and is administered during the first month after birth.

The NBAS is designed to answer a detailed array of questions such as: What is the baby's "style" of interacting? What does she hear and see, and how does she show her preferences? How well does she deal with an overload of visual, auditory, or motor stimulation? For instance, what combination of techniques does the baby make use of to soothe herself; does she attempt to comfort herself by bringing her hand up to her mouth to suck, or by turning to a soothing voice, and/or responding to touch, or to holding and cuddling? How does she show that she likes or dislikes the way she is being handled? Though this test is generally reserved for "premies" and babies who may show signs of having other problems, its initial goal was to help parents know and nurture their newborns better during the first few weeks of life.

The Newborn from Head to Toe

I honestly don't think that I had ever seen a newborn baby, much less looked at one carefully, before I met my own, but I did have an image in my mind of a pink, sweet-smelling baby with little creases on his plump wrists and ankles, cuddled against my shoulder. They say that only a mother knows the true beauty of her child, but thinking back to the day he was born, I'm not so sure. I said to my husband, "You know there is no way around it. I'll love him anyway, but this child is not beautiful." The baby looked like an undercooked, red conehead, with a little fringe of hair like a friar's. One eye was swollen shut. His ears stuck out—one more than the other—and his nose was so flattened that I was sure he could hardly breathe, and he also had no chin. My husband said, "He certainly doesn't look like anybody I know, or in fact like anything I've ever seen before." I don't want you to get the wrong idea. I didn't find any of the other newborns to be particularly beautiful either.

While you are waiting and wondering what your newborn will look like—and it's always a surprise—take all opportunities that come your way to inspect and admire, study and hold any newborn you can get your hands on. Use the following as a guide to pick out some of the special characteristics of newborns.

The Head

A newborn's head appears overly large in proportion to the rest of its tiny body. Cesarean babies often have beautifully shaped little heads, but those heads that have experienced the travail of the birth canal can look quite misshapen, elongated in the back, or even "pointy" or coneshaped on the top. These qualities usually disappear, much to parents' relief, within a day or so.

Nature has beautifully prepared the baby's skull for the passage to life. The skull bones, which are still soft and have not yet fused together, "mold" as the head squeezes through the narrow strait of the birth canal. The infused bones create two areas known as the *fontanels*, or soft spots, which are covered by a thick protective membrane. The larger of the two fontanels (the *anterior* fontanel) is near the baby's forehead; the smaller one (the *posterior* fontanel) is farther back near the crown. The posterior fontanel generally closes in the first four months, though it is sometimes closed at birth. The anterior fontanel closes between nine and eighteen months.

From certain angles and in certain lights, particularly when the baby is crying or straining to have a bowel movement, you can see the fontanels bulging and "pulsing." This is perfectly normal and is due to the blood coming to the brain with each heartbeat. If the fontanels are sunken or depressed, this can mean that the baby is dehydrated.

In addition to somewhat battered-looking features, spots and splotches are also common in newborns. Some have small red marks, caused by the pressure of forceps, on the sides and front of the skull. These generally disappear within a week or two. Others have pinkish, salmon-col-

The Newborn's Reflexes

Your newborn comes equipped with a number of reflexes. Though some are puzzling, others clearly help him to survive.

Rooting Reflex. If you gently stroke your newborn's cheek, he will turn in the direction of your touch and open his mouth.

Sucking Reflex. Gently touch the baby's lips, and he will begin to make vigorous sucking movements.

Moro Reflex. If you move the baby suddenly or make a loud noise, the baby will throw out his arms and legs and arch his back.

Babinski Reflex. Gently stroke the sole of your baby's foot from heel to toe and his toes will spread upward while his foot turns in.

Tonic Neck Reflex (the fencing reflex). When the baby is on his back with his head turned to one side, his entire body may arch away from the side that he is facing. He will also extend the arm on the face side and flex the other arm into a "fencing" position. This is a precursor to learning how to use each side of the body independently of the other.

Palmar Grasping Reflex. If you touch your newborn's palm with your finger, his hand will flex and close in an attempt to hold on.

Walking Reflex. If you support the baby under his arms and hold him upright on your lap or on a counter, he may lift his legs in steplike motions that resemble walking.

ored patches or "angel kisses" on the forehead and eyelids; these too will disappear in time. Similar markings on the nape of the neck, known as "stork bites," may, however, last into adulthood. The most noticeable mark on a newborn head can be a red blood blister known as a *hematoma.* Though rather alarming to look at, hematomas are harmless and will disappear within several weeks.

Skin

At birth, babies are covered with a waxy or cheesy white lubricating substance called *vernix,* nature's own waterproofing for the baby, who has lived in amniotic fluid those many months. When the vernix dries, it peels off in thin flakes. After that, the outer layer of skin also begins to dry and peel, leaving flaky reddened skin beneath. All this is perfectly normal, and you needn't slather the baby in moisturizing creams. This scaly phase is generally over seven to ten days after delivery. Your baby may then develop little red spots with whitish or yellowish centers. Though these are unsightly, they too are no cause for alarm and will disappear as soon as the baby's pores begin to work more efficiently—usually within two or three weeks.

Babies of African, Mongolian, Italian, Greek, and American Indian heritage often have "Mongolian spots," which are nothing more than accumulations of pigment under the skin. These generally fade and disappear entirely within a year.

Hair

Though some babies are born with a full head of hair, many others are bald or somewhere in between. Whatever the amount of hair, it will be lost—sometimes quite dramatically in little clumps. This first hair may also bear no resemblance to future hair. Some newborns also emerge with fine, downy hair (called *lanugo*) covering their shoulders and spine. This will disappear within a week or two after birth.

Eyes, Mouth, and Nose

Eyes. Your newborn may squint cross-eyedly at you through swollen, irritated eyes. The swelling, caused by pressure in the birth canal, will disappear shortly. The squint is actually an illusion caused by folds of skin at the inner corners of the eyes. These folds, which will become less prominent in the ensuing weeks, cover up some of the white of the eye near the nose, giving the baby not only a squinty but also an imbalanced or cross-eyed look.

As you study your newborn you may be wondering about his eye color. White Caucasian babies are born with dark blue-gray eyes, which change to their true color in anywhere from three to twelve months. Asian and black infants are usually born with brown eyes that remain that color.

Mouth. The baby may have a little blister on the upper lip due to possible sucking in utero. Such blisters come and go and should be left alone.

Nose. A newborn's nose can be so flat that one wonders how air gets in and out of it. Don't panic. Some of the flatness can probably be attributed to the "molding" at birth. In any case, what you see has little or nothing to do with the future shape of your baby's nose. It can take years for a nose's true character to emerge.

It may also be useful to know that a newborn baby *does* breathe through his nose. This can be noisy enough to keep you awake or just the opposite—so quiet or seemingly faint that you will find yourself checking often to see if the baby is breathing.

Hands

There is nothing quite so appealing as a newborn's tiny perfect hands, whose resemblance to a parent's is sometimes evident at the moment of birth. The hands will remain clenched into little fists during the early months, so you will have to uncurl the fingers to admire them. Do not be alarmed if the newborn's cuticles look a little red and swollen. This is because the tissue surrounding the nailbeds is tender and can be inflamed by the harder nail pushing into it. By the way, a newborn's hands—and feet—are almost always cool to the touch and may even have a bluish tinge due to inefficient circulation. This is nothing to worry about.

Breasts and Genitals

Swelling in the breasts and/or genitals of both male and female newborns is not abnormal and is caused by the high level of maternal hormones that cross the placenta during the mother's pregnancy. In some cases there is even a little milk excreted from the breasts. This may last several weeks, and no treatment is needed. Girl babies may also have a discharge of mucus or, more rarely, a slightly bloody discharge from the vagina. If your baby has been circumcised, an application of petroleum jelly to the healing area, topped with a small gauze pad after each diaper change, will prevent sticking until the incision heals.

Umbilical Stump

Sponge baths are in order for the one to two weeks that it takes for the umbilical stump to fall

How to Pick Up, Hold, and Carry a Newborn Baby

Newborns are floppy. They have poor muscle control and are most content when nestled against a human body or a mattress. What they don't like is feeling unsupported while getting from one place to the other nor do they like being moved through great expanses of space. These fears activate their Moro or startle reflex, which means that the baby will throw out his arms and legs, as if instinctively clutching for support.

You may envy the dexterity and ease with which the hospital staff handle newborns. But remember that they have had thousands of opportunities to perfect their lifts, quick turnovers, football holds, and one-handed feedings. For the novice, picking up, holding, and putting down a newborn will feel awkward at the least—if not downright frightening. But rest assured your time will come. Within weeks of putting down your sleeping baby—as you hold your breath, back away on tiptoe, praying "please, please don't wake up!"—you will have mastered what follows in slow motion.

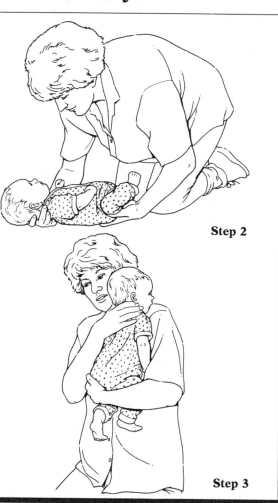

Step 2

Step 3

1. Before you pick up the baby, say something to let him know that you are there. Remember that your overall goal (other than not dropping the baby) is to keep the baby as compact, supported all over, and close to your body as possible. This is also the least hard on your back.

2. Put one hand under the baby's neck and head—wrist on neck, fingers spread out under head. Put the other hand under the baby's bottom. Let your hands rest in this position for a few seconds so that he can settle in to the new surface.

3. Lean down, bending at the knees if possible and using your arm as a support for the baby's back, and lift slowly into an upright position as you turn him toward your body. You can either hold him in this "madonna" position or continue the motion upward so that he is comfortably nestled on your shoulder.

4. To put the baby down, support the head and neck as well as the bottom and slowly lower him, turning him facedown as you go—or leaving him faceup to lie on his back.

5. Once the baby is down, keep your hands on him for a few seconds so he can settle into the new surface.

6. Never lay the baby face down on any very soft surface such as a pillow, where the baby's face sinks in. This can cause suffocation.

off. At each diaper change, simply dab the stump with a clean piece of cotton or gauze dipped in rubbing alcohol. Once the stump falls off, the belly button may ooze a bit of blood for a day or two. When this stops, tub baths are fine.

Legs and Feet

Though the newborn's legs are often bowed inward and almost always quite skinny, it won't be long before they fill out and become very appealing and squeezable.

All babies have flat feet to start out with and will gradually build up arches with standing and walking.

A Baby Is a Completely Humbling Experience

I had read somewhere in a book that over time you will notice differences in the way a baby cries. Well, I consider myself reasonably observant, but I couldn't hear any differences in the sound. I couldn't tell if she was or wasn't hungry. When you fail the quiz because you can't figure it out, then you are frustrated, and that takes even more energy. You become tired and you start thinking maybe this baby doesn't like me, maybe I'm inadequate. And here I was, supposed to be so smart. I've been advising company presidents.

I used to be very athletic, and I know the stages of physical exhaustion from physical exertion. I've been exhausted from mental activity and tension. This baby produced in me a gruesome combination of both, with an underlying solid base of fear that I was going to do something terribly wrong. A baby is a small thing. I was afraid I was going to kill her, inadvertently commit manslaughter.

The first day the baby came home from the hospital was the worst. She hadn't been a big eater,

and prior to that morning, she had eaten only an ounce or so at each feeding. Her appetite had started to pick up, and at nine that morning she'd had two ounces. The nurse said she'd probably be hungry by one. After we brought her home, she looked around for a while and conked out—comatose sleep. There was a lot of checking on our part. Is she still breathing? One o'clock rolled around, and the baby didn't wake up. In the books, they say that little babies wake up and cry, and that's how you know they are hungry. She didn't wake up, so I woke her up. The books say new babies should eat three ounces for every pound, so I figured she had to log twenty-one ounces somehow that day. The baby had three sips and clearly was not going to eat any more. She fell asleep again, a couple of hours went by, and I tried again.

I remembered reading in a book that you can't let a newborn baby sleep ten hours through the night because it's far too long for a baby to go without water, no less milk. You have to wake them up. I tried again. No luck. I was getting a little nervous, so I tried to call the doctor. I couldn't get through to his office. It was constantly busy. It got to be four o'clock, and finally I got scared. I called the nurses in the newborn nursery at the hospital: "I'm really sorry to bother you, but I wondered if there is some trick, or if something could be the matter. The baby refuses to eat."

The nurse said, "Do you mean to tell me that the baby hasn't eaten since nine o'clock this morning?" In other words, she was saying, "Are you trying to kill that kid?" That's what she's saying to me, right? So I said, "Well, I just don't know what to do. I can't get through to the doctor." The nurse said, "Wake her up. Play with her feet to make sure she's awake. Get her to eat, just a couple of ounces." She was trying to be helpful. Her first reaction, though, was the instinctive one, to question me. But can you imagine what that made me

feel like? Inadvertent manslaughter, it's what I was up to!

My sister-in-law was there that day to help out. We had those little premade bottles of formula. You take the cap off and replace it with a nipple. Before she left that night she prepared the next bottle, but she left it on the counter, so by two or three in the morning, maybe it had gotten a little spoiled. I don't know if that was the reason, but the baby was violently ill from about three to six A.M. My second attempt at manslaughter in a twelve-hour period. I couldn't believe it. If you're so damn smart, the high-powered token lady executive making it in a man's world . . . I mean it's a completely humbling experience. I had two at-

Further Reading

Brazelton, T. Berry, *Infants and Mothers: Differences in Development* (New York: Dell, 1983)

Greenspan, Stanley, and Greenspan, Nancy T., *First Feelings: Milestones in the Emotional Development of Your Baby & Child from Birth to Age 4* (New York: Viking, 1985)

Klaus, Marshall H., and Klaus, Phyllis H., *The Amazing Newborn: Discovering and Enjoying Your Baby's Natural Abilities* (Reading, MA: Addison-Wesley Publishing Co., Inc., 1985)

Leach, Penelope, *Your Baby and Child: From Birth to Age Five* (New York: Alfred A. Knopf, Inc., 1983)

Verrilli, George E., M.D., and Mueser, Anne Marie, Ed.D., *Welcome Baby: A Guide to the First Six Weeks* (New York: St. Martin's Press, Inc., 1981) tempted murders on my record, and I was in a state of high panic.

My mother arrived when Lucy was about two and a half weeks old. I slept for twelve hours straight. After she left, the baby went into a period where she'd eat two ounces, then stay awake in an agitated state all day. I would feel compelled to talk to her when I wasn't feeding her. I was so afraid not to feed her when she appeared hungry because I wanted her to develop an appetite. When I wasn't feeding her, I was washing her clothes by hand because our washing machine hadn't arrived yet, or I was cooking her damned bottles.

I finally called the pediatrician and said, "The baby is fundamentally unhappy all day. She's cranky, she's not getting enough sleep. I don't want her to go through life thinking to be awake is to be unhappy." We were going to switch to the formula without iron because he thought the iron was causing her gas. So I went out and bought a whole new batch of formula. The next day I had to use up a couple of bottles of the old stuff, even though I had new cans. She was fine. Geselle and Ilg, the child development experts, have a theory that babies go through a period of disequilibrium while they're changing stages. I'm not sure I know what a stage is, but that's the only way I can explain that behavior.

It's extremely frustrating, though, to deal with somebody who's being a pain in the neck for no reason other than the fact that she is somewhat uncomfortable. It's annoying. If you've changed her clothes three times, and she's vomited on you and urinated on you, and nothing you can do will cheer her up, it's very frustrating and not pleasant. There are times when I can understand child abuse. I can really see it. I joke with her. I say, "Listen here, stop this. You're going out the window." There are times when I've yelled—me, who is opposed to violence. My response to anger is to yell. As many as six times in the last month I may have said, "Listen, you have to stop this. This is truly offensive!" And I can see that if I were prone to violence . . . It's not in my nature to hurt anybody, however, so I don't.

The interesting thing to me, though, is no matter how mad I am, once she takes the nap and wakes up and smiles, I forget completely that four-hour stretch that preceded it. It's evaporated. Normally, if you have a fight with your husband, and even if you yell and get it out of your system, you can remember it the next morning. With these little babies, the anger just disappears. My sense of well-being is tied up with the baby. I'm so intimately involved with her that if she's happy, I'm happy. (Excerpted from Frances Wells Burck, Mothers Talking: Sharing the Secret, St. Martin's Press, 1987.)

· PART TWO ·

Feeding

• CHAPTER 3 •

Breast-Feeding

The Big Question:
To Breast-feed or Not?

Whether you plan to feed *your* baby with breast or bottle shouldn't be anyone's business but your own. But you will find that it is from practically the moment of conception on. There will be people who are absolutely dogmatic on the pros of breast-feeding. They will stress the physical and emotional benefits for the baby to the point where you may begin to feel that breast-feeding is a must, a test of your worth as a woman/mother, rather than the choice that it truly is.

There is little argument that mother's milk does have an edge over infant formulas because it is made especially to suit human babies. It is an "alive" and changing substance in the sense that its composition varies within a feeding. The foremilk, or first milk, for instance, is less rich in fat than the hind milk. As the baby completes his meal, fat contributes to a sense of satisfaction and fullness. Breast milk is also loaded with antibodies that protect the baby from many forms of gastrointestinal upset. It is easy to digest, nonallergenic, and doesn't constipate. Fewer breast-fed babies than bottle-fed babies are overweight. The baby regulates his own milk supply, and we cannot coax him into drinking an extra ounce.

Interestingly enough, it has also been discovered that adults who have been breast-fed as babies tend to have lower cholesterol levels than those who were formula-fed. Though unproven, it is speculated that the breast-fed baby, who actually consumes more cholesterol than the formula-fed baby, may develop a greater tolerance for metabolizing it as an adult. Breast-feeding also requires plenty of good hard sucking which, besides being pleasurable to the baby, helps to calm him and "organize" his behavior. Sucking on the breast has been linked to straighter teeth because infants who nurse do not thrust their tongues forward the way bottle-fed babies do. This tongue thrusting can become a habit that later interferes with the alignment of the teeth.

Breast-feeding has emotional benefits for both infant and mother. It is a continuation of the symbiotic or mutually dependent physical and emotional connection established between mother and baby during pregnancy. Its benefits to a mother's health are well-known. Oxytocin, the hormone that triggers the milk let-down reflex, causes contractions of the uterus that speed its return to prepregnant size. At the same time, suckling a baby burns around 500 calories a day, some 300 of which come from stores of body fat laid on during pregnancy.

Breast-feeding suggests convenience and economy. The food is ready-made and instantly available, which is particularly good for nighttime feedings. It is also virtually free.

Question: If breast-feeding is so beneficial to baby and mother, why doesn't everyone do it?

Answer: If we were to decide how to feed our babies in a strictly rational fashion, breast-feeding probably would be the preferred method in most cases. But new mothers don't always work this way during the early days and/or weeks after the birth of their first child—one of the most vulnerable periods in their lives.

Instead of being totally rational, we make decisions based on all sorts of feelings and attitudes that come from our unique histories. Some people regard new experiences as adventures and learning opportunities. Others come at newness with anxiety, doubt, or fear. We also decide based on how much information and support we have; how we feel about the sexual as well as "utilitarian" aspects of our bodies; how we think the baby is doing; and how we plan to share its care.

Whatever decision you make, remember that the purpose of feeding is to benefit the baby and to promote a loving relationship between two sensitive and unique people. Feeding is everything to the newborn. Besides being relief from the very real pain of hunger, it is a link to the familiar life of warmth and motion, of fullness and "surroundedness" known in the womb. Feeding is also a sensual experience. As the baby sucks, swallows, tastes, looks, touches, and listens, all of her senses come into play. Feeding is an intimate time when mother and baby come to know each other and to deepen their attachment. For the baby's sake and the mother's, mealtimes ought to be relaxed and pleasant.

A woman who wants to breast-feed, who has proper information and support, who is not in great pain or overly exhausted, and who is *reasonably* sure that the baby is getting enough to eat can provide the baby with all of the physical and emotional nourishment an infant needs. But so can a bottle-feeding mother—with some additional work and paraphernalia.

If you are *totally* repelled by the idea of breast-feeding, you probably shouldn't do it. If you are the *least* bit interested, though, why not give it a try? You can always switch to bottles or work out your own style of feeding that involves both methods. If you decide to try, it makes sense to do whatever possible to ensure that you are giving yourself and the baby a fair shot at a good experience.

Building Your Support System in Advance

One of the first things you can do is to make contact with other nursing mothers. (See Sources for Breast-Feeding Information, page 23.) While breast-feeding is a growing phenomenon in this country, it remains a fact that many of us have never even seen a woman nursing a baby before we set out to nurse our own. If you have a friend who is nursing, ask her to let you observe. Take note of how you feel. Are you curious, confused, or delighted about anything in particular? Are you embarrassed or squeamish? Ask her questions. What does it feel like? What information was useful to her, and where has she found the most support?

If you don't know a nursing mother, ask your obstetrician, future pediatrician, or Lamaze instructor for names. Or you can contact the La Leche League, the largest pro-breast-feeding information and support network in the world. La Leche answers questions, runs groups, and makes available literature and products related to breast-feeding.

Besides connecting with "real" people, read about how breast-feeding works, clear up any misconceptions you may have, and be sure to prepare your breasts in advance. (See Preparing for Breast-Feeding, page 24.)

Common Myths and Misconceptions about Breast-Feeding

Myth: *Women have breast-fed babies since the beginning of mankind, and it is a natural phenomenon that comes easily to mother and baby.*
Reality: Each mother and each baby is unique. While breast-feeding comes easily to some, for others it is a learned skill requiring practice, trial and error, patience, trust, support, and a number

of useful "how-tos." Remember, too, that breast-feeding is a "skill" that the baby may also have to learn. In utero, babies are continuously nourished through the umbilical cord. They never experience the true feeling of emptiness that we equate with hunger. Though they are born with the reflex to root—that is, to turn toward the breast, open their mouths, and latch on—as well as the reflex to suck and swallow, it takes time for them to figure out that these actions will bring food, which will in turn bring comfort. Even once the baby has caught on, he will have his own style of nursing. (See Barracuda or Gourmet, page 24.)

Myth: *In order to breast-feed you have to be 100 percent dedicated and determined to succeed.*
Reality: Most breast-feeding literature stresses the blissful aspects of the experience. For many of us these come only after we have gotten past the rough spots. Even then, it is perfectly normal to feel some ambivalence. It isn't always simple determination and hard work that make us succeed. Sometimes it takes the opposite—the ability to relax, let go, trust, or develop a wait-and-see attitude. While you don't have to be 100 percent dedicated, it is important not to go to the opposite extreme where breast-feeding becomes the "dumping ground" for all our woes and anxieties concerning our babies.

Myth: *Breast-feeding is efficient and convenient.*
Reality: Proponents of breast-feeding invariably stress the convenience and availability of breast milk at the right temperature. This is true. But let's be honest about the early weeks. Nursing a newborn can be very time consuming, especially if you happen to have a baby who does not settle down and nurse efficiently but who falls asleep, gets the hiccups, has a bowel movement,

Sources for Breast-Feeding Information

La Leche League Int'l., Inc.
P.O. Box 1209
Franklin Park, IL 60131-8209
708-455-7730 or 1-800 LA LECHE

Int'l. Lactation Consultant Assoc.
P.O. Box 4013
University of Virginia Station
Charlottesville, VA 22903

The La Leche League is a nonprofit, international, largely volunteer organization that provides information and support to any mother who wishes to breast-feed her baby. There are more than 7,000 league leaders and 3,000 groups in cities as well as outlying areas. If you live in a large city, there is probably a listing in the telephone book. You can also find out about local chapters through your hospital, Lamaze instructor, or pediatrician. Or you can write directly to the main headquarters listed above. The league reaches millions of mothers each year through group meetings, telephone conversations, their own publications, and correspondence if you live too far away to call or visit with a leader. Though they do not provide medical advice, group leaders are skilled at answering questions and helping with most problems concerned with nursing a baby. The league publishes books as well as a newsletter, which you can receive by joining for a small fee.

An exclusive audio edition of *The Womanly Art of Breastfeeding* is also available. This two-tape set offers a basic guide to breast-feeding, carefully and thoughtfully abridged from the 1987 bestselling book. ($15.95, distributed by St. Martin's Press).

The International Lactation Consultant Association can refer you to a lactation consultant who has been officially certified as a health-care provider.

---

etc. A feeding can stretch to forty minutes, if not an hour. When you are feeding ten to twelve times a day, it can seem like you are doing nothing but that because that is exactly what you are doing.

A mother offers a useful viewpoint: *"At first I was very hard on myself. Why wasn't I getting more done? All I did all day was nurse Jessica in those first few weeks. Then I realized that I was expecting too much from myself. My real job right then was to establish breast-feeding, and if nursing her a lot is what it took, I'd do it."*

Myth: *Breast-feeding will tie you down.*
Reality: All new babies tie parents down. In fact, children of any age tie parents down. This is one of the shockers of parenthood that can take years to adjust to. Newborns, whether they breast- or bottle-feed, do need to eat often, but this basic physiological necessity also ensures that the baby receives the *emotional* nourishment that contact, comfort, and stimulation provide. Read on.

Myth: *If you breast-feed, you can't give your baby a bottle.*
Reality: There is no reason why you can't combine breast- and bottle-feeding with positive results for both the baby and parents. Read on to find out how.

Myth: *Breast-feeding will change the shape of your breasts.*
Reality: Any changes that your breasts undergo are the result of pregnancy, not nursing. Exercises before as well as after the birth will help them retain their shape. (See page 134.)

Myth: *Successful breast-feeding depends on the size and shape of the breast and nipple.*
Reality: The size of your breasts has nothing to do with the amount of milk you produce. The shape of your nipple is not a problem unless it is inverted or retracted. A rubber breast shell, available through the La Leche League, can help solve this problem, particularly if you wear it while you are still pregnant.

Myth: *Breast-feeding is a reliable form of birth control.*
Reality: Theoretically, women do not ovulate for the first couple of months during lactation. But don't count on it! Use some other form of birth control. Do *not* take birth-control pills while you are lactating, though. They reduce your milk supply, and their effect on the baby's developing endocrine system is still unknown.

Myth: *Breast-feeding will leave out the father.*
Reality: This need not be the case at all. There's plenty of work and fun in baby care for the two of you to share. Keep reading if you have any doubts!

Barracuda or Gourmet— What's Your Baby's Style?

What is your baby's nursing style? Researchers at Yale University have studied breast-feeding styles and developed the following classifications:

Barracudas, as the name suggests, take a no-nonsense approach. They suck energetically for ten to twenty minutes with such vigor that they can make their mother's nipples sore.

The *excited ineffectives* are so excited that they grasp the breast but keep losing it, which makes them scream. Then the mother has to stop and quiet the baby before going on with the feeding. This hardly makes for efficiency!

Procrastinators may not initiate nursing until the fourth or even fifth postpartum day, when the milk comes in. They have no interest in sucking before that. Dr. George Barnes, who headed this study at Yale, stresses that "It is important not to prod or force these infants when they seem disinclined. They do well once they start."

The *gourmets* or *mouthers* take their time before they start. They dawdle by tasting a little milk, then smacking their lips. If you hurry them, they get furious and start to scream. Eventually they settle down to business.

Resters, as the term suggests, are babies who nurse then pause, nurse then pause. This can be frustrating for mothers because feeding can take a long time. There is no changing the baby, however. He simply won't be hurried.

Myth: Breast-feeding will ruin your sex life.

Reality: It isn't only breast-feeding that can put a damper on new parents' sex lives—though nursing mothers may experience dryness in their vaginas due to hormonal changes. It's having a baby whose needs are constant and immediate that can do in a couple's love life—temporarily, one hopes. Read "Babies, Sex, Power, and Marriage" (page 149) for more information.

Preparing for Breast-Feeding

Nipple Preparation

A decade ago, the standard advice for a woman who wanted to breast-feed was to prepare her nipples in advance—to toughen them up with various techniques so that she would not experience soreness when she began to nurse. Over the years new research on breast-feeding has suggested that preparation for breast-feeding may not be what prevents soreness—that positioning the baby on the breast may be the key. In rare cases, handling and thus stimulating the nipples has been associated with the premature onset of labor. My own experience with breast-feeding three babies was that I was much more comfortable when I followed the suggestions for nipple preparation *and* correctly positioned the baby on the breast. I have included the following suggestions because they have worked for me and for many of the contributors to this book. I suggest, however, that before embarking on any type of breast preparation, you discuss the pros and cons with your obstetrician or midwife.

- Avoid using soap or any other drying agent (such as powder, witch hazel, tincture of benzoin, or creams containing alcohol) on your nipples. These dry up the natural oils that soften and protect them.

- When you shower or bathe, gently but firmly rub your nipples with a washcloth every day. Do not use a bath brush. This can irritate nipples and make them more vulnerable to cracking.

- Go braless as often as possible, if this is comfortable for you, or cut holes in the cups of your regular bra. The friction of your clothing will help toughen your nipples, and you won't even have to think about it.

- Expose your nipples to air and sunlight (with caution) whenever possible. If you do sunbathe, lubricate them afterwards with a small amount of Massé cream or pure lanolin (but not if you are allergic to wool).

- Rolling your nipples a couple of times a day may help to toughen them as well as make them more erect, so the baby can latch on more effectively. Support your breast with one hand, then take the nipple between the thumb and forefinger of your other hand and pull out on it firmly but gently, enough so that you feel some pressure, but not so much that it hurts. Roll the nipple gently between your fingers.

- During pregnancy check to see if your nipples are inverted. The tip of an inverted nipple is flat or folded in like a slit. Take your breast between your thumb and forefinger and squeeze gently but firmly around the dark area, the areola. If the tip recedes, the nipple is inverted. If you are unsure, have your doctor or midwife check. Be reassured that inverted nipples often work themselves out during pregnancy. You can aid this process by placing your fingers on oppo-

How Does Breast Milk Compare to Formula Preparations?

In 1979 the American Academy of Pediatrics and the Canadian Pediatric Society issued a joint statement that said, "We believe human milk is nutritionally superior to formula." Though human milk may not look superior—it is thin, watery, and rather insubstantial looking compared to the creamy, rich look of formula—it is a highly complex, subtle substance. Some of its properties are duplicatable by formula manufacturers, and some are not.

Standard formula is cow's milk in which the protein and mineral content has been lowered, the carbohydrate content increased, and the butterfat replaced by vegetable oils, which are more easily absorbed and utilized by the baby. More specific differences follow.

Colostrum. Even if you nurse for only a few days, your baby will benefit from the protective qualities of this yellowish, protein-rich, pre-milk fluid secreted from the breasts before the mature milk comes in one to three days after birth. In the womb, all babies receive some protective antibodies that cross from mother to baby through the placenta. Scientists think this protection lasts for the first few months only but may be supplemented by a number of protective elements in colostrum. Among these are antibodies for such bacteria and viruses as *E. coli,* a common cause of intestinal infection in newborns; polio; mumps; and influenza. And colostrum's laxative quality helps to eliminate *meconium,* or the first thick, dark stool present in the unborn baby's bowels. This, in turn, helps prevent physiological newborn jaundice. So far, there is no manufactured substitute for colostrum.

Protein. The level of protein in infant formulas approximates that in human milk, but the proteins are different. Human-milk protein is mainly *lactalbumin,* or whey protein, which is highly digestible. Most formulas contain *casein,* which forms a harder curd that takes longer to digest. Thus, the formula-fed baby feels "fuller" and goes longer between feedings than the breast-fed baby.

All proteins must be broken down into amino acids before the body can use them. Breast milk contains combinations of amino acids different from those in formulas. For example, it has more of the amino acids cysteine and taurine, which play an important role in the development of the nervous system, the brain, and visual perception. Human milk also contains a greater number of *nucleotides,* factors that enable the body to make proteins. Finally, very small amounts of the proteins in a nursing mother's food reach her milk unaltered and thus go to the baby. This advance acclimatization to the household diet is thought to help prevent some food allergies.

Fat. Human milk and formulas have about the same amount of fat, an important energy source for the baby, but the fats in formula are vegetable oils, which the baby can absorb more easily. Human milk also has more cholesterol—which is an advantage. Though adults should limit cholesterol intake, babies need this substance. Cholesterol forms part of *myelin,* the covering on the nerves that permits muscular coordination. The high natural levels of cholesterol in human milk may also be important in helping the baby tolerate cholesterol later in life.

Carbohydrate. Breast milk and most formulas contain the same kind of carbohydrate, a sugar called *lactose,* an important source of slow, steady energy. Lactose, the least sweet of sugars, helps to create an acid environment in the intestinal tract. This helps ward off bacteria that cause infections. The *bifidus factor,* a component of the lactose in mother's milk, is responsible for the distinct, not unpleasant, rather yeasty smell of the bowel movements of the totally breast-fed baby.

Vitamins and minerals. Breast milk contains all the important minerals, but in smaller amounts than infant formulas. Human milk contains very little iron, but it seems that this iron is fully and easily absorbed and is adequate for the first six months. During this period the baby is still using up the iron stores she was born with. Infant formulas contain more calcium than breast milk and are fortified with vitamin D, which makes the calcium easier to absorb. But a mother can supplement her diet with plenty of vitamin D to increase levels in her milk. Vitamin C is important to support the growth of new tissue. Nursing babies whose mothers take in adequate amounts of vitamin C will receive its benefits in the right proportions.

site points of the areola and pulling outward several times every day. While pregnant you can also wear plastic breast shells, which put suction pressure on the breast and help draw out the nipple. These are available through the La Leche League, drugstores, and maternity shops.

• Some doctors recommend that pregnant women hand-express colostrum. Though it can be reassuring to see and feel that your milk-making system works, there is controversy over whether or not this is at all necessary. Some health-care providers feel that it helps to prevent blocked milk ducts, which can be a source of discomfort. Expressing colostrum is also a way to familiarize yourself with the useful art of hand-expressing milk. If you decide to try, do not worry that your baby will miss out on the "wasted" colostrum. The full complexity of colostrum is not achieved until after the birth of the baby and the expulsion of the placenta. (To learn about hand-expressing milk, see page 46.)

• Again, besides these simple measures, the most helpful preparation is talking to women who are breast-feeding their babies and enjoying it, and making sure that you have a pediatrician who is truly supportive of breast-feeding. (See What Are Your Health-Care Choices, page 223.) Remember, too, that the more access you have to your baby in the hospital, the better start you will have. Try to arrange for rooming-in.

The Right Bra

A comfortable, well-fitting bra is essential for the nursing mother. You will definitely want to buy two or three of these ahead of time. The bra must offer enough support, yet not be too tight. Look for fairly wide straps and flaps that can be operated with one hand while you hold onto the baby with the other. Avoid bras with plastic liners. The plastic traps moisture, which can irritate your

nipples. You might also want to purchase some washable or disposable nursing pads that fit inside the bra and absorb leaks. When purchasing bras, select two different styles. Write down the manufacturer's name and the style number along with the name and phone number of the store. In the early weeks you may discover that you like one bra in particular. When you know what you like, you can have it sent to you or have someone else pick it up. Sears, J. C. Penny, and the La Leche League offer well-designed, inexpensive nursing bras.

Comfortable Clothing

You will need comfortable clothing when you nurse. Start thinking about this in advance. The postpartum period is no time to feel like a frump or to have to go out shopping. Two-piece outfits are ideal—slacks or skirts and loose tops that can be easily lifted, that open conveniently down the front, or have side slits. A shawl, a nursing bib, or a poncho aid discreet nursing in public.

The How-to's of Breast-Feeding

How Breast-Feeding Works

The breast has a truly elegant design. When the baby nurses, he is not sucking so much as squeezing, pumping, or "jawing" on the areola, the dark area surrounding the very tip of the nipple.

This pumping action exerts pressure on the areola and sends "make milk" messages to the pituitary gland, located at the base of the brain. The pituitary, in turn, releases two hormones. The first, *prolactin,* stimulates the milk production in the *alveoli,* grapelike clusters of expandable sacs positioned radially around the breast. Prolactin, also known as "the natural tranquilizer," and the same hormone released during or-

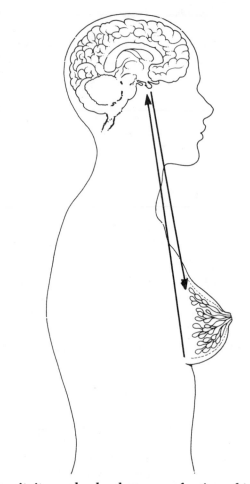

The pituitary gland releases *prolactin,* which stimulates milk production, and *oxytocin,* which causes the milk to be pushed through the nipple.

gasm, is responsible for a feeling of peace and well-being.

The second hormone, *oxytocin,* causes the cells in the ducts attached to the tissues of the alveoli to contract and push the milk forward through the ducts to the fifteen or twenty *ampullae* (located behind the areola), and out through the nipple in little jets to the baby. When a woman nurses, oxytocin causes the contracting action of the uterus, felt by some women as afterpains.

How to Get Started with Breast-Feeding

When I look back on my first few weeks of breast-feeding, I can't believe how awkward and just kind of "thick" I felt. I'm thirty-eight and accustomed to feeling a sense of mastery in my work. I wasn't used to learning something new that seemed to require getting a feel for it rather than sheer intellectual understanding.

• • •

Nursing in the beginning was a little like learning to ride a bicycle. Every action was very self-conscious, awkward, even somewhat unnerving. At first I needed my husband's confident hands to help me get Christopher onto my breast and to change sides. Once we'd get him there, he might pull off or fall asleep or get the hiccups or have to burp or have a bowel movement, and then we would have to start all over. It seems that we both mastered it in very small spurts. I often nursed him seventeen to twenty times a day! One day I realized that the baby was nursing smoothly and contentedly. Neither of us was thinking about it. We were just doing it.

Before you even put baby to breast, there are a few things you ought to know that can be com-forting and helpful. The first and most important—and perhaps the hardest to believe at the time—is that if your early experiences are difficult or disappointing or feel unproductive, they don't necessarily have *anything* to do with the totality of your breast-feeding experience. Keep remembering this, and be kind, gentle, and patient with yourself.

Second, remember that breast-feeding works on the principle of supply and demand. The single most important factor that influences the production of milk is the amount of time that your baby spends sucking. It is that direct stimulation that is most effective. Pumping or manual expression are useful, but they are not equal substitutes. Also, as the day wears on, you produce less milk.

The third most important idea to keep in mind is that there are no absolute rules about how to breast-feed. Each mother and infant is a unique pair. Read about breast-feeding, but at the same time don't hesitate to work out your own system and style. In other words, do whatever works best for *you.*

Breast-Feeding in Very Slow Motion

Once you get the knack of breast-feeding, you will wonder why anyone would spend so many words describing something that seems so simple. By the time you finish reading this, you could have nursed *four* babies! Please, don't be put off by the seeming complexity and length of what follows. Before you begin, study the diagram How the Breast Works so that you can appreciate the beauty of the milk-making system. Then read over the following steps a few times until you "get it."

Give yourself some peace. Clear the room of visitors and close the door. If the baby is screaming rather than merely fussing, try to calm him

---

Suggestions for Waking a Sleepy Baby

Brand-new babies need time to recover from the rigors of birth and can be very difficult to rouse for a feeding. If you have rooming-in at the hospital, you can nurse the baby the moment he wakes up. If you don't have rooming-in, your baby may not be awake when he is brought from the nursery for a feeding. Try requesting that the nursery alert you when he wakes. You might offer to pick up and return him yourself to reduce the nursery work load.

If the baby falls asleep at the breast during the first few days postpartum, don't panic. Just keep trying. First switch breasts. The motion and change of position might be just enough to get him interested. You can also try burping him. An air bubble may be making him feel fuller than he really is. Another way to stimulate a sleepy baby gently is to stroke the roof of his mouth with a pacifier (see pages 92–93 for the best choices). As a last resort, unwrap the baby for a diaper change—and a change of temperature. This may do the trick.

---

a little first before you begin. If you don't get anywhere with the feeding at first, relax and try again. Vary your position so that the baby stimulates different parts of your breast and has a change of view. If the baby is asleep, see Suggestions for Waking a Sleepy Baby above.

1. Read over the section on encouraging the let-down reflex to work (see page 32) before you begin.

2. Wash your hands. Don't worry about washing your breasts.

3. Have something to drink nearby. Nursing mothers need to drink six to eight glasses of fluid a day.

4. Do not hesitate to ask for help. Extra hands can be useful for positioning the baby and are absolutely essential if you have had a cesarean.

5. Get yourself and the baby into a comfortable position. (See How to Hold the Baby While Nursing, below.) If the baby's hands are covered, uncover them so that she can touch you as she nurses.

6. Now that you have chosen a comfortable position, cup your breast in your hand, supporting it with your fingers underneath and your thumb on top—so that thumb and fingers form a "C."

7. Induce the sucking reflex. In the beginning, gently stroke whichever of your baby's cheeks is nearest to you. The baby will turn toward your finger and the breast. Touch the tip of the nipple to the baby's mouth and tickle the mouth gently until it opens wide. This tickling will help make the nipple erect and make it easier for the baby to hold in its mouth.

8. Now bring the baby toward you with the arm holding her rather than moving toward her, which could overwhelm her, particularly if you are large breasted. As you move her toward you, slightly tip up the areola (this will also help keep the nipple erect), and insert as much of it into the baby's mouth as possible. This "stuffing" action is necessary in order to put pressure on all the milk ducts, so they will release equally and evenly. Remember that it is important that your areola and nipple tip be in contact with the roof of the baby's mouth (it is this contact that makes her want to suck) and that the tongue be underneath in order to achieve the correct pumping, sucking, and swallowing actions. If your baby is sucking only the tip of the nipple, she won't be "milking" the ducts. She will then pull harder in frustration and make you sore.

9. Check to make sure the baby can breathe through her nose while sucking. You don't want the baby to panic and reject the breast. You might have to depress your breast slightly with two fingers.

10. The first few sucks may be slightly painful whether or not your breasts are tender. This is normal. Breathe deeply and relax. Watch and feel the baby suck. It is productive work. The jaw, the cheeks, and even the baby's temples and ears move quite vigorously. You can hear her swallow and breathe in a regular rhythm. Nurse for five minutes to start.

11. Remove the baby from your breast. Break the suction by gently slipping the tip of your finger down between the areola and the baby's lips. Never pull the baby off your breast. This will hurt your nipples.

12. Burp the baby. (See illustration on page 29.)

13. If the baby is awake and willing, switch her to the other breast. If she is not awake, start the next feeding with the unused breast. It is best to alternate the breast you start with, so that you make sure that each breast gets its fair share of stimulation as well as emptying during the day. By switching sides the baby will also look at you from different angles, which is visually stimulating. To keep track of which breast you used last, either put a safety pin or insert a tissue in your bra on that side.

14. Now nurse with the other breast.

How to Hold the Baby While Nursing

No matter what position you take, make sure the baby is squarely facing the breast and that she does not have to strain to reach, hang on, or crane her head. Awkward positioning will affect the efficiency and pleasure your baby receives; it will also make you sore. According to Kittie Frantz, a researcher and lactation specialist who evaluated some three hundred breast-feeding mothers, "We observed a difference in the two groups—in the way the mother held the baby and the way the baby accepted the breast into his mouth. When we taught the mothers with sore nipples the techniques we observed the mothers without sore nipples to be using, they almost all exclaimed that the pain significantly lessened or, in most cases, vanished."

Lying Down This is a good position for feeding on the hospital bed and will come in handy for nighttime feedings at home. Before you start, make sure to arrange your pillows so that you get adequate neck and arm support. Cradle the baby in the crook of your arm, making sure the baby's head is slightly elevated above its feet, so that air taken in while she sucks can more easily rise and be released when you burp her. Now make sure that the baby's entire body is facing you, so that she does not have to turn her head. Also make sure that she is high enough up, so that she does not have to cling to a nipple like a mountain climber hanging from a ledge, and that she doesn't have to swallow while lying flat on her back with her head turned.

Sitting Up Make sure you have pillows on hand for back and elbow support so that you are neither leaning over the baby nor having to lift the baby too high. Place one foot on a footstool to elevate one knee, or sit cross-legged on a bed or the floor.

The Football Position This is an excellent position for cesarean mothers. The baby will not be resting on the incision, and you can nurse this way while lying down or sitting up. In order to elevate and support the weight of the baby, place a pillow under your arm on the nursing side.

Lying-down nursing position

Sitting-up nursing position

Football nursing position

Shoulder position for burping baby

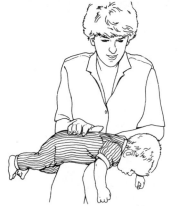

Across-the-knee position for burping baby

Sitting-up position for burping baby

This position is also very good to start with if you are large breasted, because the breast will not interfere with the baby's breathing.

Burping the Baby

Some babies need to burp more than others. You'll soon find out what kind you have. Start out burping her at least twice during a feeding. You can either place her over your shoulder or across your knees. A third method is to sit the baby on your lap with her body leaning forward over your forearm. Then pat gently between the shoulder blades. A good rule of thumb is to work on the burp for about a minute. If nothing happens, then give up and don't worry about it. Burping the breast-fed baby is an opportunity for a father to participate.

If your baby is the kind who sucks very strongly and tightly on the nipple, the air bubbles that she swallows will be very small. It may take up to an hour for the bubbles to collect into one large one, and there may be some milk on top of the bubble. Some mothers find it useful to place their baby in an infant seat after a feeding rather than flat down on stomach or back. This way gravity helps settle the milk and bring up the air. If and when the baby does finally burp, some milk or spit-up may come up. This is not the same as vomiting, and it usually looks like a lot more than it really is. So again, don't worry.

First Attempts at Breast-Feeding: Advice from Mothers

Try to breast-feed as soon as possible. If you can manage this on the delivery table, do so. Immediately after birth, babies are usually awake and receptive. If the placenta hasn't been delivered, your nursing baby may help it along by stimulat-

Correct Tongue Position for Breast-Feeding

These two illustrations show the different positions the baby's tongue takes while sucking the breast (left) versus the bottle (right).

To make the milk flow, the baby must push or thrust the areola up, pushing it against her palate. This is hard work. If you want to know what it feels like, bend your index finger at the joint and put it in your mouth and suck. Now put the same finger, unbent, into your mouth and suck. The former is much more difficult than the latter. This is the difference the baby experiences between sucking on the breast and sucking a conventional, nonorthodontic bottle nipple.

These two different tongue positions, which require two different sucking actions, can cause what is called "nipple confusion." Mothers who want to breast-feed their babies should request that the baby not be given a bottle with a conventional nipple.

ing the release of the oxytocin that contracts the uterus. And if you don't nurse on the delivery table, either because you can't or don't want to, then don't give it another thought! This doesn't mean that you haven't bonded with your baby.

• • •

I am a neonatal ICU nurse. While I was in the hospital, a bottle of water always accompanied Logan at feeding time. A lot of nurses believe that the baby must have some water, or he will be fussy in the nursery. If the bottle returns full, they feed it to the baby. By emptying half the bottle myself, I made sure that breast milk was all he got.

• • •

Don't let the hospital get you down. I'd say my experience was totally negative. The baby hardly nursed for the first three days and was fed bottles in the nursery because of a mix-up. I was asleep during the one breast-feeding class, and I had terribly sore breasts. I thought, "I'll never be able to do this. It's all over." Guess what! It all worked out.

• • •

I never saw a drop of my milk. It did not squirt across the room the way my roommate's in the hospital did. This is perfectly normal, but I suppose I expected that it would come spraying out just like a cow's.

• • •

I am an o.b. nurse and advise many new mothers on breast-feeding. Most are surprised that breast-fed babies nurse as frequently as every two or three hours but are even more surprised to learn that there are plenty of newborns who nurse every hour or sometimes even more in the evenings when your milk supplies are low. Also, my ten-month-old still nurses every two hours in the daytime.

• • •

We have a spare bed in our baby's room. I lie down and nurse him there at night, and then I often doze off. I feel fairly rested in the morning.

• • •

If your baby is crying a lot and you're nursing him a lot, ask your doctor if you can come in for a weight check. There's usually no charge for this, and it can give you a big boost in confidence.

• • •

When you nurse on the first breast, the other breast may let down and start to leak. To stop the leaking, press on the other breast with your free hand or forearm.

• • •

My milk came out so fast that the baby choked and spluttered. To slow it down I would lie down with him directly on top of the breast.

• • •

My only piece of advice is to give a supplemental bottle often enough so that the baby will take one. I didn't and am now stuck nursing her all the time. She's five months old. She absolutely refuses a bottle, and I've tried them all. I remember one evening when I wasn't feeling well and didn't want to nurse her. She woke up screaming, and I told my husband to "do something" with her because I was too sick to nurse her. There was nothing he could do, so between trips to the bathroom, I managed to feed her. It was an awful experience, and I only pray it doesn't happen again until she's weaned.

• • •

If you don't feel you have adequate access to your baby [in the hospital] in order to nurse him, have your pediatrician put it in writing to the nursery staff that you want your baby brought to you more often. And always smile and be pleasant, no matter what, when you insist on anything.

Answers to Common Questions about Breast-Feeding

Question: How do you know the baby is sucking properly?

Answer: Look at the illustration of the correct tongue position for breast-feeding (page 30). Then check to make sure your baby's ears are wiggling when he sucks and that his lower lip is out rather than tucked in. Gently draw his lips aside to see if his tongue is visible. Because it should be underneath the nipple, you should not see it. Also, if he can be easily removed from the breast, he's not on right.

Question: What do you do if a baby has been given a bottle, or you have been using a nipple shield, and he then refuses the breast?

Answer: In her excellent book *Breastfeeding: A Heartstart* (New York: Dell, 1987), Ilene S. Rice suggests the following for babies trained on the conventional nipple: "The baby is imprinted to suck a rounder, longer, firmer, and better-defined (rubber) nipple. A baby has greater stimulation to suck when his hard palate is stroked. When the baby finally does go to the breast with its previously learned artificial nipple suck, he will use the tongue and cheek muscles (with little effort) as trained to withdraw the milk from the bottle. When no milk comes, or it does not come as readily, the baby pulls off the mother's nipple and cries."

The author suggests offering a Nuk exerciser (see page 62 for specifics about this product) to retrain the baby. "As you talk gently to the baby, stroke the Nuk against his hard palate, [the] roof of the mouth. Hold the exerciser there and keep stroking the palate. Often the baby will spit it out. Try again. It may also help to express milk onto the Nuk before offering it to the baby. Each time the attempt is made the baby will learn to

accept the reprogramming with less frustration and crying. When you do nurse the baby again, express milk as he sucks by combing down on your breast to aid the let-down reflex."

Question: How long should I nurse on each side?

Answer: Generally women have been advised to start with short frequent feedings so that their breasts do not become sore. Start with five minutes per side. This way you can be sure that the let-down reflex has gone into operation and the baby has gotten some of the richer hind milk. Each day add five minutes to each breast time until you are nursing twenty minutes on one breast and then twenty minutes on the other. If you start to get sore, give the baby shorter, more frequent, feedings. (See pages 39–40 for more details on dealing with soreness.)

Question: How long does it take for the baby to empty each breast?

Answer: It is useful to know that a hungry baby can get most of the milk from the breast in five or so minutes and almost completely empty it in seven or eight minutes. (It's never totally empty.) But babies often want to nurse much longer, and should be allowed to if possible. The sucking not only calms and comforts them, it builds your milk supply.

Question: How often should I feed the baby?

Answer: In the early weeks, the best policy is not to worry about how often the baby eats. All babies are different. Some will nurse on an orderly two- or three-hour schedule. Others may astonish you by sleeping for five hours between feedings and then want to be fed almost hourly for the next several feedings. And then there are those growth spurts that keep you wondering. If

To Encourage the Let-Down Reflex to Work Before You Begin Nursing, Mothers Advise . . .

Peace and quiet are essential. Don't be shy about clearing the room of visitors, turning off the TV, and putting out the "Do Not Disturb" sign. In the beginning, at least, it's best to have nothing else on your mind but feeding that baby. Later you can do all sorts of things when you nurse. You should see me! I made an entire cake one-handed while I nursed Jonathan.

• • •

I noticed in the hospital that a warm shower aimed directly onto my breasts helped release my milk. Applying a warm moist washcloth to my breasts fifteen minutes before I expected to nurse also seemed to help.

• • •

I massage my breasts to literally help move the milk down. A massage involves motions similar to breast self-examination. Starting at the top of the breast and pressing firmly toward the chest wall, move your fingers in a circular motion on one spot, then move on to a new area, spiraling in toward the areola.

• • •

I use a combing, stroking motion, from the top of the breast down toward the areola.

• • •

I can't relax when I'm thirsty, and nursing makes you thirsty. I sit down with a glass of water, fruit juice, or herb tea at my side before I nurse.

• • •

I make a conscious effort to relax by closing my eyes, breathing deeply, and envisioning the milk being made in the beautiful, grapelike clusters of alveoli, then flowing freely through the ducts and out to my baby. People have been known to fight diseases with this kind of visualization. Why shouldn't I use the same technique to enhance nursing?

• • •

I was very, very tense. Syntocinon nasal spray, a synthetic form of oxytocin, brought my milk down immediately. My doctor wrote a prescription for this. I only needed it for the first week or so. Not only was it physically helpful, it was tremendously *confidence boosting.*

---

you can just give yourself over to the process for the first month, some order will begin to emerge.

Question: *What is the primary factor influencing milk supply?*

Answer: The primary factor is nipple stimulation, which in turn stimulates the release of prolactin, the milk-making hormone. Frequent, unrestricted sucking is what makes milk. A newborn may want to nurse twelve or fifteen times a day. It may be encouraging to know that prolactin levels are at their highest for the first two weeks after birth.

Question: *What is the key to successful nursing?*

Answer: Lots of sucking and a well-functioning let-down reflex, which is what moves the milk forward. To work smoothly, the let-down reflex needs practice and conditioning. So be patient, and give it a chance.

It can be helpful to remember that the pituitary gland, which releases oxytocin, is connected to the hypothalamus, the "seat of the emotions," and its output is not automatic. Instead it depends to a degree on the woman's emotional state. A nursing mother almost always produces plenty of milk in her alveoli as long as the baby sucks and causes the release of prolactin. But if she is an emotional wreck from fatigue or tension, the let-down reflex may not work. This is why it is so important to be rested and relaxed.

Question: *What does the milk let-down reflex feel like?*

Answer: Some women experience no sensation when the milk lets down but may notice that the other breast is leaking. Others describe the let-down as anything from a slightly tingly feeling like pins and needles to a stronger, more painful, sensation accompanied by afterpains in the uterus. And others feel it as an erotic sensation. Remember that the let-down reflex works in both breasts at the same time. This information can be useful when certain problems, such as engorgement, arise and when you want to pump your breasts. Read on.

Question: *How long does it take for the milk to let down?*

Answer: This varies from woman to woman. Some, generally those who have established a comfortable nursing pattern, will feel the let-down reflex operate before they even put the baby to the breast. Her cry or even a thought about her can trigger it. For the novice, however, the let-down reflex must become a conditioned response. In the beginning it can take three to five minutes of nipple stimulation before the milk lets down. Again, that is why it's important to nurse the baby for at least five minutes on each breast to start.

The big question: how do you know the baby is getting enough to eat?

Yes, intellectually I know breast-feeding is supposed to work on a supply-and-demand basis. The more your baby needs, the more often he will nurse, and the more milk your body will make to meet his needs. But it can be hard to be cool about these things when you're nervous, and your baby is fussy, and you realize that this 6-pound person's life is entirely in your hands. You don't want to starve the kid as you lie back repeating the litany "trust your body! trust your body!"

• • •

An Expert Replies:
Some mothers find it difficult to stay calm about their baby's feeding when they have no idea how much milk he is getting. The correct advice is "leave it to the baby; he will take what he needs

if you just feed him whenever he wants." But if you are worried, you may find it hard to follow this advice. In fact, worry over whether the baby is getting enough is one of the most common reasons mothers change to bottle-feeding: It is a relief to be able to see 3 or 4 ounces vanishing into the baby.
—Penelope Leach
Your Baby and Child:
From Birth to Age Five

• • •

A quick, easy way to reassure yourself that your infant is getting enough milk is to check the number of wet diapers. If he has six to eight really wet ones a day, he is probably getting plenty of milk. Frequent bowel movements are also a sign that [your] baby is getting enough to eat. For the first six weeks or so, a breast-fed baby will usually have two to five bowel movements a day.

From time to time, your doctor will weigh the baby as a way of measuring physical progress. Some babies never lose an ounce from the day they're born and put on weight with the greatest of ease. Most babies lose some weight during the first week but get back to birth weight by two to three weeks of age. After that, a pound a month, or 4 to 7 ounces a week, is usually considered an acceptable gain, although some babies gain as much as a pound a week. Family characteristics and the baby's individual makeup need to be considered. Remember—healthy happy babies come in all shapes and sizes.
—La Leche League International
The Womanly Art of Breastfeeding

WARNING! DON'T OFFER BOTTLES AND DON'T CHECK THE BABY'S WEIGHT YOURSELF. If you don't have people who are supportive of you, listen to the following mothers.

Growth Spurts

It can be very, very helpful to know that there are a few ages when many babies—even babies fed with formula—quite predictably go through growth spurts. These are at seven to ten days, three and six weeks, and again at around three months. There are subtle differences in the ways we can look at this. Instead of thinking in terms of not being able to provide the baby with what she needs, think in terms of the baby wanting more, you being sensitive to that need, and responding by nursing more frequently. Continue to drink plenty of fluids—at least eight glasses of noncaffeinated drinks per day—and be sure to rest. These spurts come at times when when we think we have "recovered" from childbirth and when we think we should be able to resume aspects of our prebaby lives. But watch out. You have to make a conscious effort to slow down and to rest (see Relax and Build Your Milk Supply, page 42).

My mother, who had come to help, was driving me crazy. She insisted that every time Jack cried, it was because he wasn't getting enough milk. She said I looked frantic and exhausted and that she was here to help me get some rest. Her anxiety was infectious. I began to believe her. Finally I called my pediatrician. He said, "If you are incredibly anxious about whether or not your baby is gaining, bring him in for a weight check, but do not do it at home. Home scales are not accurate." We took him in at two weeks. He'd gained. What a relief!

• • •

Do not test your baby for hunger with a bottle after you have finished nursing! If someone else is pressuring you, ignore them. The need to suck is so strong in most babies, and the ease of sucking on a conventional rubber nipple is so great, that most babies will gobble up what is offered, leaving you feeling guilty and discouraged and confused.

• • •

Don't watch the clock or worry about schedules. Your friend who is bottle-feeding will report that her baby eats every four hours, or sleeps five and six hours at a stretch at night. But it takes time to breast-feed. My baby kept falling asleep. Your attitude toward time has to change. Slow down, give in; this is not a productivity contest.

What to Eat and What Not to Eat When You Breast-Feed

What does it take to make breast milk? Information, support, a willingness to try, a degree of rest and relaxation, and good eating habits. Most pregnant women, concerned for the health and well-being of their unborn babies, eat very carefully. But all too often they begin to neglect their diet once the baby is born. They don't have the time and leisure to think about themselves now that their focus is outward to the baby.

Breast-feeding uses between 400 and 500 calories a day; double that amount for twins. Lactating women need between 2,200 and 2,500 calories per day, including six to eight glasses of fluid, to make breast milk and meet their own and their baby's nutritional needs. Whether or not you are nursing, it is *never* a good idea to crash diet. It doesn't work, and it's not good for your body. Crash dieting also mobilizes the fat in a woman's body and releases chemicals or toxins stored there, such as PCBs and pesticides, into her breast milk. It also depletes a woman's stores of calcium and protein, which are needed to feed her bones, muscles, and vital organs. If you don't eat properly, you also run the risk of becoming even more tired, which affects the way you feel about yourself, your baby, and motherhood in general.

The truth is, it does not have to be difficult to eat well and at the same time lose the weight you have gained during pregnancy. Choose good, high-energy, low-fat foods, not those with empty calories. Remember that it is safe—as well as realistic—to lose about half a pound a week. You can do this by eliminating as few as 100 calories a day and increasing your activity level. In this way the weight will come off gradually, which is the way it went on. Weight lost gradually is much more likely to stay off than pounds lost in a hurry. Following are some recommendations for a good healthy diet, very similar to the diet recommended for pregnancy. The main difference is that a lactating woman needs less protein than she did during pregnancy. (If you are nursing a low-birthweight baby, see Breast Milk for Low-Birthweight Babies, opposite page).

Protein. You will need between two and three servings of protein a day. Any of the following foods constitute one serving:

2 ounces lean meat, fish, or poultry
2 eggs
1 cup cooked dried beans or peas
8 ounces tofu
¼ cup peanut butter or ½ cup peanuts
½ cup cottage cheese
2 cups milk, yogurt, or soy milk
¼ to ½ cup pumpkin or sunflower seeds, almonds, or walnuts

Fat. Fat has a bad name in the American diet, but when you are breast-feeding, it is no time to go on a super-low-fat diet. It is essential that you eat two servings a day; any less will affect the quality of your breast milk. Breast milk with a lower fat content is less caloric and filling for the baby. Fat also plays a vital role in your baby's brain development (see How Does Breast Milk Compare to Formula Preparations, page 25). One serving equals approximately 12 grams of fat. Knowing this, you can watch your fat intake by reading labels carefully and being aware that certain foods, such as nuts, chocolate, and avocados, are very high in fat. Eat these foods in moderation, and limit servings of butter, margarine, mayonnaise, or vegetable oil to 1 tablespoon.

Grains and Breads. Grains and whole grain breads not only have the advantage of being high-energy foods; they also contain iron, which the lactating mother needs to feel her best. Four servings per day are the minimum. Any of the following equals one serving:

1 slice whole-grain bread
½ English muffin
½ bagel
½ hamburger roll
1½ cups wheat germ
¼ cup bran
½ cup cooked lentils, beans, or split peas

1 ounce dry pasta
½ cup cooked rice or other grain such as barley, corn, oatmeal, bulghur, or quinoa
2 cups popcorn, made without oil

Calcium-Rich Foods. It is not necessary to drink gallons of milk to make milk, but you do need four to five servings of calcium-rich foods a day. Choose from among the following, each of which equals one serving:

1 cup skim milk or buttermilk
1 cup low-fat plain yogurt
1½ ounces hard cheese
1½ cups cottage cheese
¼ cup grated Parmesan cheese
3 ounces canned salmon
8 ounces tofu
1 cup cooked bok choy, kale, mustard greens, collard greens, or broccoli
¼ cup tahini (sesame-seed paste)

Vitamin C–Rich Foods. You'll need at least two servings a day of foods rich in vitamin C. If your breasts are sore, add an additional serving because this essential vitamin helps to repair tissue. Each of the following constitutes one serving:

1 orange or 4 ounces orange juice
½ grapefruit
½ cup strawberries
¼ papaya
¼ cantaloupe
1 tomato or 1 cup tomato juice
1 cup cooked broccoli, Brussels sprouts, collard greens, or kale
1 green pepper or ½ red pepper
1 cup chopped cabbage

Vitamin A–Rich Foods. Select two to three servings a day from among these green leafy and yellow vegetables and fruits. One serving is equal to any of the following:

1 cup raw or ¾ cup cooked pumpkin, winter squash, sweet potatoes, carrots, broccoli, spinach, asparagus, or green pepper
1 cup cantaloupe, papaya, peaches, or watermelon
2 apricots

Other Vegetables and Fruits. Choose one to two servings of the following to round out your diet. The following constitute one serving:

¼ head lettuce
1 cup bean sprouts or snow peas
1 small potato
½ cup zucchini
1 apple, banana, peach, or pear
1 medium slice pineapple

Iron-Rich Foods. To feel strong and energetic, keep up your stores of iron. The following foods are rich sources:

red meat and organ meats
blackstrap molasses
all types of dried beans (especially black beans and garbanzo beans)
dried fruits (especially prunes and apricots)
spinach, peas, and beets
whole grains and wheat germ

Fluids. It used to be that nursing mothers were advised to drink gallons of fluid a day to keep up their milk supply. But research has shown that excess fluids do not influence milk production. Drink at least 6 to 8 cups of fluid a day, and more

Breast Milk for Low-Birthweight Babies

Though breast milk provides the mother's disease-fighting antibodies, it is often not nutritious enough to prevent growth problems in low-birthweight infants. As an experiment in changing the nutritional balance of breast milk, researchers at the Children's Nutrition Research Center at Baylor College of Medicine in Houston put ten mothers of babies weighing 3½ pounds or less on very-low-fat, high-carbohydrate diets: 5 percent of the total calories consumed from fat and 80 percent from complex carbohydrates. In order to achieve this balance the women cut way back on high-fat dairy products, red meat, and rich desserts and substituted fruits, vegetables, and cereals. Not surprisingly, the milk reflected these changes. It contained more medium-chain fatty acids, which are thought to improve fat absorption by low-birthweight babies. This diet would not benefit infants of normal weight, but if you have a low-birthweight baby and are breast-feeding, a change in your own diet is worth discussing with your baby's doctor.

only if you are thirsty. A good way to remember to drink is to have a small glass of water, seltzer, low-fat milk, or fruit juice beside you when you settle down to nurse.

Vitamin Supplements. Continue to take your pregnancy vitamins while you are nursing just to ensure that you are getting the correct minimum daily requirements. But remember: Vitamins are no substitute for eating good, healthy food.

Answers to Common Questions about Diet and Breast-Feeding

Question: Does the breast-fed baby need vitamin supplementation?

Answer: According to the *Journal of Pediatrics,* there are reports of breast-fed infants with rickets, a disease characterized by a softening of the bones. The reason: Breast milk tends to be low in vitamin D. Supplementation is one way to ensure that the baby gets adequate amounts of this essential vitamin. Another way is to get the baby out in the sunshine, which helps the body to manufacture its own vitamin D in the skin. How much sunshine is enough? Doctors estimate that an infant wearing only a diaper needs thirty minutes of sunlight per week. Fully clothed but without a hat, babies require about two hours of sunlight per week to produce adequate amounts of vitamin D. Remember to use a sunscreen to protect the baby's skin from the harmful effects of ultraviolet rays.

Question: Is it necessary to drink lots of milk in order to produce breast milk?

Answer: No. Even though cow's milk is a good source of calcium, it is also a common allergen for adults as well as for some breast-fed babies whose mothers consume large quantities. Some other good sources of calcium are yogurt, hard cheese, cottage cheese, molasses, tofu, cabbage,

collard greens, kale, sesame seeds, liver, almonds, Brazil nuts, canned sardines, and canned salmon.

Question: Aren't there some foods that mothers should avoid while breast-feeding?

Answer: Traces of everything you consume can appear in your breast milk some four to six hours after you have eaten them. As stated above, the prime offender seems to be cow's milk if you are milk sensitive. Other potentially allergenic foods are citrus products, eggs, and wheat products. Some mothers eliminate onions and garlic, as well as foods in the cabbage family such as broccoli and Brussels sprouts when their babies are fussy. There is no hard evidence, however, that babies mind these foods.

Question: I've heard that beer is good for nursing mothers. Is that so?

Answer: Beer and stout both contain brewer's yeast, which is rich in B-complex vitamins, iron, and protein—all substances that help combat fatigue. You needn't drink beer, however. You can purchase brewer's yeast at the health-food store, but go slowly. Brewer's yeast doesn't suit everyone, and it can make a baby gassy.

Harmful and Potentially Harmful Substances That Affect Breast Milk

Medications

Medications taken during lactation do not affect the baby nearly as much as those taken during pregnancy. It is estimated that as little as 1 to 2 percent of a given medication passes to the baby through your milk. Therefore, it is not considered harmful to take an occasional aspirin, aspirin substitute, or antihistamine. With any other drugs, to be extra safe, always check with your

baby's doctor, who should have access to a publication called *Drugs in Pregnancy and Lactation: A Reference Guide to Fetal and Neonatal Risk,* edited by Gerald Briggs (Baltimore: Williams & Wilkins, 1986). The doctor can also call the La Leche League's main number in Illinois (312–455–7730) to ask additional questions. Whatever you do take, make sure you do so *after* you nurse the baby. This way the medication will have the greatest amount of time to pass through your system before you nurse again. If it is necessary to stop breast-feeding while you are taking a particular medication, you can pump your breasts, throw out the milk, and feed the baby formula or milk from a milk bank or your own milk previously frozen and stored (see page 48 on pumping and storing, and the section Working and Breast-Feeding, page 43, for information on introducing supplemental bottles).

Caffeine

This substance, found in coffee, tea, soft drinks, and chocolate, also passes from the mother's milk to the baby. Large amounts can make the baby tense and fussy. Try to limit your intake of these beverages to a cup or two per day. If you miss the "kick" that caffeine provides, try exercising instead (see pages 135–139).

Cigarettes

Can you smoke and breast-feed your baby? Of course you *can,* and some mothers do—knowing that it would be better for their own health as well as the baby's not to. Like any other ingested substance, nicotine, a stimulant, does pass in small traces to the baby. Though there is still no hard evidence that this is dramatically harmful to the baby, one surmises that it could make a baby irritable or tense. It is also suspected that smoking may reduce milk production as well as the amounts of vitamin C transmitted in the breast milk to the baby.

What is clearly harmful to the baby are the "passive effects" of smoking. Inhaling smoke from other people's cigarettes, cigars, and pipes increases the likelihood that a baby will have respiratory infections. Dropping ashes on the baby is also a possibility, no matter how careful you think you are being. If you can't give up smoking entirely, consider cutting back to under ten cigarettes a day. Smoke only after you nurse and do so outdoors or in a room away from the baby.

Alcohol

Moderation is the key here. In the past it has been suggested that new mothers sit down with a glass of wine or beer to relax as they nurse. This isn't necessarily the best advice, however. Small amounts of alcohol will reach the baby, which may not be a problem as long as drinking is moderate. What is moderate, however? Certainly no more than two drinks a day. Of equal danger is the fact that alcohol can act as a depressant for the mother or can become an escape from the very real stresses that new parenthood brings. Though it's certainly not easy, it's better to face these stresses head on and try to deal with them rather than run from them. (See The Transition into Motherhood, page 143.)

Marijuana

Why take a chance? Though the evidence is by no means in yet, we do know that heavy marijuana smoking alters brain-cell chemistry in adults. We also know that even if you smoke only occasionally, certain unhealthful elements, including THC, are stored in your fat cells and remain in your body for long periods of time. These same elements will appear in your breast milk in small quantities. THC also lowers the levels of prolactin, the "mothering" hormone responsible for milk production.

Cocaine

Though we don't yet know exactly how damaging cocaine can be to a nursing baby, we do know that even a single dose can kill an adult. This powerful drug also passes through to breast milk and puts the healthy development of the baby's still delicate nervous system at tremendous risk. DON'T USE COCAINE, ESPECIALLY DURING THE NURSING PERIOD. If you do use it, stop nursing immediately and enter a drug treatment program to give you the support you will need to overcome your addiction, to face the pain in your life, and to deal with the issues that parenthood presents.

Mothers Talk About Common Breast-Feeding Problems

All breast-feeding literature is supportive and encouraging, as it should be. Nursing a baby can be a wonderfully close and satisfying experience, with as many benefits for the mother as there are for the baby. But there can be a dark side, which falls into the category called "common problems." There are usually many good, practical suggestions for dealing with these problems that work more often than not. But little mention is made about how deeply these common problems can undermine a new mother who is heavily invested in the notion of success and who is used to having it if she works hard and diligently enough. Her sense of competence and well-being can be truly shaken if things don't go as planned.

If these problems did not coincide with the initial shock of new parenthood and the demands of newborn care, they might not seem so great, and we would be better equipped to handle them. But alas, they usually come in the beginning! There are some practical ways to approach the problems, but attitude is important, too. Don't be hard on yourself! Know that you are not alone. Before you try any of the suggested approaches, pause and listen to the supportive advice from the following women.

Problems are common in the first days and weeks. Almost everyone I know had at least one and weathered it. My nipples were very sore. I even cried. I thought it would never end. One day I noticed that I wasn't wincing when I put Lee to my breast. Things had gotten better. The bliss you read about can be real. I felt it on many occasions, but not until breast-feeding was well established.

• • •

You need support when you breast-feed. You really need support if you have a problem. Surround yourself with positive people who aren't going to tell you to give up. Be ruthless! Stay away from the doubters. Don't let them in the house! You don't need them.

• • •

Breast-feeding is not a test for "mother of the year." You don't have to love every minute of it to do it. In fact, some days you don't have to like it at all, and there's nothing wrong with admitting it. It doesn't mean that you don't want to do it, or can't succeed.

• • •

I had mastitis and was sure that I would have to stop nursing. My La Leche League leader gave me the following advice. She said, "When you call your doctor, tell him what is going on, but make sure that you state positively that you know it is possible to continue to nurse. Stress that you have a specific problem that needs to be solved with his help." I followed this advice and got positive results. If you come across as doubtful, a doctor who is not terribly well informed about breast-feeding may feel that he is helping you out by suggesting that you stop. You don't want an out as much as you want help and support.

· · ·

There are as many ways to breast-feed as there are mothers and babies. I've nursed three babies. The first time I was not a purist. My daughter had plenty of bottles. That was for my benefit, not hers. I wasn't confident. Whenever she cried, I blamed it on inadequate breast-feeding. However, she thrived in spite of me. With the others, I never gave them bottles. They thrived, too.

· · ·

Amity was born seven weeks early. I was determined to breast-feed her, and I did by pumping with an electric pump rented from the La Leche League. I went through a great deal to succeed and want to lend my support to other mothers in the same situation. If you have a premature baby, you may have to fortify yourself against people who don't understand why you want to make the effort to nurse when, in their eyes, you should simply be happy to have a baby at all. In other words, who are you to be so fussy, or "fanatic," as one relative put it, about how the baby eats. They also don't believe the baby will get enough to eat. Why didn't they say things like, "Isn't it wonderful that you are trying!" Amity had some scary ups and downs before we brought her home. I think what got me through was saying over and over, as I pumped away, sometimes crying in fear, anger, and fatigue, "I'm doing the right thing! I'm doing the right thing!" I wish I could be there in person with my arm around every mother who needs understanding. Take it from me, you're terrific for trying.

· · ·

Give it a chance. I was very doubtful about the whole business. I took it one day at a time. I had some problems. I was terribly engorged and got a plugged duct, and the baby wasn't latching on properly. Later he wasn't gaining the way the doctor thought he should. I set little goals. I'd say to myself, "We'll see if we can get past this. In three days or by next week if things aren't better, maybe I'll stop." I always knew that I could switch. This approach worked for me. I never saw breast-feeding as an all-or-nothing process. I saw it as a choice, not a "must" or a "should."

· · ·

I say hang in there. The best parts are yet to come.

· · ·

Tell the women who read your book that it does get better. In fact, don't tell them once. Keep telling them it gets better! It gets better! It gets better! Tell them that a hundred times.

The Most Common Breast Problems While Nursing

Sore Breasts

Breast soreness can be caused by a number of things, but the treatment is almost always the same. In *The Womanly Art of Breastfeeding* (New York: NAL, 1983), the La Leche League, which has helped many thousands of nursing mothers with sore breasts, says: "Whatever the cause of a sore breast, there are three basic steps involved in treatment: apply heat; get plenty of rest; and keep the breast comfortably empty by frequent nursing. These procedures may sound deceptively simple, but immediate action can mean the difference between a few hours of discomfort and several days in bed." I agree with this advice and so do the contributors to *Babysense*.

Engorgement

Engorgement or swelling of the breasts is very common when the milk comes in, two to five days after the baby's birth. It can also occur when the baby sleeps through a feeding or when you are weaning and drop a feeding. The painful, overfull feeling is caused by the increased flow of blood and lymph and very high levels of the hormone prolactin. It is prolactin that produces large quantities of milk in the alveoli. Engorged breasts feel hard and warm, and they hurt! In fact, the breasts can be so full that the nipples flatten, and the baby can have difficulty latching on. And that hurts, too! If the engorgement is not relieved, the swollen tissues can actually begin to hinder the milk production as well as its release to the baby. This can be frustrating to the baby, who then may keep pulling off the breast, causing added soreness to the nipples.

It sounds worse than it is! Engorgement is not a serious problem, but as you can see, it can undermine your comfort and feelings of confidence and be the start of various vicious cycles.

For engorgement, prevention and cure are very similar. The best way to avoid engorgement is to nurse frequently as soon and as often after the birth as you can. Nurse in varying positions, on *both* breasts, to empty them. This will "milk" all the ducts located behind the areola. If you are already engorged, relief should come if you can get your breasts to "leak." To do this, encourage your let-down reflex to operate fifteen minutes before you nurse (see page 32). Heat is best for this and usually releases the milk spontaneously. Use warm wet compresses on your breasts; a hot shower is even better. Never use ice! If you do not have access to heat, then gently stroke your breasts with a "combing" motion (see page 46) until they begin to leak.

This release of milk will relieve you of some of the fullness and will help soften your nipples and make them less flat and more erect so that the baby can grab on. Your milk will have already let down, so the baby will not have to work so hard to get it. All of these activities will stimulate blood and lymph circulation and open the milk ducts.

If you are engorged, *do* continue to wear a bra. It will serve as a gentle compressor to keep fluid from entering breast tissue—much in the way that support hose help with swollen ankles. At the same time, check to make sure that the bra is not squeezing you too tightly in any one spot. Don't go overboard on fluids at this time. Stay between six and eight glasses a day. Don't pump your milk with a breast pump for relief as this will stimulate your nipples to send the "make-milk message" to the brain. You don't want to increase your supply when you are engorged. Whatever you do, don't use a nipple shield (see Say No to Nipple Shields!, on this page.)

Plugged Duct

Sometimes only one area of the breast will become engorged because the baby has not "milked" the ducts in this area. The area will appear red and feel hard or lumpy. This can be painful, but it is not serious unless left untreated. Then it can lead to a breast infection, which is hard on both you and the baby. If you have a plugged duct, regard it as a warning to slow down, rest, and take the time to nurse fully on each breast.

The treatment for a plugged duct consists of heat and gentle firm pressure or massage on the engorged or plugged area several times a day. Nurse frequently, using the affected breast first to make sure that it is emptied. Make sure that the baby is positioned correctly (see How to Hold the Baby While Nursing, page 29), with as much of the areola in her mouth as possible, so that she milks all the ducts. The La Leche League also suggests that you get on your hands and knees and "hang" over the baby, and nurse from above. This way you will have gravity on your side to help unplug the duct. Do whatever works! Last but not least, double-check that your bra is not constricting your breasts.

Breast Infection

If you have the soreness or lump described above as partial engorgement or a plugged duct accompanied by flulike symptoms, you probably have a breast infection. Do not panic! This does not mean that you have to stop nursing your baby or even take a break. Your baby will not be harmed because of the infection-fighting agents, or antibodies, in your breast milk. The treatment is the same as for plugged ducts. Your own doctor or your pediatrician may prescribe antibiotics and will know which are safest for a nursing baby. If there are doubts, check *Drugs in Pregnancy and Lactation: A Reference Guide to Fetal and Neonatal Risk,* edited by Gerald Briggs (Baltimore: Williams & Wilkins, 1986). Remember, too, that the baby's stools may be looser when you are on antibiotics, and he may get diaper rash. Be sure to take the full course of the medication. It is tempting to stop once your symptoms are gone, but don't, or the infection is likely to recur. (See pages 237–238 for more information about antibiotics.)

Sore Nipples

One of the most common problems with breast feeding is sore nipples—particularly if you are

<hr>

Say No to Nipple Shields!

Nipple shields look like bottle nipples that fit over the breast. Sometimes they are suggested as a way to protect a sore breast and give it a rest. They are also sometimes offered as a way to make it possible for a baby to latch on when nipples are engorged and flat, or inverted.

So what's wrong with nipple shields? They seem like a good idea, but they aren't because they don't solve problems. They only delay the effective solution and in doing so can cause other problems. Here is how: Without the direct contact of your baby's mouth on your nipple, it will not be stimulated enough to send the "make-milk message" to your brain. This, in turn, will affect your milk supply. Furthermore, the bottle-style nipple shields can cause "nipple confusion" (see page 31), which can lead to rejection of the breast. If it is absolutely necessary to use a nipple shield, make one out of a Nuk-style nipple.

<hr>

fair skinned. The nipples are tender and *really* hurt when the baby sucks on them. Though this is not a serious problem, it certainly *feels* like one—and don't let anyone tell you otherwise! If it is any comfort at all, you should know that soreness almost always goes away with time.

Breast-feeding experts used to feel that soreness occurred primarily because of lack of nipple preparation and toughening, or from not building up nursing time gradually. Now there is research to suggest that positioning the baby improperly on the areola is the real culprit (see page 30 for tips on correct nursing positions).

Soreness can lead to other problems. Pain, or even the thought of pain, is anxiety producing, and this can inhibit the milk let-down reflex. When the milk doesn't let down, the baby may not feel satisfied and may vigorously pull off the breast, causing even more tenderness and pain.

If you have prepared your breasts in advance, nipped engorgement in the bud, and have correctly positioned the baby on your breast every time you nurse, your chances of developing sore nipples in the first place are greatly reduced. If it's too late, take heart. The following seven-step plan of attack plus the tincture of time should help.

1. Breast milk itself, gently massaged onto the painful nipple, is said to have wonderfully curative properties. Use heat to stimulate your let-down reflex so that you leak a little milk. Others have found relief by rubbing small amounts of Massé cream or vitamin E oil from a capsule onto the nipple.

2. Check your diet, and make sure that you are getting plenty of vitamin C, which helps repair tissue. Don't be a martyr. Your goal is to establish breast-feeding, not to suffer. Remember, you can take aspirin in small quantities to help with the pain. Slow, deep, abdominal breathing can also help bring relief.

3. After each feeding, air-dry your nipples by leaving the flaps of your nursing bra open. You can also cautiously expose them to sunlight for five-minute periods three or four times a day. Or you can substitute a reading lamp with a 40-watt bulb, placed at a distance of a yard. Do not use soap or any other drying agent on your nipples.

4. Carefully go over the mechanics of correctly positioning the baby on the breast (see page 30). It cannot be stressed too often how important this is. If the baby's tongue is rubbing on the tip of your nipple, which sometimes happens when she falls asleep at the breast, this improper sucking or pacifying can cause you a lot of pain. So check the tongue position. If the baby needs additional sucking, offer a Nuk-style pacifier.

5. Unfortunately, sore nipples can hurt so much that one is tempted to cut back on feedings and give the nipple a chance to heal. But this is not the best approach. Instead, nurse frequently and for shorter durations, keeping in mind that the baby can empty a full breast within seven minutes. Don't wait for the baby to become ravenously hungry. He will suck more vigorously than ever or even pull on your breast, which will add to your discomfort.

6. Check to see if the baby has thrush, a mouth infection usually contracted in the birth canal. To check for thrush, look for white, milky patches on the tongue and cheeks. Milk wipes away easily. When you attempt to "wipe off" thrush, there will be a raw patch of skin underneath. Thrush can not only make a baby's mouth sore and affect his sucking comfort, but also make a mother's nipples sore. Treatment with an antifungal medicine is needed for baby's mouth as well as the mother's breasts, so that the two do not continue to pass it back and forth.

7. Do not use nipple shields! Nursing mothers are sometimes offered these in the hospital on the theory that giving a sore nipple a chance to rest will help to cure it. (See Say No to Nipple Shields!, page 39.)

Undersupply of Milk

Here I'd been sailing along thinking this breast-feeding is a snap. Isn't it great. It's so easy once you get past the beginning. We went everywhere. We could do everything. What's the big deal? I felt like mother earth herself nursing him at parties, on park benches. We even went to the movies. Do you want to know what guilt feels like? He had lost seven ounces on our first visit to the doctor.

• • •

My mother kept saying the baby was hungry, and I guess she was right. I feel so discouraged.

If your baby is not gaining at the rate your doctor feels is appropriate for a *breast-fed baby,* you may suspect that you are producing less milk than the baby needs. Before you panic, pause for a moment and know that you have your child's best interests at heart and that you will not let him starve. Do *not* waste time feeling guilty. Instead, direct that energy toward dealing with the problem, and above all, stay away from negative people. This is just the opportunity the doubters are looking for. Following are some observations you can make and actions you can take.

• Is your baby going through a growth spurt? These tend to occur at about ten days, three weeks, six weeks, and again at three months; however, they can happen at other times, too. The baby will be hungry. Wanting to nurse more often is a logical response. Give yourself over to this, and at the same time try to rest, relax, and eat well.

• If you look carefully at your own activity level, you may notice that it has changed. Often, a woman starts out breast-feeding and gives herself entirely over to it as she rests and recovers from childbirth. During early postpartum, she exists in a kind of "time warp"—up at night, sleeping late, taking naps, not getting dressed until two in the afternoon. Then, as the baby begins to settle in and Mom feels a little less dazed, she begins to come back to earth and re-enter "reality." The shopping and meals have been neglected, and so have the plants. She's probably also begun to feel a little stir crazy and wants to get out of the house. She begins to add elements of her former life—her "real" life—to her day. Even though her sleep is still interrupted at night, she may not feel the need for or, more to the point, feel she can *justify* a nap during the day. Without realizing it, she's not making as much milk as the baby needs because she is overly tired.

The best approach is to *slow down.* Experts on breast-feeding, including the La Leche League, recommend giving yourself over almost entirely to increasing your milk supply for twenty-four to forty-eight hours. This means doing little else but nursing and resting, eating, and drinking properly. You may have to ask for help—help in caring for the house, for other children if there are any, or for yourself. Asking for the last can be especially hard for a competent woman who is used to caring for herself as well as others. Babies can, if we let them, teach us how to set priorities. In the grand scheme, what is more important—a clean house, a cooked meal, a visit with a friend, a completed piece of work, or this time in your life with *this* baby, a time that will never come again?

• Keep notes on how often you are feeding the baby. (See page 276 in the record-keeping section.) The best way to make more milk is for the baby to stimulate your breasts by sucking. If your baby is the sleepy type (he falls asleep during feedings and is able to last for long stretches between them), chances are your breasts are not getting adequate stimulation. Even though it can seem perverse to wake a sleeping baby, do so if you must. Feed the baby at least every three hours during the day, and do not let him sleep for more than five hours at night. If you are working away from home and don't have access to the baby, try to pump your breasts more often.

• If your nipples are sore, remember: Do not reduce the amount of nursing, because this can affect your milk supply. Instead, nurse more often for shorter periods of time, and follow the other suggestions for relieving the discomfort (see pages 39–40).

• If your breasts are engorged, this too can affect your milk production. See page 38 for ways to deal with engorgement.

• Check to see if the baby is sucking effectively (see page 30 on positioning the baby on the breast and checking for correct tongue position). His tongue should be under your breast so that he can effectively "jaw" as much of the areola as will fit into his small mouth. This is how he "milks" the ducts and stimulates the breast to make more milk. If he has been using a bottle with a standard-shaped nipple, he may be suffering from nipple confusion. A call to The La Leche League or to a lactation consultant may be in order.

• Make sure the baby is nursing from *both* breasts. To further encourage milk production, switch from one breast to the other at least twice during a feeding. Watch carefully to see when the baby's sucking and swallowing slow down, then switch, even if it has only been four or five minutes.

• Is your baby using a pacifier instead of your breast to get most of his sucking satisfaction? If the baby is fussy, try putting him to the breast, even if he has already just eaten.

• Is your baby taking a bottle? If so, try eliminating it, and nursing him instead, or consider using a supplemental nutrition system (see illustration opposite.)

Question: If the baby isn't getting enough breast milk, shouldn't I offer supplementary bottles?

Answer: You can always do that, but why not wait and see if you can build up your milk supply first? Some experts suggest allowing at least two weeks, one to build up the supply and the second to observe the changes in behavior of the baby. The problem with offering a bottle is that one bottle tends to lead to another. Bottles have a subtle way of undermining your commitment as well as your confidence. And the rubber nipple is much easier for the baby to suck milk from than your breast. Your baby might grow confused or, just as difficult, may come to prefer the bottle and reject your breast. Then you will be in the difficult position of denying the baby something he seems to want.

Supplemental Nutrition System. **This cleverly designed device allows a nursing mother to supplement her baby's feedings with milk from her own breasts, milk from a breast milk bank, or infant formula as the baby continues to stimulate her breasts by sucking. Thin tubes attached to the supplement are taped to her breasts. As the baby sucks, he receives milk from both the breast and the tube without causing nipple confusion that can occur when he sucks on a bottle nipple.**

Nursing After a Cesarean

There is no reason why you can't breast-feed after a cesarean. At first it may seem difficult to comprehend how you will manage to nurse and protect your tender incision at the same time. But it is possible, and so will be rolling over, sitting up, and standing. You will just have to go slowly and accept help in the beginning. The most remarkable aspect of a cesarean is the rapid recovery. By the time you leave the hospital, you will marvel at your agility, sprightliness, and independence.

Nurse as soon as possible. Though one hears about cesarean mothers who are able to breast-feed on the delivery table, most new mothers who have had major surgery need some time to heal and rest before they feel up to it. Remember that there is no reason to be a martyr. Make sure your physician knows you are breast-feeding. Then take the pain medication offered. It will not adversely affect the baby. In fact, the American Academy of Pediatrics takes the position that the benefits of nursing far outweigh the effects of your analgesic on the baby. Deep breathing will also help you to manage your discomfort. If you get up and walk as soon as possible, this will help to move the gas out of your intestines, get your circulation going, and generally speed the recovery process.

Cesarean Mothers Offer Suggestions and Support

I found it helpful to have my husband spend the daytime in the hospital with me. I slept most of the time, but when the baby stirred, he was right there to wake me and to help me position her on my breast. When he had to go back to work, my mother-in-law took over for an afternoon. After that I was able to manage on my own.

• • •

At first I felt really uncomfortable and out of it, and quite tearful and lonely in my single room. I found that when Caity was with me I felt better. Instead of thinking about myself and my miseries, I thought about her. Despite my awkwardness, she seemed to know how to nurse perfectly well, so we got off to a better start than I ever would have imagined.

• • •

Fortunately the hospital I gave birth in was very sensitive to cesarean mothers. They put us together in the same rooms, and we had a real sense of camaraderie as we struggled with our IVs, our bed rails, and our bedpans. It's deadly to compare your birth experience with the woman down the hall who delivered vaginally and is dancing around the hallways and drinking champagne two hours after she's delivered.

• • •

I have to admit that I was disappointed, even though a healthy baby is what is most important. My attitude, however, is that very often there is an upside to disappointment, and in this case it was Tom's early and intense involvement with our baby. I am usually a real "take over" type of person and consider myself more competent than most people. I really wasn't up to much for the first day but felt wonderful knowing that Tom was doing many of the things for Emily that I couldn't. He was able to stay in the room for a good part of each day with us. While I dozed, he held her a lot and really tuned in to her. He watched the way she slept and noticed just how she became wakeful. His large hands were really helpful when it came to putting her onto the breast. He burped her and changed her. In fact, it was he who proudly showed me how to diaper her properly. He was also my advocate, making sure that I got what I needed from the nursing staff, whether it was extra pillows or a consultation with the pediatrician. I feel like I loved him more than ever, and part of that came out of my allowing him to take care of me as well as the baby. The three of us were very close by the time we went home.

• • •

Warn women to take it easy at home. I didn't. I think I was trying to be supermom too soon. You've experienced a great deal. Think of the tremendous changes your body and your psyche have been through, first with pregnancy, then birth involving surgery, and then gearing up for nursing. You really do need to allow yourself to rest and to do nothing but take care of the baby.

This is pretty easy the first week at home when everyone is reinforcing you with "Oh let me do this for you," but once that initial flurry is over, you still have to be able to ask for help and let a lot go.

Working and Breast-Feeding

If you want to be a working mother and a breast-feeding mother at the same time, there is no reason why you shouldn't try. Giving of yourself in this special way can help reinforce that complex and mysterious bond you feel with your baby. Breast-feeding, its physical and emotional benefits, are gifts that only you as a mother can offer, which for many women is meaningful compensation for leaving the baby. Breast-feeding can also offer a relaxing, peaceful, and welcome respite from the hassles of work. It also offers a pure and direct way of connecting with your baby before leaving for work and reconnecting at the end of the day.

Nursing while working does require extra time, effort, tedium, some sacrifices, and a real commitment on the mother's part. The crucial variables seem to be determination, timing, a degree of flexibility, preparation and practice, and the conviction that you can work out your own system. Research shows that the best odds for success come from part-time work combined with pumping begun sometime after the baby is sixteen weeks old, but many women do it differently. Whatever works for you is best, be it pumping and offering only your own milk, or partially weaning and supplementing with formula.

Whatever method you adopt, be sure to read the section on working mothers (page 181), and aim to streamline your life as much as possible. It is worthwhile for all new parents—but especially the working nursing mother—to cultivate

Comfortable Nursing Positions for Cesarean Mothers

For the first couple of days after you give birth, do not be shy about asking for assistance from nurses or spouse. Lie on your side, with the bed elevated slightly and the railing up. Put a pillow between your legs to take the pressure off your abdomen, and another pillow behind you to cushion your back against the railing. Make sure the baby is level with your breast and directly facing it, so that he does not have to turn his head. Nurse from the first breast for five minutes. Then, to get from one side to the other, have your assistant hold the baby while you use the guardrails to roll over and get repositioned on the other side. As you get stronger, you will be able to roll over while holding the baby on your chest.

Other comfortable positions, once you are a little bit more agile, are the standard "madonna position" and the "football position" (see page 30). Make ample use of pillows to protect your incision as well as to raise the baby to a comfortable level facing the breast.

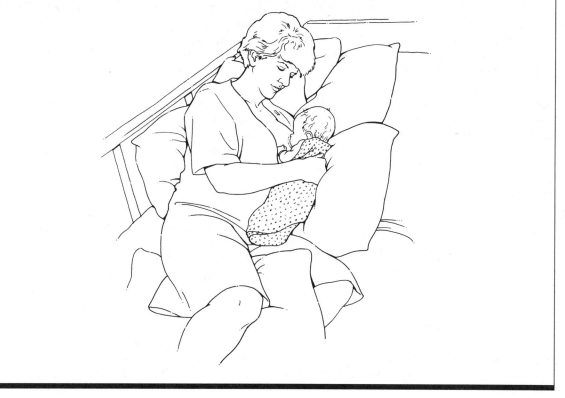

the attitude that her child's babyhood represents a very short period in the entire nurturing spectrum. There will be time later to catch up with all the undone tasks and to give to others beyond spouse and baby. But until then she needs to say no to just about anything extra. (See Mothers Under Stress: Relax and Build Your Milk Supply, page 42.)

Question: *How does employment affect breast-feeding?*

Answer: To find out, Dr. Kathleen Auerbach surveyed 567 married and single employed nursing mothers. The most important factor, she found, was how soon after her baby's birth the mother returned to work. Mothers who rejoined the work force when their babies were at least sixteen weeks old typically nursed longer than those who returned sooner—most likely because the mothers were experienced at breast-feeding and their milk supply was solidly established.

Not surprisingly, Dr. Auerbach also found that part-time working mothers, who miss fewer feedings, tended to nurse their babies longer than full-time working mothers. A third variable was whether or not the mothers expressed their milk when they missed a feeding. The mothers who did so were more likely to nurse longer than those who didn't by supplementing with formula instead.

Preparations and Practical Considerations

• In some European countries, where breast-feeding has always been the norm, many businesses allow nursing mothers breaks so they can go to nearby child-care sites to feed their babies. The United States has not come this far, and it is still up to us individually to make the best arrangement we can. There is certainly no harm in asking your employer to be flexible. Is it possible to work part-time, to bring work home, or "ease" back into a full-time job, starting with a few hours a few times a week and gradually building up? Each nursing mother who can work out a satisfactory arrangement with her employer is setting a precedent for all who follow.

• If you plan to work and nurse, choose a child-care arrangement that will support you. A baby-sitter who knows how important nursing is to you will make the extra effort sometimes required to keep the baby content until you arrive with full breasts at the end of your workday. For instance, if you use family day care, are you welcome to arrive early and nurse the baby before going off to work and to do the reverse at the end of the day? You might also consider finding child care near work so that you can go to the baby at lunchtime.

• Eat well and remember to satisfy your thirst when you are at work, preferably with decaffeinated drinks.

• Dress in simple, loose, washable clothing. If you are pumping, choose two-piece outfits that are easy to lift and will not look wrinkled or out of shape. If you leak, wear breast pads and keep extras at your workplace as well as an extra top just in case.

• It is useful to master the art of hand-expressing milk—either to collect milk, to relieve overly full breasts, or to stimulate your milk supply. (See How to Hand-Express Milk on page 46 for details.)

• If you plan to pump your breasts, spend some time finding the best breast pump for your needs. Talk to your friends and see what worked best for them, or call the La Leche League and see if they have a group of working mothers. (Also see Choosing a Breast Pump on page 47.)

• Once you have chosen a pump, practice in advance. You will probably feel awkward at first, just as you did when you began to nurse. Give yourself a few weeks to master the techniques in the privacy, peace, and quiet of your own home.

Be patient! Do not be discouraged by the small amount you get on the first few tries. You need time to adjust physically and emotionally. Remember, you are not a machine! You are a living, breathing, sensitive human being. When you are actually nursing your baby, it is the stimulation of your baby's sucking as well as your emotional response that triggers the let-down reflex. But when the baby isn't there, you must trigger the reflex artificially.

After your practice sessions at home, try to think ahead about a quiet, private place at work where you can do your pumping. When you return to work, go there, do a few minutes of slow deep-breathing exercises, and gently massage your breasts before you begin. Warm washcloths will help to trigger the let-down reflex, as will looking at a photograph of your baby. Some women even play tape recordings of the sounds their babies make while nursing. If you are having trouble relaxing enough for the let-down reflex to operate, remember Syntocinon nasal spray. This synthetic form of oxytocin will trigger it.

• Introduce your baby to an alternate feeding method. There is controversy over the best time to introduce a bottle (see Introducing Bottles to the Breast-Fed Baby: Three Points of View, opposite.) If he is over five months, you might want to try a cup and forget about bottles.

• If you find that you cannot maintain enough milk to satisfy your baby's nutritional needs when you are nursing, you don't have to give up breast-feeding. The emotional benefits will still remain if you decide to nurse part time. Nurse the baby first, and then offer a supplement.

Question: *What if the baby refuses the bottle?*
Answer: *Be patient! Let someone else try. Never force it.*

A: Nurse the baby when she is drowsy. Take the baby off the breast very slowly. Gently slip the bottle into the baby's mouth, stroking the top of her palate with the nipple.

A: I resorted to the tiniest bit of jelly to sweeten the nipple.

A: I expressed breast milk onto the nipple, so it tasted right.

A: I had my husband feed Jenny my milk in a bottle. At first she refused. After three tries, she accepted it. We tried once a day.

Dropping Feedings

If you plan to replace missed feedings with formula, without expressing milk, you will be partially weaning your baby (see pages 50–52 on weaning). The best advice to follow for your sake and the baby's is to go slowly. Give yourself at least five if not seven days to eliminate each feeding that comes during your working hours. In this way your body will gradually learn to make less milk at those times.

Many women whose babies drink formula during working hours nurse exclusively at night and on weekends. Their breasts are somewhat full on Mondays, but they handle this by hand-expressing some milk and wearing breast pads to absorb leakage. Be sure to check your breasts often for plugged ducts, and remember to use a variety of positions when feeding the baby to offer the most stimulation to all parts of the areola.

Introducing Bottles to the Breast-Fed Baby: Three Points of View

Your milk can be given to the baby by bottle, spoon, cup, or eye dropper. You don't need to introduce the bottle in baby's first few weeks just because you'll be returning to work later on. Some babies refuse to take a bottle from mother when they know the breast is right nearby, but they soon become accustomed to taking a bottle from the sitter.

—La Leche League International
The Womanly Art of Breastfeeding

Generally, introducing the bottle at about six weeks of age avoids problems. By this age, most babies are competent nursers and yet they're still flexible enough to try something new. Furthermore, the mother's milk supply is well established by now and flows easily enough to keep her baby happy.

—Marvin S. Eiger and Sally W. Olds
The Complete Book of Breastfeeding

The time to decide whether you are going to be a breast-feeding purist is right in the beginning. While many breast-feeding advocates say, "Don't let a bottle in your house," I disagree with this approach.

You simply don't know [in the beginning] how you will feel about full-time nursing when your baby is six or eight months old. Unless the baby has already become used to the rubber nipple in the first three months or so, he may balk. If he's not yet able to drink from a cup, you'll need to be there to feed him when he's hungry. If you offer a biweekly or weekly relief bottle consistently, and don't get lazy about it, you will have the insurance of having an alternate feeding method should you have to be away.

—Frances Wells Burck
Babysense (first edition)

How to Hand-Express Milk

This technique is useful for women who must be separated from their babies. It is also often recommended as part of a treatment program for certain common problems such as sore nipples, overfull breasts, and underfull breasts. For your first practice session, pump or express before your baby nurses, when your breasts are full. This will give you confidence. Before you begin, read through the suggestions for stimulating the let-down reflex on page 32. Also drink a glass of water, milk, or juice before you begin.

Step #1: Wash your hands, then position a clean, wide-mouthed plastic cup, jar, or thermos under your breast at the right height so that you are not straining your back. (Use plastic. More of the leukocytes or white blood cells that fight infection in breast milk will cling to glass than plastic and will be lost to the baby. Plastic also doesn't break.)

Step #2: Cup your breast in one palm and use your other hand to gently stroke or "comb" downwards from the upper portion of the breast, stopping at the areola. Work clockwise all around the breast, using this same motion.

Step #3: Place your thumb above and two fingers underneath, about midway on your breast.

Step #4: Slide fingers and thumb down to the edge of the areola in a firm, squeezing motion as you push back against your chest (easier to do than to describe!). The milk should squirt out in jets.

Step #5: Use this same sliding, pressing, squeezing motion as you move to different points clockwise around the breast.

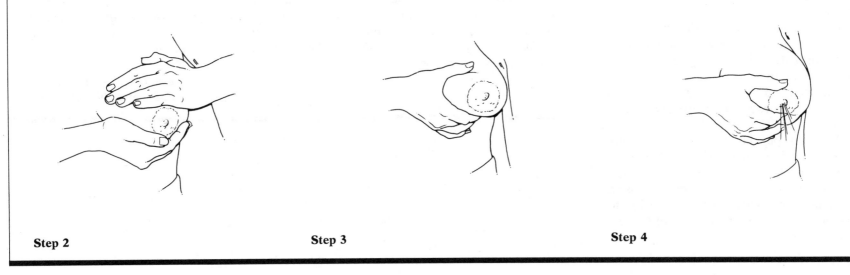

Step 2   Step 3   Step 4

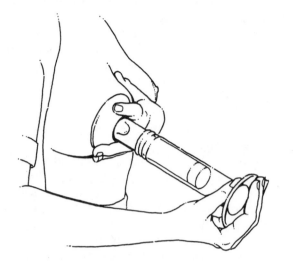

Syringe-style breast pump

Trigger-type breast pump

Choosing a Breast Pump

Breast pumps come in a variety of sizes, shapes, and prices. If you are going to rely on one every day for several months, give your choice careful consideration. A pump you are comfortable with will make a difference in how good you feel about your commitment to continue nursing. Besides cost, consider portability, cleanability, breakability, and, of course, the ease with which it is operated.

Bulb-type Breast Pumps. These look like bicycle horns and consist of a rubber bulb attached to a plastic or glass cup. Though these are inexpensive and widely available at most drugstores, they are not recommended. They do not work efficiently. They also can hurt and, because the cup is not large enough to fit over the entire areola, they can cause damage to the breast tissue. Finally, they are virtually impossible to clean, so that any milk collected runs the risk of being contaminated.

Syringe-type Breast Pumps. The most popular type of breast pump, these work with a gentle, firm action that is quite simple to master. These pumps are made up of two cylinders, one of which slides back and forth inside the other, to create suction on the nipple. The beauty of this pump is that the larger cylinder, which serves as a collection container, can be fitted with a nipple and used as a bottle.

Trigger-type Breast Pumps. As the name suggests, the suction action of this pump is created by squeezing a trigger. The advantage is that it can be used one-handed, though you must be quite dextrous and have fairly large hands to manage comfortably. One problem is that the breast opposite the dominant hand will be emptied more efficiently than the other. Inefficient pumping can cause plugged ducts, which can lead to infections. These pumps are also made of glass. Although they are easy to clean, they are highly breakable.

Battery-Operated Breast Pumps. Though these pumps have their advocates—they can be used one-handed and are portable and nonbreakable—most don't offer the control or the efficiency one would expect. Most of these pumps

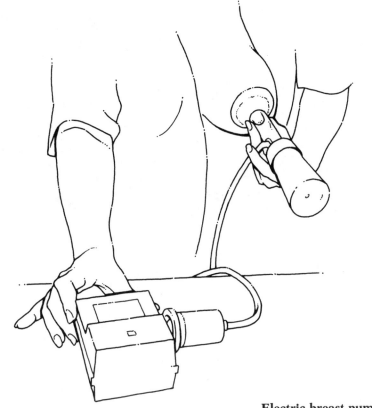

Electric breast pump

Question: *How long is it safe to keep expressed breast milk unrefrigerated?*

Answer: The *Journal of Pediatrics* reports that expressed breast milk can safely remain unrefrigerated for up to six hours. Breast milk's natural bacteriostatic qualities inhibit the growth of bacteria.

Question: *How long can you store breast milk in the refrigerator?*

Answer: Breast milk can be stored in the refrigerator for up to forty-eight hours. This milk will maintain its leukocytes, or antibodies that help ward off infections. Express the milk into a sterile container and transfer it to a separate storage container, bottle, or plastic nurser bag. Remember that breast milk separates, so gently shake it before serving.

Question: *How long can you store breast milk in the freezer?*

Answer: Milk kept longer than forty-eight hours must be frozen. You can freeze breast milk for up to two weeks in the freezer compartment of a refrigerator or up to three months in a separate-door freezer. It can be stored for up to two years in a deep freezer that remains at a constant 0°F. Be sure to label containers with the time and date.

Question: *How do you freeze breast milk?*

Answer: After you express the milk, cool it in the refrigerator. There will be less waste if you freeze milk in small quantities—from 2 to 4 ounces. You can add fresh breast milk to frozen breast milk as long as you add less fresh so that it does not thaw the frozen milk. If you are using the rather fragile plastic nurser bags, double

use up batteries at an alarming rate, which drives their cost much higher than that of your initial investment. If you buy one, check with the La Leche League for the best brands.

Electric Breast Pumps. Although efficient, fast, and easy to use, these pumps are very expensive and therefore generally found only in hospitals, or for rent through pharmacies, medical supply houses, and the La Leche League. Some women get together and rent one of these jointly to keep at their workplace. One hopes that someday it will be standard practice for employers to own and operate one of these as a benefit to their breast-feeding employees.

Note: No matter which pump you use, be sure to read the directions carefully, wash your hands before you start, and clean the pump thoroughly after each use. To be even more efficient, you might consider using plastic breast shells. As you pump one breast, you can collect the milk that lets down from the other breast in a sterile breast shell. These cuplike devices, which can be purchased at drugstores or through the La Leche League, should not be worn for any longer than the ten or fifteen minutes that it takes to pump. The warmth of your body can cause bacteria to grow in the collected milk.

them. Before you seal them, squeeze out the air on top, and fasten them at least an inch from the milk to allow for expansion. Place upright in a container until the milk is frozen solid. If you use bottles, again allow for expansion. Do not tighten caps until milk is completely frozen.

Question: *How do you thaw frozen breast milk?*

Answer: Start by holding the container under cool running water. As the milk begins to thaw, add warm water, then hot water until the milk is gently heated. Then gently shake. The milk is not homogenized and will separate. Do *not* use the top of the stove or a microwave oven. Both weaken the germ-fighting properties of breast milk.

Question: *Once the milk is thawed, for how long can it be used?*

Answer: Thawed breast milk that has not been heated can be used for up to twelve hours as long as it is refrigerated. Milk at room temperature must be thrown away after half an hour.

Question: *Can you refreeze thawed breast milk?*

Answer: No, but if it has been refrigerated you can give it to your baby within twelve hours.

Question: *How do you transport breast milk?*

Answer: The most convenient way to transport it is in a clean, wide-mouthed plastic thermos. (If you plan to freeze the milk, the thermos should be sterile; use a dishwasher or follow the instructions for sterilizing on pages 58–61.) Place ice cubes in the thermos to chill it. Then empty them out before use. If you can't get the milk into a refrigerator within six hours, place it in an insulated bag or a portable cooler surrounded by ice or ice packs.

How Other Mothers Have Worked and Nursed Their Babies

I work full-time as a floor supervisor at a small manufacturing plant. We need the income, and if I miss a day of work, I miss a day of pay. I didn't nurse my first child, because I didn't think I could do it and work. He had bad allergies, though, and I decided I was definitely not taking any chances with my second. At the time I gave birth to Alex, another woman on my floor had been nursing her baby for six months. I called her up, and she told me just how she did it, right down to which breast pump to buy and how to transport the milk and negotiate with the supervisor. We get two fifteen-minute coffee breaks plus lunch. Well, she had asked for two longer breaks and a shorter lunch, and would go to the nurses' station and pump her breasts. She put the milk into a little Igloo cooler with ice packs that she kept in her locker. At first it took me a long time to pump, but after about two weeks, I could do each breast in five or six minutes flat. By Friday I wasn't getting as much milk because I was pretty worn out by then. But then I would nurse all weekend and be up to full capacity by Monday. Remember to keep up your fluid intake at work. I feel proud of myself. Also, Alex hasn't been sick once this year with anything more serious than a cold!

• • •

I have a demanding full-time job in a law firm. I am the primary breadwinner in the family, and I could not afford to stop working. Fortunately, my husband is an artist with great flexibility. If I had an important meeting that I could not schedule for later, I'd lock my office door, drape myself with a towel to collect leaks, and pump my breasts into a large measuring cup. Then I would transfer that into a chilled thermos to take home. On weekends I pumped and stockpiled breast milk in the freezer.

Usually, however, I took a short, early lunch hour. My husband would drive Lila down and pick me up on the corner outside my office building. Then we'd go and park. I'd nurse, cuddle, and love the baby with one hand while I ate my sandwich with the other. Then Tim would drop me off. Sometimes I'd meet my fast-track cohorts on their way out for their fat-cat martini lunches. I never told them where I went or why. I enjoyed having the secret. Humor is essential.

• • •

I work at home as a graphic designer. During the last trimester of my pregnancy, I began to plan on how I could continue to work and nurse the baby. I decided that I would let several of my clients go and kept one major one who needed a catalogue every three months. I knew exactly what was required at every phase and knew that I could get it done at night when Pat was home to baby-sit if necessary. A lot depends on the kind of baby you have. It turned out that Oliver was a baby who slept a great deal. I would nurse him, then put him back into his crib to sleep, and leave the intercom on. Then I'd go right downstairs and get to work. When he got older, I hired a woman to watch him when he was awake, but I had to let her go because she didn't want to bring him to me to nurse and kept offering him bottles instead. No matter how clearly I explained what I wanted, she kept undermining me, so I found another person who has been terrific and is still with us.

• • •

I think when you are a single working parent you need all the support and encouragement and help you can get. I had waited long enough to have her and was determined to nurse Leeanne to maintain the closeness. I knew that I would have to go back to work. The summer she was born I spent a great deal of time looking for a baby-sitter within a block of the school where I taught. Through La Leche, I found a lovely woman who had young children and was at home. I'd nurse Leeanne in bed in the morning. At Gail's house, I would sit and nurse her again. At lunch break I'd race back with my sandwich in a bag and then return again right at the end of the school day. Before we'd get into the car to go home, I'd nurse her. This period of intense nursing did not go on forever, but sometimes it felt that way. There truly were days when I felt it wasn't worth it. I was bone tired, but Gail was so helpful. She never said, "See, you're crazy to have had a kid and then try to nurse her, too." She allowed me to be negative, whereas I sometimes felt some of my fellow teachers were waiting for me to fail. I remember once that I couldn't leave the school for some reason to get to Gail's, and she brought the baby over to the teacher's lounge. I'll never forget that gesture of generosity. Sometimes what women will do for each other truly amazes me. When I think about it I'm very proud of both of us.

Weaning from the Breast

When you are pregnant, people will ask, "Are you going to nurse your baby?" Then it seems that within a few short months after the baby is born and is nursing smoothly and contentedly at your breast, those same people will want to know when you are planning to stop. One discovers that any answer (including "I don't know") is bound to evoke a story or an opinion. One can only conclude that weaning a baby is just as charged an issue as breast-feeding itself.

There are a few *real* truths about weaning, however. One is that any amount of breast-feeding is good, and the advantages of breast-feeding do not cease at any definite time. You are not a failure if you nurse for a very short period. You've given the baby the benefit of a good start on colostrum, rich in nutrients and antibodies.

You've also given yourself something, too: a new experience from which you have grown and learned—even if it's negative. On the other hand, if you decide that you want to nurse your baby for a prolonged period, that too is fine. You are not a weirdo who has to hide in a closet. There is no evidence to suggest that either a little nursing or prolonged nursing produces either insecure people or extraordinarily secure people. Whatever you do, you don't have to justify your actions to anyone. It is easy to say, but hard to do—but nobody should make the decision about weaning for you.

The second truth is that how you go about weaning the baby, and how you deal with your own feelings, are much more important than when you wean or why. It is helpful, however, to look at weaning as a process rather than simply an end to breast-feeding. Weaning need not be synonymous with the notions of "taking away" or "giving up." Instead, weaning really means replacing breast milk—or complementing it—with formula, cow's milk, juice, or solid food. It is best to go slowly and gently with this process—to eliminate one feeding at a time over a period of weeks or months. This way the baby can gradually adapt to another feeding method, and you won't suffer a great deal of physical discomfort due to engorgement and abrupt hormonal changes.

The third truth about weaning is that it is perfectly normal to feel ambivalent about it. You may want to give up or cut back on breast-feeding for all sorts of reasons—some grounded in fact, others quite arbitrary. In other words, you don't have to be totally rational or logical about this decision.

Remember, too, that nothing about weaning need be written in stone. Allow yourself the luxury of flexibility. As you watch for your baby's cues and listen to your own feelings, you may decide to proceed at a different pace than you had originally envisioned, or even change your mind entirely. For instance, if a colicky baby has a good day, and a mother is able to complete a few tasks or have a few moments to herself, weaning may not feel so urgent. This is why going slowly is such good advice.

Question: How did you decide to start weaning your baby?
Answer: I have four children and breast-fed each of them for only a month, a rather maverick approach nowadays. My theory is that this first month is the most important in terms of health benefits for the infant and the mother.

A: I nursed Caroline for a month, then stopped because I was feeling so tired and overwhelmed. I thought that nursing contributed to this. But after I stopped I was still tired and overwhelmed, and then I also felt guilty. I guess that every new mother is entitled to the luxury of saying, "I'd do things differently with a second child." And that's what I say. I am perfectly aware that it is stupid to feel guilty, by the way.

A: My nipples were very sore, and I gave up after six weeks. I dropped a feeding every three days. It was quite painful because I was very engorged.

A: My husband put a lot of pressure on me to stop when Jessica was three months old. Our sex life was so bad—because I was so tired—that he said, "It's either bottles or divorce." I had hoped that I would feel less tired and better about myself physically after weaning Jessica, but in all honesty, I didn't. I was still overweight, exhausted, and depressed. We eventually got some counseling, and that is what helped the most.

A: I don't feel that I made the decision. I went back to work when Ellie was four months old. I tried pumping, but it just began to feel like one more thing that I had to do on top of everything else. I'd jump up at the end of a long meeting and race to the ladies' room, and then a colleague would be knocking on the door, wanting to speak with me and asking me how long I would be. Fortunately, the baby didn't seem to suffer. She wasn't too interested in nursing at that point. After a couple of minutes she'd pull off the breast, look around, play with my shirt, or fiddle with her hands. Because I wasn't pumping and because she wasn't sucking enough at her morning and evening feedings, I couldn't keep my supply up. So it all ended rather more abruptly than I had hoped or anticipated. For about a week I felt sad about it and cried, but then I felt fine.

A: Rachael has been nursing part-time since I went back to work when she was five months old. I haven't thought of this as weaning. At fourteen months she now nurses only in the morning or takes a few sips throughout the day if she's having a bad day.

A: I weaned Caitlin at six months. I had one friend who had a baby when I was pregnant. She planned to nurse for six months, and I think I adopted that as my idea of what seemed right. I also told myself that I didn't want to be "tied down" after that time. Of course I now know that breast-feeding isn't what ties you down. It's the baby who does. I wish that I hadn't been so arbitrary.

A: Abigail weaned herself cold turkey at ten months. I had to go to a funeral and left her with her grandmother for a full day, which I hadn't done before. When I came home—in agony, my

The Timing of Weaning: Different Points of View

There's no single optimal time for weaning, as we can see from the great range of weaning ages around the world.

—Marvin S. Eiger and Sally W. Olds
The Complete Book of Breastfeeding

There are lots of mothers who either aren't able or don't want to nurse until a baby is ready to be weaned to the cup at about five or six months. . . . The physical advantages of breast milk, its purity, its easy digestibility, are most valuable to the baby at first. But there is no age at which they suddenly become of no benefit. The emotional advantages of breast-feeding will not cease at any definite period, either. One sensible time to wean to the bottle is at about three months. By this age, the baby's digestive system will have settled down. She will be about over any tendency to colic. She will be pretty husky and still gaining rapidly. But if a mother would like to stop at one or two months, those are satisfactory times to wean, too. It is a little safer not to wean in very hot weather.

—Benjamin M. Spock and Michael B. Rothenberg
Dr. Spock's Baby and Child Care

There are at least three lags in interest in breast-feeding that originate in the infant. The first is at four or five months and is associated with the sudden widening of interest in his surroundings. The second accompanies the tremendous motor spurt at seven months. The third occurs between nine and twelve months in most babies. A few never lose interest and probably have to be pushed away. When a baby begins to lose interest after nine months, it seems appropriate to me to take him up on it. He has had enough nutritional sucking, and I do not find that many need much more extra nutritional sucking after they have had nine months at the breast. The spurt of motor development and independence that will be coming around a year is geared to a natural separation from the mother, and weaning seems indicated by then.

—T. Berry Brazelton, M.D.
Infants and Mothers: Differences in Development

Since the baby has emotional needs which can easily be satisfied through the closeness of breast-feeding . . . it is hard to understand why we must set a specific time for ending this important, intimate relationship.

—La Leche League International
The Womanly Art of Breastfeeding

breasts were so full!—she refused to nurse and turned away angrily every time I lifted up my shirt to offer. I was in shock, but that was it. She wouldn't budge.

A: *I felt very conflicted about weaning Andrew because he loved it and I loved it. It was so simple and easy. This may sound crazy, but I didn't want to overprotect him the way I felt my husband's mother had done with Adam. Somehow, extended nursing reminded me and Adam of this overprotectiveness. But on the other hand I really wanted to keep on nursing because I kept thinking, "What if we only have one child and this is the only time in my life that I'll have this experience?"*

When Andrew was thirteen months old, he'd really become interested in having sips of orange juice from our glasses at breakfast. Adam kept saying, "Why don't you get him one of those tip-proof cups?" I did, and Andrew hated it. He'd knock it on the floor every time I put it in front of him. I admit that this made me feel a little gratified. Then Adam decided that Andrew wanted a glass, not a cup. He got out one of those plastic champagne glasses, which was very easy to hold. The baby was so thrilled. He was really in charge, sitting there with his own glass. He was ready to go on to something new.

When I realized this, I felt okay about ending nursing. I think I had been looking at weaning him as depriving him of something he deserved—and which I, of course, enjoyed—when in reality, something new and exciting, the control he had over that plastic glass and the fun he had with it, was taking its place. Isn't it incredible what we can put ourselves through when we become parents? On the one hand I laugh at myself a lot for being so silly about so many things. But then I also say, so what, you're entitled to have doubts and needs yourself. You're only human, after all.

Suggestions for Weaning

Following are some points to consider before you begin the process.

• If you think you might wean before your baby is eating solids (around six months), then you will want to introduce a bottle before you do so. The earlier you do this once breast-feeding is established, the surer you will be that the baby will accept a bottle. Every baby is different, but to be safe, once your milk is flowing, offer at least a bottle per week so the baby doesn't forget what the bottle is and reject it.

If you don't want your baby to have bottles, try offering sips from a cup after about five months. If you worry about the reduced amount of milk your baby takes from the cup, remember that you can substitute other milk products such as yogurt, cheese, and cottage cheese.

• Watch your nursing pattern, and decide which feeding will be the easiest for the baby and you to give up. The thought of getting up in the freezing cold and preparing a bottle on a dark November morning may seem too chilling a prospect compared to cuddling and snoozing as you nurse until sunup. On the other hand, a late-night feeding is often the ideal time for a father to offer the frequent nurser a bottle. If you are planning to go back to work, you would obviously focus on eliminating those feedings during the times you will have to be away. Try to pace it so that you eliminate no more than one feeding a week.

• Be alert to your baby's cues and level of interest in nursing. The baby who once nursed so vigorously that beads of sweat appeared on his brow may go through a phase when he appears to be almost goofing off. (See Watching for the Baby's Cues on opposite page.) This is a good time to wean.

• Nursing can be so much more than simply feeding the baby; it becomes an integral part of nurturing. Through it we establish contact, feel close, soothe and comfort, as well as calm and put the baby to sleep. For these reasons many women worry about how they are going to mother without it. (See below on finding substitute comforts for the breast.)

Substitute Comforts for the Breast: Mothers Advise

I was most concerned about naptime. I'd always nursed Zack lying down on my bed after his lunch. Then we would fall asleep together for about an hour. At seven months, I decided I wanted to begin the weaning process. I realized I'd have to change the pattern of putting him to sleep. First I began nursing him in the rocker in his bedroom. At least I was upright! If he started to get drowsy, I'd put him right into his crib. After about a week of that I gave him a bottle as I rocked him. Then he got a cold and didn't want the bottle, so we went back to nursing for another week. But once he was over that I found that he was happy to have his bottle right after lunch, and sometimes he even wanted to hold it himself.

• • •

Bedtime was the hardest for Jamie. When we got down to that last nursing time, I let my husband take over. He'd read him a book and sing him a song, then wind up his music box, cover him with his special quilt, and pat him to sleep. This ritual took quite a bit of time, and there was one rough evening when I left the house and took a long drive, feeling like a mean and guilty mother. It's painful to deny your child something that you know you could give him.

• • •

My baby was still an avid nurser at fourteen months. Her interest never lagged, and I was be-

ginning to feel like a human milk machine. My friend suggested that I begin weaning her once the weather got good and we could be out in the park with the other babies. This turned out to work very well. I brought a snack, a thermos of apple juice, and I always had a couple of those small Dixie cups in my bag. These were especially good because she could hold them easily. There she would sit up on the park bench like a real little kid.

• • •

I had planned to breast-feed Arianna for six months but ended up nursing her for eighteen. By that point, we were able to discuss it. She was very interested in babies because my sister had just had one. We talked about how Willie nursed, and how tiny he was and how big she was. I didn't offer the breast. Then I got her a doll, who she pretended to nurse. About a week later, I noticed that she hadn't asked to nurse. Usually she'd come and pull at my shirt. That was it. The end of an era!

• • •

I think distraction works best when you are weaning an older baby or toddler. We read lots of books and went to see the cows in our neighbor's barn. Thank goodness it was summer. The wading pool helped too.

When Nursing Is Over— The End of an Era

Some mothers, but by no means all, undergo a mild depression or sadness when they wean their babies. This may be caused by the hormonal changes the body undergoes when the demand for milk is lessened. If nursing has not met your expectations, the sadness may be related to feelings of inadequacy. To hear that it is pointless to

---

Watching for the Baby's Cues

I tried to wean Ann at five-and-a-half months, but she wouldn't take a bottle. I tried everything: putting my own milk into the bottle, different kinds of nipples, juice, having her father give it to her. I also tried sweetening the nipple with jelly. She refused. She'd laugh, and then scream and cry. We were having a real battle, and I remember spending an entire afternoon indoors trying to dribble 4 ounces of milk into her. I was frantic. Finally a friend said, "Is it worth it? The baby is obviously just as stubborn as you are. You've had such a good breast-feeding experience, why end it with a battle?" She was right. I gave up. I waited a few weeks. One day I just handed Ann the bottle to play with. She put it in her mouth just like she puts everything else in her mouth. Once I knew she'd take it, I wasn't nearly as uptight about weaning her and nursed her for two more months, offering bottles a couple of times a week.

• • •

Max began weaning himself when he was getting his first tooth. He just didn't seem to want to suck then.

• • •

Drew would take a few sips, then become distracted, pull off the breast, smile at me, stare at his hands, or at the dog, or at his brothers. He could hardly be bothered to nurse because there was so much to look at. He wouldn't stay horizontal and would wiggle and twist into the most vertical position he could muster. I decided to drop the daytime feedings and nurse him only in the morning and before bedtime when it was peaceful.

• • •

At ten-and-a-half months Dena was feeding herself entirely. One morning Bill left his orange-juice glass on the counter near the high chair. I turned around for a second and when I looked back, there she was drinking from it, grinning away.

---

be sad probably won't help, because if you feel this way no one is going to change your mind for you. But do consider that nursing is only *one* of the ways that we nurture our children and is a brief time in a child's life in which we will make countless other nurturing gestures.

If nursing has been a positive experience, you may feel not so much a sadness as a poignancy.

After all, a very complex and mysterious aspect of your relationship with your baby comes to a close with weaning. It is the end of the pregnant cycle, the end of an era when you have truly shared your body with another human being. Consider, however, that weaning need not be viewed as loss but rather as completion and a moving on to something new.

Breast-Feeding Resources

Association for Breastfeeding Fashions
P.O. Box 4378
Sundland, CA 01040
(818) 352-0697

"Breastfeeding Your Baby: A Mother's Guide." (One-hour video produced by Medela, Inc., in cooperation with La Leche League International, available through the La Leche League, see page 23)

Eiger, Marvin S., and Sally W. Olds, *The Complete Book of Breastfeeding* (New York: Bantam, 1987)

Fredericks, Carlton, *Carlton Fredericks' Guide to Women's Nutrition* (New York: Putnam, 1988)

Kitzinger, Shelia, *Breastfeeding Your Baby* (New York: McKay, a subsidiary of Random House, Inc., 1989)

La Leche League International, *The Womanly Art of Breastfeeding* (New York: New American Library, 1983)

Mason, Diane, and Diane Ingersoll, *Breastfeeding and the Working Mother* (New York: St. Martin's Press, Inc., 1986)

Rice, Ilene S. *Breastfeeding: A Heartstart* (New York: Dell, 1987)

• CHAPTER 4 •

Bottle-Feeding

Bottle-feeding is a perfectly fine way to nourish a baby, and there are still plenty of mothers who cannot envision themselves doing anything else. It has some clear advantages. You can monitor exactly how much the baby is drinking, eliminating one of the largest and most difficult areas of uncertainty for the breast-feeding mother. A bottle-fed baby is also more likely than the breast-fed one to "last" longer between feedings because infant formulas take longer to digest than breast milk. With bottles, it is very simple to share feedings with Dad, a grandmother, or a baby-sitter so that you can sleep or even go out dancing without wondering whether the baby will have enough to eat. You can also wear what you like and not have to worry about leaking, or lifting your blouse in public. Though it's important for your health to eat and drink sensibly, you can consume what you like as well as diet as you please. The bottle-feeding mother's body is her own. Though she may still be too tired for frequent passionate lovemaking, she can take birth-control pills without harming the baby. And because her body will return to its prepregnant state by the end of postpartum, she will not suffer

from a dry vagina due to hormonal changes, like the breast-feeding mother.

If you do decide to bottle-feed, what is most important is that the experience be relaxed and pleasurable, a time when the baby and adult feel close and attuned to each other. Nowadays there is tremendous pressure to breast-feed. When you decide to bottle-feed, some people may question your choice and try to make you feel guilty. Don't let them! Your dissatisfaction will put a barrier of tension between you and your baby. When you are feeding your baby, what counts more than your method is your attitude and the quality of your attention. Your baby will thrive if you are happy. (See Bottle Feeding with Love and Care, page 62.)

Mothers Talk About the Decision to Bottle-Feed

Question: Why did you decide to bottle-feed your baby?

Answer: We bottle-fed Aaron because it seemed the normal way to feed a baby. I was bottle-fed,

and so were my brothers and sisters and all of my cousins. My friends use bottles for their babies, too. It's just what the people I happen to know do.

A: We bottle-fed both of our adopted children. It was a wonderfully cuddly and cozy time for the babies, for me, and for my husband. When I was tired, or when my older child needed my attention, it was especially nice to have Daddy be able to perform the bedtime ritual with Meredith. An older sibling can participate, too, which I think helps to create a bond.

A: I had planned to breast-feed, even though I had doubts. Then I had a cesarean and was very weak and in pain and had problems getting into a comfortable position to nurse Chris. My nipples cracked and bled and the baby cried constantly. Any apprehensions I had before grew worse. After five days I decided to quit and spent that whole night crying. I'd read so many books that said "If you don't breast-feed, forget it!" I felt so selfish. One of my roommates had the same problem. We talked and talked, and that helped.

A: I had a very hard first six weeks—a hard labor, small pelvis, torn and strained ligaments in my hips as a result. It took a week to walk again and a month to sleep lying down. After ten days of this, plus blisters on my nipples, a poor let-down reflex, and zero sleep, I switched to bottles, which was a smart move for all three of us. My husband could help out. I resent all the indignant reactions of the breast-feeding advocates. I agree breast is best, but mine was a rather extreme case. I don't like being judged!

A: I knew I'd have to go back to work at six weeks. I breast-fed for the first month, then over the next two-week period totally switched to bottles. This worked out well for the baby, for me, and my sitter.

A: Lucy was born prematurely. Though I would have liked to have nursed her, I just couldn't deal with it at the time with all the running back and forth to the hospital. I was so grateful to be feeding my own baby in my arms without any monitors or tubes on her, that the farthest thing from my mind was feeling bad about the fact that she was taking a bottle instead of my breast. To feel loving and close is what counts.

Types of Milk

Milk must meet all of the baby's nutritional needs for the first four to six months. If you do not offer breast milk, then your pediatrician will help you choose from among several standard milk- or soy-based formulas especially designed for babies. These have the right proportion per ounce of calories, protein, carbohydrate, and fat. If your water is unfluoridated, ask your doctor about formula fortified with fluoride. If you have a history of milk allergies in your family, discuss this with your pediatrician. Do not switch to a soy-based formula without his or her approval. (See Food Allergies and Babies, page 68.) Formula also comes with an iron supplement for babies who are not taking it in drop form. Your baby is not yet ready for pasteurized milk, whether it's whole, 2 percent, 1 percent, or skim. It's way too high in protein for an infant, and the milk curd is too hard to digest comfortably.

When you use commercial infant formulas, preparation is very simple. If you buy a six-pack of prebottled formula, you need only add a sterile nipple and collar. This is the luxury route, however. Formula in a quart can, or concentrated formulas to which you add water, are less expensive. The powder-based equivalents are even more economical.

Useful Equipment

• Six to eight glass or plastic bottles or a nurser set (either 4-ounce or 8-ounce size) with nipple collars, caps or discs, and covers
• at least a dozen nipples (see box on Nuk-style nipples, page 62, and see note below)

• sturdy bottle brush and nipple brush
• heat-resistant quart measuring cup with a spout
• long-handled spoon
• large pot with a tight-fitting lid and pie plate with holes poked in it as a rack, or a sterilizer with a rack purchased at an infant supply store
• tongs for lifting hot bottles
• can opener
• small jar with a screw-top lid with holes punched in the top for sterilizing nipples
• timer (optional)

Note: Bottle and pacifier nipples are made of either rubber or silicone. Rubber nipples present problems that parents may not be aware of. Heat, sunlight, and saliva cause them to deteriorate and become sticky after two or three months of use. There is also concern about cancer-causing agents called *nitrosamines*, added to the rubber to give it strength and resilience. Though there is no evidence that this chemical harms babies, recent changes in the manufacturing process are reducing nitrosamine levels. Until more is known about potential hazards, to be on the safe side the FDA recommends that before using these nipples, parents should boil them five or six times for five minutes each time, changing the water with each boiling.

Silicone nipples are both heat-resistant and virtually nitrosamine-free. Because they are firm, they do not become the sticky, porous, bacteria collectors that rubber nipples can become. They also hold up well in the dishwasher. They can, however, split and tear and can be bitten in two by babies, according to the Consumer Product Safety Commission. Be sure to inspect these nipples carefully for tears and scratches before each feeding.

Useful equipment: cannister of formula; plastic nurser; easy-to-hold bottle; glass bottle; bottle caps and rings; long-handled spoon; nipple brush

Keeping Germs at Bay

It takes time for all babies to develop immunities to the common germs in the environment. A newborn who does not breast-feed will miss out on the powerful germ-fighting properties of colostrum. Whether or not you sterilize bottles, you will need to make a consistent and conscientious effort to create as bacteria-free a climate as possible. Before handling any equipment or milk, be sure to wash your hands *with soap* and dry them on a *clean* towel. Damp sinks are ideal places for bacteria to grow. Carefully scrub and rinse yours clean, or have a special dishpan that you can use just for your baby's bottles. Don't use your bottle or nipple brush for any other purposes, and hang them up, brush side down, so that they will dry more quickly after use.

As soon as a bottle is finished, fill it with cold water until you have time to get back to it. A tablespoon of vinegar in the water will dissolve the filmy deposits on bottles that have been sterilized in hard water. Whether you sterilize or not, you will still need to wash your equipment thoroughly with soap and hot water before adding the milk.

All About Bottle Nipples

Give special attention to nipples because the butterfat in milk causes the rubber to deteriorate. It is a good idea to rinse nipples before you actually wash them or sterilize them. A pinch of salt in the nipple cuts the butterfat and will help to open any clogged holes. Shake salt down inside the wet nipple to form a paste. Then squeeze and roll the nipple between your fingers to force the paste through the hole. Scrub with a nipple brush, then turn inside out and rinse thoroughly. Invert bottles and nipples to dry on a clean rack or towel. Store dry nipples in a clean, closed container.

Question: How rapidly should milk flow out of the nipple?

Answer: When the bottle is inverted, the hole should be large enough so that the milk will come out in a series of rapid drops, but not in a continuous stream. If the hole is too small, the baby may get tired from sucking and fall asleep before she is truly satisfied. If the hole is too large, the milk will rush out so fast that the baby may experience a feeling of choking and will swallow air along with the milk. She may also drink so fast that her sucking needs may not be satisfied, leaving her full but still fussy and discontented. You may wonder whether the baby is still hungry. The breast-fed baby feeds on average for at least twenty minutes. One assumes this is what a baby needs, not only nutritionally but to meet her sucking needs.

Question: How do you get the right-size hole in the nipple?

Answer: To make a small hole larger, stick the blunt end of a needle into a cork, then heat the point over a flame until it is red-hot. Slowly stick the needle into the nipple, then quickly pull it out. Repeat this procedure until the hole, when tested, allows the milk to flow in steady drops. To make a large hole smaller is somewhat chancier. Try boiling the nipple for three minutes.

Sterilizing Methods

There are two methods of sterilization: the *terminal* and the *aseptic.* (See pages 60 and 61 for instructions for each method.) A dishwasher will also adequately sterilize bottles and nipples as long as the water reaches 140°F, and the machine does a thorough job of rinsing.

Answers to Common Questions About Transporting Bottles

Question: How long after a bottle has been taken out of the refrigerator can you still use it?

Answer: During the time when a bottle is at drinking temperature or room temperature or pleasant outdoor temperature, any bacteria that may have gotten into the formula will be able to multiply rapidly. That is why it is unwise to give a baby a bottle that has been sitting around the house or carriage or car for several hours, whether it's a full bottle or one that has been partly consumed.

If you will need to feed the baby a couple of hours after leaving home, put the bottle, as soon as you take it out of the refrigerator, into an insulated bag designed to keep things cold or wrap it in ten layers of newspaper (which is a plenty good insulator!).

If you have a young baby who sometimes goes to sleep after half a bottle and then wakes up in a couple of hours for the rest, you can promptly put the half-finished bottle back into the refrigerator. I wouldn't use such a bottle more than twice.

—Benjamin M. Spock and Michael B. Rothenberg
Dr. Spock's Baby and Child Care

Alternative: You can avoid the whole refrigeration process by using powdered formula premeasured into a bottle. Carry a thermos of sterile water, and mix up formula as you need it.

How to Prepare Formula

When you are making infant formula either from scratch or from powdered or concentrated bases, it is imperative that you follow the instructions to the letter. With powder-based formulas, use the scoop provided. Level the powder off with a clean knife.

When working with liquids, use a clean or sterile glass measuring cup and view it from eye level. Also, because water evaporates, be sure to measure it *after* it has been boiled. If you are using disposable bags and nurser frames, don't measure quantities in the bags. You cannot get an accurate reading. Use a measuring cup to mix, then pour into the bag.

Again, follow instructions carefully. If you make the formula too strong by not adding enough water, or by using more powder or liquid base than called for, you can actually harm your baby. She will be getting too much fat, protein, and minerals, and more calories than she needs without enough water to satisfy her thirst. She'll cry. You'll think she is hungry and perhaps offer even more overconcentrated formula. And so the cycle goes. If you err in the opposite direction and dilute the formula with extra water, your baby will not be getting enough calories to satisfy her true hunger.

Question: Is it necessary to warm bottles?

Answer: No. Several years ago Bellevue Hospital in New York City performed a study with premature babies to see whether warming their bottle affected the babies' well-being. Half of the babies were fed warmed formula and the other half formula straight from the refrigerator. The results: There was no significant difference in spitting up, diarrhea, cramps, or weight gain between the two groups.

If you do warm a bottle, do it right before a feeding, because warm milk is the ideal place for bacteria to grow. An easy way to warm a bottle is to place it in a coffee can containing hot water from the tap; or simply run it under warm tap water. Be sure to test a few drops on your wrist. It should be just barely warm. There are devices

To Sterilize or Not: Two Points of View

Sterilization of formula and bottles is no longer routinely recommended for people who use reliable city or town water supplies and who have adequate refrigeration in their homes. If you use well water, or for any other reason have any question about your water supply, or if you're not sure about your refrigeration, check with your doctor, public-health nurse, or health department to see whether or not you have to sterilize. . . . Those who don't have to sterilize can substitute thorough soap-and-water washing and rinsing for sterilization. You can use your dishwasher for bottles and bottle caps after you've rinsed them, but nipples should be washed by hand.
—Benjamin M. Spock and Michael B. Rothenberg
Dr. Spock's Baby and Child Care

• • •

There are bacteria everywhere. We all carry germs on our hands and our clothes. We breathe them, eat them, and excrete them. Most of them are harmless. Very few types will make us ill unless we take in such a large number all at one time that our body's defenses are overwhelmed.

A new baby, especially one who is not breast-fed, has few defenses against common germs. It takes time for him to build up immunity to them. In an ordinarily clean home, he will cope with the germs that he sucks off his hands or breathes in the living room. But when he is feeding it is different. Milk, especially milk which is around room temperature, is an ideal breeding ground for germs. So while he might pick up a few off his own fingers and deal with them perfectly well, he will pick up an enormous, and possibly overwhelming, number from a bottle which has been left standing around in a warm room. . . . Sterilize everything you use in **measuring, mixing, or storing** *the made-up milk. That means measuring spoons, mixing jars, and the water in the feeding itself.* **Sterilize bottle, nipples, and nipple covers.**
—Penelope Leach
Your Baby and Child: From Birth to Age Five

Solution: Make up your own mind based on information from your pediatrician or health-care provider, observations of your own baby, and on your own temperament. If it makes you nervous not to sterilize your baby's bottles, then sterilize them. If it doesn't worry you, then don't.

The Terminal Method

With this method, the prepared formula is sterilized along with the bottles and the nipples. It is a good way to sterilize a single bottle.

1. Wash all of your equipment with hot, soapy water. Rinse well and drain dry.

2. If you are using a can of formula, clean the top of the can with hot soapy water. Pay special attention to the can opener, which can harbor bits of food and rust.

3. Either mix the formula base and water in individual bottles or make one large batch in a clean measuring cup or pitcher. In either case, use cold water from the tap. The formula will be sterilized along with the bottles in step #5.

4. Put rings and caps on loosely so that steam can pass under them.

5. Place bottles upright in 3 inches of water in a spaghetti pot or sterilizer. Make sure the bottles are close enough together that they can't tip over. Cover and boil for twenty-five minutes.

6. Remove bottles. When they are cool, seal the caps tightly and store in the refrigerator immediately.

The Aseptic Method

The aseptic method of sterilization requires that all equipment (bottles, nipples, caps, rings, discs, spoons, funnels, tongs, measuring cups, can openers, etc.) be sterilized before you fill the bottles with sterile formula (either powder or concentrate mixed with water that has been boiled and then cooled).

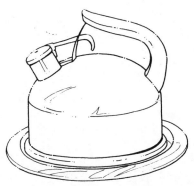

1. Before you even begin to sterilize your equipment, start preparing the water that you will need to mix with the formula plus an extra half ounce for evaporation. Bring the water to a boil for three minutes, then set aside to cool.

2. To sterilize equipment, boil it for twenty-five minutes in a sterilizer, covered saucepan, or spaghetti pot.

3. After sterilizing your equipment, mix the formula. The formula base and sterile cooled water can be mixed either directly in each individual bottle, or in one large batch. In the latter case, use an oversized measuring cup and a long-handled spoon. A funnel will help you get the formula into the bottles without spills.

4. After you have mixed the formula and filled the bottles, place inverted nipples on them. Be careful to touch only the outer rims of the nipples.

5. To store, tightly screw caps or discs on the bottles and refrigerate immediately.

Nuk-Style Nipple and Exerciser

The Nuk nipple or other brands in the same style are recommended by many pediatricians and hospitals because they more closely mirror the shape of a human nipple than the traditional baby-bottle nipple. This nipple is especially designed to stimulate the baby's hard palate on the roof of his mouth. This type of sucking is hard work. It not only exercises the jaw but also feels good and releases tension. The nipple collapses and expands easily and allows the baby to control the rate of the flow of milk with less tongue thrusting. The flat passage also encourages the baby to close his lips entirely around the nipple and breathe through his nose rather than his mouth. The nipple fits all standard bottles. Nuk also makes a pacifier called the Orthodontic Exerciser. This pacifier, similar to the bottle nipple in design, has advantages over the traditional pacifier for the same reason that the bottle nipple does. It doesn't fall out of the baby's mouth as easily as the traditionally shaped pacifier either.

on the market that are particularly handy for night bottle feeding. These bedside bottle holders, which keep a bottle chilled, will warm it up in an instant.

Note: Do *not* warm bottles in the microwave oven because the heat is uneven. Shaking the bottle does not always eliminate hot spots. Even if you test the bottle with a few drops on your wrist, there may be hot spots elsewhere that could scald your baby.

Bottle-Feeding with Love and Care

Feeding is a significant event for a baby. It is a time of warmth, touch, and contact when all of the baby's senses come into play. There is the pleasure of sucking and becoming full, of listening to, looking at, touching, and coming to know and trust the special person(s) in the baby's life. To make bottle-feeding intimate and relaxed, try the following.

1. Find a chair or bed to sit on that offers good support for your back as well as the arm that cradles the baby's head.

2. If the baby's hands are covered, be sure to expose them, and if you are comfortable doing so, unbutton your shirt so she can have contact with your skin.

3. Cradle the baby in your arm, making sure that she is tilted upward so that her head is well above her stomach. Never feed a baby who is lying flat on her back. Not only is it hard to swallow, it is also thought that babies fed in this position are more susceptible to inner-ear infections.

4. As you hold the bottle, use the index finger of that same hand to gently stroke the baby's cheek closest to your body. The baby should then turn her head toward your finger. Then gently touch the baby's lips with the nipple, making

Correct position for bottle feeding

sure the bottle is tipped upwards so that the nipple entirely fills with milk.

5. The baby will draw the nipple into her mouth. (Make sure that it is well back into her mouth.) She will then begin to suck. If the nipple collapses from the strong suction, gently pull on it to release the vacuum and allow air to reinflate the nipple.

6. Burp the baby midway through a feeding (see page 29).

7. After you pause for a burp or a diaper change, change arms or sides as a nursing mother would when she changes breasts. This stimulates the baby by providing a different point of view.

8. See page 276 for a space to make notes on early feedings.

Question: Is it okay to prop bottles?

Answer: No. Besides the fact that this is a potential choking hazard, the baby would miss out on the love and cuddling she needs and deserves in order to develop a sense of trust.

Staying in Tune with the Bottle-Fed Baby

I chose bottle feeding so that I could see how much milk Laura was drinking. If she seems to want more or less than what I have decided is the appropriate amount, then I begin to think something is wrong. Why is she eating so little? Is there something off with the formula? Is she coming down with a cold? If she eats more than what I consider usual, then I feel guilty. Maybe I haven't been feeding her enough in the first place. Isn't it ridiculous?

• • •

The most helpful thing my pediatrician told me was to forget about feeding schedules in the early weeks. Breast-fed babies aren't stuffing themselves in the first couple of days, so why was I making myself crazy stuffing a bottle into my sleepy baby's mouth?

One of the best aspects of breast-feeding, even though it can be one of the hardest for many mothers to deal with, is that we simply don't know how much the baby is getting. It can be hard for us to accept, but nature intends babies to be self-regulating or in charge. They demand a lot if they're very hungry and less if they aren't. This is the way it ought to be for a bottle-fed baby, too. Offer the baby a bottle when she seems hungry. When she stops sucking vigorously and pauses, wait a few seconds before you remove the bottle. Don't jiggle it or rotate it in the hopes that you can nudge her into taking another ounce. Leave it up to her.

Remember that a newborn has been used to having his hunger needs continually satisfied through the umbilical cord in utero. He literally doesn't know what it feels like to be empty or even half-empty. In the beginning his needs for food will not necessarily be what we consider to be regular. As he adjusts to this new way of eating outside the womb, over the weeks he will be able to feel and then signal more clearly when he is really hungry as opposed to just a little hungry. But remember, this takes time.

Question: How do I know when the baby is full?

Answer: We have to allow ourselves to be open to what our babies are trying to tell us. With time we become more and more sensitive to their cues. Mothers have noted . . .

A: When Lucy is full, I have noticed that she begins to slow down with her sucking. The nipple slips forward just a little bit. Then we stop.

A: Mark is very clear when he has had enough. He spits the nipple out and clamps his little mouth shut.

A: Jack falls asleep when he is full. No amount of wiggling or jiggling will wake him.

A: I have trouble knowing exactly what is going on, but Katie will drink and stop and look content. It's just a look. I can't really describe it except to say she looks satisfied.

A: Seth is a gobbler. His bottle is gone in two seconds flat. Then he belches. That's it. He's had enough.

Question: *Why shouldn't the baby be on a four-hour schedule like he was in the hospital?*

Answer: *Offered feedings only at 6 A.M., 10 A.M., 2 P.M., 6 P.M., and 10 P.M., he will eventually expect food at these natural intervals. The difference is that these early weeks will be miserable for you all. The baby will wake and cry. If you do not feed him because it "isn't time," you will try every other method of comforting him, which will be hard work. Because what he really wants is food, and because he will get hungrier and hungrier while you are working away at other methods of comfort, nothing you do will really soothe him. By the end of the session you will be feeling that unhappy mixture of guilt and anger and helpless despair. To crown it all, when the clock does at last say "right time" and you give him a feeding, he will probably not suck well or take enough milk to keep him happy until the next scheduled meal. All that crying will have tired him and filled his stomach with air. He will probably fall into exhausted sleep after an ounce or two and wake up again an hour later to repeat the whole performance.*

So don't fall into the trap of thinking that if you feed your baby whenever he seems hungry he will get into the habit of demanding food frequently. He does not wake from habit, he wakes from hunger. When he is mature enough not to be hungry so often he will not wake up and cry.
—Penelope Leach
*Your Baby and Child:
From Birth to Age Five*

Question: *Is it possible to overfeed a newborn baby?*

Answer: *I discovered that I was actually feeding our two-month-old way too much. He was a gobbler and a gulper and could consume an entire 8-ounce bottle in about ten minutes. Then he would howl and howl. I assumed he was still hungry, so a little later, when I couldn't stand the crying any more, I'd feed him again. One day he ate 48 ounces. My pediatrician was aghast. She explained that even a four-, five-, or six-month-old baby needs only 24 to 26 ounces of formula a day.*

She said to me, "Think of a baby's stomach being about the size of a lemon" (see page 91 for illustration). Imagine trying to fit so much milk into that. The stretching would be painful. He will cry. Perhaps mistakenly you will feed him again. Look at the vicious cycle that begins.

Question: *Should I give my bottle-fed baby water?*

Answer: Both breast milk and formula should supply all the water a baby normally needs. With a breast-fed baby, sucking from a bottle may be confusing, and it may decrease the baby's sucking needs. In some instances water is prescribed for medical reasons. If this is the case, your pediatrician will inform you. If you do offer water, don't use sugar water. There is no reason to cultivate the baby's sweet tooth.

Question: *Can bottles ruin a baby's teeth?*

Answer: Yes. If you regularly put your baby to bed with a bottle of formula or juice, this will become part of her bedtime ritual. When her teeth come in and she still wants her bottle at bedtime, she will be a candidate for *bottle-mouth syndrome:* When the baby falls asleep with a bottle, the bacteria in her mouth can feed on the residue of formula left on her gums. The production of saliva, which ordinarily bathes the teeth, slows down at night, leaving these bacteria free to produce acids that can then eat away at the baby's teeth. To avoid this, don't put the baby to bed with anything but water in the bottle. Breast-fed babies who nurse on and off in the mother's bed all night run the same risk of developing tooth decay.

• CHAPTER 5 •

Introducing Solid Foods

Deciding When to Start

Just when you are beginning to settle in with your new baby, and she has demonstrated that you can both sleep for five glorious hours in a row (maybe), you may begin to feel pressure from well-meaning people to start offering solid, "real," or "grown-up" foods.

In the not-too-distant past it was common for babies to eat cereal at one month, fruits and vegetables at three months, and meats at four months. Perhaps this reflected an urgency to make the baby grow up sooner, which was considered a positive development. Or it may have reflected the notion that food and love are equivalent, that is, the more work and complexity we put into our children's meals, the more we demonstrate that we love them.

And then there are the tired parents, who want to believe that something—anything—a little cereal, perhaps, will help their baby sleep through the night. Alas, such a tempting theory! Who isn't susceptible? But studies have proved that there is *no* connection between feeding a baby solids and his or her sleeping through the night.

Question: When is it appropriate to introduce solids?

Answer: The consensus is that babies do not need to be introduced to solid foods until they are between four and six months old. Until then, breast milk or formula are perfectly adequate. They are "real," complete foods supplying the right balance of protein, fat, and carbohydrate in the easiest-to-digest form.

Breast milk and infant formulas also supply the vitamins and most of the minerals that an infant needs (with the possible exception of Vitamin D); see page 25. Breast milk contains small quantities of iron, vitally important for the production of hemoglobin that carries oxygen from the lungs to all the cells in the body. Nature, however, makes up for this dearth by supplying enough iron in the newborn's liver to last until he is between four and six months old. It is also important to note that the iron in breast milk, though limited in quantity, is very efficiently absorbed by the baby.

Between four and seven months, the pediatrician usually performs a routine blood test for anemia and may or may not suggest introducing

---

Solids, Bowel Movements, and Diaper Rash

When you introduce solids, expect the quality of your baby's bowel movements to change in consistency, color, texture, odor, and frequency. For more details see The Poop on Poop, page 244. Also, watch for diaper rash. (See page 125.)

---

some foods rich in iron, changing to an iron-fortified formula, or adding iron drops.

Introducing solids to the baby before four months isn't overtly harmful, but it's neither necessary nor particularly helpful. It can interfere with his desire to suck, which in turn can decrease a nursing mother's milk supply just enough to confirm her worries that the baby is not getting enough. Solids may also crowd out room for milk without making up for its nutritional loss. Until a baby is at least three months old, these more complex foods, along with their vitamins and minerals, pass largely undigested through his system. In the meantime his immature kidneys have worked much harder to process out the wastes than they do with milk. Many experts also believe that delaying some of the more allergenic foods for as long as possible will minimize the likelihood of allergies.

But just as important, the early breast and bottle feedings provide the kind of closeness—the holding, rocking, and cuddling—that the baby needs. As soon as high chairs, spoons, and dishes are introduced, feeding becomes, in addition to more work for parents, more businesslike and less intimate.

Question: *If milk is so good, what makes babies ready to eat solids?*

Answer: Milk is fine in the sense that it is a nutritionally complete food. But milk is largely water. A baby's stomach is small, and it can hold only so much liquid at one time. The baby eventually needs a more concentrated source of calories in order to satisfy his hunger. And that's what solids are—a more concentrated source of calories.

Just as important as the baby's physiological readiness for solids is his developmental readiness. The period between four and six months coincides with the time that the baby's most intense desire to suck begins to taper off. The pacifier may be rejected (seemingly mysteriously), and nursing periods may shorten. The baby may seem easily distracted and may prefer to participate in the action around him than concentrate on nursing. By this age, too, the muscles used for swallowing are strong from all the sucking. The baby is now able, with a bit of practice, to move food from the front to the back of the

---

Watch Your Baby, Not the Calendar

I first tried to get Birch to eat some cereal when he was five months old. I was getting a little nervous about being the sole source of his diet, even though he was doing fine on breast milk alone. I gave him a demitasse spoon full of cereal and milk, and he spit it out and cried. I waited a couple of days and tried again. He still hated it. I tried altering the consistency. No luck. I tried applesauce. No luck. He howled. Then I tried bananas. He wouldn't have them! My mother said, "I never heard of a baby not liking bananas! What's wrong with him? Call the doctor!" I had visions of never being able to wean him. After three weeks of experimenting, I finally said the hell with it. Two weeks later Kim casually offered him a spoonful of his plain yogurt. He loved it. It's been smooth sailing ever since.

• • •

I wasn't going to be rushed with Harry. But at five-and-a-half months he grabbed my older son's spoon and started banging it with such a racket that my husband said, "I think he's trying to tell us something. He wants what we have." Oatmeal it was.

• • •

When Jessica was two months old, my sister-in-law kept on saying, "Give her some cereal. If you wait too long she will become balky." So I talked to my friend who had had six babies. "Hogwash!" she said. Then I brought it up at the well-baby visit with my pediatrician, who said she had never seen any evidence of a baby becoming balky because a parent waited too long. Balkiness had more to do with personality or temperament than with the timing of solids. She had absolutely no interest in the puréed foods I offered her starting at six months. When she was almost seven months, she picked up a breadstick and began to jaw it. From then on she was open to trying just about everything as long as I didn't force it on her.

---

mouth. The younger baby who pushes it right back out is telling you that she is not yet ready.

The baby's interest in the world around her has also increased tremendously. She may enjoy sitting up for longer periods of time; she will reach out for objects—at first using the palm to clutch at what she wants and bring it somewhat awkwardly to her mouth. In time this action will be refined to a more delicate grasp between thumb and finger known as the *pincer grasp*. She has also begun to vocalize and socialize, to wiggle and kick and roll, and is generally feeling curious and experimental. Her parents, at this point, are probably feeling more relaxed and experimental, too.

How to Start and with Which Foods

There are no hard-and-fast rules about what solids to introduce when. Your pediatrician may offer guidance based on observations of your baby's age, weight, and growth patterns and on how often she is taking milk feedings. These are all considerations that you can take into account,

Good Advice about Introducing Solid Food

I think it's a great mistake to get into an argument with babies about their first solid food. Sometimes a long-lasting feeding problem starts in this way. Even if it doesn't last, it's bad for parents and babies to go through an unnecessary fight.
— Benjamin M. Spock and
Michael B. Rothenberg
Dr. Spock's Baby and Child Care

Food is an area where mothers can make themselves absolutely crazy. I know because I was one of them. I wanted my baby to be healthy and well nourished. I remember going to all sorts of lengths to make my first baby eat vegetables because vegetables to me were synonymous with good nutrition—and good mothering! If she refused to eat her peas or carrots, I worried. I wheedled and coaxed and played choo-choo with the spoon of food. When that didn't work, I'd steam and purée the carrots, then hide them in meat loaf or cottage cheese or applesauce. It never occurred to me that the fruit she loved provided her with all of those vitamins and carbohydrates that in my mind had to come from vegetables. With my other babies I had no time to steam and purée. I simply offered them what was on hand and didn't worry. The youngest loved all vegetables, including cooked mushrooms. The middle baby, like her older sister, couldn't be fooled.

but try to be open and flexible. Remember that during the first year, your baby's primary task is to develop a sense of trust, and feeding is a time when this is happening. If meals are full of tension, frustration, and rigid scheduling, this can instill attitudes and behavior about food that may last a lifetime.

It can be helpful for you and your baby if you regard the first solid feedings as purely experimental. Moving to solid foods is not an opportunity to get the right amounts of the correct nutritional "stuff" into the baby. It is simply one more way to broaden your baby's discovery of the world through all of her senses—sight, smell, taste, touch, and even sounds she makes as she eats and plays.

It's also useful to see the introduction of solids as part of a transition that will last for several months until the baby is actually feeding herself table foods with her own hands. The goal, as with bottle-feeding or breast-feeding, is to allow the baby to lead the way and to be "self-regulating." If you think of this period between milk feedings only and total self-feeding as a purely transitional time, it should be easier to be flexible. For instance, it is not a step backward if the baby suddenly decides she doesn't love bananas anymore or only wants to nurse for dinner—particularly if you mistakenly feel that every step forward depends on you and your ingenuity rather than on the baby's wishes. Your job is not to make the baby eat; it is to provide a reasonable array of healthy food choices in a relaxed climate for experimentation.

Question: *Which solids are best to start with?*
Answer: Many pediatricians and authors of books on baby care insist that baby cereal—starting with rice, then moving to oats, barley, then wheat—mixed with breast milk, formula, or regular whole milk (if the baby is at least six months

old), is the best first food. These cereals are quite easy to digest. They provide carbohydrates for energy and are also fortified with iron, which the baby will begin to need. On the other hand, they are also very bland, and there is no guarantee that the baby will like them. What can happen is that the desperate parent ends up sweetening the cereal with fruit to interest the baby. This is not a good idea unless you have already introduced fruit and know that the baby is not allergic to it.

If the baby hates cereal, try vegetables, starting with the sweeter ones such as carrots or yams. Then move on to fruits. Meat and egg yolks, more concentrated sources of calories and iron, are usually introduced last. Start each food by offering only a teaspoon or two at first and work up to two or three tablespoons. Introduce only one food at a time, for three or four days, watching for any signs that may indicate an allergic reaction. (See Food Allergies and Babies, page 68.) Be sure to write down each food that you offer and the date you offered it. Otherwise it's easy to forget. (See pages 276, 298, and 299 in the Recordkeeping section.)

Warning!

Never mix solid food with milk and feed it to the baby from a bottle with an enlarged nipple hole. This can cause choking, and just as important, it is the equivalent of force-feeding, which is physically and psychologically damaging to your baby.

Food Allergies and Babies

It can be difficult to know when a particular food is disturbing your baby. That is why you need to go slowly and introduce one at a time, keeping notes. The most common allergenic foods are cow's milk, wheat, egg whites, beef, soy, corn, citrus, and chocolate. Infants are very sensitive, however, and can react to many other substances, including minuscule amounts of chemicals and pesticides used in processing a wide variety of foods.

Food allergies manifest themselves in various symptoms. Sometimes they are upper respiratory. The baby will have a runny nose, a cough, or even an ear infection or croup. The baby's digestive system may also give you a clue; the baby may vomit, or there may be a sudden change in bowel habits, ranging from diarrhea or frequent, watery stools, to constipation. Other babies show that they are allergic through changes in their skin: rashes, including diaper rash; blotches; hives; eczema; or swelling around the eyes, which may also become watery, red, crusty, or oozy.

If you suspect your baby is allergic to a particular food, talk to your health-care provider about eliminating that food from her diet, making sure that you substitute a nutritional equivalent. (Note: if you suspect your baby is allergic to cow's milk, do not automatically switch to soy formula without your doctor's approval. Many who are allergic to cow's milk are also allergic to soy. Also, some of the soy milks on the market are not nutritionally sound for babies.)

Tuning In to Feeding Styles and Fullness

Question: At what point during a breast or bottle feeding should I offer solids?

Answer: At first, regard solids as a supplement to milk feeding. Offer milk first. That way the baby will not be overly hungry when you offer her solid food and will be more likely to be in a good mood. Then offer the solids, regarding them as purely experimental. Tune in to your baby's feeding style just as you did when breast or bottle feeding. If the baby doesn't like the high chair, hold her or try an infant seat. Match your pace to the baby's interest and enthusiasm. And look for your baby's way of saying she's had enough.

Question: What is a baby's feeding style?
Answer: Let the baby lead the way. Watch for her cues. Parents explain . . .

A: Lucy hated it if I wasn't shoveling the food right in. She was impatient, smacking her lips very intensely. I almost felt like I needed to have two spoons going at the same time.

A: In the beginning I had to hold Willy when I fed him solids. He wouldn't eat sitting in his infant seat. He'd cry. He was willing to taste only minuscule amounts of rice cereal from one of my grandmother's tiny demitasse spoons, just at the tip of his tongue so that he could suck it back into his mouth.

A: Lally looked bored and would start to play with her hands after a taste or two. I used to worry. I'd call the pediatrician and ask, "Why doesn't this child like to eat more? Everyone in my family likes to eat, and the same is true in my husband's family. We're eaters." The doctor reminded me that I'd asked why it took her so long to nurse. He said that we had agreed then that her temperament is cautious, if not rather "quietly strong willed." This was Lally, and didn't we love her for it—for sticking to her guns? He also pointed out that the rate of a baby's growth slows down dramatically in the second half of the first year. It has to, or she would end up as a giant.

A: The nurse practitioner suggested that we start our baby on rice cereal because it was least likely to cause an allergic reaction. Malcolm seems to hate it and spits out more than I put in. I tried peaches instead, and he didn't spit quite so much out. I concluded that he just doesn't like rice cereal. I don't blame him. It tastes like cardboard.

Be sensitive to when the baby has had enough. Mothers elaborate . . .

My baby clamps her mouth shut. That's it. No more!

. . .

More gets spit out than goes in. Then I know that Celia is done.

. . .

Jackie slows down and turns her head to one side. She usually makes a humming kind of sound when she eats. When she's had enough, she quiets down.

. . .

He becomes very distracted and looks from side to side for some new action.

. . .

I have a hard time telling when Abigail is done because she likes to eat so much. I slow down. If she doesn't complain, I stop.

Spoons, Dishes, and Bibs

Spoons. The traditional long-handled baby spoon, with a small, flat bowl works well, but so does a demitasse spoon or even a wooden tongue depressor. For first experiments, put a small amount of food on the very tip of the spoon, then place it between the baby's pursed lips. Allow her to suck the food into her mouth. Don't be discouraged if some dribbles out. Moving food to the back of the mouth is a skill that has to be learned.

Sometime after the baby's first birthday she may become proficient at using a spoon herself. But give her a spoon before this to distract her, and let her practice. Self-feeding with a spoon is easiest with a wide-bowled or swivel spoon with a short, preferably crooked, handle.

Dishes. Eventually, your baby will love to play the drop-it game. Enjoying her sense of power and her newly developed ability to let go of objects, she'll drop her food, her spoon, her plate, and everything else you put on her high-chair tray onto the floor. For this reason plastic bowls or plates with a rim are a must. Those with rubber suction cups on the bottom are even better.

Bibs. Plastic molded bibs with a pocket at the bottom look like armor, but don't let this put you off. They are extremely practical. They do not require laundering as much as they do a good scrubbing. And there are no strings to choke on. If you and your baby don't like molded plastic, choose a cloth bib that snaps rather than ties for safety reasons.

The Basics of Baby Nutrition

There is nothing like a baby in the family to make parents become concerned about nutrition. Good nutrition is one of the most important factors in your baby's life. A healthy diet is the best form of preventive medicine and the foundation for future eating habits. Food is also the raw material for growth. In the first year the baby does more growing proportionally than he will ever do again and expends tremendous amounts of energy absorbing information as he strives to reach, turn, creep, sit, stand, crawl, and finally walk. One of the many bonuses of becoming concerned about a baby's diet is that we usually become more aware of our own nutritional habits and needs as well. If you aren't a purist, you can start over! Ban the junk food, the artificial sweeteners, the caffeinated beverages, and overly fatty and heavily salted foods, and you'll be ahead—at least for a while.

Once the baby has become used to a variety of solids, parents begin to be concerned about offering good meals and snacks in the right balance. Dr. Myron Winick, president of the University of Health Sciences/The Chicago Medical School and distinguished professor of pediatrics and nutrition, suggests that by the second half of the baby's first year, parents aim to create a varied diet in which about 30 percent of the calories come from protein, 30 percent from carbohydrates, and 40 percent from fats. Note that this differs considerably from the proportions recommended for adults. Because they are still growing so rapidly, infants need a greater percentage of protein and fat in their diets than we do.

While these guidelines are useful, it sometimes feels like they have little to do with reality. We soon realize that babies, like adults, have likes and dislikes and their own styles of eating. They don't necessarily embrace the notion of a balanced meal. It's good to keep in mind that flexibility—rather than dogma or panic—is called for. Infants, toddlers, and young children need to eat often to fill their small stomachs and recharge their batteries. Nutritious snacks can make up for what has been left out or refused from a meal.

On those days when your baby will eat only breadsticks, remember the oft-quoted experiment by Dr. Clara Davis. This brave woman allowed a group of year-old babies to choose freely from a sampling of healthy, natural foods. With no adult interference, the babies selected what they wanted. Taken on a day-to-day basis their diets were indeed lopsided, but over the course of a month, they ended up being very well rounded. In other words, likes and dislikes will almost always add up to a diet that is right for the baby if we can only step back, have faith, and give him a chance.

One of the many delights of having a baby is witnessing the true miracle of growth. Though our baby's growth is partially determined by genetics, it is food provided with love, concern, and care that fuels that growth. Food—proteins, carbohydrates, fats, vitamins, and minerals—along with oxygen, constitutes the raw material. Of these nutrients only two—vitamins and minerals—are ready for immediate use. The others must be chemically broken down into simpler components before cells can utilize them. How the body makes use of food is another of those "simple" miracles that we take for granted. Di-

Mothers Share Bib Tips, and More . . .

If your baby starts to cry when he sees the bib coming at him, try standing behind the high chair as you gently explain what you are doing. This way you can also see better and get the bib on faster.

• • •

Roll up your baby's sleeves when she begins to self-feed or, if it's really a mess and the weather is warm, let her go topless, then pop her right into the kitchen sink for a quick rinse.

• • •

Spread yesterday's newspaper under the high chair and in a five-foot radius around it to catch spills, then remove a layer after each meal. Or use an old shower curtain. Wash it in the shower at the end of the day.

• • •

To soften dried, encrusted baby food on the high chair, use a teaspoon of dishwasher detergent to a quart of hot water. Scrub with a plastic pot scrubber or steel-wool pad. Then rinse thoroughly.

• • •

Once every week or two I put the high chair in the bathtub, scrub it down, then turn on the shower for a rinse.

• • •

Caitlin kept slumping in the high chair. A piece of foam underneath her bottom gave her enough traction so that she didn't slide.

• • •

I know this sounds nutty, but I'll tell you anyway. I put a hat on Matthew before I feed him. (He's used to it!) Better to wash the hat than shampoo his head every day.

• • •

I never give Pete a new food at dinner. If it's going to upset his system, I want to know about it during the daylight hours!

• • •

I make my own health-food cereal for Marissa. I mix two parts baby cereal to one part wheat germ. Then I add some banana or sugarless applesauce. She loves it.

• • •

Be sure to label the contents of your homemade frozen baby-food cubes. They all look alike! Date them, too.

• • •

At my sister's suggestion, I bought a garlic press and a Mouli Grater especially for pureeing small quantities of Alex's food. (A chilled piece of meat is much easier to grate than a warm, just-cooked piece.) These compact items are also perfect for travel because they fit neatly into his diaper bag.

gestion, starting in the mouth, but doing the bulk of its work in the stomach and small intestine, transforms these large nutrients into usable small units. Proteins are broken down into amino acids, carbohydrates into simple sugars (glucose), and fats into fatty acids and glycerol. From the digestive sites in the alimentary canal, the processed chemicals, as well as the unprocessed vitamins and minerals, are absorbed into the bloodstream or the lymph system and carried to the cells. In the cells the amino acids, fatty acids, glycerol, and minerals will be assembled into new compounds that will form structural components such as cell membranes. The glucose in the diet will be used mainly to supply the energy for this complex assembly process. The vitamins serve as catalysts to speed up the synthesis of the new compounds.

Proteins

Proteins are the builders and maintainers and are the most important group of compounds in the body. Besides being the body's main structural elements, they form the enzymes that control and create the thousands of chemical reactions and help convert food into compounds the cells can use. For example, they preside over each step in the complex process by which sugars are broken down to give energy. Proteins also form antibodies to fight infection and form the hemoglobin that carries oxygen to all the cells in the body.

The greatest amounts of protein are needed when the body is building new tissues—during pregnancy, lactation, and especially during infancy. Unlike some other nutrients, protein is not stored in the body in large quantities for very long. This is why it is so important that a baby receive an adequate amount every day.

In order to be of use to the body, proteins are

broken down by digestion into amino acids and then absorbed into the blood. These amino acids (twenty-two in all) are then used as building blocks in cells to form replicas of themselves. Of the amino acids, fourteen are created by our metabolisms and are called *nonessential* amino acids. The remaining eight are called *essential* amino acids and are the ones to be most concerned about because they must be gotten from food.

Foods that provide all eight of the essential amino acids in the right proportions are known as *complete* or *high-quality protein foods.* High-quality proteins are found in breast milk, infant formulas, cow's milk, eggs (start with yolks and whites separately to see if the whites cause an allergic reaction), cheese, yogurt, meats, poultry, and fish. Milk is probably the most common high-protein food in a baby's diet during its first year. To add variety to the baby's diet, use the following chart to substitute milk products for milk.

Useful Milk Equivalents

1-inch cube Cheddar-type cheese	= ½ cup milk
½ cup yogurt	= ½ cup milk
½ cup cottage cheese	= ⅓ cup milk
2 tablespoons cream cheese	= 1 tablespoon milk
½ cup ice cream or ice milk	= ⅓ cup milk

An incomplete or low-quality protein is either missing one or more of the essential amino acids or has an incorrect proportion of them. Low-quality proteins are found in some vegetables, seeds, and grains. By combining two complementary sources of lower-quality protein, you can increase usable protein and add variety to a baby's diet. But you must know what you are doing. Books such as *The New Laurel's Kitchen* (by Robertson, Flinders, and Ruppenthal, Berkeley, CA: Ten Speed Press, 1986) or *Diet for a Small Planet* (by Frances M. Lappé, New York: Ballantine, 1982) can help you to choose foods that complement each other correctly. For example, 1¼ ounces of cheese, when served with ¾ cup cooked rice, yields 20 percent more usable protein than when it is served alone. Other good combinations of lower-quality proteins are grains with milk or other dairy products (cereal with milk, pasta with cheese, grilled cheese on whole-wheat bread, whole-grain French toast, milk with rice pudding). Grains and legumes also complement each other (rice with beans or lentils, peanut butter on whole-wheat bread, cornmeal with beans, baked beans with brown bread). Seeds complement legumes (for instance, sesame paste with garbanzos or red beans).

Carbohydrates

Carbohydrates are the starches and sugars the body needs to supply energy for protein synthesis, and the fibers or roughage necessary for proper digestion and elimination. Many important functions depend on carbohydrates as their primary fuel. The brain, for example, relies on glucose, among other things, to help produce the chemical transmitters and the energy the brain needs to do its work.

Like all other forms of energy used by people,

The Joys of Yogurt

Yogurt is one of the healthiest, most versatile, and most convenient foods for babies. It has a protein value almost as high as milk and is rich in B vitamins and in certain healthy bacteria that create an environment in the intestinal tract that is inhospitable to many harmful bacteria, such as those that cause dysentery. Because it is predigested by the bacteria, yogurt is easily digested and assimilated into the system in about an hour; milk takes three or four hours to digest. Yogurt stores well in the refrigerator and can be served at any meal; it can be used as a base for cereals, fruits, or vegetables, a thinner for pureed meats, or a base for drinks. And what the baby doesn't eat, you can eat. It's also great for travel.

the energy we receive from our diets originally comes from the sun: It is stored in seeds, grains, roots, tubers, and fruits. Carbohydrate foods, with the exception of table sugar, supply many of the essential vitamins and minerals, such as iron, calcium, B vitamins, vitamin A, and vitamin C, that a baby needs.

Carbohydrates can be thought of as protein conservers. If too few "energy foods" are consumed each day, valuable protein will be converted to carbohydrates for fuel instead of being used for the growth and repair of tissues. Proteins and carbohydrates should usually be eaten together at the same meal to keep this protein-sparing action working efficiently—though, once again, as long as the baby is drinking milk, this will occur automatically. The baby's first carbohydrates are sugars called *lactose*, found in breast milk or infant formulas. Later his carbohydrate needs can be met by cereals, whole grains such as rice and barley, whole-grain breads, vegetables, and stewed or fresh fruits.

Whenever possible, buy whole-grain breads and whole-wheat pastas. Most breads and pastas available today are not made from whole grains. Instead, they use "enriched" flour, which means that about one-third of the iron and niacin (one of the B vitamins) is removed in the process of refining the flour. They then are replaced, but many of the other nutrients, such as calcium, potassium, and magnesium, are not totally restored. In addition, the protein of the wheat germ, rich in essential amino acids and B vitamins, is discarded in the making of white bread and pastas.

The difference between the nutritional value of white and brown rice is also astonishing. Brown rice has almost four times the protein and calcium value of white enriched rice, and more than twice as much iron.

Another excellent whole-grain product is wheat germ. The embryo (germ) of the wheat kernel is the most nutritious part of the plant. It is rich in B-complex vitamins and is the best-known source of vitamin E, as well as being a good source of complete protein. Wheat germ must be stored in the refrigerator or oxygen will combine with the oils in it that contain vitamin E, and it will turn rancid. Add it to cereals, yogurt, meat loaves, stews, pancakes, and so on. Avoid it, however, if your baby has an allergic reaction to wheat products, as some do.

Sugar

A preference for sweet foods is inborn in all of us. At birth the newborn will choose sugar water over plain boiled water. But try to stick to the natural sweeteners in fruits and vegetables such as yams and carrots. There is much more nutritional value in a fresh peach than in the peach cobbler found in the baby-food section of the supermarket. Table sugar is one of the few foods that supplies no vitamins or minerals—only calories that can crowd out room for other nutrients, destroy appetite, cause cavities, and make a baby fat. It may also increase the body's need for thiamine (a B vitamin) and the trace mineral chromium. Avoid raw honey during the first year. It can contain botulism spores, which under some conditions produce the poison that can cause the deadly botulism infection.

Fat

We have become a very fat-conscious society! The message is everywhere. "Eat more fiber, less fat, and watch out for your cholesterol consumption." This is good advice for adults but not for infants, who need a higher percentage of fat in their diets than we do. Fats are part of every cell in our bodies. They supply a concentrated source of energy—twice as much as either proteins or carbohydrates. They also carry the fat-soluble vitamins A, E, and K, as well as fatty acids needed for the development of the nervous system and healthy skin. Fat is also necessary to cushion the vital organs and to insulate the body from loss of heat. Premature babies have not had time to lay down a protective layer of fat; that is why such care must be taken to keep them warm.

Babies get most of the fat they need from dairy products, including breast milk and formulas, and meat. The American Academy of Pediatrics has specifically stated that children who have graduated from breast milk or infant formulas to regular pasteurized milk should be given whole *(not 1 percent, 2 percent, or skim)* milk until they are at least eighteen months old. Skim milk can actually endanger an infant's health. It is a very concentrated source of protein, which puts stress on an infant's immature kidneys.

Cholesterol is a controversial subject nowadays. Some cholesterol is important to the body's metabolism, but the body produces all the cholesterol it needs. Cholesterol forms the raw material from which vitamin D, bile salt, and sex and adrenal hormones are made. But we also now know that cholesterol is transported through the bloodstream by different kinds of lipoproteins, or blood fats. High levels of high-density lipoproteins (HDLs) reduce one's risk of suffering from heart disease or a stroke. High levels of low-density lipoproteins (LDLs), on the other hand, may lead to increased risk. Only a blood test for HDLs and LDLs can determine whether you need to modify your diet or your child's for cholesterol control. If cholesterol is a problem in your family, by all means ask your pediatrician about this test. In the meantime, many nutritionists and pediatricians continue to advise limiting consumption of egg yolks, which are particularly high in cholesterol, to two or three per week.

Vitamins and Minerals

People cannot manufacture vitamins in their bodies and must get them from a variety of foods or from synthetic sources. Vitamins help the body utilize nutrients and promote normal growth of tissues, and they are essential for the proper functioning of nerves and muscles. They are also part of the reproductive and digestive processes, and they may well help the body resist infections. Minerals are important because they give strength and rigidity to certain body tissues and assist with a number of other bodily functions. Vitamins and minerals work together in many combinations, as shown in the chart on

Vegetarian Babies

Growing numbers of vegetarian parents want to feed their babies in a like manner. In the early months, breast-feeding is best along with a vitamin supplement. When it's time for solids, the vegetarian baby can thrive as long as her diet is well planned. The vegetarian diet is low in caloric density because it contains so much fiber in relation to fat. To get adequate quantities of protein and fat, the baby has to eat much more unless some fat and dairy products are included with her meals. Vegetarian diets that include milk, cheese, and eggs (particularly the yolks) will provide plenty of complete protein, vitamin B_{12}, and calcium, and some iron, which is so vital to your infant's tissue, muscle, and bone growth. In addition to these sources, add calcium-rich tofu and whole-grain breads and cereals, including wheat germ, brown rice, and whole-wheat and vegetable-based pastas. Dark leafy green vegetables can supply many necessary vitamins and minerals; ground nuts or nut butters can provide essential fats. If dairy products and eggs are taboo, parents will have to add a calcium supplement and possibly a B_{12} supplement to the baby's diet. This is best done under the guidance of your health-care provider. To cook legumes correctly, see the box on pureed palate pleasers on page 78.

pages 74–75 (chart is adapted from *Our Bodies, Ourselves,* by The Boston Women's Health Book Collective, Inc. [New York: Simon & Schuster, 1976]). Though each is described as having a rather specific function, they seldom act independently.

Question: *Do babies need vitamin supplements?*

Answer: Supplementation with vitamins A, C, and D is often recommended for the breast-fed baby. Infant formulas are fortified in adequate amounts to meet the RDAs of these vitamins, so vitamin supplements are unnecessary for the bottle-fed baby. After the breast-fed baby is eating a varied diet of solids, these supplements are usually discontinued, but check with your pediatrician. If your water supply is not fluoridated, you might also want to ask your pediatrician for fluoride supplementation.

Baby Food in Jars

Those commercial baby foods that look so appealing in their little color-coded jars went through hard times when consumers learned that some contained substances that were harmful to babies. Under pressure from consumer advocates, baby-food companies have removed the worst of these additives—the salt, *MSG,* and *most* of the sugar—though some continue to add modified starches to fruits and mixed dinners. Many of the overly sweet desserts, which babies don't need, still contain sugar.

For busy parents who read labels carefully, these foods can be a real convenience, especially the beginner varieties, which are highly pureed and quite bland. They have been processed quickly to retain nutrients. If you use these, check the expiration dates as well as the lids, which are vacuum sealed. If the button on the lid

A Recommended Reading List for Vegetarian Parents and Babies

Elliot, Rose, *Vegetarian Mother and Baby Book: A Complete Guide to Nutrition, Health, and Diet During Pregnancy and After* (New York: Pantheon, 1987)

Ewald, Ellen B., *Recipes for a Small Planet* (New York: Ballantine, 1975)

Lappé, Frances Moore, *Diet for a Small Planet* (New York: Ballantine, 1982)

Robertson, Laurel; Flinders, Carol; and Ruppenthal, Brian, *The New Laurel's Kitchen: A Handbook for Vegetarian Cookery and Nutrition* (Berkeley, CA: Ten Speed Press, 1986)

Yntema, Sharon K., *Vegetarian Baby: A Sensible Guide for Parents* (Ithaca, NY: McBooks Press, 1980)

is down and pops up when opened, the jar is safe. Generally the vegetables and meats are the best buys and the mixed dinners the worst. Introduce these foods slowly by adding a new one every four to seven days and never feed the baby directly from the jar. The enzymes from his saliva will spoil the leftovers. Keep in mind that packaging, special portions, and textures have been created to keep a child on baby food long past the time when he could begin to feed himself finger foods that come from your own table.

Nutrients: Their Functions and Sources

Nutrient	Chief Functions	Important Sources
Vitamin A (fat-soluble) Extra vitamin A is stored in the liver—that is why animal livers are such a good source.	Helps prevent infection. Helps eyes adjust to changes from bright to dim light (prevents night blindness). Needed for healthy skin and certain tissues, such as the lining of eyes and lungs.	Liver, whole milk, fortified margarine (A is added), butter, most cheeses (especially Swiss and cheddar), egg yolks, dark-green and yellow vegetables (especially carrots, parsley, kale, and orange squash), apricots.
Vitamin D (fat-soluble)	Needed for strong bones and teeth (regulates calcium and phosphorus in bone formation). Essential for calcium absorption from the blood.	Sunlight shining on bare skin, vitamin D fortified milk, fish-liver oil, sardines, canned tuna.
Vitamin E (fat-soluble)	Helps preserve some vitamins and unsaturated fatty acids (acts as an antioxidant). Helps stabilize biological membranes.	Plant oils (especially wheat-germ oil and soybean oil), wheat germ, navy beans, eggs, brown rice.
Vitamin C or ascorbic acid (water-soluble) C is easily destroyed by air and heat. Like many other water-soluble vitamins, it is *not* stored in the body, so we need some every day.	Needed for healthy collagen (a protein that holds cells together). Helps wounds to heal. Needed for normal blood-clotting and healthy blood vessels. Needed for iron absorption. Spares or protects vitamins A and E and several B vitamins. Needed for strong teeth and bones.	Citrus fruits, green and red peppers, green leafy vegetables, parsley, tomatoes, potatoes, strawberries, cantaloupe, bean sprouts (especially mung beans and soybeans).
B vitamins (water-soluble) include thiamine (B_1), riboflavin (B_2), niacin, pyridoxine, folic acid, cobalamin (B_{12}), choline, etc. Folic-acid deficiency is common during pregnancy. It may also be caused by birth-control pills. Riboflavin is destroyed by sunlight, so use milk containers that keep out light. Fatigue, tension, depression are often signs of a B deficiency.	Needed for steady nerves, alertness, good digestion, energy production, healthy skin and eyes, certain enzymes involved in amino-acid synthesis, maintenance of blood.	Whole-grain breads and cereals, liver, wheat germ, nutritional yeast, green leafy vegetables, lean meats, milk, molasses, peanuts, dried peas and beans.

Nutrients: Their Functions and Sources *(Continued)*

Nutrient	Chief Functions	Important Sources
Calcium Calcium is more easily digested when eaten with acid foods (such as yogurt or sour milk).	Needed for building bones and teeth, for blood clotting, for regulating nerve and muscle activity, for absorbing iron.	Whole and skim milk, buttermilk, cheese, yogurt, green vegetables, egg yolk, bone-meal powder, blackstrap molasses.
Phosphorus	Needed to transform protein, fats, and carbohydrates into energy in the body. Makes up part of all the body's cells. Needed for building bones and teeth.	Milk, cheeses, lean meats, egg yolks.
Iron Daily intake is important. Children, teenagers, pregnant and menstruating women are especially likely to have iron deficiencies.	Makes up an important part of hemoglobin, the compound in blood that carries oxygen from the lungs to the body cells.	Lean meat, liver, egg yolk, green leafy vegetables, nutritional yeast, wheat germ, whole-grain and enriched breads and cereals, soybean flour, raisins, blackstrap molasses.
Iodine	An important part of thyroxine; helps the thyroid gland regulate the rate at which our bodies use energy. Affects growth, water balances, nervous system, muscular system, and circulatory system.	Iodized salt, seafood, plant foods grown in soil near the sea.
Magnesium	Required for certain enzyme activity. Helps in bone formation.	Grains, vegetables, cereals, fruits, milk, nuts.
Potassium	Needed for healthy nerves and muscles.	Seafood, milk, vegetables, fruits.
Sodium, chlorine, fluorine, and other trace minerals. Most of our diets now contain too much sodium, largely because of sodium compounds used in processed foods and excessive use of table salt.	Varying functions, many of them not well understood.	Meat, cheese, eggs, seafood, green leafy vegetables, fluoridated water, sea salt.

Answers to Common Questions About Commercial Baby Food

Question: How long can I keep an opened jar of baby food in the refrigerator?

Answer: Jars of fruit and juices have a refrigerator life of one to three days; meats and vegetables one to two days. A good, efficient refrigerator should maintain a temperature of 38 to 40°F and will keep foods fresh for the maximum amount of time; a refrigerator set at 50°F for the minimum.

Question: Can I warm baby food in the jar?

Answer: Even if you intend to use the whole jar for one meal, the jars are *not* heatproof. Use another warming appliance and warm only the amount you intend to use for that meal. Keep in mind that heating causes some vitamin loss and creates an opportune climate for bacteria to multiply.

Question: How can I tell if the food is spoiled?

Answer: Spoiled baby food does not necessarily smell and/or taste bad. If you have kept it longer than the amount of time suggested above, then assume that it will not be good for the baby. If it has liquified or has any signs of mold on it, throw it out.

Making Your Own Baby Food

If you don't like the idea of using commercial baby food, and you have the time and the inclination, you can always make your own. There is nothing mysterious or complicated about the process, and there are some advantages to homemade food. You can be in control of exactly what goes into it. It should go without saying, but I'll say it anyway: Be sure not to add sugar or salt.

You can choose high-quality fruits, vegetables, grains, and meats and leave out the unnecessary fillers such as water and cornstarch still found in some commercial baby foods. Store-bought baby foods also tend to have the same consistencies. We want our babies to experience differences in colors and textures—to feel and taste the rich creaminess of a banana, the tartness of an apple, and the lush stringiness of a peach. Also, if you puree portions of the food *you* eat before seasoning, there is a good chance that the baby will easily move to your table foods, which is the ultimate goal.

When you make your own baby food, you can also save money. All you need are a few standard kitchen implements, which you may own anyway, and/or an inexpensive and portable baby-food grinder small enough to fit in the baby's diaper bag or your pocketbook. There is no question that making baby food does take some time compared to opening a jar of prepared food. But if you cook ahead and freeze meal-sized portions, or grind up part of your own dinner before you add the seasonings, you will save a great deal of time. Also, keep in mind that the longer you wait to introduce solids, the shorter the time period will be when your baby needs finely pureed foods, which are the most time-consuming to make.

There are only a few recipes included here (see A Selection of Pureed Palate Pleasers, page 78). Everyone knows how to mash a banana and to thin it with liquid if it seems too bulky for the baby. No baby profits from elaborate sweet desserts such as the puddings or cobblers that the baby-food manufacturers would have us believe are good for our babies. Many of the foods you eat, such as stews and soups, can be pureed to become "combination" dinners. Cereals, scrambled eggs, cottage cheese, mashed potatoes, and yogurt are excellent vehicles for vegetables if your baby is horrified at the sight of a spoonful of string beans.

The number of months that a baby will allow the parent to be in control of her feeding—that is, putting pureed foods into her mouth with a spoon—are very few. That's especially true if you encourage self-feeding as soon as the baby shows signs of being able to pick up anything and everything and putting it in her mouth. For this reason, it's not recommended that you spend a great deal of money on elaborate feeding equipment and special cookbooks.

Useful Items for Making Your Own Baby Food

• A blender, food processor, food mill (which will separate out skins and seeds), or a small hand-operated baby-food grinder or new garlic press for pureeing, and/or a sieve to put blended or milled foods through as a final step if a smoother consistency is desired.

• A small vegetable steamer, colander, or sieve for steaming rather than boiling vegetables and fruits. Many vegetables and fruits contain vitamins C and A, which are water-soluble and easily destroyed by overcooking.

• A pot with a tightly fitting lid, or a pressure cooker to save time, and/or a pan for braising or stewing meats. A cast-iron pan will add a little absorbed iron.

Simple Guidelines for Preparing Your Own Baby Food

All the advantages of making your own baby food can be lost if the food is not handled carefully. Make sure you work with clean hands, clean utensils, and especially a clean cutting board, butcher block, or wooden counter. The grooves and scrapes in these surfaces trap bacteria, including salmonella, which is found in raw eggs, chicken, and fish. Scrub work surfaces daily with hot soapy water, rinse well, and dry carefully. Bacteria thrive in damp places. Also watch out for chipped enamel pots and chipped china because acidic foods like tomato sauces, juices, fruits, vinegar, and tea may leach toxic substances into the exposed china or metal. Make sure that your can opener is clean and that the tops of cans are scalded with boiling water. If you taste the food, don't put the spoon back in the pot without washing it.

For thinning. Baby-food manufacturers add plain water for the proper consistency, but you can add the steaming water from fruits and vegetables, which contains the vitamins lost during cooking. You can also add breast milk; formula; cow's milk; yogurt; meat, vegetable, or soup broths, or stew juices. To sweeten you can use apple or orange juice.

For thickening. Baby-food manufacturers use modified starch or cornstarch, neither of which is particularly well digested or nutritious for babies. You can add wheat germ, whole-grain cereals, cottage cheese, farmer cheese, cooked egg yolks, yogurt, or mashed white or sweet potatoes. Add these thickeners a little at a time until the desired consistency is reached.

Fruits. Handle all fruits gently. Crushing or bruising releases an enzyme that destroys vitamin C. Bananas are often the first fruit a baby eats. Choose ones with brown spots on the skins because these are the ripest. Simply mash with a fork, and thin or thicken as desired. Other fresh fruits need to be softened by steaming or baking. When it is practical, cook the whole piece of fruit in its skin, which helps keep soluble nutrients from dissolving in the cooking water. Baked apples, for instance, are delicious (see page 78). If you can't cook the whole fruit, then peel, cut, and

steam the pieces in a vegetable steamer over an inch or so of water in a tightly covered pot to retain vitamins. Steam until the fruit is soft enough to mash with a fork, then push through a sieve, baby-food grinder, etc. Puree according to the baby's desire or ability to handle lumps.

Vegetables. Try carrots, zucchini, and other types of squash, peas, beans, and sweet potatoes first. You can bake the potatoes. Cut the other vegetables into small pieces and steam them in a vegetable steamer over 1 or 2 inches of water in a tightly covered pot. Use this water as a thinner when pureeing vegetables. The approximate ratio of vegetables to liquid is 2 cups of fresh vegetables to between 1/3 to 1/2 cup of liquid.

Certain vegetables, such as spinach, lettuce, carrots, beets, turnips, celery, and collard greens, may contain excessive amounts of nitrates from the soil. In babies under four months, nitrite inhibits the blood's ability to carry oxygen. Remember, too, that certain vegetables, such as beets and spinach, will change the color of the baby's bowel movements. Pieces of raw vegetables of any type can cause choking. Cooked corn, unless it is pureed, can also cause choking.

Meats, fish, and legumes. Meats can be steamed, broiled, baked, poached, stewed, or braised, but not fried. Chicken is a good meat to start with because it is easy to digest. Again, be sure to wash hands, sink, cutting surfaces, and knives carefully after handling raw chicken and fish. Meats cooked in soups or stews are flavorful and tender. It is quite difficult, as well as unnecessary, to approximate the lumpless consistency of commercial baby-food meats. In most cases you will need to add some liquid (see the box on pureed palate pleasers, page 78).

Don't soak or boil dried legumes for long periods of time because vitamins will be destroyed. Instead, boil them for two minutes and let them

stand for two hours. This is equivalent to fifteen hours of soaking. Don't rinse after soaking. (See the box on pureed palate pleasers, page 78.)

Warming the Baby's Food

Warm food has more flavor than cold food. You can place the food in a special baby warming dish, in one or two small Pyrex dishes in a pan of water on the burner of your stove, or in a multiple egg poacher. Do not use the microwave oven, because it will heat the food unevenly. Even with stirring there is no guarantee that you will totally eliminate hot spots.

Storing, Freezing, and Thawing Baby Food

After preparing the baby food, cool it quickly in the refrigerator; there is less chance for bacteria to form in a cool environment. If you freeze food in ice-cube trays or in squares of aluminum foil,

A Selection of Pureed Palate Pleasers

Baked Apples. Preheat oven to 350°F, then wash and core apples. Wrap each apple in a square of aluminum foil, and seal tightly. Bake for 30 to 45 minutes, testing with a fork for desired softness. Remove foil, skin, and core. Mash apples. Count on two to three apples to produce 1 cup of mashed apple. You can use the same method for pears, which will reach the desired softness within 15 to 30 minutes.

Pureed Meats. Cut meat into ½-inch cubes. Trim off all fat. Add 1 cup of stock (either meat or vegetable) to 1 cup of meat. Simmer until meat is tender—45 minutes to an hour. Drain stock, reserving the liquid. When you puree, use ½ cup of cooking liquid for each cup of meat. Freeze extra portions immediately.

Pureed Legumes. Carefully rinse and pick over 1 cup of any legume. Soak in water overnight or bring to a boil for 2 minutes, cover, and then allow to sit for 2 hours. Drain off the soaking water or the cooking water, then add 3 cups fresh water and bring beans to a boil. Reduce heat and simmer, covered, until beans are tender (anywhere from 30 minutes to 2 hours, depending on your choice of legume). Skim the surface often as beans are simmering. Puree with ¾ cup milk. Freeze unused portions immediately.

Sweet Potatoes. Scrub potatoes and bake at 450°F for 40 to 50 minutes, testing with a fork for desired softness. Allow to cool. Peel, then mash with a fork, adding vegetable cooking juices, milk, or a bit of apple juice. Acorn squash can be substituted for sweet potato.

Vegetable Purees. Follow directions for steaming vegetables on page 77. Place steamed vegetables and a little of the steaming water in a food processor or baby-food grinder and puree to a soft consistency. To add flavor and protein, try adding an equal amount of baked or steamed potato to the steamed vegetables and puree together. Thin mixture with milk to desired consistency. Freeze unused portions immediately.

Combination Dinner. Place 1 cup cooked meat, ⅔ cup cooked vegetables, ⅓ cup cooked white or brown rice, and 1 cup stock in a blender or food processor. Puree, and freeze leftover portions immediately. Yield should be approximately 3 cups.

---

be sure to label and date them; then seal them in plastic bags. Food stored in the freezer is good for one month. A small amount of vitamins C and A are lost in the freezing process, but this is far less than what is lost by storing baby food in the refrigerator over a period of a few days.

When you thaw the food, do so in the refrigerator. Thawing at room temperature allows bacteria to grow. If you are in a hurry, you can thaw by submerging food in a plastic bag in cold water and gradually adding hot water.

High Chairs

You will get a lot of use from a high chair all the way through toddlerhood, first with the tray and later without it at the family table. It is worth choosing carefully. The most important feature in a high chair is safety. According to *Consumer Reports,* as many as 9,000 people a year, including adults, are hurt by high chairs. Babies left unattended and/or unrestrained with a belt can stand up, fall, or slip out. Sliding trays can pinch fingers or, if not properly snapped in place, fall off, bringing the baby down with them. A crawling or standing baby can pull over an unstable chair. Next to safety, cleanability is crucial. The more streamlined the chair, the fewer places for food to lodge. Following are some points to look for:

Don't be deceived by beauty! My sister gave me a beautiful wooden high chair that was totally impractical. It was hard to clean, the seat was too deep, and Joe kept sliding down so his chin was on the tray. The footrest wasn't adjustable, and his feet kind of hung there. I gave it back and bought a metal and vinyl chair whose tray was easy to remove and which I felt comfortable scrubbing down once a week in the shower.

• • •

My sister lent me her deluxe, super-duper high chair with a reclining seat. I don't recommend spending the extra money for babies not yet ready to sit up. A portable infant seat serves the same purpose and besides, they don't need to eat until they are ready to sit up anyway.

• Buy only a certified high chair. This means that the chair has met voluntary safety standards set by the Juvenile Products Manufacturers Association (JPMA). These chairs meet standards for stability, and restraining belt and tray safety.

• For overall stability, check to make sure that the base is wider than the seat of the chair. Models vary tremendously. Shake the chair to test it.

• Look for a strong, adjustable, easy-to-operate safety and crotch strap to prevent the baby from standing and sliding down in the chair. Another suggestion to keep the baby from sliding and/or slumping is to put a piece of foam under him for traction. Bathtub stickers work quite well, too.

• Modern high chairs have removable trays, an essential feature for thorough cleansing in the sink. Make sure that the latches for holding the tray are easy to operate, by feel rather than by sight. An even greater safety advantage is a chair with a tray latch that can be operated with one hand while you hold the baby with the other. Look for a lip on the tray, so that spills don't reach the floor so quickly.

• Make sure that the backrest is high enough to support the baby's head and that the footrest is adjustable. The vinyl padding on the seat should be thick so that it won't puncture and tear. Check to see if the heat-treated seams are smooth.

• If you are considering a collapsible or folding chair, the locking device must be strong and reliable. Collapse the chair in the store to be sure just how large it is when folded. If you are plan-

High chair

Add-on chair

ning to put it in a closet or a car trunk, take measurements with you.

The safest high chair isn't safe if you aren't careful every time you put your baby in it. Use the seat belt, and never leave the baby unattended. Check the tray-lock mechanism every time you put the baby in, and watch out for fingers—your own and the baby's. Be sure to position the chair away from chairs, tables, walls, counters, electrical outlets, etc. (See the safety chapter, page 207.)

Booster Seats and Portable Add-on Chairs

These seats seem appealing. Besides being small, portable, and relatively inexpensive compared with a high chair, they allow the baby or small child to eat right at the family table. Unfortunately, many booster seats are not safe because they don't secure firmly onto an adult-size chair. Others lack safety belts. These features are of crucial importance, so insist on both.

Hook-on chairs work on a cantilever principle. The chair frame slides onto a tabletop and is held in place by friction, the weight of the child, and either suction cups or a spring-latch locking device. If you plan to buy one of these seats, choose very carefully. Look for good, strong frame locks to hold the seat in place, seat and crotch straps, a nonslippery seat surface, and no parts that can pinch or break off and be swallowed by the baby.

When you use the seat, follow directions to the letter. According to *Consumer Reports*, the most common accidents occur when parents put an adult-size chair under the hook-on seat, hoping that this will provide additional support for the child. The child can then push down on the chair, lifting the seat and causing it to dislodge from the table. The seats are also dangerous if used on glass, single-pedestal, card tables, on the leaf of a table, or a table that is thicker than specified by the manufacturer.

Self-Feeding

Your baby will probably let you know when he is ready to try feeding himself before you start wondering when to encourage him. He may flatly refuse to let you put a spoonful of pureed peas into his mouth by clamping his jaw and shaking his head. Alternately, he may simply grab the spoon out of your hand. Or he may gradually express an interest in feeding himself over a period of months.

Signs of readiness may begin to appear between seven and ten months and coincide with his newly found mobility and dexterity. Sitting increases his scope and view of the world, and creeping and crawling his range to explore new territory. His fine motor skills and eye and hand coordination have come together to the point where he can pick up small objects and put them into his mouth. Now everything goes in, including the dust balls. If only babies worked as hard at feeding themselves as they do at cleaning floors, there wouldn't be as many high-chair horror stories as there are!

Self-feeding is a great stride forward in a baby's independence, and it should be encouraged. However, it can be difficult for parents whose experience has consisted of neatly spooning pureed foods into their baby's mouth. First of all, self-feeding is messy, and there is nothing efficient about it. When the baby is in charge, food is a truly sensual delight—to be poked and smeared, and to be squeezed through the fingers, then worn as a cosmetic on the face and hair. It

takes a strong stomach—and a sense of humor—to witness a meal.

Keep telling yourself that eating should be pleasurable, not a grim duty that we impose on our children. Let the baby dip her hands into a bowl of yogurt or applesauce as you continue to offer some on the spoon. Also, be sure not to present the baby with too much food. Place two or three pieces of soft, "gummable" foods on the high-chair tray. (See Finger-Food Palate Pleasers, page 81.) Never turn your back on these early experiments because the baby could gag or start to choke. (See Responding to Choking, and Gagging, page 82.) You will notice, too, that a lot of the food may end up on the floor. The baby is not doing this to drive you crazy. Once he has developed his picking-up skills, he then begins to work on releasing his grasp. He's also becoming aware of cause and effect: If he drops a spoon, a clattering sound will follow. If he throws a piece of toast on the floor, the dog will gobble it up. He will also notice if you are upset by the way he eats. So grin and bear it, ending meals promptly when they become all play.

Another major concern about self-feeding is the quantity of food that actually ends up in the baby. Babies who feed themselves eat less than they did when a parent wielded the spoon. This is normal and (as hard as it is to believe) appropriate for the baby's growth and development. Remember that on average, children triple their birth weight in the first year by consuming about 50 calories per pound each day. Then their weight gain slows down. If it didn't, the child would weigh 180 pounds by the age of three! By the second year the child needs 30 to 40 calories per pound, and 20 to 35 calories per pound thereafter.

Another concern for parents can be that the baby's consumption of milk may also drop or vary considerably from day to day. The nursing

Foods That Babies Can Choke On

As many young children die each year from choking as from poisoning. Following is a list of the foods that are the most common causes of choking. Be sure to show this list to your baby-sitters or anyone else who feeds your child.

- hot dogs
- candy
- nuts
- grapes
- popcorn
- raw apple pieces
- raw carrot pieces
- cookies, breads, and biscuits that don't dissolve in the baby's mouth almost immediately
- lumps of peanut butter

baby may appear to find the world more interesting than the comfort of your breast. The bottle-fed baby may take a few ounces, then push the bottle away. This is normal. According to nutritionist Ellyn Satter, author of *Child of Mine*, 16 ounces of milk a day is adequate for the baby who eats an ounce of meat a day. Remember, too, that you can substitute other high-calcium foods for milk. (See Useful Milk Equivalents, page 71.)

From seven months on your baby experiences a growing curiosity and excitement about everything in his world. Self-feeding is part of this exploration and discovery. We tend to worry overly much about getting the right nutrients

Finger-Food Palate Pleasers

For many babies, complete self-feeding is a gradual and erratic process. One day the baby will show interest, the next he may not. Place one or two pieces of these soft, "gummable" selections on the high-chair tray. Continue to offer favorite pureed foods by spoon, but don't coax and wheedle.

- cheese, milk, and egg custards cooked to a firm consistency
- small chunks of soft cheese, large-curd cottage cheese, or farmer cheese
- small frozen yogurt bits
- macaroni-and-cheese, or well-cooked pasta (in addition to plain, try whole-wheat and spinach)
- grilled cheese on whole-wheat bread
- small ground beef, lamb, or veal balls poached in broth, rather than sautéed, to retain their softness
- cooked crumbled hamburger or meat loaf, fortified with finely chopped vegetables and wheat germ
- very soft stewed or braised beef, chicken, veal, lamb, etc.
- any soft, carefully deboned fish (sole is particularly good)
- French toast made with whole-wheat bread (make sure that the eggs are thoroughly cooked)
- whole-wheat pancakes
- eggs, hard-boiled, soft-boiled mixed with bread for firmness, or scrambled (add steamed vegetables and cheese for combination omelets)

- bits of tofu
- bananas
- avocados
- tomatoes with skin and seeds removed
- white and sweet potatoes, and winter squash cooked to softness and shaped into small balls
- small pieces of steamed zucchini
- small pieces of steamed carrot
- small pieces of steamed broccoli and cauliflower (no stalks)
- peas with skins broken
- small pieces of steamed string bean, strings removed
- small bits of sugarless, dried cereal that soften quickly in the mouth
- small pieces of rice cake
- cooked cereals shaped into small balls

(*Note:* Peanut butter is on the list of dangerous foods for babies. Its thick, sticky texture can cause choking. When the time comes for this childhood staple (when your child is about two years old), be aware that peanuts can contain aflatoxin, a carcinogen found in a common mold. Commercial peanut butter is strictly monitored for this. Salt also protects peanuts against mold. Fresh peanuts waiting to be ground at your local health-food store can develop mold. Ask how fresh the peanuts are when they are ground for use. Taste a few if you have any doubts. Refrigerate fresh peanut butter and use it up quickly.

into our babies when what we really need to do is let go, offer high-quality foods, and leave the rest to the baby. He won't starve, even if he appears to survive on air and breadsticks. To reassure yourself, take a good look at your child. Is he curious, energetic, and vital?

Responding to Choking and Gagging

Question: *Your ten-month-old is eating a piece of bread. She suddenly starts gagging. Do you know what to do?*

Answer: First of all, don't panic. Remember that choking and gagging are fairly common occurrences in babies and don't usually lead to a blocked airway. The following suggestions are reprinted directly from "Choking Prevention and First Aid for Infants and Children" from the American Academy of Pediatrics (AAP) and the American Trauma Society (ATS):

1. Find out if the child can breathe, cry or speak. See if the child has a strong cough. (A strong cough means there is little or no blockage. It may also dislodge the item if there is blockage.)

2. If the child is breathing, coughing, or speaking, carefully watch him. *Do not start first aid if there is a strong cough or if there is little or no blockage.* This can turn partial blockage into complete blockage.

3. Begin the following first aid if:
- the child cannot breathe at all
- the child's airway is so blocked that there's only a weak cough and loss of color

For Infants Under One Year Old

1. Make sure you or someone else has called for emergency medical services.

2. Place the infant face and head down on your forearm at a 60-degree angle. (A) Support the head and neck. Rest your forearm firmly against your body for extra support.

Note: If the infant is large, you may want to lay the child face down over your lap. Firmly support the head, holding it lower than the trunk.

3. Give four rapid back blows with the heel of your hand, striking high between the shoulder blades.

4. If the blockage is not relieved, turn the infant over. Lay the child down, face up, on a firm surface. Give four rapid chest thrusts over the breastbone using *two fingers.*

5. If breathing does not start, open the mouth with thumb held over tongue and fingers wrapped around lower jaw. This is called the tongue-jaw lift. It draws the tongue away from the back of the throat and may help clear the airway. If you can see the foreign body, it may be removed with a sideways sweep of a finger. Never poke the finger straight into the throat. But *be very careful of finger sweeps* because they may cause further blockage.

6. If the infant does not begin to breathe right away, place your mouth over the mouth and nose of the infant. Attempt two quick, shallow breaths. Because of the infant's size, use quick and short breaths.

7. Repeat steps one through six.

For Children Over One Year Old

1. Make sure you or someone you know has called for emergency medical services.

2. Place the child on his back. (B) Kneel at his feet. Put the heel of one hand in the midline between the navel and ribcage. Place the second hand on top of the first. Then press firmly, but gently, into the abdomen with a rapid inward and upward thrust. Repeat this six to ten times. These abdominal thrusts are called the Heimlich maneuver.

3. If breathing does not start, open the airway using the tongue-jaw lift technique. If you can see the foreign body, you can try to remove it with a sideways sweep of the finger. *Be careful, though, because finger sweeps may push the object further down the airway.*

4. If the child does not begin to breathe right away, attempt to restore breathing with the mouth-to-mouth technique described in step 6. If this fails, repeat a series of six to ten abdominal thrusts.

5. Repeat steps 1 through 4.

Note: In a larger child, the abdominal thrusts (Heimlich maneuver) may be performed when the victim is standing, sitting or lying down (C).

Avoiding Frustration Over the "Balanced" Diet: Tips from Mothers

Molly's repertoire got smaller and smaller. Finally she would eat only pureed chicken, bananas, and teething biscuits. I did give her vitamins but stopped offering her a lot of other foods out of pure frustration. When we left her with my mother for a day, she reported that Molly had gone on a vegetable binge. I felt so guilty! Even if the baby seems to be on a food jag, don't forget to offer other things anyway. One day the baby may just take them.

• • •

M. F. K. Fisher, the great food writer, suggests balancing the day rather than the meal. With our baby I found that it wasn't so much a matter of balancing the day as of balancing the week.

• • •

I caught myself playing "Open your mouth, Hadley! Here comes the choo-choo full of spinach." I said to myself, "Why is a forty-two-year-old woman, who has had a complex relationship with food—and her pushy mother—all of her life, trying to stuff her eight-month-old daughter with

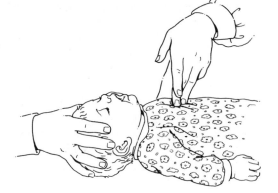

Position baby so his head is lower than his body

Use two fingers to give four rapid thrusts over the breastbone.

If the infant does not begin to breathe right away, place your mouth over the mouth and nose of the baby, and attempt two quick, shallow breaths.

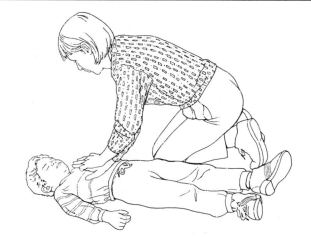

Press firmly on the midline between navel and ribcage. Give six to ten rapid thrusts.

The tongue-jaw lift: Wrap your fingers around the child's lower jaw, open the mouth, and hold your thumb over the jaw.

Mouth-to-mouth technique for a child is the same as for an infant.

spinach?" I decided I don't want to repeat old patterns.

• • •

I finally learned that a meal can be only one food or even none. A baby doesn't have to get all the nutrients from each meal each day the way food charts would have us believe. I kept seeing those brightly colored four basic areas of nutrition that I grew up with—the bright, shiny eggs next to the neat slices of white rather than whole-wheat bread and those beautiful fresh fruits! If I didn't get a fresh fruit in, I was in a state of near-panic. If she concentrated on vegetables, I would push the meat. I could never just be happy letting her eat what she wanted to eat. I've finally come to realize that Anna will get all she needs in her own way, even if she seems to eat several meals in a row of all carbohydrates. Letting go of this controlling urge is difficult. I wanted to be a "good mother" and provide good food. I had trouble accepting that offering it is where my job as a "good mother" ends.

• • •

Besides eating practically nothing and dropping most of it on the floor, Ellie, ten months, won't stay sitting down in the high chair. She wants to stand up all the time. For a while I fed her in her stroller. Then we went back to the high chair. She seems pretty content to sit there now.

• • •

It's always so easy for me to talk about my fifth baby, when I remember so clearly how I felt with the first. I really didn't think he would survive without three solid meals a day on a set schedule. I sang and danced and wheedled and coaxed. Meals were really tense, and I was reluctant to feed Jason between meals because I wanted him to be hungry at the next meal. With each succeeding baby I have become more and more flexible. I feed them healthy snacks, or parts of meals that they wouldn't eat during their regular meals.

Maybe I'm just worn out from motherhood, but I don't worry. I spread the New York Times out in several layers in a five-foot radius around the high chair and throw a layer away after each meal. When he stands up in the chair, I take him out, the meal is over.

• • •

My twins have totally different food preferences. Emma is on an egg kick, only the yolks, thank you. She wears them in her hair. Jonathan wants nothing but Cheerios and your basic ripe banana. He likes to fingerpaint with yogurt, but very little gets in the mouth. I have no time to be uptight or to make them special gourmet treats. People stop me with my double stroller, and say, "What beautiful, healthy babies you have!" I agree. Something's working, and it's not my cooking!

• • •

In retrospect I feel that I was overly worried about Nancy's diet because she was a low-birthweight baby. In those early weeks every single half ounce that she gained represented a kind of victory in her fight for survival. And then there would be setbacks when she didn't gain. That experience stayed with me when I started her on solids. I found that I was monitoring her and worrying more or less constantly. Rather than talk about this to my pediatrician, I kept my worries to myself. I might have benefited by her support if I'd been able to be more open about my concern.

• • •

No one needs to create a feeding problem today. We have too many substitutes for foods that a child needs. The substitutes make it possible for a mother to stay out of her child's feeding conflicts. His nutritional needs are completely met by 1) a pint of milk or its equivalent in cheese, ice cream, or calcium substitutes (one teaspoon is equivalent to eight ounces of milk); 2) an ounce of fresh fruit juice or one piece of fruit; 3) two ounces of iron-containing protein, such as one egg or two ounces

---

Is Your Baby a Juice-Aholic?

Would you let your baby nip at a bottle of sugary cola? Probably not, but if he swigs all day from a bottle of apple juice, he's getting just as much sugar. Large quantities of fruit juice also promote stomach pain, bloating, and diarrhea. Too much juice can spoil his thirst for milk, which supplies him with essential fats. For most babies the diarrhea clears up when their diets are balanced; that is, when juice is kept at a maximum of 6 to 8 ounces and milk between 18 and 24 ounces a day. After that, offer water.

---

of meat (one half jar of baby-food meat or a small hamburger); and 4) a multi-vitamin preparation. (This last may even be unnecessary, but it makes me feel one can forget whether a child has eaten green, yellow, or any vegetables.) With these four requirements a child will grow and gain weight normally. No more is necessary."
—T. Berry Brazelton, M.D.
Infants and Mothers:
Differences in Development

From Breast or Bottle to the Cup

Many parents want to wean their babies directly from the breast to the cup. This way they avoid bottles altogether, which is a mixed blessing. Bottles, while they do provide the pleasures of food and sucking, can become oversized security objects, "crutches" to quiet a fussy baby or toddler. There certainly aren't many two-, three-, and

Helpful Books on Nutrition and Feeding Your Baby

Boston Children's Hospital Staff, and Baker, Susan, *Parent's Guide to Nutrition* (Reading, MA: Addison-Wesley Publishing Co., Inc., 1987)

Brody, Jane, *Jane Brody's Nutrition Book* (New York: Bantam, 1987)

The Bureau of Nutrition, *Feeding the Toddler, Building Good Eating Habits in Young Children,* and *Nourishing Food for the Child and Family* (New York, NY 10013: Department of Health, City of New York, 93 Worth Street) (Available to residents and nonresidents of New York)

Kenda, Margaret E., et al., *Natural Babyfood Cookbook* (New York: Avon, 1982)

Natow, Annette B., and Heslin, Jo-Ann, *No-Nonsense Nutrition from Toddlers to Pre-Teens* (New York: McGraw-Hill, Inc., 1984)

Satter, Ellyn, *Child of Mine: Feeding with Love and Good Sense* (Palo Alto, CA: Bull Publishing Co., 1986)

Satter, Ellyn, *How to Get Your Kid to Eat . . . But Not Too Much* (Palo Alto, CA: Bull Publishing Co., 1987)

Zaphiropoulos, Hirschman, *Are You Hungry?* (New York: New American Library, 1987)

Need information on the sodium content in products or meals? Call Mrs. Dash, Sodium Information Hotline at (800) 622-DASH.

four-year-olds carrying cups as security objects, and you will never be accused of prolonging your baby's "infantilism" if you move straight from breast to cup. Though toilet training is and ought to be a distant prospect when you have a baby, a cup-drinking two-year-old is easier to help along than a child who carries a bottle and nips at it all day. There are other advantages as well. If you forget a bottle, you are sunk. A cup is replaceable, and a small thermos is very portable.

A baby who is used to a bottle may not take the cup very seriously, so if you bottle-feed, try introducing the cup as early as five months—before the baby becomes too opinionated. You will have to be patient when you start. If he balks, try again in a few days. If he balks again, wait a few weeks. Offer plastic cups in the bathtub for pouring. You'd be surprised what happens in that non-pressured situation. If the whole cup business turns out to be a fiasco, don't get discouraged. Just remember that everybody who goes to nursery school knows how to drink out of a cup. It does happen eventually.

• First, choose a nonbreakable cup, because it will likely end up on the floor. Some baby cups have no handles, and some have two handles for easy grasping. A rubber band or two around the cup will give it better traction in a baby's wet little hands. Spouted lids are optional. These keep spills at a minimum but require a semisucking action that your baby might or might not take to. Put only a small amount of liquid into the bottom.

• Some mothers reserve fruit juice for cups only. Its good, sweet taste is an incentive to keep trying. Breast milk or formula are also good choices. If one doesn't work, try another.

• Have the baby sitting up as well as covered with a large bib. At first, more of the liquid will dribble out of the baby's mouth than actually goes in.

• The bathtub is a good place to try a cup. The interest level may be high, and spills no problem.

• Call it quits when the baby shows the least bit of disinterest.

· PART THREE ·

Comforts

• CHAPTER 6 •

Crying

How I wish there were a magical force that would penetrate the baby and make her stop crying!

• • •

There is nothing quite like the sound of your own baby crying! Poignant, insistent, unnerving, and frustrating if it goes on and on. We *wish* the baby wouldn't cry, though we realize that it is the only way she has to communicate her needs. Few parents can (or would want to) ignore their baby's distress. Most of us have been roused from deep sleep, through closed doors, when we are rooms or even floors away by our baby's cry. We become so attuned to the signal that we sometimes "hear" the baby's crying even if we've left her at home for a walk around the block.

As hard as it is to feel your baby's distress, crying does serve some purpose. The newborn is still a very disorganized person whose complex systems have not yet adapted to life outside the womb. On top of this, she is barraged by all sorts of new and overwhelming stimuli. Crying serves as an outlet for this tension. It is also a way of blocking out the disturbing stimuli she is not yet mature enough to handle. Crying and sleep, at

opposite ends of the spectrum, are barriers against stimulation and, as odd as it may sound, they are attempts at ordering the baby's world.

One of the burning questions about crying is whether you should rush to soothe the baby or leave her to "cry it out." Sometimes babies do just need to cry. But as you read this section, you'll see that with younger babies, at least, the burden of opinion and evidence is to err on the side of comforting.

Question: *How do parents feel when their baby cries?*

Answer: *I called the pediatrician almost daily for the first two months. I felt as helpless as the baby did. The doctor finally lost his patience one day and said, "I don't know any better why your baby is crying than you do. Sometimes they just cry because life is tough!"*

A: *Every time she cried I became frightened and panicky. I had read that mothers could tell the difference between different kinds of cries. As I could never tell, I felt terribly inadequate.*

A: *An inconsolable baby will reduce even the most composed adult to a state of frenzied helplessness.*

—T. Berry Brazelton, M.D.
What Every Baby Knows

Interpreting Your Baby's Cries

Though a baby can always make herself heard, she can't always make herself understood. If you don't know why your newborn is crying each time she cries, join the club. You do not fall into the "parent without instincts" category. Some experts on infancy insist that we are supposed to be able to distinguish a hunger cry from a tired one, or a cry of pain from one of apprehension in a mere three weeks. Though there is surely some truth to this for all of us *eventually,* in the beginning most of us simply have to rely on the logic of trial and error as we wait for this knack to develop.

Sensing how to meet a baby's needs works two ways. With each day her behavior becomes slightly more organized, and her cues clearer as she adjusts to life outside the womb. And with each day parents become more skilled at reading the baby's cues, and more relaxed.

In the meantime, it should be comforting to know that even if you take the "wrong" approach in your attempt to soothe the baby—should you diaper her when what she really needs is sleep, or burp her when she's starving—your efforts *do* make a difference. Answering a baby's cries promptly and consistently and not leaving her to "cry it out" give her a sense that she is not alone and that you care.

You Won't Spoil the Baby!

A dialogue between two mothers:

Ann: They are all telling me, "You'll spoil her if you keep picking her up. She's not hungry." I feel ganged up against by my own mother, my mother-in-law, and my husband. Even my sister who has older kids agrees. Of course I'm frazzled.

Martha: Tell your busybody relatives to butt out!

Ann: But they've had fourteen babies among them, and they're worried about how tired I am.

Martha: Tell them if they are so worried about you, they can go wash the dishes or empty the garbage instead of dispensing advice.

Ann: What if we spoil . . .

Martha: Are you some kind of a creep because you want to pick up your own crying baby and try to make her feel better?

• • •

There appear to be two philosophies on why babies cry. One is that they never cry without a good reason and that they need attention. The other is that they cry for no good reason and will be spoiled by too much attention. I instinctively believe in the first philosophy. When we hear our baby cry, it is very difficult not to go to her and want to pick her up and comfort her as best as we can. Yet it is fascinating to note how many parents believe that it is wrong to follow this instinct.

According to a survey at the University of South Dakota School of Medicine, nearly two-thirds of the mothers and four-fifths of the fathers polled agreed that a baby under age one can be spoiled. The majority of those parents believed that this is done by "allowing him to have his own way." Most of the parents polled also felt that while there were no long-term ill effects of "spoiling," in the short term, spoiled babies are "demanding, obnoxious, and overindulged." Responding to an infant and, in particular, picking her up when she cries is, in the minds of many parents, the way that spoiling begins.

"Demanding, obnoxious, overindulged." In other words, the baby is capable of manipulating an adult into giving her something that won't be good for her. The baby is therefore better off being unhappy. Does that make sense? This reasoning may explain an older child's tantrum, but it gives the baby much more credit for rational thinking than she is capable of. Babies simply don't have those mental abilities to manipulate their parents—yet.

Perhaps parents assign that power to the baby because it's easier to regard the baby as spoiled rather than face those horribly uncomfortable feelings that her cries arouse in us. An infant's helplessness brings us head on with the tremendous responsibility we have assumed when we have a child. This can be frightening, and it can also remind us of our own powerlessness. Rather than accepting these negative feelings, which are perfectly legitimate, a part of us would rather "blame" the baby.

The Research on Spoiling

A growing body of research on infants supports the notion that babies will *not* be spoiled if we comfort them when they cry. A well-known study done by Mary Ainsworth and Sylvia Bell at Johns Hopkins University confirms that babies who are tended to quickly will cry less frequently and for a shorter duration than those who aren't. The researchers also noticed that by the end of the first year, the babies who had been "spoiled" by some people's standards were more independent and better at communicating and at getting adult attention through means other than crying.

Question: On the average, how long do newborns cry every day?

Answer: Plenty. T. Berry Brazelton, the well-known pediatrician, researcher, and author, has conducted studies at Boston Children's Hospital on just this question. His research shows that normal babies start out by crying for a period of one to one-and-a-half hours a day up to three weeks. They then build up to two hours (and some to as much as four hours) by six weeks.

Why Do Babies Cry?

During the early months you'll probably spend a good deal of time wondering why your baby is crying. The first and simplest reason that comes to mind is hunger.

Question: How does the baby feel when she is hungry?

Answer: "His hunger is a ravenous hunger, the tensions it produces are intolerable, and the satisfaction of this hunger is imperative."

—Selma Frailberg,
The Magic Years

Crying and Feeding: Schedule or Demand?

The Dilemma:

"You mean he's not on a schedule?" my mother who was visiting kept saying. "He was on a schedule in the hospital, wasn't he? If you pick him up every time he cries and feed him, no wonder he has a stomach ache, and no wonder he then needs to be picked up and held all the time—even when he's not hungry." But I can't not feed him if he's hungry, can I? If I try to feed him and he eats, and no disaster occurs, I have to conclude that he was hungry, don't I? You can't make a baby eat who doesn't want to eat, can you? How can you overfeed a two-week-old infant who is nursing?

Consider the following:

Question: Can you overfeed a baby?
Answer: No, every baby will stop sucking when he is full, and you won't be able to get another drop into him. If you attempt to force food into him beyond this point, he will only vomit.
— Virginia E. Pomeranz, M.D., with Dodi Schultz
The First Five Years: The Relaxed Approach to Child Care

• • •

In a study in Cambridge, England, Martin Richards and I found that mothers varied greatly in how they interpreted their babies' crying. In the first place, many were at a loss to explain it, particularly in the case of persistent crying in the evenings. In the second place, most breast-feeding mothers tended to assume that crying showed that the baby was hungry. Although a few mothers responded by feeding the baby regardless of how long it had been since he was last fed, many breast-feeding mothers felt that if adequately fed he should be happy for three to four hours, and hence this more frequent crying must be a sign that their milk supply was inadequate. This "inadequacy" was the most common reason for giving up breast-feeding. But in fact the babies of the successful breast-feeders, who continued to feed for over six months, cried just as frequently in the early weeks as did the babies of those mothers who gave up: It seems that it is a general feature of the early stages of breast-feeding for babies to sleep for short periods and to take frequent feeds. We found that mothers who were willing to feed their newborn babies when they cried were more likely to be successful breast-feeders later.
— Judy Dunn
Distress and Comfort

• • •

A baby's digestion is such that a full meal, taken calmly over a reasonable period—in twenty-five minutes, say, rather than in sips over an hour—will probably last him for between three and four hours. But that is once he is settled, once his digestion has begun to have a pattern. He has, after all, to learn to accept comfortable fullness and near emptiness, rather than the constant topping up of nutritional needs which went on in the womb. Furthermore, he has to accept our diurnal rhythm, to accept a long period unfed during the night. All this takes time. Because it takes time, the much-disputed question about whether babies should be fed "on demand" or "on schedule" makes very little sense.
— Penelope Leach
Babyhood

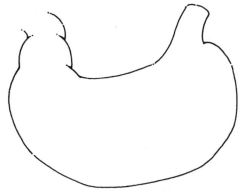

Actual size of an infant's stomach at birth (sometimes a picture is worth a thousand words!)

If a baby is hungry, a pacifier, sugar water, rocking, singing, or fun and games will not fulfill that need. Few of us ever experience true hunger pains, but when a baby does, it is excruciating. We wouldn't think twice about feeding a baby who wanted to eat if we *really* knew she was hungry. The notion of schedules, particularly hospital schedules, where babies are fed at three- or four-hour intervals, can give a distorted picture of what feeding patterns in newborns are really like. During the first two or three days of a baby's life she may be too sleepy to eat as often as she will in the future. Remember also that a baby experiences a constant state of fullness in utero. Anything short of that is a new and even painful experience. Until she is several weeks old, a breast-fed baby in particular usually can't last for four hours between feedings.

Because a nursing mother can't see how much the baby is taking, her first thought as she feeds the baby for the tenth time that day is that she doesn't have enough milk. Almost everyone worries about this in the beginning, and we all need some reassurance. *It cannot be stressed enough that two hours, even an hour, between some feedings is not uncommon in the early weeks, and that if the baby begins to go without eating for longer intervals at night she may well have to make up for this by eating more often during the day.*

Is the Baby Crying Because She Needs to Be Burped?

It never occurred to me that I wasn't burping Andrew enough, that twice a feeding was inadequate, until the pediatrician suggested that I do it every three to five minutes, working on a burp for about a minute. After a few weeks, when his digestive system settled down, I didn't have to be so careful.

Sometimes a baby will cry because she needs to be burped, even if you have already burped her a half hour ago when you fed her. A newborn may eat in gulps and swallow a lot of air. The air forms in tiny bubbles that take time to gather together into one large bubble that can be burped. If you suspect your baby is this way, sometimes holding her upright against your shoulder after a feeding, or placing her in a semi-upright position in an infant seat, will help the bubble collect. A pacifier may also help to bring up the bubble (see the discussion of pacifiers that follows as well as page 93).

Is the Baby Crying Because She Needs More Sucking?

Babies need a lot of sucking. Sucking, associated with eating and feelings of warmth and fullness, is pleasurable to a baby. It is also good exercise and seems to relieve tension. Sucking helps to deepen and regulate breathing, to relax the baby's muscle tension, and to quiet random movements. Jerome Bruner, an infant researcher, notes that sucking also relaxes the movement of the gut and reduces the number of eye movements the baby makes if given something patterned to look at. Sucking also can help babies stay asleep. Studies show that noises and disturbances that might ordinarily wake a baby and lead to crying just make a baby with a pacifier suck more vigorously.

Before you introduce a pacifier, encourage your baby to suck her fist. If the baby can master this, she will have the freedom to comfort herself if and when she needs to. After you lay her down on her stomach, gently place her hand beside her mouth, then touch it to her lips to see if you can induce the sucking reflex.

If your efforts to teach the baby to suck her fist do not succeed, continue to try, but at the same time don't hesitate to use a pacifier between feedings. The orthodontic designs are preferable for both breast- and bottle-fed babies because they require that the baby work hard at sucking, which in turn helps to release tension and organize her behavior. Besides lessening the chances of "nipple confusion" for the breast-fed baby, orthodontic pacifiers don't fall out of the baby's mouth as easily as the conventionally shaped nipples.

Some experts suggest that parents remove the pacifier once the baby is asleep. In this way she won't come to rely on it to remain asleep, and you won't have to replace it in her mouth quite so often. If that works, fine. But if it doesn't, then leave it in the baby's mouth when she sleeps and don't worry about dependency.

If this approach doesn't seem appropriate, it can be useful to examine further what you really feel about this so-called dependency. Do you regard a pacifier as a crutch? Or have you been repelled at the sight of a two- or three-year-old with a "plug" in her mouth? It may be useful to know that a baby's most intense desire to suck comes in the first four to six months. After this point, many naturally lose interest in the pacifier as their interest in the world around them broadens. It can be the parents who are hooked on the "plug" to quiet their infant. You can avoid this by not "force-feeding" the pacifier and by being sensitive around the fourth month to signs of lack of interest. If the baby is fussy, there is a whole range of other comforts to offer. Read on.

Question: Will sucking a pacifier or thumb hurt the development of my baby's teeth?
Answer: "Sucking is one of the baby's natural reflexes. Thumb sucking usually decreases after age two. Only past age four can it create problems with normal dental development."
—The American Dental Association

Safe Pacifiers

Before you buy a pacifier, gently but firmly pull on it to make sure that it is sturdily constructed. Any parts that are loose may come off and are potential choking hazards. Look for a shield large and firm enough to keep the baby from drawing the entire pacifier into her mouth. The ventilation holes in the shield should be small enough not to entrap a baby's tiny fingers and the shield and handle no more than $^{63}/_{100}$ inch (somewhat less than three-quarters of an inch) in length, a measurement set by the Consumer Product Safety Commission. Never use a bottle nipple, or any other makeshift device, as a replacement. NEVER TIE A PACIFIER AROUND A CHILD'S NECK WITH A CORD OR RIBBON! In fact, don't attach it to anything. Be sure to check all pacifiers regularly for deterioration because they can come apart, and small pieces of them could choke the baby. If you discover cracks, tears, or gumminess of texture in the nipple, throw the pacifier away immediately. Also remember to keep the pacifier clean just as you would a bottle nipple. Finally, if your baby has thrush, it's best not to give her a pacifier until the infection clears up. Then discard old pacifiers or boil them.

Is the Baby Crying Because She Needs a Diaper Change?

A newborn almost always needs a diaper change if you consider a "damp" diaper a wet diaper. The diaper is probably not what is disturbing the baby unless it is making her cold or causing a rash. Yet a change may help anyway. In one experiment using agitated but well-fed babies, nurses picked up and changed the entire group. In half the group, they simply removed and then replaced the wet diaper; in the other half they put on a new, dry one. *All* the babies settled down. Wetness made no difference at all. The babies apparently settled because of the warmth of the nurse's touch, the motion, and the change of position. By all means, change the baby's diaper!

Is the Baby Crying Because She's Too Warm or Too Cold?

The first time Caitie slept for more than three hours in a row, I thought she was dead! We'd placed her swaddled (see page 96 for instructions) in a basket on the kitchen table in the country, where we have a wood-burning stove. The wood stove was going all afternoon while we had friends over. It must have been a combination of the company, our feeling relaxed, and the warmth of the stove. This made sense to me. After all, she'd been inside me for nine months at 98 degrees.

Most of us run the risk of overdressing rather than underdressing our babies. This is just as well because newborns would rather be too warm than too cold. They have only rudimentary abilities to regulate their own temperatures in different environments. Moreover, they have very little insulating fat to keep them warm.

Peter Wolff, an English researcher who has made one of the most extensive inquiries into why babies cry, found that those who were kept at 88 to 90°F cried less and slept more than those kept at 78°F. Wolff concluded that the colder temperatures probably weren't the cause of the crying, but that since babies sleep more deeply when warm, the colder babies may be more responsive to stimulation and therefore more likely to cry for other reasons.

Dr. Spock, a firm believer in fresh air and cool houses, suggests that parents keep indoor temperatures between 68 and 72°F. If your house is cool, remember when you undress the baby for a diaper change that the baby may get chilled. Adding more clothing to an already cold baby will not warm the baby up but only insulate the cold. So, warm the baby up close to your body, then wrap her up again. And don't hesitate to put a little cap on your newborn, just as they do in many hospitals. Humans, especially those with minimal hair, lose more heat through their heads than through any other part of the body.

Is the Baby Crying Because She's Startled?

Sometimes a baby will cry because her *Moro reflex* is acting up. A newborn may be startled by a loud noise or any sudden change of position—particularly if her head drops back. When this happens, she throws out her arms and legs, cries, then draws her arms together as if to cling to her mother. This response is thought to be a holdover from primitive times, when the infant had to grasp her furry mother for survival, protection, comfort, and mobility. Each time the baby cries, she may startle, which upsets her and makes her cry again. Thus the cycle can perpetuate itself. If you pick the baby up and hold her securely, swaddle her, or simply place a firm hand on one of her extremities, you can help break the startle-crying, startle-crying cycle.

Is the Baby Crying Because She Is Overstimulated?

We sometimes forget that a newborn can become overstimulated by the hectic world around her and, ironically, by all of our efforts to comfort her. Each baby has her own stimulation threshold. While some babies can sleep right through the Fourth of July festivities, others can be set off by something as seemingly innocent as a bright light or a dog or a child moving around in the room. They may become even fussier if handled and constantly jiggled. Some signs of overstimulation that appear to lead to crying are back arching, gaze aversion, hiccupping, and even vomiting unexpectedly. If you learn to look for these cues, you can put the baby down in a quiet place before she becomes overstimulated. If she's already over the edge, she may need a chance to blow off steam on her own without a parent's intervention.

Is the Baby Crying Because She Needs to Be Held Closely and Carried?

Through the work of Drs. Rene Spitz and John Bowlby, we have long known that the human need for touch is as important as that for food, warmth, and shelter. Spitz and Bowlby studied orphaned infants in institutions. The babies were kept warm, clean, and well fed, but because of shortages in caretakers they were otherwise deprived of touch—of cuddling, stroking, and holding. One out of every three babies was listless, withdrawn, and very slow in mental and physical development. Some actually died of what appears to have been emotional neglect or despair.

New research continues to support what Bowlby, Spitz, and many mothers have always known: that babies who are carried in slings or pack carriers seem to cry less than babies who aren't. Simply being quietly and closely held, without necessarily being talked to or looked at, can comfort a fussy baby. It can also be comforting to a parent to experience this physical and emotional closeness and to know one is attending to the baby, with hands free for other tasks.

Is the Baby Crying Because the Parents Are Tense?

We're fighting a lot with each other. It seems like Jessica has done nothing but cry, nurse, and poop in her diaper all day. I've finally got dressed at about four in the afternoon. My breakfast dishes sit in the sink along with a half-drunk cup of coffee. John arrives home tired. The baby is just gearing up when he walks in. If he's cheerful, it annoys me. How can he be so damn cheerful? If he's tired, that annoys me too, because how could he be as tired as I am? There is something so infuriating about him telling me it's my *anxiety that's making her that way. Apparently he read it in some book. Do you know* anyone *who is capable of relaxing around a screaming baby?*

There is no hard evidence that tense parents make their babies cry, but one suspects parental tension is not helpful. The only solution is a little "time out," either as a couple or separately. A walk around the block, a bath, or half an hour to lose yourself in a magazine or a book, does miracles (see You Deserve a Break, page 165).

Is the Baby Crying for Some Inexplicable Reason?

You have investigated every possible reason for crying. The baby is not hungry because she was fed forty-five minutes ago. She is not being poked by a diaper pin, doesn't have a wet diaper, isn't too cold or too warm, and isn't tired of being in the same position because you have switched her from back to stomach, from stomach to back, from prone to tilted. You've burped her, or tried to, several times, and she's still crying. She isn't bored because you've shown her the view from every window.

You're very tired and beginning to feel inadequate. The sun is on its way down, or perhaps it has already dropped beneath the horizon. The term *colic* flashes through your mind. But you can't quite face that. After all, this doesn't happen every day—maybe every other day, sometimes for twenty minutes and sometimes for two hours. The only alternative answer is, to coin a "Spockian" phrase, "periodic, irritable crying," which is usually further explained as "unexplained." Following is a selection of age-old comforts (some of which will probably be familiar to you) and further reasons why they work.

Age-Old Comforts for the Crying Baby

Swaddling

You can't carry the baby all the time when he fusses. Swaddling can be an effective alternative because it provides the baby with the sensations of constant touch and warmth. A study done by infant researcher Yvonne Brackbill showed that constant stimulation, through sound, light, swaddling, or warm temperatures, increased the amount of time the infant spent sleeping, decreased the amount of time spent crying, slowed the heart and breath rate, and quieted random movements.

Brackbill also found that if two or more approaches were combined, such as swaddling and sound, the results were even better. When she

The Benefits of Carrying a Baby

The evidence continues to mount that carrying a baby has many positive short- and long-term effects.

- In a study published by *Pediatrics,* the official journal of The American Academy of Pediatrics, ninety-nine mother/infant pairs were assigned to either an increased carrying group or a control group. Infants from four to twelve weeks who were carried an extra three hours a day cried 50 percent less than the infants in the control group. The carried infants also nursed more frequently and were generally more content.

- Dr. William Sears, author of *The Fussy Baby: How to Bring Out the Best in Your High Need Child* (Franklin Park, IL: La Leche League International, 1985), speculates that carrying helps to settle the "disorganized" baby partially because of its positive effect on his vestibular system, which keeps the body in balance. This system, located behind each ear, is similar to three tiny carpenter's levels, one oriented for side-to-side balance, another for up-and-down, and a third for back-and-forth. A baby who is carried about moves in all of these directions, and the fluid in these "levels" stimulates tiny hairlike filaments that send messages to the muscles in the body to keep it in balance. The unborn baby has a very sensitive vestibular system that is constantly stimulated because the fetus is in almost continuous motion. To put it simply, Dr. Sears believes that carrying is a comfort because it "reminds" the baby of the womb.

- Carrying the new baby appears to have further benefits. In addition to soothing, it seems to increase future bonding between mother and infant. In their study at Columbia College of Physicians and Surgeons, Drs. Nicholas Cunningham and Elizabeth Anisfeld gave soft baby carriers to half of a group of women and plastic infant seats to the other half. When they evaluated the children one year later, they found that 83 percent of those using the baby carriers were rated "securely attached" to their mothers, versus only 38 percent of those using the seats. Bottle-feeding mothers take note: The researchers also discovered that the mode of carrying had a greater positive effect on mother/infant bonding than did breast-feeding alone.

- Animal studies are teaching us even more about the lifelong health effects of touch. A Stanford University neurobiologist, Robert Sapolsky, has found that rats touched often in infancy were smarter—that is, they ran mazes better in old age—than rats who were not handled. Autopsies showed that the fondled rats suffered little degeneration in the part of the brain responsible for learning and memory. It seems that these rats were better able to deal with stress and actually exhibited an inhibition of the "stress hormones" that usually damage cells.

- This concurs with studies done by Drs. Marshall Klaus and John Kenell at Case Western Reserve. Well known for their research on maternal-infant bonding, the doctors have also looked at the connection between touch and intellectual development. They matched control groups of infants whose mothers had offered a great deal of cuddling and holding within twelve hours of birth with children who did not receive as much physical contact. When followed up at intervals in their lives, the children who were touched more evinced superior language skills, higher reading-readiness scores, and significantly higher IQs.

- In another study at Duke University researchers found that baby rats separated from their mothers and deprived of instinctual maternal licking failed to produce growth hormones. The researchers surmised that the orphaned rats may actually have produced high levels of endorphins, or natural painkillers, in order to help them survive the maternal deprivation. These endorphins, they suggest, block growth hormones.

- Experts debate whether the findings of animal studies like the above are applicable to humans. But a study of premature human babies by a team from Duke University and the University of Miami seems to suggest that touch and growth are related. The researchers found that massaging premies resulted in a 50 percent increase in their body weight and enhanced their neurological development.

How to Swaddle a Baby

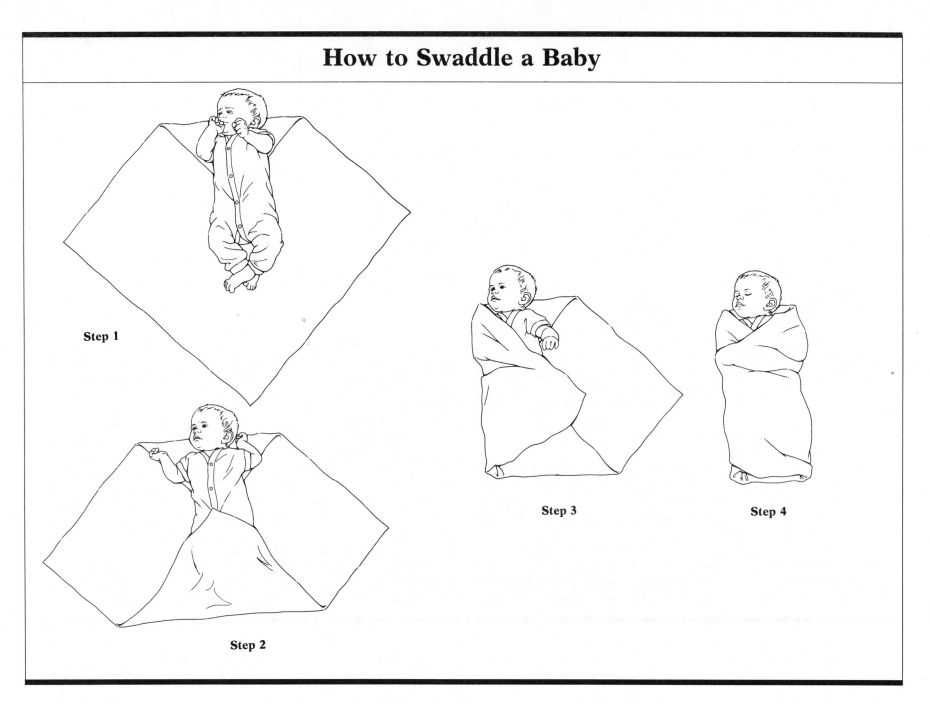

Step 1

Step 2

Step 3

Step 4

Automatic Baby Swings

Does your baby start to fuss the minute you sit down to eat your dinner? Many parents assure themselves a moment of peace by putting the baby in an automatic swing. The swing supplies that comforting, rhythmic rocking that often seems to help. These swings consist of a baby seat suspended by tubular support arms in an A-frame structure. The mechanical swinging unit is built into the crossbar on top and is powered either by batteries or by a wind-up mechanism. More elaborate units offer a cradle as well as a seat.

Before you buy a swing, see if you can borrow one and try it out. They have some drawbacks, which may or may not be of concern. One disadvantage: The long legs, necessary for stability, require up to 12 square feet of floor space. You may not have the room. The swing will also be useful only until the baby sits up. At that point she will be large and coordinated enough to reach and grab the frame leg, upset the balance, and possibly topple out. The models with cradle attachments roll the baby from side to side rather than from head to foot, which is the more natural movement. But many parents absolutely swear by these swings.

If you do buy one, look for the swing with the longest run per single winding. Consumers Union does not recommend battery-operated models because some have had problems with the electric motor. Check for overall stability by shaking the swing, and make sure that all plastic or vinyl seams are smooth. If you buy a cradle/swing model, check that the bottom or "floor" of the cradle is sturdy and well attached.

Safe Usage. Use the safety belt, and never leave the baby unattended in the swing or cradle. Give the swing up once the baby is old enough to sit up on her own. Also, remember that any device that physically separates baby from parent or caretaker should be used sparingly. A swing is no substitute for human warmth and touch.

compared the effects of different kinds of continuous stimulation, she found that swaddling was overwhelmingly the most effective. Here is one way to swaddle a baby so that the wrapping won't come undone.

Rocking

The age-old custom of rocking a fussy baby is certainly worth a try. Like swaddling, rocking is a source of consistent, mild stimulation. It may also re-create the gentle motion the baby felt in-side the womb (see The Benefits of Carrying a Baby, page 95). Ashley Montagu, author of *Touching: The Human Significance of the Skin* (New York: Harper & Row, 1986), also suggests that the rocking motion helps to develop the efficient functioning of the baby's gastrointestinal tract by improving the muscle tone of the intestine.

If you own a cradle but find you are instead constantly walking the floor to quiet the baby, you may not be rocking the baby fast enough. The most effective rate of rocking appears to be sixty rocks per minute—quite a fast pace to maintain. Sixty paces a minute, on the other hand, is a relatively slow walk for an adult. If the baby is rolling instead of rocking, try placing two rolled blankets or towels on either side of him.

Baby Massage

A gentle massage can soothe, relax, and possibly act as a fussing preventative. Stroking the baby's skin with a little oil is not only pleasurable but also stimulates her circulatory, digestive, and respiratory systems. The massage need not be a planned activity. Seize a quiet moment between feedings or after a bath or diaper change when she is feeling content. Make sure the room is warm. Many newborns don't like to be undressed, so you may try massaging one part of the baby at a time, leaving the rest of her dressed. Whatever oil you use—baby oil, coconut oil, or even vegetable oil—test a small amount on your baby's skin first, waiting a half an hour or so, to be sure the baby is not allergic. Then warm the oil in your own hands before you begin. Put the baby on a comfortable surface—the changing table, your bed, or resting on your own raised thighs. Move your oiled fingers in slow, gentle circular motions over the surface of the baby's skin. Start with shoulders and arms. Then move to chest, stomach, thighs, lower legs, and feet. If the baby enjoys this, turn her over and work on her other side. Stop if she seems to be getting restless or disturbed.

Tips from Parents on Comforting a Crying Baby

Question: *What do you do if the baby continues to cry for some inexplicable reason?*

Answer: *I just nursed Jack all the time. If he was hungry or not, nursing always quieted him.*

A: We had a beautiful antique cradle that we bought for Benjamin at an auction. He rolled instead of rocked, and he hated it. So we often took turns walking him. Sometimes we just let him cry because we couldn't figure out what was the matter with him. One night I was so exhausted, discouraged, and dismayed by this eight-pound power figure who had transformed my life that I called my sister long-distance. We went over every possible reason for his crying. She finally sug-

gested that we get out of the house with him and go for a walk. It worked, for that night at least.

A: Harry loved his pacifier. With my first baby, I was too pure to use it. This time I felt comfortable trying whatever worked. God forbid if you lose that pacifier, though. Then you're really up the creek!

A: We experimented with different pacifiers until we found one that Jenny liked. It was quite soft. We bought five of them!

A: Our baby sucked her fist. When she got in a real frenzy, I would try to touch her hand to her mouth so that she would get the idea that she could help comfort herself.

A: We developed what we called the "straight-jacket and wedge" to cure Caitlin of her twilight miseries. We swaddled her tightly and laid her on her side with her back against the side of the basket, and wedged a stuffed rabbit against her stomach to hold her in place. Apparently, it made her feel secure, but until we figured this out, she thrashed around so much that there was never any hope of calming her down. You have to swaddle the baby correctly, though, or it just makes her angrier.

A: I'd take Nicky into the bathroom and turn the water on in the tub full-blast to run a nice warm bath. Sometimes the sound of the water settled him, but if it didn't, I'd take him into the tub with me and rest him on my knees. The water helped a lot. Of course we couldn't stay there forever, but at least this worked for a little while.

A: Anna was definitely a motion baby. The only way I could settle her was to rock and hold her,

and sing to her, mostly songs that I had made up for her myself like "Quiet down, quiet down, quiet down, I'm so tired" to the tune of Brahms's lullaby. I had a rocking chair that squeaked and went along with the melody. The only problem was that I couldn't do anything else while I was rocking her, like read, because the chair had no arms. When we bought a hammock, life improved significantly because I could put her next to me or on me without having to hold her. Then I could read or crochet, or even sleep a little myself.

A: David rocked Matthew back and forth in the cradle. He was studying for his bar exam and often read aloud in an appropriately monotonous voice. He'd sit at his desk and push the runner on the cradle up and down with one foot. His power of concentration amazed me. I think he bored the baby to sleep!

A: I wore Tasha in the Snugli baby carrier almost constantly. It was absolutely the only thing that worked. I cooked dinner this way, did housework, and sometimes even slept like this at night.

A: We walked and walked and walked and walked—back and forth, pretty fast. When I got tired I would try to sit and make my legs move as if they were walking, but I couldn't fool Binkey. It had to be the real thing, The Baby Walk.

A: My La Leche League leader suggested I either vacuum with the baby in the soft front carrier or put her in an infant seat on top of the dryer. The baby seemed to like the combination of noise and warmth. Make sure you secure the seat, because the vibrations can move it.

A: I felt terribly exasperated when my first baby cried. I tried this, I tried that, in an almost frantic effort to get her to stop, as if her crying would engulf me. When I think back, what I remember is the gesture of putting her back down in her crib with this sense of relief once she was quiet. With my other two babies, my body remembers the gesture of leaning over and scooping them up, holding them close, that's all, giving them what they needed, and what I needed too. Now that they are older, that real physical contact is what I remember—not their crying.

And finally:
Dr. T. Berry Brazelton feels that babies need to "blow" at the end of the day as a common response to what he calls an overloaded nervous system. The prescription he recommends in *What Every Baby Knows* follows:

1. Try to find the reason for the crying and satisfy yourself that nothing will readily stop it.
2. Calm down and force yourself to quit fussing over the child.
3. If it is a young baby, put her down for ten minutes at a time. Let her fuss for that period, then pick her up, hold and "contain" her, feed her sugar water or water, and bubble her. If she is still jumpy and itchy, put her down to fuss for another ten minutes, then repeat the cycle. At the point when you think she's cried it all out, swad-dle her, or place her on her abdomen to let her go to sleep. She may need a milk feeding before you put her to bed. If so, feed her in a quiet, darkened room and soothe her afterwards. Until she's ready, this won't work, so you'll have to learn to read her cues.

4. If the child is older, try leaving her alone for a while, then introduce one quiet activity at a time. Try for quick periods, even if the child does not nap. Before meals, bedtime, or a family time together, try to institute familiar, soothing routines, such as reading, rocking, or music. Watch for cues of overload.

Conclusions

The newborn baby has spent the greater part of his life in the womb, curled up in a small, warm place, bathed in amniotic fluid. He has heard the rhythm of his mother's heart and felt the movements of her body. It is therefore not surprising that swaddling, walking, rocking, patting, or even taking the baby into the bathtub often calm him. These sensations are familiar, and thus reassuring. Who knows whether they actually relieve the discomfort or simply take the baby's mind or, more to the point, his body off it?

We sometimes think of such comforts as techniques for soothing a fussy baby. But an infant who isn't particularly irritable or demanding needs them, too. Touching, talking, holding, cuddling, and rocking are loving ways to communicate, stimulate, and help instill a sense of self as the infant begins to find his place in the world.

It may seem an elusive and mysterious concept, but in the beginning of life outside the womb the baby still does not distinguish between his own physical sensations and those imposed from the outside. Through the repetition of physical contact with another person who satisfies the baby's basic needs for food, warmth, and motion, the baby begins to differentiate himself from that source of relief or comfort. As he starts to become an individual, he begins to separate the "me" from the "you" and all else. He comes to realize that he has an impact on his surrounding world and that he can find comfort for himself.

Each time his cries are answered, he learns that the world is a reliable and caring place. When you hold and feed, or cuddle, your baby, you offer close companionship, affection, conversation, and games. This emotional nourishment is as important as the physical, because it is the basis for trust and love. With this foundation the baby is ready to go on to learn about the world around him.

CHAPTER 7

Colic

Colic is perhaps the most dreaded word in the English language to the parents of an infant whose crying can seem endless. It's tempting to ask, "Why us? What are we doing wrong?" The truth, however, is that colic remains a mystery. Nobody knows exactly what it is or how to eliminate it. Some techniques seem to work some of the time for some babies, but, like Job's boils, colic may be something you just have to endure.

Question: *What is colic?*
Answer: *One guess is that both conditions [irritable crying and colic] are due to periodic tension in the baby's immature nervous system.*
  —Benjamin M. Spock and Michael B.
    Rothenberg
    Dr. Spock's Baby and Child Care

A: The infant susceptible to colic is an active, driving baby who is hypersensitive to the climate and stimuli around him. As his exasperating period of fussing creates tension in those around him, they overreact. They try too many ways to quiet him, feeling there must be a magic way or there must be something wrong that they should

correct. Often there are three generations at work on each other. The tension around the infant builds up, he reacts to it with more of his own, his intestinal tract begins to reflect his increased tension—and what starts out as a two-hour period rapidly grows to four, eight, then twelve hours. His intestines are as hyperactive and hyperreactive as the rest of him to the increasing fatigue and breakdown in the family. This pattern becomes a vicious circle, and we call it "colic."
  —T. Berry Brazelton, M.D.
    Infants and Mothers

A: *. . . colic means: inconsolable crying for which no physical cause can be found, which lasts more than three hours a day, occurs at least three days a week, and continues for at least three weeks.*
  —Marc Weissbluth, M.D.
    *Cry Babies—Coping with Colic:
    What to Do When Your Baby
    Won't Stop Crying*

A: *What is colic? It's pure misery for the baby. I've fed her, but she still cries—piercing screams*

that go on for hours. They reach a crescendo, and I think surely it's over for tonight. She'll maybe quiet down for a few minutes as she gasps for air and her whole little body shudders. Then her face starts to screw up again and her fists clench. Her body gets beet-red and she flails her arms and legs. If I feed her, she'll suck frantically for a moment, then push my breast away, enraged as if I've tried to trick her, and I guess I have because I know she's not hungry. Burping her when she's like this is almost impossible because she arches her back and screams even louder. The pacifier won't stay in her mouth because it's always open with the howling. Sometimes she responds to walking and rocking. During the day, she's really terrific. I take her out and everyone tells me what a beautiful, adorable baby I have. She smiles at everyone. But Fred and I are basket cases.

A: *No one knows exactly what colic is, but I can honestly tell you that whatever it is, Ben's colic was the most difficult experience I have ever had in my life. Sometimes he would scream for six or seven hours at a stretch. I needed constant reassurance from my pediatrician that he was okay,* *that one out of five babies suffers from this, and that he would indeed outgrow it. Mainly, though, I needed to hear that I was not a bad mother, that I didn't cause this. My pediatrician was great. She kept telling me I was a heroine, that I deserved a medal. And do you know what? She was absolutely* right.

A: My nerves were shot, and so were Don's. We slept in separate rooms and moved like zombies in slow motion. The sound of colic is unbelievable. When other mothers complain about crying, they have no idea. The sound is unbearable. This has a higher pitch. It is screeching. They do not know how incredibly frustrating it is not to be able to help. Until you go through it, you can't understand. Besides robbing me of all shreds of self-confidence as a mother, and wearing me to the bone physically, I found the unpredictability of colic impossible. We never knew when it would strike. Some mornings it was at 10 A.M. Other days he'd build up from 4 in the afternoon to 10 at night. You can't plan anything.

A: What do you tell people when they ask about the baby who you have planned for and wanted for years and years? We got a lemon?

One Parent's Colic Story

The tighter I held her, the more she stiffened, arching her back and pummeling her heels into my midsection. And her continuous high-pitched shriek made my skull reverberate. It had been going on for nearly five hours. Seldom in my life had I felt so rejected by anyone. My six-week-old daughter had colic.

In my seven years as a family practitioner, I have counseled hundreds of anxious parents of colicky children. I've reassured them that colic is uniformly benign; that, although there are many treatments, none consistently works two nights in a row; and that colic always disappears magically, blessedly, by four months of age. These facts weren't helping me at the moment. Put her down! a small voice inside me reminded. Your frustration is just making it worse. Yes, right, I remembered. I loosened my white-knuckled grip on her tiny arm, noting with horror the indentations my fingernails had imprinted into her skin. God, I thought, how can such a small, helpless infant, my own beloved flesh, evoke such nearly uncontrollable hostility in me, her daddy, a physician?

From the start, Julia was a different child from her older sister, Laura, who had been a quiet and placid newborn. Laura's cry had been gentle and beseeching, stirring me to pick her up and cuddle her, but Julia's shriek made my hair stand on end and made me want to leave the room.

"I hate her!" I heard myself confess. I was sitting among six trusted colleagues during a meeting of our family-practice support group at the hospital. Under the deft and gentle guidance of a clinical psychologist, we meet weekly to discuss the psychological aspects of our patients' illnesses. Recently, the group has evolved into a forum for exploring our own personal and family stresses as well. "I'm embarrassed to say it, but when she's screaming, I feel like shaking her till she shuts up!" Even within this privileged and safe setting, my words sounded almost criminal. My colleagues listened supportively, quietly asking questions. No one spoke judgmentally, but it was soon evident that no one else in the room had experienced such prolonged negative feelings toward his own young children. I felt terribly alone.

A peculiar pall settled over my medical practice. The usual enthusiasm I brought to my encounters with patients was replaced by vague feelings of inadequacy and illegitimacy. I felt like an interloper in my own office. I began to have particular trouble facing the parents of my pediatric patients. How could I, a confessed daughter-hater, deign to advise other parents about colic—or any other subject, for that matter? It became increasingly difficult to put on my white coat each morning.

And then something more unsettling began to gnaw at me. Subliminal at first, the terror soon became palpable. I struggled to identify its source. The physician support group again:

"What are you afraid of?"

"I don't know. I feel so out of control. That's very scary to me, especially in medical situations."

"What do you feel the need to control? Your patients?"

"No, no! Their illnesses. Their suffering. I realize it's just an illusion," I quickly added, "but I'm sure that is one of the attractions medicine has always had for me. And now my family is having its first medical 'crisis' of sorts, and I'm finding out I don't even have control over a simple case of colic! What's going to happen when someone I love really gets sick? I'll probably be just as naked and terrified as everyone else." I paused. Beads of sweat had formed on my brow.

"What are you feeling right now?" our psychologist asked me. Long pause. My heart was racing.

"I feel like the eight-year-old I used to be who stayed up at night until 3 A.M., nauseated with the fear that someone would die: my parents, my best friend . . . me." So that was it! Gradually, I began to understand what had happened. The hostility and self-doubt I had been feeling were only icing on an emotional layer cake. Julia's colic had reconnected me unconsciously to my childhood fear of death. With the help of the group, the insight slowly emerged. I felt terror's grip begin to loosen. My heart quieted. And by the end of the hour, I felt better than I had in weeks.

That night, I had a dream about a wizened medical-school professor who examined me on my deathbed and announced to his coterie of interns and students: "The lad obviously suffers from a case of existential colic, poor fellow. There's no cure!" I awoke and laughed out loud. Perhaps the colic's spell was broken.

Over the next several weeks, like a violent storm finally spent, the intensity of the colic began to ebb. In its aftermath, Julia was slow to show love and affection. She never became a cuddly child. She continued to scream to get her needs met. We were frankly just a little worried.

But now, at two years, she has miraculously, unaccountably turned out just fine. She is a rough-and-tumble toddler with an infectious belly laugh and a mischievous grin. She takes positive delight in testing her own limits and those of her parents. She clearly loves being alive.

Her daddy's death fear has not disappeared, of course. It still gnaws at me. Yet I've found that I can live with it now that it is out in the open. I am relieved to say that it has lost its power to paralyze me with nausea, as it did in my childhood, or to insinuate itself unconsciously into my adult life as a lurking occult presence.

I am awestruck by the power of what happened. I still marvel that a disorder I used to describe as "uniformly benign" could send me on such an intense emotional trip. If a case of colic could do this to me, I must assume that other common and mild disorders that bring patients into my office can do the same to them. An earache, a laceration, a wheeze, all may have the power to tap into unconscious fears: of loss of

control, of suffering, perhaps even death. Thanks, Julia. I'll try to remember that. In the meantime, when anxious parents bring a fussy infant into my office, I no longer reassure them blithely that it's just a simple case of colic. When it's your own child who's afflicted, colic may not be such a simple matter.

(Dr. Joel C. Berman is a family physician practicing in Penacook, New Hampshire. This article originally ran in the *New York Times* magazine section ["About Men," November 29, 1987].)

Coping with Colic

It's clear from the definitions of colic that it is not a disease but a condition—one extreme of what is considered normal infant behavior. All babies cry some of the time for reasons that we cannot understand. One out of five, however, experiences so much "unexplained crying" with such intensity that it is called "colic."

Colic usually strikes within a few weeks after birth (in premature babies it is delayed), when the baby's crying pattern becomes so long, intense, and agonized that it can no longer be interpreted as the generally disorganized behavior of the newborn.

If your baby truly has colic, and you haven't already consulted your pediatrician, by all means do so. Colic should not be diagnosed at home, just in case there is something else going on. Parents also should know that there is one drug that has been approved by the FDA called Dicyclomine sold under the name of Bentyl. This is available by prescription, and you may want to ask about it.

Rest assured, however, that your pediatrician will not be the only person offering you advice. Friends, neighbors, relatives, even strangers on the street, once they hear that your baby suffers

from colic, may start telling you why your baby has this condition and what to do about it. What they suggest will be well meaning but not necessarily accurate.

Question: *How do parents feel about colic?*
Answer: It is exceedingly difficult not to have an intense emotional reaction—frustration, rage, fear—when you have been listening to your baby's high-pitched wails hour after hour after hour. You may feel like shaking the baby, a less violent act than throwing or striking the baby. Don't act on those feelings, of course—but acknowledge them.

There is actually a condition called "shaken baby syndrome" that has been linked to permanent brain damage and, in a few cases, death. Injuries from shaking can be as severe as those from a direct blow, even though they produce no visible bruises on the body's surface. When an infant is grabbed by the arms or shoulders and shaken, the head moves back and forth. Infants under two years of age have weak neck muscles that are unable to support the head adequately. They also have disproportionately large skulls in order to allow the brain room to grow. Symptoms of "shaken baby syndrome" are sleepiness, irritability, vomiting, and loss of appetite. If you are afraid that you will hurt your baby, leave the room and calm down. If you are alone, call someone on the phone whom you trust. A reassuring adult voice may be all the support that you need at the moment.

The National Child Abuse Hotline (800-4A-CHILD) is also available twenty-four hours a day, seven days a week. Specially trained counselors are available to help anyone who feels they are in danger of hurting a child.

Colic: Myths and Reality

Myth: It was assumed that Lilly screamed at the top of her lungs for at least three hours a night because of my general anxiety as a new parent.

Reality: Studies show no evidence that colic strikes first-born babies more than second, third, or fourth babies. And according to Dr. Marc Weissbluth, author of *Cry Babies—Coping with Colic: What to Do When Your Baby Won't Stop Crying* (New York: Berkley, 1986), who has made perhaps the most thorough investigation on colic, "the theory that an infant can 'pick up' tension from his parents . . . is one of those oft-repeated ideas which has no basis in fact. [T. Berry] Brazelton says that tension in the people around a crying infant makes the infant's intestinal tract act up, causing the pain, gas, drawn-up knees, etc., of colic, as though colic were some sort of infantile ulcer! [Allison Clarke] Stewart says that when a tense, anxious, or ambivalent parent holds a baby, the tension is communicated through all the baby's senses (including smell!). This is folk medicine at best. At worst, it is another twist on blaming the mother's behavior, personality, or her perfectly natural anxiety."

Myth: My sister implied that Jonathan had colic because I wasn't nursing him. A breast-fed baby wouldn't have suffered the way he did.

Reality: There is no evidence that breast-fed babies are immune from colic. Just as many seem to have the condition as do formula-fed babies.

Myth: My pediatrician changed the formula twice, assuring us that the colic would end. We had a quiet evening and thought we were home free. But the next evening Dena began again."

Reality: According to the *American Journal of Diseases of Children,* there is no difference in the incidence of colic among babies fed soy milk formulas, cow's milk formulas, breast milk, or breast milk supplemented by formula.

Myth: As a breast-feeding mother I was told to eliminate certain foods from my own diet. These were chocolate, eggs, nuts, and shellfish. Citrus fruits had to go and so did gas-producing vegetables such as broccoli, cabbage, and cauliflower.

Reality: This is one of the most common myths that you will hear if you are nursing a colicky baby. There is absolutely no hard evidence that foods that cause gas in a nursing mother also cause gas in the baby.

Question: What does *cause colic?*

Answer: There is some speculation that colic is caused by disorganized sleep patterns or *asynchronic* sleep patterns that are out of synch with other vital functions such as breathing. Dr. Marc Weissbluth speculates in his book *Cry Babies— Coping with Colic: What to Do When Your Baby Won't Stop Crying* (New York: Berkley, 1986) that some babies may have to cope with more asynchrony than others. "These babies might not be able to breathe regularly enough to keep themselves asleep," he says. "They may sometimes have to fight for air." Dr. Weissbluth proposes that crying is a way of compensating when breathing becomes disordered during sleep. When the baby cries, he inflates his lungs with air, a way to get plenty of vital oxygen into his bloodstream. Colicky crying is therefore perhaps not a grieving cry as we adults may hear it, but instead a breathless gasping for air. If we believe that the paroxysms of crying—as unnerving as they are—serve a very necessary function, then they might be just a bit easier to accept.

Suggestions for Soothing a Colicky Baby

Remember, colic is not your fault. You did not do anything to deserve a colicky baby. It is a condition that passes and is the result of an immaturity that is outgrown with time. Colicky babies are healthy babies. They eat and grow at a normal rate. Like any crying babies, they should not be left alone to "cry it out."

The way you view your colicky baby may also make a difference in the way you cope with the situation. When we view the colicky baby simply as miserable, demanding, or even "bad," these terms all imply negative value judgments. Instead, try to think in more neutral terms. The La Leche League uses the term "high-need" baby. All babies have needs, and we don't hold that against them. Colicky babies are going through a period of high needs. Naturally, this is hard to deal with. High needs place tremendous demands on parents, for whom it is a true challenge to summon up the necessary strong doses of heroism, patience, and maturity. Let yourself be angry about the lack of sleep and frayed nerves, but don't let this keep you from connecting with the baby.

Following are some age-old techniques that you can employ to head off or temper the crying bouts as much as possible. A combination of them *may* work—at least some of the time.

Question: *How did you manage your baby's colic?*

Answer: *I learned by trial and error. My pediatrician suggested that we try to keep all stimulation at a minimum, so I fed Amelia in a darkened room, kept her swaddled, and moved her with great gentleness when I picked her up. We also played a record of a heartbeat that my neighbor lent me. I think the boring rhythmical sound helped.*

A: First on the list is for parents to remain allies with each other. It's nobody's fault, and you need each other to talk to rather than vent your feelings upon. Colic brings tremendous tension into a house.

A: My advice is to sleep when the baby does or at least lie down and relax. To hell with housework. It takes all your energy, mental as well as physical, to help the poor thing through the night. It does end.

A: Unfortunately, one of the hardest aspects of Christopher's colic was that my husband was really turned off. All the comforting was left to me. I felt abandoned, and John felt useless. Parents should remember that anyone can walk a screaming baby. It doesn't always have to be Mom! It has taken months to repair the situation. Now that Christopher is six months old, he and his father are beginning to have fun together.

A: Once I convinced myself that Walker was perfectly healthy, I made sure I got out of the house every day. I took my screaming baby along with me in the Snugli. Sometimes I'd just walk and walk through the mall. Yes, people sometimes glared at me, but I held firm. I had to continue leading my life because I knew that if I didn't, the resentment toward the baby would build and build and build.

A: We found that having a plan helped. I was so exhausted, I finally said to Chris, "You have to sit

Fennel Tea: Placebo or Not?

Following is an old West German recipe for anticolic tea. Some people swear by it. Pour 4½ cups hot water over 1 teaspoon fennel seeds. Let the seeds steep for 10 minutes. Strain the seeds carefully and, when the liquid cools, feed an ounce or two to the colicky baby from a bottle. According to Varro Tyler, former dean of the School of Pharmacy at Purdue University, the volatile oil in the fennel seed has a carminative effect, meaning that it dilates the blood vessels in the alimentary canal, expelling gas, facilitating digestion, and producing a warming effect.

The 55-Mile-an-Hour Crib!

Taking a baby for a car ride has long been a home remedy for fussiness. Now there is a device to simulate the calming action of the car. This device, called a Sleeptight, comes in two parts, a vibration unit that mounts beneath a crib and an audio unit that attaches to the crib's side. Together they simulate the sound and vibration of a car going 55 mph. In a three-year-long Ohio State University study, the device was tested on sixty colicky babies. Many stopped crying within seven seconds after the machine was turned on. Eighty-five percent quieted within twelve minutes, and 97 percent showed "decreased stress," meaning they went from sobbing to whimpering, from whimpering to being quiet. Whatever works! (The device is available through Sleeptight, Inc., 3613 Mueller Road, St. Charles, MO 63301; call 1-800-325-3550 for information on price and shipping.)

down with me and help me figure this out for the day." At breakfast I'd make this crazy schedule with his help of all the things I would do. Chris would call from his office to check in, so that I didn't feel so alone with Amanda's screaming.

A: I needed to love this baby so much. He was just so different from what I had expected. I had read that babies who are carried a lot cried less. Even when Matthew wasn't crying, I carried him in the Snugli when I did my chores around the house. This felt good to me, and I like to believe that it felt good to him, too.

The End of Colic

No, I will never forget Jessica's colic. My favorite memory naturally is the last night of it. It was Fred's night on, and my night to sleep. But it was so noisy, I had to get up and see what was happening. I went into the living room. There was a bottle of Jack Daniel's on the coffee table and a seedy-looking glass with a cigarette butt in it. The moonlight was streaming in the window, framing the cradle. Jessica was sound asleep. Fred was swaying back and forth in his Jockey shorts and black socks, rocking the cradle with one foot while he played his guitar. He was singing, "Your time is up. Your time is up. Your three months are over, or we're giving you away," in his best country-and-western style. That, believe it or not, three months to the day, or should I say night, was the end of one of the most horrendous periods in my life.

P.S. Once past the newborn stage, colic or no, parents become more skilled at interpreting their infant's cries. It isn't simply that we know the baby and feel more at ease trusting our instincts. The baby has also become a better communicator.

By three months the quality of the infant's cries has changed. She'll cry, but then she will pause and look toward the parent or care giver to see if the crying has been noticed. By six months the baby will cry as she looks directly at you as if to say, "Give me comfort right now." Between six and twelve months, the baby's crying becomes even more elaborate. She cries, looks, and gestures all at once. For instance, as she sobs, she'll stretch out her arms to be picked up and held.

If you can't get to the baby at that moment, a reassuring word will offer some comfort. Just as important, she will come to know that her needs are valid and that her efforts to communicate are heard. This builds trust and self-esteem.

Difficult Babies Grow Up to Score High on Intelligence Tests!

According to a study published by the *American Journal of Psychiatry*, a group of scientists from Laval University in Quebec, Canada, discovered that "difficult" babies may grow up to score higher on intelligence tests than their quieter playmates as long as they come from middle- or upper-income families or families with "superior communication skills." Dr. Michael Maziade divided seventy-five four-month-olds into groups according to temperament: "easy," "average," or "difficult." Difficult babies were defined as those who were cranky, unsootheable, intense in their emotional reactions, and unresponsive to new stimuli.

Researchers theorize that parents pay more attention to the demanding babies than to the "easy" babies. The extra verbal stimulation helps to speed intellectual development.

Books to Help Get You Through Colic

Jones, Sandy, *Crying Baby, Sleepless Nights* (New York: Warner Books, 1983)

Kirkland, John, *Crying and Babies: Helping Families Cope* (New York: Methuen, Inc., 1985)

Kitzinger, Sheila, *The Crying Baby* (New York: Viking, 1989)

Sears, William, *Fussy Baby: How to Bring Out the Best in Your High-Need Child* (Franklin Park, IL: La Leche League International, Inc., 1985)

Weissbluth, Marc, *Cry Babies—Coping with Colic: What to Do When Baby Won't Stop Crying* (New York: Berkley, 1986)

Young, Carol, *Crying for Help: How to Cure Your Baby of Colic* (Rochester, VT: Thorsons Publishers, Inc., 1986)

• CHAPTER 8 •

Sleep

There never was a
Child so lovely but his
Mother was glad to see him asleep.
—Ralph Waldo Emerson

Sleeping Through the Night: The Impossible Dream?

Question: What is the single most-talked-about aspect of baby care?
Answer: Sleep.

Question: Why is sleep such an important aspect of a baby's life?
Answer: The quantity and quality of sleep affect a baby's health, alertness, and sense of well-being. Yes, of course, we know this! But let's get to the heart of the matter. How much the baby sleeps is the difference between having cheerful and alert parents or members of the living dead, who bumble and stagger through the days in a dulled, pained state of lethargy bordering on confusion. How much the baby sleeps can affect just about everything in your life—the division of labor in your family, your work, your creativity, your problem-solving abilities, your self-expectation and self-esteem, your marriage, your sex life, your social life, your relationship to friends

and community. In short, the way your baby sleeps—well or not so well—affects your general effectiveness as a human being in the world.

Question: How much do newborns sleep?
Answer: Many parents have expectations about how much their newborn should sleep and even more about what to do with the free time they so desperately need. Your baby's sleeping habits may reflect those of the "average baby" we read about who supposedly sleeps somewhere around sixteen hours a day in three- or four-hour stretches with periods of wakeful alertness in between. Or he may sleep sixteen hours a day in very short stretches, with a great deal of crying in between, so that it doesn't feel like sixteen hours. Or he may startle you by sleeping for six hours one day—so that you are constantly checking on him to see if he is alive and thus do not take advantage of the delicious benefits of this break—and then not repeat the behavior for weeks and weeks. And then there are the babies who sleep for a mere ten hours a day, and those

on the opposite end of the spectrum who sleep as much as twenty-two hours. In other words, with newborns there are no average formulas. As long as the baby is healthy, everything and anything goes.

Question: What does the term "sleeping through the night" mean?
Answer: "Sleeping through the night" no longer means what it once did before you had a baby. It is now a euphemism for sleeping from, say, midnight until perhaps 5 A.M.

Question: Don't most babies sleep through the night by six weeks or by a certain weight?
Answer: This is really an individual matter. According to a study done by the American Academy of Pediatrics, 70 percent of babies don't stop waking at night for a feeding until they are at least three months old. Some 13 percent do not sleep without waking and crying at night until they are six months old. And we won't even talk about the other 17 percent!

Question: Isn't there anything I can do to make my baby sleep through the night?

Answer: You can take some measures early on to help foster good sleep habits (see Aiming the Newborn Toward a Full Night's Sleep, page 109), but, for the most part, the baby will sleep as much as he needs to sleep, and there is nothing that you can do other than to be responsive to his cries and wait for the passage of time. Sleeping in longer and longer stretches occurs as his neurological system matures and adapts to the world outside the uterus.

Question: Shouldn't I let my newborn "cry it out" at night?

Answer: No. Your newborn is not yet ready to "cry it out," and he doesn't yet know the difference between day and night. That term refers to the older, bigger baby (read on!) who does not need to eat as often as a newborn and has more resources to comfort himself than a newborn has yet developed. If you are breast-feeding, it's important to feed the baby often, be it day or night, in order to build up your milk supply. Though this can be tiring, a good milk supply will ultimately help your baby to sleep through the night when he is physiologically ready.

Question: Won't feeding the baby cereal help him to sleep through the night?

Answer: No. (See page 65 on introducing solid foods.) There is some evidence, however, that holding and carrying the baby will help him to cry less and sleep for longer periods at a time. (see The Benefits of Carrying a Baby, page 95).

Question: What is the best sleeping position for a newborn baby?

Answer: The typical newborn sleeps best on his stomach on a firm mattress. He will not suffocate, because he can turn his head from side to side. Pillows, however, or anything else that is soft, could suffocate him! Pediatricians think it is much more important to satisfy the baby's natural urge to repeat a comfortable pattern in sleep than to worry about some of the pros and cons presented for each sleep position, so use whatever works best.

Question: Once you get the newborn to sleep in your arms, how do you then put him down without waking him?

Answer: This is tricky, and everyone has to perfect his or her own method—by setting the stage, developing their timing, taking advantage of serendipity, ruthlessly analyzing their errors, and being willing to start all over. A parent offers the following suggestions:

Have your systems and strategy ready to go. Before we even begin, my husband turns on the classical-music station low in the baby's room and warms the bed with a hot water bottle. I've learned that an ice-cold sheet is enough to wake a baby. Though I have nursed standing, swaying, rocking, and jouncing, it's hard on your back. So nurse or bottle-feed near the baby's bed, in a chair that you can get out of without waking him, and so that you will not have to carry him very far before putting him down. If you use a carriage or a bassinet, have it right at your side. If you are using a standard-sized crib, raise the mattress so you don't have to lean over too far. Keep the baby close to your body as you lower him, while turning him with ever so slow a motion facedown. I make the depositing action simpler by swaddling him before I nurse him for what I hope is the last time that evening. This way he is contained in a cozy, easy-to-handle bundle, and the chances of him startling himself awake are greatly reduced.

Whatever you do, don't blow it by tripping over some piece of furniture in the dark as you are making your breathless exit on tiptoe. Have a night-light glowing at all times. That comes first, along with warming the bed. And don't forget to turn on the intercom, too, if you have one. Or better yet, maybe it's best not to know. I know this sounds complicated, but . . .

What Bedtime Can Be Like After Six Months

The baby has been pulling on his ear, a sign that he is tired after a long day, and you are even more tired. You long for adult companionship and conversation, some time alone with your mate or another verbal adult, a chance to put your feet up, to read a magazine, and to have a pleasant, uninterrupted, if late dinner. Or forget dinner—a chance simply to stare aimlessly at the television screen while you "veg out."

After feeding and changing the baby, you've held and cuddled him, then wound up the music box that plays a gentle lullaby. His eyes are looking a little droopy as you kiss him good night and place him in his favorite position into his cozy crib. Then you quietly switch off the light and turn casually to leave—on tiptoe. Maybe even before you've had a chance to complete your exit and begin to feel pleased with yourself for pulling it off, you hear a whimper. Your heart rate speeds up slightly as you scurry away without looking back. By the time you've reached the kitchen and angrily banged a pot or two, there is no doubt in your mind. The baby is not asleep. He is awake and is letting out intermittent, half-hearted cries.

Your jaw tightens. But you have hope. He's just settling down, after all. You glance casually at the nearest clock. The cries are no longer intermittent and have grown louder. But you turn the water on in the kitchen so that you can't hear so

Aiming the Newborn Toward a Full Night's Sleep

Parents advise . . .

Night feedings are very businesslike, and stimulation is kept to a minimum. I don't turn on the lights. I nurse for a short time, no more than six or seven minutes per breast, then I burp him and put him back down in his cradle.

• • •

I get totally organized for the night ahead of time. I have the bottle ready in an insulated bag, a thermos of hot water to warm it, and an electric blanket plugged in by the rocker in his room.

• • •

I want Nelson to associate bed with sleeping at night, so during the day I put him to nap in the carriage. When he's awake he's in the infant seat or the Snugli.

• • •

By the second baby I learned not to pop up every time I heard a peep. Sometimes she will wake momentarily, let out a little squeak, and then fall back to sleep for another hour.

• • •

After the last feeding before midnight, I burp Jonathan very carefully and leave him sitting at an angle in his infant seat for a few minutes, hoping that his stomach will be nice and settled.

• • •

We wake Matthew at midnight for a feeding even if it hasn't been that long since he's eaten. Then we hope he will go for at least three or four hours more.

• • •

Gully's in bed with us. I've found that we both get a better sleep if I put him to my breast and nurse him before either he or I fully awake. There have been studies done of the sleep cycles of lactating mothers. Apparently baby and mother have more or less the same periods of deep and light sleep. He never wakes me out of a deep sleep, so I therefore feel rested the next day.

• • •

I don't change diapers at night unless Lulu has had a bowel movement because I've found that undressing her wakes her up fully. I put a good coating of Vaseline on her bottom to protect her from diaper rash at the last feeding before midnight when I go to sleep.

• • •

By the third or fourth day after leaving the hospital I noticed that Aaron would suck on his fist. Whenever I put him in his carriage after a feeding, I make sure his hand is close to his mouth. This way he can suck when he wants to for comfort.

• • •

I don't mind getting up at night with Jack. I work all day and have two other children. It is quite chaotic in our house in the early evenings, and I prefer to visit with the baby at the nighttime feedings when it is peaceful. I'm also so busy during the day that this is the only time when I can really nurse him for a long, uninterrupted period of time and keep up my milk supply. We enjoy this time together. I function well enough with interrupted sleep, perhaps because I know it will end. I didn't know that with my first baby.

• • •

We've worked out a system. I handle all feedings during the week so that Charlie can sleep and get up refreshed for work the next day. On weekends he gives a relief bottle or brings the baby to me for a nursing. On Saturdays and Sundays I take long naps to catch up on my sleep.

• • •

I think your own attitude is very important. Before I had a baby, I had a very rigid idea about the amount of sleep I required. It had to be at least seven hours a night or I wasn't very pleasant to be with. Enter baby. What a shock! I got one who doesn't sleep much at all. I will complain to anyone who will listen. But I've had no choice but to learn that I can live with a lot less sleep and still function quite well.

• • •

By the time Evan was three months old, I was pretty worn out from feeding him two or three times a night. The pediatrician suggested we try to stretch it by having my husband try to soothe him, because he'd come to associate waking at night with breast-feeding. This actually did help—at least to the point where he was waking only once.

well. You rattle the pots and pans some more as you glare at the clock again. Three minutes have passed. You turn off the water. The crying has become more persistent.

You consult your mate. "What time is it?" The baby is screeching now. You sit, take a deep breath, and control the tears of rage and disappointment that are beginning to cloud your vision. You grope for the silverware. Five minutes have gone by. "I can't take it," you growl. "It's not fair. *You* set the table!" Scenes from your former life flash through your mind—impromptu dinners at the Chinese restaurant around the corner, a carefree drive or stroll afterwards, or perhaps a visit with friends, or a movie, or two movies, with a beer and chicken wings—and affection—afterwards.

Now the cries have turned into loud, pathetic wails. There are seconds of silence when you know the baby is shuddering, struggling for air. You tell yourself, "We must stand firm!" Before you became a parent, you had visited couples with no backbones whose "spoiled" babies would not go to bed and were up at all hours dominating the adults' attention, ruining the evenings. It wasn't cute. In fact, maybe it was even the end of your friendship. You vowed, "This will *never* happen to us."

Your mate has set the table and slyly located your dog-eared copy of Dr. Spock. He quotes, "*Section 346. Chronic resistance to sleep in infancy—going-to-bed type. This is a difficulty that develops insidiously. In most cases it grows out of a case of colic or irritable crying. It can be thought of as a form of spoiling. A baby girl has been miserable with colic most evenings for her first 2 or 3 months. Her parents have found that she is more comfortable when they carry her around. This makes them feel better, too. But by the time she is about 3 or 4 months old, it gradually dawns on them that she doesn't seem to be in so much*

pain or misery any more—her cry is now angry and demanding. She wants her walking because she's used to it and thinks she's entitled to it. She almost glares at her mother when she sits down for a well-needed rest as if to say, 'woman, get going!'

"*A baby who becomes engaged in a nightly struggle to keep parents walking has to train herself to stay awake, and she succeeds step by step as the months go by—first to 9 p.m., then to 10, 11, even midnight. Her parents say her lids often close and her head droops while they're carrying her, but that as soon as they start to lay her down she wakes with an indignant yell.*"

"No, no" you plead, wiping a tear of frustration from your cheek. "Tell me honestly, it hasn't gotten that bad yet—has it?"

Your mate reads on without answering: "*The habit is usually easy to break once the parents realize that it is as bad for the baby as it is for them. The cure is simple. Put the baby to bed at a reasonable hour, say good night affectionately but firmly, walk out of the room and don't go back. Most babies who have developed this pattern cry furiously for 20 to 30 minutes the first night, and then when they see that nothing happens, they suddenly fall asleep! The second night the crying is apt to last only 10 minutes. The third night there usually isn't any at all.*" He concludes with Dr. Spock's final bit of advice. "*It's sometimes worthwhile to explain the program to touchy neighbors in order to reassure them that it will take only a few nights and to ask their indulgence.*"

"What do you think about that?" he asks you. You glower at him. "Well, I think the guy's on to something," your mate says.

"Be quiet!" you yell. He needn't have read it. You already know the passage by heart. You also know real-life, true horror stories to back it up, but it isn't the same when it happens to you. The baby's full-throttle shrieks are now punctuated

by gasps. You turn to the clock. Seven minutes. It feels like an eternity. "I'm sorry!" you sigh. "I apologize for flying off the handle. Look, let's stay friends. We need each other."

The rice is ready, moist and steaming. As you reach for a plate and serving spoon, you realize that you have no appetite. It's the noise. Now your heart is pounding. The child is choking, possibly even dying. How can you eat your dinner under these circumstances? He is, after all, only a baby, and now you are worried. Surely he's suffering. It is *you* the baby wants. How cruel can you get? Dr. Spock may be a renowned pediatrician, but he is not a psychoanalyst. These early feelings of abandonment will shape his psyche for the rest of his life. Really.

Now it's bad. You begin to sink into the slough of despond. You feel yourself crossing the hard line of resolve into that dangerous, gray area called ambivalence.

The rice is on the plates. Your day began at 5:02 A.M. You need and deserve nourishment and peace. Why is the baby now gasping in-between coughs? You rattle the pots and pans in the sink. You turn to your mate for support, but he is wavering, too. He asks, "Do you think that anything is wrong?" You glare at the clock. A full nine minutes have gone by—you've never let him cry this long. Your mate says, "He is after all only a baby, and he's my son." Dr. Spock is an ogre. What does he know about babies? He hasn't actually lived with one in years.

To let the baby cry it out or not? Rest assured, you are not alone . . .

My main problem with Geneve is sleeping at night. And I've yet to find a solution or attitude. I'm unwilling to spend two hours getting her to sleep, and I'm equally unwilling to let her cry and cry. She can work herself into all kinds of anxious, fearful, hysterical, emotional states. Most of the time I nurse her to sleep (she's seven months old), which I'm told is a bad habit to get into. But she often wakes up as I move her to the crib, and then I stay in the room with her. When she gets sleepy and starts to cry, I rub her to sleep. Sometimes the rubbing doesn't do any good, and after a while I leave and she cries herself to sleep, but sometimes I can't stand the crying or she starts to get hysterical and I go back in. Sometimes she's more than amenable and goes to sleep, sometimes my going back starts the whole cycle all over again, and sometimes going back isn't enough, doesn't seem to comfort her, so I pick her up and either that works and she calms down and goes to sleep (frequently only to wake as I put her back in the crib . . . oh God, oh God) or it doesn't, and I burst into tears of frustration and we both have a good cry. This doesn't happen all the time, or even most of the time, just often enough to make me feel that I really don't know what the hell is going on!

Some Suggestions, Philosophical as Well as Practical, on Sleep

If a baby is busy, restless, struggling at bedtime, and yet you know he yearns to rest, see if you are not busy, too—with ten thousand thoughts. The thoughts can be anything—he's got to sleep, he needs it; he's got to sleep, I need it; I have to get some time to myself; maybe if I do this; maybe he wants that; why won't he sleep? Is it so? Then try to acknowledge that, at least for the moment, neither you nor the child has any needs beyond the awareness of love. Corny? Well, just try it. . . . For just a few minutes do not think of what you have to do or what you want to do or what the baby needs.

—Polly Berends
Whole Child—Whole Parent

• • •

We understand that the older infant finds it painful to be separated from beloved persons. We grant him the right to protest; at the same time, this pain, this discomfort is something he can learn to tolerate if it is not excessive. We need to help him manage small amounts of discomfort and frustration.

—Selma Fraiberg
The Magic Years: Understanding and Handling the Problems of Early Childhood

No matter how tired or impatient you may feel, try to give yourself over entirely to the baby before he goes to sleep for the night. Your full presence and calm and loving attention coupled with a regular ritual is the first and best way to bypass bedtime dilemmas. This will not only make it easier for the baby, it will also make it easier for you in the long run. If the baby cries and protests, knowing that you have given your all will help calm your guilty or ambivalent feelings, and that is half the battle.

Many going-to-bed problems begin in the second half of the first year. By this age the baby is firmly attached to you and may feel a genuine sense of loss when he has to give you up. This, coupled with great advances in motor development that require a tremendous outlay of energy, can make the baby overstimulated, adding to his going-to-bed difficulty.

Establishing a Bedtime Ritual

The baby can manage the transition from wakefulness to sleep with some help and understanding on our part. The best way is to develop a soothing and comforting bedtime ritual that mother, father, or a baby-sitter can perform. Plan to spend about half an hour. It's worth it!

You might, for instance, give the baby a massage or a warm bath, take a walk around the room saying good night to toys and stuffed animals, or look at a picture book together. Then wind up a music box or put on a favorite lullaby tape. If none of these activities appeals, then think of something you do like that is pleasurable to both of you. Otherwise, your baby will pick up on your impatience. The idea is to be fully present, so that the baby has "enough," then go. If you think leaving a night-light on or the door open a crack may offer the baby a feeling of security and connection with the daytime world he has given up, then do so.

Question: Don't the warmth and closeness of nursing or giving the baby a bottle get him to sleep, as many mothers swear?

Answer: It's hard to give up this kind of a ritual when it not only works but also feels good to all concerned. The problem is that the baby can become dependent on these activities in order to fall asleep. This might be fine at bedtime, but not if the baby begins to wake at night, which many do during the second half of the first year. The baby who is used to being nursed to sleep will not know how to settle down on his own when he wakes at night. He will cry for you and the things he's come to associate with falling asleep.

If you enjoy the warmth and closeness of holding, rocking, or feeding the baby to sleep and are prepared for the possible consequences, then so be it. Know, however, that if and when you want to change this routine, both the baby and you may experience some discomfort and displeasure.

Question: What alternatives are there to nursing, holding, rocking, and cuddling the baby to sleep?

Answer: You can encourage the use of a "transitional object" at bedtime. If you always introduce the same special blanket, cloth diaper, doll, stuffed animal, etc., when you put the baby to bed, he may become attached to it and comforted by it. Though objects can never be a true substitute for human contact and comfort, they can be useful, especially at times of separation such as bedtime. Remember, too, that the thumb is a "built-in" transitional object that is always there for the baby. Sucking offers comfort when he must give up the day and the pleasure of being with the people he loves.

Question: Is a bottle a good transitional object?
Answer: Almost everyone agrees that putting the baby to bed with a bottle is not a good idea. When the baby lies flat on his back and drinks, the milk can leak into the eustachian tubes, which connect the ears to the throat. This can cause ear infections. The lactic acid in the milk can cause cavities. A pacifier or bottle of water are somewhat better alternatives. But keep in mind that these objects can easily get lost or fall out of the crib or be purposely dropped by the ever more wily baby who is bidding for your attention. When you go to replace the objects, you are apt to be annoyed—and worse, you may stimulate the baby to even greater wakefulness.

Question: What if the baby is still having trouble settling down for the night although you've tried a bedtime ritual and encouraged the use of a transitional object?
Answer: You might have unrealistic expectations about the amount of sleep he needs. Check his nap schedule. Babies who sleep late in the afternoon may have a second wind in the early evening. As he approaches his first birthday, it may be time to consolidate two or three short naps into one long nap after lunch. It may be hard to accept, but consider, too, whether you

are confusing your own needs for privacy and peace with your child's need for sleep. If you have been on duty all day and need a break from the baby, you may find that you are hustling him off to bed when he's not really tired yet. You may then have to spend another hour going back and forth, growing more and more frazzled and resentful, when attempts to settle him don't succeed. A question you might ask is, are you getting enough off-duty time to yourself? Can your husband or someone else put the baby to bed so that you can have some time alone? And are you getting out without the baby? By six months you could probably use some regular time away.

Night Waking, Six Months and Over

Question: Why do babies wake up in the middle of the night?
Answer: According to recent studies, sleep cycles in infants are regular and characteristic. An active, noisy baby may be active and noisy in his sleep. Three- to four-hour cycles usually make up the night's sleep. Each cycle can be broken down into various types of sleep. In the middle of each is approximately sixty minutes of deep sleep. The hour on each side of this deep sleep may be a lighter, dreaming state in which movement and activity (or dreaming) come and go. Then, at regular intervals through the night, an infant comes to a semi-conscious, semi-alert state. In this period, he may suck his fingers, cry out, rock or bang his head, move around the bed, practice his newly learned tricks, fuss, or talk to himself, and then settle into his conditioned sleeping position to get himself to sleep again. When his parents are nearby and respond to these cries and activity, they quickly become a necessary part of his pattern of getting himself back to sleep. It is important for us to "condition" them to use their own

resources for sleep as early as we can. This is an important part of acculturation.
—T. Berry Brazelton
Infants and Mothers: Differences in Development

Despite good advice, your better judgment, or all the wishes in the world, your baby still isn't sleeping through the night. When he woke the first couple of times, maybe you went to soothe him either by nursing or offering a bottle, a pat on the back, or a close cuddle in the rocking chair. You might even have included a walk around the house and a look at the stars as well. Perhaps you took another tack and let him cry for five, ten, even a ghastly twenty minutes. (How you all suffered!) Then, feeling guilty for having been so cruel and heartless, you gave up and went to offer comfort, at the same time wondering whether if you'd waited just *two* more minutes, he would have stopped—and learned his lesson—that is, to go back to sleep all by himself . . . like a "good" baby.

Now you feel so tired that the only solution may seem to be to pick up the baby and crawl right back into your own bed with him in your arms. But this is not ideal unless you're used to it. After all, he's wiggly and damp, and he snores, albeit delicately. The fear that he will fall onto the floor, or that you will roll over and crush him, saturates your dreams and keeps you on the very edge of sleep—far from the deep, restful state you so desperately need and crave.

It is now clear that you are suffering from night after night of interrupted sleep. You have circles under your eyes. Your attention span and temper are both short. You've lost your sense of humor, and life has begun to lack luster. You're ready to acknowledge that maybe you should have followed the warnings in the books you've read (some specifically devoted to babies and sleep) and the advice of your pediatrician or that of friends and relatives whose raised eyebrows and growing lack of sympathy for your fatigue have begun to be offensive. "We told you so," they say if not with words, with their tone, and with their looks of mock concern. "We told you so," they say again. "You really blew it!" You are finally willing to admit from the very core of your being that you've got a sleep problem on your hands.

Here follows the best advice you will ever get.

Don't waste a *single moment* punishing yourself or letting all those scolds punish you either! Put your innocent mistakes, misguided decisions, your good will, generous heart, desire to please, the whole kettle of fish, behind you. You are not the first parent this has happened to.

It is possible to start afresh!

Different Approaches to Dealing with Night Waking

There are different ways of dealing with night waking, and each family has to decide what they think is best for their baby and for themselves. Various parents and experts will tell you that you can eliminate the problem in anywhere from three nights to two weeks. This is probably so—if you truly know where you stand on the issue. It is worth trying to think it through carefully. Look for your own ambivalences, and lay them out on the table for examination. This way you can approach the problem with more clarity and confidence.

The Hard-Line Approach

The hard-line approach consists of letting the baby who wakes at night cry herself back to sleep. In *Dr. Spock's Baby and Child Care* (New York: Dutton, 1985), Drs. Spock and Rothenberg

say of the no-nonsense, hard-line approach, "This can usually be accomplished in two or three nights by letting her cry and not going to her at all. . . . The baby must not see the parents when she wakes up. If she sees them, even though they pretend to be asleep, this angers her and stimulates her to keep up the crying indefinitely." If the baby sleeps in the same room as her parents, then her crib should be shielded from view.

The Middle-of-the-Road Approach

With variations, this approach calls for waking and feeding the baby at a set time late in the evening before the parents go to bed. If he then wakes and cries later at night, the parents at least know he is not hungry. The idea behind this approach, like the hard-line approach, is to help the baby become more self-sufficient at comforting himself and putting himself back to sleep. This approach differs from the hard-line approach in that a parent is initially present to offer verbal reassurance so that the baby does not feel totally alone with this challenge. When he cries, a parent may go to him, and without picking him up, may say something in a calming and reassuring voice for a set amount of time. Then the parent leaves. If the baby continues to cry, the parent may return, check to see if the baby is okay, offer more verbal reassurance for a shorter amount of time, and then leave again. The intervals between contact grow farther and farther apart. The baby, who has been gradually and thus humanely weaned from mother's or father's reassuring voice and presence, eventually learns that he can put himself back to sleep on his own.

The Family-Bed Approach

At the opposite end of the spectrum are people who believe that sleep problems can be avoided if parents and babies sleep together in the same room, if not in the same king-size bed. Advocates of the family bed argue that we are a contact species. Our closest animal relatives, apes and monkeys, rarely leave their infants alone day or night. Physical attachment, at first a means of surviving the threat of predators, has become the foundation for healthy emotional development. Contrary to what we might fear, the baby who has a parent available during the night as well as the day will not be overly attached. In fact, the opposite will be true. She will ultimately be able to let go more easily because she has had enough given to her. In the busy and complex world we live in, sharing a bed is also a way of spending "quality time" as a family: It lets fathers as well as mothers be physically and emotionally close to their children. This system works well for those parents who have no ambivalence about it and are able to meet their own needs for intimacy outside of the family bed.

Questions You Can Ask Before You Take Action

• Is the baby physically comfortable? Warm enough? Cool enough? Free to change positions? Is he hungry, teething, suffering from diaper rash, coming down with a cold, or getting over an illness? Has he recently been immunized? Are there any signs that he is allergic to something in his food or in his environment? Has his child-care arrangement changed? Have you been away from him more than usual? Have you taken him on a vacation where he has slept in a strange bed? Has he recently made a motor leap—say learned to pull himself up to stand, to walk, etc.? Any of these factors can contribute to night waking. It helps to be aware of them.

• Is the baby taking more than two naps a day? Perhaps he needs less sleep at night as a result. Too many daytime naps also mean that he is missing out on a lot of action and opportunities for stimulation. Are the baby's naps the only time you have to yourself? Is there another way that you could schedule time for yourself other than the baby's sleep time? Or is the baby not getting a real nap? Does he doze on the fly—in his car seat or stroller?

• Is the night waking affecting the baby? Does he seem tired and cranky the next day? Such a baby is probably not as alert to all the wonderfully stimulating aspects of life around him as a rested baby.

• When a baby wakes and cries at night, there seems to be little disagreement that he's feeling something akin to unhappiness. Will this hurt the baby emotionally if we don't intervene? No expert or parent really knows the answer. Some people can live with uncertainty. Others can't. Still others say, "Even if I don't know whether this hurts the baby, I do know that it's hurting me. I can't function as an effective parent unless I get a full night's sleep." Where do you stand on this? And why?

• The hardest question to face about continued night waking is a surprising one. What's in it for Mom? What's in it for Dad? There are few of us who are not susceptible to guilt and ambivalence about our roles as parents. For instance, myriad hidden agendas may be operating to keep a working mother and her baby from getting a full night's sleep. Is she trying to convince herself that she is an attentive mother if she's there for a wakeful baby at night? Or if the baby wakes at night, is this proof that he misses her? Does she want to stay home with her baby? If she is tired and worn out on the job and can't handle it effec-tively, isn't this justification to quit or be let go?

• Can continuous night waking come between parents and affect their marriage? Without knowing it consciously, a husband and wife can use their child's sleep problems as a way to avoid the real issue—intimacy between them. Children change us and upset our routines in ways that nothing else ever will, and as long as we have a problem like night waking to keep us busy and apart, we don't have to look further into ourselves and each other. In not looking, however, we're missing an opportunity to learn something that will add to our stature as individuals, as partners in a marriage, and as parents.

Early-Morning Waking

The sun has just peeped over the horizon as you are roused from a deep, comfortable, much-needed sleep. The baby is up, the crib is rattling, and you can hear the toys hitting the floor. With the last thud there is one long sweet moment of silence. As you savor it, you know that your time is up. This is when you consider making blackout curtains or having them made to order if you don't sew. This is when you wish you'd started having children earlier. By now they would be seven years old and able to make their own breakfast, and maybe even bring you a glass of orange juice in bed. You certainly deserve it! Until this phase passes—and it does seem to be cyclical, perhaps having something to do with the seasons, with teething, with a change in child-care arrangements, or with the mastery of a new motor skill—the only fair and reasonable solution is for parents to take turns getting up early. If you are a single parent, you must endure. To make up for this very real sacrifice, force yourself to be good to yourself in other ways. Ask for and accept help from friends and relatives. Can you list three things that you would enjoy doing?

Useful Books on Sleep

Ferber, Richard, *Solve Your Child's Sleep Problems* (Princeton, NJ: Princeton University Press, 1985)

Sammons, William A.H., *The Self-Calmed Baby* (Boston: Little, Brown & Co., 1989)

Schaefer, Charles E., *Teach Your Baby to Sleep Through the Night* (New York: Putnam Publishing Group, 1987)

Thevenin, Tine, *The Family Bed* (Garden City Park, NY: Avery Publishing Group, Inc., 1987)

Then make a *concrete* plan to do at least one of them within a week.

A Place to Sleep: Cradles and Bassinets

Many parents wonder whether to invest in a cradle or a bassinet when the baby is very small. Of the two, a bassinet is the more practical. Its wheels and enclosed sides offer both mobility and security. Look for a wide base and a sturdy bottom. Cradles, though homespun and romantic, tend to be expensive. They also roll the baby from side to side instead of rocking him from head to toe, by far the preferred motion. If you *must* have one (I did for my first baby!), look for one with a wide base and sturdy bottom. If you're choosing an antique, make sure the spindles are no more than $2\frac{3}{8}$ inches apart and that there are no dangerous cutouts or finials that might inadvertently trap the baby. Instead of a cradle, consider investing in a rocking chair, which the whole family can enjoy for many years.

Choosing a Crib

Babies spend a considerable part of their lives alone in their cribs. For this reason, the crib you choose must be absolutely safe—you won't be there every moment to monitor what is going on. Thanks to the Consumer Product Safety Commission's 1973 safety standards, full-size cribs must meet stringent criteria that govern the width between slats, interior dimensions, mattress size, the height of the sides, the safety of the hardware and wood or painted surfaces, and the simplicity of assembly instructions.

Still, accidents do occur in cribs, both new and secondhand. By the time your baby moves to a regular-size bed as a toddler, his crib will have taken a lot of wear and tear from shaking and bouncing. Parents must monitor the condition of the crib daily. Following are some suggestions for choosing a crib and using it safely.

• Cribs come with either one or two drop sides, which you can lower to reach in and pick up the baby. Be sure the locking and releasing mechanism works smoothly, can be released with one hand, and is out of reach of a curious baby or toddler who is playing on the floor.

• Check the teething railings on the crib sides. They should be firmly fixed to the rails so that the baby cannot pull them off.

• If you are buying an antique cradle or crib or are using a hand-me-down that was made before 1973, check the following dimensions with a tape measure. The distance between slats must be no greater than 2⅜ inches. Fully raised sides must measure at least 26 inches from their upper edge to the top of the mattress support in its lowest position. The height of a lowered drop side is important, too. It should be at least 9 inches above the mattress support when set in the highest position.

• Do not buy a crib with corner posts higher than ⅝ inch. If you have a secondhand crib, unscrew any knobs or posts, or saw them off. Posts and decorative finials on cribs can catch on a baby's clothing and have been known to kill by strangulation. Also check that the headboard does not have any cut-out designs, or a space between corner posts and end panels in which a baby could become entrapped.

• Consider choosing a crib with adjustable mattress supports, which will allow you to lower the mattress as your child gets taller. Check it periodically, particularly if you have moved it, to make sure that all four mattress-support hangers are firmly secured to the frame. If one slips out of place, that corner will sag, and the baby may become dangerously trapped.

• If you are buying a new mattress, don't be taken in by a persuasive sales pitch for the most expensive one. Babies are light, and the cheaper mattresses made of urethane foam are perfectly adequate and hypoallergenic. They are also lightweight and easy to lift when changing crib sheets. Make sure the mattress fits snugly. Any gaps between mattress and bed frame could trap the baby's arms, hands, legs, or even head. Also check the seams and surface of the plastic mattress cover to make sure they are free of tears. If not, invest in a waterproof mattress protector, available at baby products stores.

• Never use any kind of plastic garbage bag to protect the mattress—it can cause suffocation.

• Any crib manufactured before 1978 may be coated with paint or varnish that contains lead. Some babies chew on all surfaces. If you have any suspicions, write to the manufacturer or refinish the crib with paint approved for use on children's furniture.

• Finally, check before buying on how easily the crib can be assembled. If you aren't handy, consider having it delivered already assembled.

Save assembly instructions. If you are reassembling a secondhand crib, always refasten wood screws with the next-larger screw size.

Optional Purchases

Crib Bumpers. These offer protection for the baby's head. They soften corners where babies like to snuggle and keep arms and legs from dangling between slats. Patterned crib bumpers are more interesting for a baby to look at than plain. Make sure the bumpers fit around the entire crib and tie or snap in at least six places. Cut off any excess length from the straps or strings so that the baby will not chew on them. Remove bumpers as soon as the baby stands up. They can offer a foothold for climbing up and out of the crib.

Sheets. You will need at least three fitted crib sheets—one for the bed, one for the drawer, and one for the laundry. When the baby is still immobile, small flannel-fronted plastic pads are also useful for protecting parts of the sheet from the baby's face and diaper area.

Crib Extenders. When your baby gets taller, you can place these handy extensions on the side rails of the crib in the hopes of preventing him from climbing out. Generally, children who reach 33 inches in height should be put in a regular bed to sleep.

Safe Use of Cribs

Never place a crib near a window where cords from blinds, shades, or curtains could strangle a baby. Don't hang stringed toys or mobiles over the crib within reach of the baby. These, too, can strangle.

Portable Cribs

Portable cribs are smaller and lighter than full-size cribs. They come in two styles. The wooden ones look like regular cribs; those made with metal frames and fabric or vinyl resemble playpens. Portable cribs have some advantages. They can be moved from room to room—through doorways—and can be folded to fit in the car trunk for travel. They range in weight from 11 to 30 pounds. Unfortunately, they also have many drawbacks. Not all are regulated under federal safety standards. Many have flimsy floors and finger entrapment hazards. Choose carefully and continue to check the crib often. Following are points to consider.

• **Wooden Portable Cribs** are bulkier and heavier than mesh cribs. They do, however, offer different positions for the floorboards, including a diaper-changing height that can be very handy. Check to make sure that the floorboards are sturdy and that there are no gaps between panels that could trap a tiny finger or toe. Instead of drop sides, these cribs have a hinged, spring-operated, fold-down section halfway up one of the sides. Check this for ease of use and strength. The mattresses for these cribs tend to be thin foam with vinyl covering, which may tear easily and need to be replaced.

• **Metal-Frame Mesh Cribs** fold in a variety of ways. Some have hinges like playpens. Others require that you first assemble a lightweight frame and then mount the crib's fabric in place. The drop sides on some mesh models present a suffocation danger. If you inadvertently leave the drop side in the down position, the baby *could* roll into the pocket created by the loose mesh and the floor of the crib. On some models, the sides aren't rigid, and a strong baby or toddler may be able to pull them down into a sagging position and climb right out. Check the mesh often for tears. A baby can get a button or even a tooth caught in a mesh hole.

• **Usage.** Don't use these cribs for anything but sleeping. They are not made to double as playpens for the active and awake baby. Never leave the side down on mesh models because the baby could get trapped and suffocate. Keep large toys out once the baby can stand and, of course, keep the crib away from windows and long cords on shades, blinds, or drapes.

Beware of Crib Toys!

Eager to stimulate their baby, parents often hang mobiles and crib gyms over the baby's bed. These are fine for the immobile baby, but once she can get up on her knees and reach them, she can become entangled. Take them down at that point. Don't leave stuffed animals with features that the baby could pull or chew off in the crib with her—or any large toys that could offer a foothold up and out once she is standing.

• CHAPTER 9 •

Bathing and Clothing

Bathing Your Newborn

Some parents actually enjoy bathing their newborn. For others the bath can be a nerveracking ordeal. For these people, not even twenty Red Cross baby-care courses or hospital demonstrations could dispel the fear that their floppy, slippery, tiny baby will slide through their fingers and onto the floor. If you or your baby don't feel comfortable with baths at first, or if you don't have time to give your baby a daily bath, don't worry about it. It is not necessary to scrub the baby from head to toe every day. What is crucial, though, is to keep the diaper area meticulously clean.

When you do give the baby a bath, remember that if the baby screams, which is perfectly normal and natural, it is not because you are incompetent. It is probably because he does not like the insecure feeling of being unwrapped. After all, he's just spent nine months in a body-temperature environment.

The bath is a good opportunity for a father to get involved with some hands-on, down-and-dirty baby care. A man's hands are often bigger than a woman's, which can make it easier for him to hang on to the baby in the famous football hold (see illustration on page 120).

Getting Organized with the Right Supplies

The bath will go more smoothly if you get everything organized and within reach before you undress the baby. It's easiest if these supplies are kept in one basket, box, or pan. Don't rush. Allow yourself plenty of time to give the baby a bath. If the phone rings, ignore it, or wrap the baby in a towel, pick him up, and take him along to answer it. *Never* leave him unattended.

Question: *When is the best time to give the baby a bath?*

Answer: The best time is a short time after he's had a meal, so that he's neither hungry nor so full that he's likely to spit up from the handling and the excitement.

What to Have on Hand
- mild soap
- tearless baby shampoo
- fine-toothed baby comb
- soft washcloth
- cotton balls for eyes (optional)
- towel, preferably a hooded baby towel
- skid-proof surface to line tub or sink (a towel or rubber mat)
- clothing
- diapers
- diaper-rash ointment if needed
- blunt nail scissors

How to Give a Sponge Bath Until the Navel Heals

Choose a warm, draft-free location and a waist-high surface (a kitchen or bathroom counter or tabletop). Have everything ready before you begin. Place the baby on a towel or a large baby-shaped sponge, and have a tub or bowl of warm water nearby if you aren't near the sink. Some newborns panic when they are completely naked, and if this is the case, keep the baby's diaper on when you wash his top and an undershirt on when you wash his bottom. This is sometimes referred to as "topping and tailing."

1. *Face.* Don't use soap on the baby's face. Start with the baby's eyes. Take a clean cotton ball and dip it in warm water. Gently wipe from the inside corner of the eye outward. Do the same for the second eye, using a fresh cotton ball. Don't forget the creases under the baby's chin.

2. *Ears.* Ears clean themselves naturally, as do all orifices on the baby. Don't put anything smaller than your elbow into your baby's ears! *No Q-Tips!* Wipe the outer ear with a washcloth folded over your finger, and clean well behind the ears.

3. *Nose.* You can soften, then gently remove dried mucus from the baby's nose by using the corner of a damp washcloth.

4. *Arms and hands.* Be sure to wash in all the creases of the baby's hands, wrists, and elbows. These can collect an amazing amount of lint. Dry carefully.

5. *Back and neck.* Gently turn the baby over on his stomach and wash his back and neck, making sure you get into the neck creases. After you turn him back over, you can put his shirt back on if the weather is cool.

6. *Navel.* Don't wash with water until it is healed. Dab with a cotton ball dipped in rubbing alcohol several times a day. Be sure to fold the diaper, bikini style, below the navel so that it remains exposed to the air. When the navel is healed, it should be washed at each bath. You'd be surprised what accumulates there!

7. *Bottom and legs.* Be sure to wash in all the creases on legs and bottom, and dry thoroughly with a towel.

8. *Genitals (girls).* Gently spread the labia and wash with soap and water from front to back. There is usually a whitish, cheesy material that accumulates in the folds of the labia. This is perfectly natural and will go away on its own. It does not have to be scrubbed away.

Genitals (boys). Until the circumcised penis heals, do not expose it to water. Instead, keep it covered with a dab of Vaseline and a small sterile piece of gauze. Once healed, wash the penis as you would any other part of the baby. If the baby is not circumcised, there is no need to pull the foreskin back to clean the penis. It will clean itself and is best left alone.

9. *Head and hair.* You need not wash your newborn's hair more than once or twice a week. You can wash hair at the beginning or at the end of the bath. Use the sink for this. Before you shampoo, you may want to rub a little baby oil on the baby's head, then comb off any crusty material, which is called *cradle cap.*

To keep him warm and feeling secure, you might also want to wrap him in a towel so that only his head is bare. Hold him football-style (see illustration), or place him on his back on the counter by the sink. Apply tearless baby shampoo or plain, mild soap, and do not be afraid to scrub the fontanel—it is covered by a tough membrane. Rinse. If baby is on the counter, you need only rotate him, so that his head, supported in your hand, is over the sink beauty-parlor style.

10. *Fingernails.* Keep the baby's nails short so he won't scratch himself or you. Cut them when he's drowsy or asleep. Tiny babies have thin, almost transparent nails. If you put a little cornstarch under each nail, you will be able to see what you are cutting.

Using the Big Bathtub

Once the baby is sitting up well, you can use the big bathtub. You may discover that there is nothing better for holding his attention than water,

Football position, for washing baby's hair

the most available and the cheapest of all toys. A bath, as commonplace as it seems, is truly a learning experience for a baby. Think about the variety of sensations he gets from the water alone. There are the tactile pleasures—the temperature difference between the water and the air, and the sensual, free, semiweightlessness of his body. Water also provides some of the most dramatic evidence of cause and effect. Look at the power he has to influence his environment when he splashes, makes waves, blows bubbles, and pours. And if you have any doubts about his abilities to drink from a cup, give him one in the bathtub and see how he practices.

Before you begin, get all of your supplies together, preferably on the floor near you. If you sense that your baby might be overawed by the height and expanse of the big tub, and if you have been using a small plastic baby tub, start by putting it in the big tub. You will have to kneel on something soft and lean over the tub. Until the baby sits up really well you will need to keep the lower part of your arm across his upper back, cradling his head and supporting one shoulder as you wash him with the other in order to help him feel secure.

Bathtub Safety

- *Never* leave the baby alone in the tub. If the phone or doorbell rings, bundle him in a large towel and take him with you.
- Remove all objects such as soap, razors, and shampoo from the sides of the tub.
- Make sure that your water temperature is below 130°F or 55°C (see page 215 on baby proofing). Always turn off the hot water first, and then the cold, to ensure that any last drips are not hot ones.
- Consider installing nonskid bath stickers on the bottom of your tub for better traction.
- Tub spout covers will protect your baby's head should he slip and fall against the spout.
- Special bath chairs, which keep the baby in an upright position, can be handy, but they can provide a false sense of security. Again, don't turn your back or leave the baby unattended, even for a second.
- Finally, the bathroom is a high-risk area, so be sure that yours is thoroughly baby-proofed (see page 215 for suggestions).

Question: *What if the baby is frightened by the water?*

Answer: Don't assume that the baby will get past his fear if you keep trying. He'll only get more frightened. Go easy. Offer sponge baths instead. Don't try for a while. Babies change rapidly and forget their fears. In three or four weeks he will be much more "grown up" and may have forgotten his fear and feel much more experimental.

Parents Share Their Bath-time Tricks

Once the navel has healed, the baby can have a tub bath. By the time he is wiggling and kicking, the bath may become the highlight of his day. Parents elaborate.

I always undressed the baby, then wrapped her immediately in a towel to warm her up again before I put her in the water.

• • •

I found the kitchen or bathroom sink the most convenient place to give a tiny baby a bath. Special baby bathtubs, when full, are very heavy to lift and empty. They also aren't useful for very long and have to be stored someplace. Fill the sink with a couple of inches of water and test the temperature with your elbow or wrist. Your fingers are not an accurate gauge. Place a towel, a piece of foam, or a rubber mat in the bottom of the sink to provide traction. Add a couple of inches of warm water, being sure to turn the hot water off first. Then wrap the spigot with a towel or use a spigot guard so that the baby will not be hurt if you accidentally brush him against it. Then lower the baby in by slipping your hand under the baby's back, supporting his head with your wrist or arm, with the fingers of your hand crossing to the baby's armpit on the side away from your body (see illustration). This way you have the other hand free to soap and rinse the baby, one part at a time. A totally soapy baby is impossible to hold on to.

• • •

I gave Jessica a bath by placing her in her infant seat in the kitchen sink. This way I didn't have to worry about holding on to her. The seat was plastic, and it didn't matter if it got wet. Instead of the cushion, I used a towel to soften it.

• • •

Before I shampoo Vanessa's hair, I dab a little petroleum jelly on each eyebrow. This keeps the soap from streaming down into her eyes.

• • •

Cold shampoo can be a real shock to a baby. I warm the plastic bottle by immersing it in the bathwater.

• • •

I took Nickey into the tub with me. I had to compromise on the temperature, but in the middle of August this was no great sacrifice. Your legs are the perfect resting place for the baby. Just leave a thick towel on the floor by the tub to put the baby on before you get out.

• • •

I like the Tubby, which looks a little like an inner tube. I never had any fears bathing Karina in it. At ten months she still enjoys playing in it on a hot day. Because it's inflatable, it's easy to store or take to the beach.

The Safest Ways to Hold a Baby During Bath Time

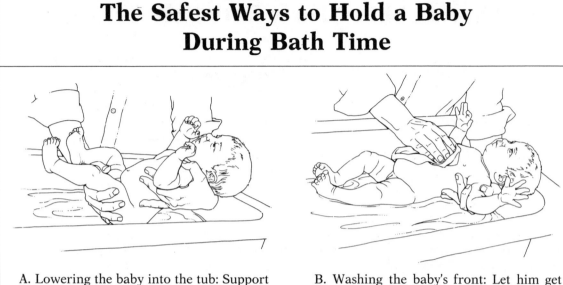

A. Lowering the baby into the tub: Support head and shoulders by keeping your thumb over the baby's left shoulder and your fingers under his arm; support his buttocks by grasping the left thigh with your right hand.

B. Washing the baby's front: Let him get used to the water for a moment before you begin soaping his front. Clean folds on neck, arms, legs, and crotch area. Rinse well.

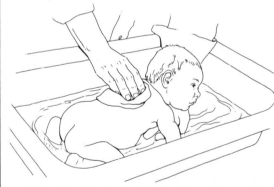

C. Washing the baby's back. Turn him on his back, supporting his chest with your forearm, and gripping his shoulder, soap his back and clean between the buttocks. Rinse well. You can lift him from the tub in this position.

D. The football hold for washing the baby's hair. Support the baby's head and body with your right arm and hand, tucking his hips and legs against your side. Use your left hand to lather the head; rinse thoroughly.

Clothing Your Newborn: Buyer Beware!

It is hard not to get carried away when picking out baby clothes. Because miniature shirts, dresses, and nightgowns are so appealing, it's easy to overstock. Late in pregnancy, who isn't driven by the need to be thoroughly prepared? But it really isn't necessary to buy *everything* at once. Control yourself. The baby's wardrobe should be based on your budget, the season of his birth, the gifts and hand-me-downs you receive, the time you have to spend caring for the clothes, and—most important of all—your access to a washing machine.

If keeping costs down is a priority, you will find that clothing sales are usually held in January, March, April, and July. Visits to thrift shops, the Salvation Army, and tag sales can also be very rewarding. Secondhand clothing is soft and comfortable and is past the point of shrinking and fading. For ideas on brightening up recycled clothes, see page 129. Diaper facts can be found on pages 124–128.

Facts and Opinions About Baby Clothes

The "average" baby will double his weight in five months, triple it in a year, and grow about eight inches in the first year.

I didn't have any friends or relatives with babies, so I put myself in the hands of a department-store sales clerk. I spent close to $150 on clothes, at least three of everything in yellow, white, and bilious shades of aqua. After Betsy was born, it took me about a week to figure out what was easy to get on and off her and what looked good. I put the rest away, so I wasn't reminded of my folly. To start out, I'd recommend buying a few really useful *things like stretch suits and front-opening T-shirts and, at most, one of each of the other things.*

• • •

If possible, control yourself. When people ask you what you want, tell them honestly. I wanted a good snowsuit. They are expensive, but two of my friends got together and gave me one. When you do buy, don't take your credit card with you! Take a set amount of cash to the store. Buy the least number of items on the list to start with, and just wait for the gifts to come in.

The True Story on Baby-Clothing Sizes

Age/Size	Weight Range	The Better Choice
up to 3 months	up to 10 pounds	6-month size
3 to 6 months	up to 14 pounds	12-month size
6 to 9 months	up to 18 pounds	18-month size
12 months	up to 24 pounds	24-month size
18 months	up to 28 pounds	2T (toddler)
24 months	up to 34 pounds	3T

Suggestions for Buying Baby Clothes

• When you buy baby clothes, skip the three-month size and start with six-month. Granted they will be a little big, but your baby will quickly grow into them. Always choose weight rather than age as a guideline.

• Choose clothing that provides easy access to the diaper area; preferably, the garment should open down the front. If clothes go over the head, look for large neck openings or snaps on the shoulders.

• Look for snaps and metal zippers. Plastic zippers stick when they get wet: tiny buttons are difficult to handle. Velcro seems like a great idea, but it wears out quickly with all the laundering baby items require.

• Aesthetic appeal and comfort are also important. Are the seams well constructed and soft? Check sleepwear carefully for rough seams and loose threads that can entangle tiny fingers and toes. Bright colors are hard to find for newborns, but they are certainly more interesting for the baby to look at. They also look cleaner far longer than pastels.

• Clothing with room to grow is practical. Look for tucks, pleats, and yokes that can be let out; plastic that stretches; cuffs that you can roll up; and hems and shoulder straps that can be let down.

• Unfortunately, baby-clothing sizes have not been standardized throughout the apparel industry. One six-month size may be so large that it fits a one-year-old; another might barely fit your four-month-old. The best way to get accurate sizes beyond the newborn stage is to take your baby with you and hold the piece of clothing up against her. When you measure your baby's height, make sure the baby is stretched out to her full length. Wash new clothing soon—even if it looks too big for your baby to wear at the moment. Some garments shrink quite a bit, and will thus be ready for use sooner rather than later.

The Layette

Basics

4 to 6 knit undershirts, T-shirts, or snap-bottom body shirts that won't ride up. An undershirt and a diaper are all a baby needs for comfort and freedom of movement in the summer. In winter a shirt will provide extra warmth under a stretch suit or a gown. Choose snap or tie-front-opening shirts for easy newborn changes. Over-the-head shirts are fine for the older baby.

4 to 6 stretch suits. My collaborators agree that the stretch suit is the best buy in baby clothing. A one-piece suit with front snaps from neck to crotch to toes combines the assets of booties, tights, and shirt.

Stretch suits can be worn day or night and stretch enough to fit all babies. You can even cut the feet out to make them last longer. Stretch suits are available in both summer and winter weights. The quality varies; you get what you pay for. If this is your first baby, and you are planning to have more, you might want to invest in the better-quality suits.

1 or 2 nightgowns. These long-sleeved, front-opening gowns are useful in cold weather and usually cost less than stretch suits. They are either sewn shut on the bottom or have a drawstring to "bag." (Buy only the latter for accessibility to the diaper area.)

1 or 2 blanket-sleepers. These are very useful once the baby starts traversing the crib at night. The blankets will fall off, but the baby will still be warm in a blanket-sleeper. These come in two styles: bags for babies who do not yet stand up, and coverall designs with built-in feet for later. If you start out with a bag, invest in a "grow sleeper," which has tucks that can be let out as the baby grows.*

1 or 2 sweaters. These common gift items are useful, especially during transitional seasons. Look for tightly knit sweaters so that the baby's fingers don't get caught in the weave. If you choose a cardigan, periodically check to make sure that the buttons are sewed on securely. Winter sweaters that zip up the back and have hoods attached are very practical.

1 or 2 hats. A hat is a must. In summer, the entire baby, including the head, should be kept out of the direct sun, so choose a wide-brimmed hat. Unfortunately, almost all baby hats have strings that tie under the baby's chin. They hate this! A good winter baby hat is a knitted "helmet," basically a bag with a small opening for the baby's face, like skiers wear—no strings to tie and then have untied by the baby.

1 or 2 pairs of booties. There is one well-designed type that won't fall off—the one with an elastic in the back of the heel and a tie around the front. Knee socks are a good alternative or supplement to booties in the winter.

1 bunting or snowsuit. A bunting is a bag with sleeves made of snowsuit fabric. It is a luxury

---

* Many parents favor all-cotton sleepwear for their babies, reasoning that this is the most natural and absorbent material available. They may also turn to all-cotton because they remember the dangers of TRIS, a flame retardant used between 1972 and 1977 on children's synthetic sleepwear. It was discovered that TRIS was carcinogenic, and it has since been banned. Many people don't know, however, that cotton itself is quite flammable, and that is why cotton children's sleepwear is not available in this country. It should be reassuring to know that since February 1978, all children's synthetic sleepwear must meet flammability standards *without* containing chemical flame retardants.

item because a baby who is still small enough to put up with bagging can be wrapped in a blanket. A bunting is inconvenient if you use a front pack carrier or a car seat. Some convert into snowsuits. Buy one of these, or skip the bunting altogether and put the money into a good snowsuit. A snowsuit that is easy to get on and off is crucial for your sanity in the winter. Optional snap-on mittens and feet are also very useful for babies who have the ability to pull off mittens and don't yet wear shoes. Look for fabrics that are not too slippery; it's hard enough to hold onto a wiggly baby as it is. Also look for zippers that the salesperson swears are infallible.

Overalls. These are for later, so you needn't purchase them right away. By the time the baby starts crawling around the house, stretch suits won't provide enough knee padding or warmth on cold floors. Two to four pairs of overalls with snap crotches are very useful. They come in two designs—a coverall with buttons or snaps at the shoulders, which tend to stay on the round shoulders of the baby, or the old-fashioned style with bib front and straps, which tend to fall off the baby's shoulders. The latter, however, are more practical because the buttons can be moved down the straps as the baby grows taller. If you twist the straps several times to make them shorter, these overalls will not slide off the baby's shoulders. Some parents choose only solids, so that the overalls match a variety of print shirts.

Items That Look Great
but Aren't Too Useful

Kimonos. These mysterious garments look like long bathrobes. They can be worn with the opening either down the front or down the back, the theory being that if the baby is lying on his back, the kimono is worn with the opening down the back and is spread out and away from the

diaper area, so that it doesn't get wet. When he's on his stomach, the kimono is worn with the opening down the front. Long before the baby outgrows this garment, however, he will become an active wriggler and kicker. A kimono bunches up and gets in the way because it is so long.

Sacque sets. These two-piece suits have a short, front-opening top and matching waterproof-lined pants. They are common gift items and are usually quite dressy. But they are quite useless in cold weather unless you put tights on underneath, which makes changing the baby a more complicated process than most of us wish to get involved in on anything other than special occasions.

Towels and Linens

2 or 3 receiving blankets, useful for swaddling, as a light covering, or a portable changing surface
3 crib sheets
1 or 2 waterproof pads
1 blanket or quilt (wait for the gifts!)
2 hooded terry-cloth towels
2 baby washcloths
1 dozen cloth diapers to be used as burping pads, changing surfaces, etc. (optional)

Question: Should I wash new baby clothing before I use it?

Answer: Yes, it's a good idea. Most clothing has been treated with chemicals, some of which remain in the fabric permanently, some temporarily. Most of these are not harmful, the possible exception being a chemical containing formaldehyde, used to give permanent-press qualities to nearly all the cotton and rayon clothing on the market. Since the negative effects of formaldehyde have been discovered, the amount used in fabric has been significantly reduced.

Nevertheless, some people are sensitive to even small amounts, which are almost entirely removed after a few washings. You will also definitely want to wash the all-cotton items because they may shrink. Otherwise, you won't know their true size.

Changing Tables

If you plan to buy a changing table, there are three basic styles to choose from: wheeled, folding models with baskets for clothes and diapers; railed, wooden tables with open shelves; and fold-down or hinged adapters for the top of a dresser. If none of these appeals, you can change the baby on a pad or small mattress on the floor. Even more practical and convenient is making a changing area on top of a dresser or table. Cover a piece of thin foam with vinyl for a soft surface. Hang shelves for diapers above. Keep clothing below in drawers. If you are buying a dresser for this purpose, choose one with drawers that slide easily. This is important for your own convenience as well as for that of your child, who will eventually be taking her own clothes in and out of the drawers. Other convenient features are a towel rack for hanging towels and clothes, and as a support and distraction for the baby when she insists on standing; a paper-towel or toilet-paper dispenser; a mirror (to distract the baby); and a laundry bag hung from hooks at the end of the changing table.

The most important features of a changing table are sturdiness and stability. Look for a table with some weight and a wide stance. Shake it. When your baby is older and crawling, and pulls himself up to stand by holding onto the table, you don't want it to tip over. Of the three types, the fold-down version is the least desirable. If the baby is placed on the outer edge, the entire dresser can tip, bringing the baby down

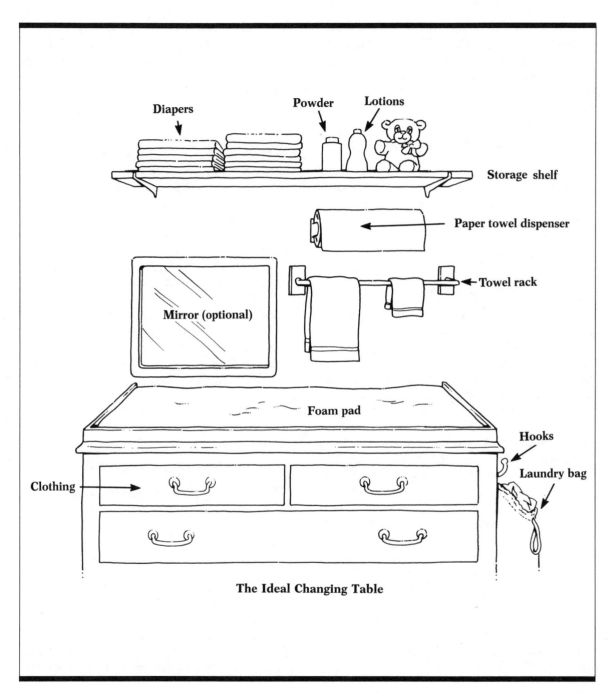

The Ideal Changing Table

with it. Other safety features include a safety strap as well as a guardrail or edge around the table; the higher, the more protective. Though open shelves under the table are more convenient than the rather deep baskets, they are also more accessible for a crawling baby.

Safe Use of Changing Tables

Babies unexpectedly fall off of changing tables all the time. Never leave the baby unattended, even with the safety belt in use. Gather up what you need ahead of time. If the phone or doorbell rings, take the baby with you.

Everything You Ever Wanted to Know About Diapers

Diapers are a huge part of your baby's wardrobe. If you aren't a pro at putting them on to start with, you will be within about a week. It is mind-boggling to realize that you will change between six and seven *thousand* diapers before your child is toilet trained. A newborn will use up to twelve or thirteen diapers a day, putting the weekly amount somewhere around one hundred. Fortunately this amount lessens as the baby gets older.

There are three approaches to diapering. The least expensive and most time-consuming is to own your own diapers and wash them. A diaper service is the middle-of-the-road approach. Disposable diapers make up the luxury route. You can, of course, combine all three; many parents do. Some decide to use a diaper service for the early months, disposables for outings, and then buy cloth diapers and launder them until the baby is toilet trained. By far the greatest number of parents opt for the convenience of disposables for the duration.

If you decide to use a service, choose one *before* your baby is born. If you decide to start with disposables, it's still a good idea to have a dozen or so cloth diapers on hand. They are useful in emergencies, can double as towels or burping pads, and can be used to keep portions of the baby's bed and your lap dry.

Cloth Diapers

Cloth diapers are by far the most economical approach to diapering a baby. You will need about four dozen. Besides the fact that this will cost about a third of the price of disposables, it makes sense ecologically. Biodegradable disposables are now on the market, but their manufacture still depletes forests. One wonders, too, where all the nonbiodegradable diapers go. The answer is to the landfill—and they make a lot of landfill!

Cloth diapers come in three types of fabric: cotton gauze, bird's-eye, and terry cloth, widely used in England. The styles also vary: flat, pre-folded, or fitted. My collaborators seem to prefer the prefolded, gauze kind because they are the softest and require the least work. See "Coping with the Laundry" on page 128 for suggestions on washing diapers.

Diapering Accessories

Pins. You will need several pins, preferably with strong metal locking heads. Pins with plastic heads are fine as long as they are reinforced with metal. The pins that most often hurt babies are those with plastic ducks and rabbits on the heads. They can chip apart and scratch the baby. To keep pins sliding easily, poke them into a bar of soap left in its paper wrapper, so that the soap flakes don't scatter.

Clips. It takes a practiced hand to use a diaper clip, but once you master it, it's fast, and you will never poke the baby or yourself by accident.

Warning about Powder and Diaper Wipes

According to the American Academy of Pediatrics, baby powder, oils, and lotion serve absolutely no medical purpose. Powders, if inhaled, can also cause pneumonia. If you do decide to use powder, choose a cornstarch rather than a talcum base, or use plain cornstarch. Don't shake the can over the baby. Instead, pour a bit on your hands first, then rub it onto his skin. Remember to close the cap. Never let the baby hold the can.

When choosing a diaper wipe, avoid those containing alcohol, which dries a baby's skin. Inexpensive alternatives are warm water and soap, a moist washcloth, or paper wipes cut into four sections. These can be washed until they wear out.

Keep pins and clips in a safe place. They are swallowable.

Diaper covers. These wool covers, modern versions of the old-fashioned "soakers," are worn over cloth diapers instead of plastic pants. They absorb moisture rather than trap it next to baby. Many come with Velcro closures so that diapering is quick—the ads say "a ten-second job"! Buy half a dozen to start with.

Rubber pants. Start with half a dozen. These prevent leakage onto a baby's clothing and bedding, and your lap. But they keep the baby wetter than diaper covers because moisture that might otherwise evaporate or be absorbed into the baby's clothing is trapped, increasing the likelihood of diaper rash.

The best pants are made of soft nylon, which doesn't get stiff with repeated washing and drying. Dry at low heat.

Diaper liners. A diaper liner can be useful for reducing wear and tear and staining on cloth diapers. After you fold the diaper, place the liner inside, then pin the diaper together. These also cut down on rinsing.

Diaper ducks. These are hooks that attach to the back of the toilet seat. You attach the diaper to the hook, flush, and then use it to wring the water out before you put it in the pail.

Diaper pails. Consider buying a diaper pail with a foot-operated pedal to keep your hands free. Also look for a comfortable handle (full pails are heavy!) and an efficient pouring spout. A medium-sized pail will be easier for you to carry when full. These hold between thirty and forty diapers. Some have compartments designed to hold the deodorizing cakes. Numerous injuries are caused by diaper pails. Children have been known to drown in them as well as suffer from eating the cake deodorizers. Look for a pail with a locking mechanism. Otherwise, once your baby starts crawling, keep the pail out of reach.

A Plug for Diaper Services

If you want to save time, a diaper service can give you several free hours a week that you would otherwise spend washing, drying, folding, and carrying heavy diaper pails. Diaper services use special soaps, bacteriostats, and rinsing agents that insure against bacterial buildup or soap residue from washing to washing. Diaper services also usually provide newborn diaper sizes, a boon to any new mother who has never diapered a baby before. Services are more cost-effective than most parents realize, only slightly above the cost of owning and washing your own. There are more diaper services than ever as parents have become more conscious of the ecological and cost benefits.

Disposable Diapers

Disposable diapers dominate the diaper scene for the obvious reason that they are very convenient. They eliminate work, time, and equipment. The biggest drawback is that they are expensive. Look for an absorbent, well-fitting product that won't leak.

Regardless of what the directions say, don't flush these diapers, especially if you have a septic tank. When you put them in the trash, fold them so that the plastic layer is outside and seal them in plastic bags. A study done by the Environmental Protection Agency showed a significant number of intestinal and polio viruses in the stools of babies recently immunized with live polio vaccine. This can be a real hazard for sanitation works and for animals as well.

Question: *Are ultraabsorbent diapers safe?*

Answer: Ultraabsorbent diapers have crystals embedded in the padding that form a gel when wet, and it is this gel that prevents urine from contacting the baby's skin. The absorbent material is the same one used in ultraabsorbent tampons, which were suspected of causing toxic shock syndrome. TSS bacteria thrive inside the body. Diapers are worn on the outside of the body. The official word according to the Centers for Disease Control, the Consumer Product Safety Commission, and the U.S. Food and Drug Administration is that there is no link between ultraabsorbent diapers and TSS.

Diapering and Dressing Tips from Parents

Be sure to comparison shop for disposables. It is worth it. Go to the supermarket, department store, and discount store and check the prices. I buy in the next state and save on taxes.

• • •

We buy our diapers by the case, and we use the least expensive brands. Try these at different ages.

Preventing Diaper Rash

Wet and soiled diapers are the primary cause of diaper rash in babies. If rashes persist, check your diet if you are nursing and check the baby's diet for possible sources of irritation or allergy. The acid in fruit juice, for example, can be an irritant. Prevention, however, is the best approach to diaper rash. Change wet diapers often. If the baby has had a bowel movement, obviously change the diaper as soon as you can. Wipe with a warm wet washcloth, then rinse with warm water. Dry thoroughly. If the baby does develop a rash, try a baking-soda soak using 1/2 teaspoon baking soda per gallon of warm water. Also, leave the baby diaperless for short periods of time when practical.

Desitin or A and D Ointment© are both good products for relief of diaper rash. If diaper rash persists, contact your doctor. There are certain kinds of fungi that you cannot clear up without prescription ointments (see page 240 for treating diaper rash).

Four Ways to Fold a Diaper

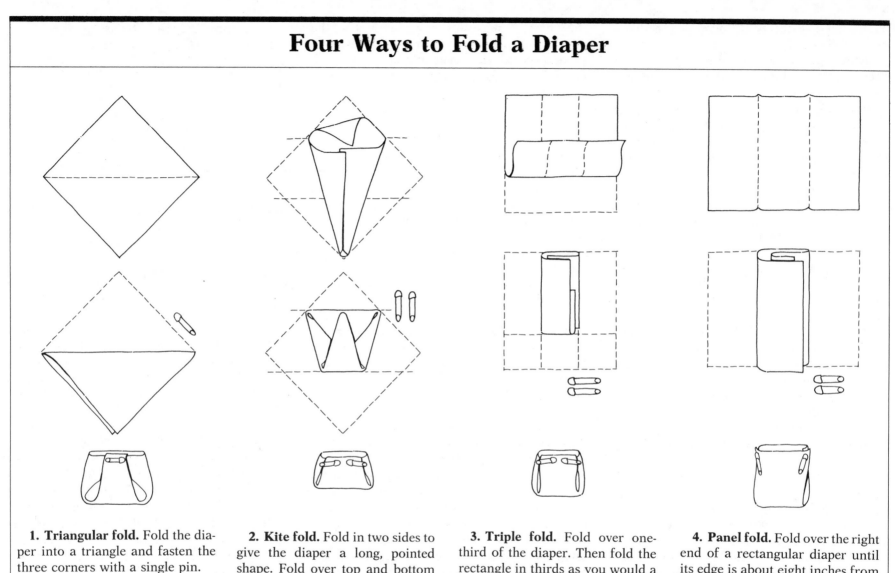

1. Triangular fold. Fold the diaper into a triangle and fasten the three corners with a single pin.

2. Kite fold. Fold in two sides to give the diaper a long, pointed shape. Fold over top and bottom flaps; secure with two pins. This method provides a thick center panel.

3. Triple fold. Fold over one-third of the diaper. Then fold the rectangle in thirds as you would a letter. Fasten the diaper with two pins. The extra thickness should go at the back for girls and in the front for boys.

4. Panel fold. Fold over the right end of a rectangular diaper until its edge is about eight inches from the left edge. Flip the right end back over itself about three inches, then fold the left side over to meet the far right edge, as if you were closing a book.

For instance, the newborn generics in one store were not very good, whereas the toddler size were. The most expensive are not necessarily that much better.

• • •

I clip coupons, save proof-of-purchase symbols, and watch for sales. I've also asked all my friends and relatives who don't have babies to save their coupons for me. This way I hardly buy any at full price.

• • •

Change the baby often. Highly absorbent paper diapers are deceptive. They don't seem wet, so you don't change them as often as you should, and then the baby gets a diaper rash.

• • •

I bought three dozen irregular or "seconds" in diapers and they have worn very well. I've thrown out only one after a year's use.

• • •

I use cotton terry-cloth diapers and Biobottoms. I would never go the pin-and-rubber-pants route again. I recommend buying one or two of each style diaper cover to determine which fit your baby best and which are easiest for you to use on a wiggly baby before investing in more.

• • •

I use diaper liners with my cloth diapers. I throw away the poopy ones, but the wet ones go right into the diaper pail and get washed along with the diapers. This way I reuse them several times.

• • •

I put the changing table in the bathroom because there was space. It is warm in the winter, and I can easily dunk dirty diapers in the toilet, and have the sink for warm water.

• • •

I hung a set of three-tiered wire baskets over the changing table for diapers, ointments, and T-shirts.

• • •

I don't use a changing table. Instead I use a small mattress on the floor. It's safer, and it's good exercise for me to get up and down.

Dressing the Baby

Dressing a newborn feels awkward. Most of us approach the task quite gingerly, wishing we had an extra pair of hands to hold up that wobbly little head, help guide those tiny fingers through narrow sleeves, and at the same time keep the baby covered. (Newborns don't like to be naked!) Following are a few suggestions from mothers to make dressing babies of all ages easier.

I use the changing table for diapering the baby but have found that he cries less if I cuddle him on my lap to change his shirt. This keeps him warm and makes him feel secure. When you are using a pullover shirt, stretch the neck wide and lift it over the back of the baby's head without touching his face. Then work on each sleeve. I put my hand down the sleeve, grab his hand and pull it up through the sleeve. This is easier than trying to stuff a little hand down a narrow sleeve.

• • •

Hang a safe baby mirror behind the changing table. You'll get lots of mileage out of it. You can play all sorts of fun games like "Who is that beautiful baby in the mirror?"

• • •

When Lally got into the really wiggly stage, she rolled off the changing table when my teenage sitter was dressing her. The girl turned for one second to pick up the powder that fell on the floor. It is second nature to me to keep a hand on her at all times, but remember to caution your baby-sitters. Or you can put a quilt on the floor and change the baby there.

• • •

I always sing and play with Samantha when I dress her. I blow on her stomach, I count her toes, I kiss her on the nose and generally have a good time. We both love it.

• • •

Don't always put clothes on your baby in hot weather. My baby Kevin is very sensual and loves to be naked.

• • •

I keep a small toy basket hung on the wall by the changing table, and I hand her a toy to keep her busy. I rotate the contents so that she is never bored.

• • •

I give up! Mark at ten months is so wiggly at this age that it's a battle to dress him. I now try to dress him as he stands in his crib. At least it's safe.

• • •

Snowsuits are an effort to put on, especially over the baby's feet. Try putting a largish plastic bag over the shoe. The snowsuit will slip right on. Then immediately put the bag away to safeguard against suffocation.

Question: *How do you know how much clothing to put on the baby?*
Answer: A good rule of thumb is to dress the baby the way you would dress yourself. If it is hot, remember that it takes a while for the newborn's sweat glands and pores to start working efficiently. He'll probably have some odd-looking blotches already. Overdressing him may give him prickly heat as well. If you are wearing a sundress and sun visor, a sunsuit and hat with a big brim are fine for your baby. Remember, too, that a baby's skin burns easily. Sunscreens are not recommended for the first six months, so cover him well in light clothing. His head especially needs protection from direct sun if he's

going to be exposed to it for more than a few minutes. Put a sun visor on him, or a hat with a big brim.

Until babies are about six months old, they can't yet shiver—to let you know they are cold as well as to generate more body heat. Be sure to cover the baby's head because a bare head loses body heat. Layers are also the most practical and versatile way to provide the right amount of warmth. When you put the baby in the car, simply peel off the outer layer and the hat.

Snowsuits with built-in mittens and feet will help to keep hands and feet warm but remember that they will never be as warm as the rest of his body. A pediatrician will assure you that this is nothing to worry about (see chapter 18, especially pages 193–194, on mobility).

Coping with the Laundry

I never knew what laundry was until I brought Jack home from the hospital. It amazes me that one 6-pound person could make a task I never gave a moment's thought to into such a big job. I now kiss the ground that my washer and dryer sit upon!

How to Wash Diapers

Wash diapers at least every other day. Here is one tried-and-true method that works:

1. Rinse and wring out dirty diapers in the toilet, then collect them in a diaper pail containing one of the following: a diaper-soaking product; 1 teaspoon of Borax (not boric acid!) dissolved in 1 gallon of water, or 1 to 2 tablespoons chlorine bleach to a gallon of water. These substances will fight bacteria that produce ammonia and will help remove stains.

2. Pour diapers and soaking solution into your machine and set the dial to spin out the excess liquid (this is the final spin on most washing machines). Then set the machine for soak or prewash. Add detergent.

3. To complete the wash, add more detergent and chlorine bleach, and set the controls for hot wash and cold rinse. Water temperature should be at least 140°F.

4. If you want to give diapers an extra rinse, use the permanent-press cycle. Some parents add ¼ cup of vinegar to the final rinse to cut detergent residue. If you wish to use fabric softener, add it to the final rinse. Use it sparingly, however, because it tends to reduce diaper absorbency.

Miscellaneous Laundry Tips

Once your baby starts eating solid foods, the laundry will take on a new aspect. Following are some suggestions for stain removal:

• **Vitamins and medicine.** Treat these with an enzyme presoak product or rub detergent directly onto the stain. Wash in hot water using chlorine bleach and detergent.

• **Baby food and spit-up.** Soak garment in cold water. Rub detergent into stain while still wet. Wash in hot water using chlorine bleach. If the garment can't be bleached, soak it in warm water and an enzyme presoak product.

• **Formula or milk.** Soak garment in cold water, then wash in hot water using chlorine bleach. Try enzyme presoak if the garment can't be bleached.

• **Fruit juice.** Soak garment in cold water first. If that doesn't work, soak it in warm water with an enzyme product.

• **Mystery stain removal.** See page 129.

Secondhand is Beautiful (A Story)

When Anna was three months old, I began to feel like I was going stir-crazy. I felt confined to the house because of the cold weather, tired from her night waking, and very lonely. I still hadn't adjusted to a nonworking life and missed the routine and friends from my old job.

A La Leche leader put me in touch with a neighborhood woman, Judi Weber, who had a baby, Justin, near Anna's age. Judy, an ex-stockbroker, had recently opened a recycled clothing store for infants and toddlers. She had rented a small storefront and initially stocked it with clothing from thrift shops and the Salvation Army. She also took in some new, handmade items from local women—tie-dyed shirts and crocheted hats, bags, and sweaters. Used toys and larger pieces of baby equipment like cribs, high chairs, playpens, car seats, and rocking chairs were also sold on consignment.

Once the store had been open for a few months, Judi started a credit system by which parents could trade their children's outgrown clothes for credit to be used toward 50 percent of a new purchase. With this incentive, there was always plenty of inventory and turnover. Nothing cost more than $4 or $5, and many items went for less than $1.

I was delighted when Judi offered me a job two afternoons a week. I was able to bring Anna with me, which was good for both of us. In the back room she and Justin took naps in a playpen and Port-a-Crib (also available to customers when not in use). The floors were carpeted and baby-proofed for crawlers, and we never had to worry about the secondhand toys remaining perfect. Anna and Justin became close friends over the months and were seldom bored with each other or the customers.

Budget Baby had a lot to offer parents as well.

Because we encouraged browsing and talking, the store soon became a meeting place. We had a comfortable old porch swing where mothers could nurse and rock their babies, sit and talk, or eat their lunches out of paper bags. A bulletin board had information on baby-sitting, day care, playgroups, pediatricians and clinics, exercise and Lamaze classes, and current newspaper clippings. Eventually Judi stocked some books on baby care and nutrition and gave a psychologist friend use of the store to run a group for new mothers one evening a week.

My salary wasn't large, but I really enjoyed using my imagination to renew some of the old clothes that came in. When I'd worked full-time all those years before Anna was born, I hadn't had the time to knit, crochet, embroider, and sew, and I felt great using these skills again.

But more important, the store helped me to make new friends with women in the community. The playgroup that Anna has belonged to for over a year is made up of Budget Babies, and the cooperative nursery she'll go to the following year grew out of parents I met through the store as well.

As for myself, the work at the store convinced me that I enjoyed business and might even be successful with my own enterprise.

I've recently finished an evening course in running a small business and am thinking about opening a health-food store and restaurant geared mainly for children. I think every neighborhood would benefit from a place like Budget Baby. Does your community have one? (Bette Lacina)

Shoes

Question: *Why are stiff, high, hard-soled, difficult-to-put-on shoes made for babies?*

Answer: There is no good reason. Babies do

Tips for Secondhand Clothing

If you borrow or buy secondhand baby clothing, you will save a tremendous amount of money. Baby clothes are worn for such short periods of time that they tend not to wear out the way an older child's clothes do. The clothing might not be perfect, however.

- If snaps aren't working properly, give the stub of the snap a gentle tap with a hammer. Then try snapping them again.
- Use empty disposable-diaper boxes to store outgrown baby clothes as well as hand-me-downs for future use. The diaper sizes on the box makes them easy to identify. No labeling is necessary. Add a fabric softener square to keep the clothes smelling fresh.
- Here is a recipe for a "home-brew" fire retardant, which you might want to use on handmade sleepwear that is not made with fire-retardant fabric:

9 ounces Borax
4 ounces boric-acid solution (available at your drugstore)
1 gallon warm water

Combine all three ingredients. Soak clean clothing in the solution until it penetrates the fabric thoroughly. Dry as usual.

- Mystery stain removal for when all else fails and you're *determined* to remove a stain: Spread stained material over a bowl of boiling water. Apply a few drops of oxalic acid solution (1 teaspoon of crystals, available at a hardware store, dissolved in 1 cup of water) to the stain. Rinse quickly and very thoroughly by dipping into hot water.

not need ankle support; if they did, nature would have provided it.

Because a baby's feet provide as much sensory stimulation as his hands, it makes no sense to cover them up unnecessarily. Babies do not need shoes until they walk outside, and then shoes that simulate bare feet are best. Sneakers are a good choice. They provide good traction, they are flexible, and are cheap. If you buy inexpensive shoes, you are much more likely to replace them at the right time, which should be every two to three months.

After a baby is standing and walking there's a real value in leaving the child barefoot most of the time when conditions are suitable. The arches are relatively flat at first. The baby gradually builds up the arches and strengthens the ankles by using them vigorously in standing and walking. . . . When you always provide the baby with a flat floor to walk on and always enclose the feet in shoes (with their smooth insides), especially if the soles are stiff, you encourage the child to relax the foot muscles and to walk flatfooted.
— Benjamin M. Spock and
Michael B. Rothenberg
Dr. Spock's Baby and Child Care

How to Find Shoes That Fit

• Always take the baby with you to the shoe store, so he can try on the shoes. He's much more likely to be relaxed if you, rather than a stranger, hold him and put the shoes on him.

• Socks are important for the fit of the shoe. If you are buying winter shoes, bring along a pair of heavy socks for fitting.

• After putting on both shoes, let the baby walk around the store so that you can see if his walk is normal.

• Make sure there is ½ inch of space beyond the longest toe and a baby finger's width at the heel. Feet grow in both directions. If you can't feel the toe space, the shoe is too hard and inflexible.

• Request extra, longer laces, which will make it easier for you to tie the necessary double bow.

· PART FOUR ·

Living with Motherhood

• CHAPTER 10 •

Postpartum

Understanding the Changes

Most of us live through the postpartum period, the six-week to three-month period during which our bodies return to their prepregnant state, without fully grasping the dramatic physical and emotional upheaval we are experiencing. After birth, your body undergoes as many physical changes as it did during pregnancy, but they occur more rapidly, and far less attention is paid to them. While a pregnant woman turns inward with a new awareness and sensitivity to each development, once the baby is born, he takes center stage.

The postpartum period is also a time of far greater *emotional* stress than pregnancy. Besides coping with the rigors of childbirth and the constant physical and psychic demands of newborn care, a new mother has just made the greatest maturational leap of her lifetime. To help manage this dramatic period, know what is happening to your body and put it into perspective as you take steps to ensure and maintain your health. We all know that our physical well-being

is connected to our emotional well-being. Now that you are someone's mother, the stakes are even higher.

Question: What changes does the body undergo during the postpartum period?
Answer:
Hormonal activity. During pregnancy the placenta produces very high levels of estrogen and progesterone, which keep the baby attached and nesting in the uterine wall. After the delivery of the placenta, hormonal levels drop dramatically and immediately while the level of prolactin, the breast milk–producing hormone, increases. The level of the hormone produced by the thyroid gland also drops to a point below your normal pregnancy levels. The endocrine system will remain out of balance as long as a woman is nursing. Because of the unusually high levels of prolactin and the lowered levels of estrogen, there will be a decrease in vaginal lubrication, which can be alleviated by using a lubricant such as K-Y Jelly. Though there is no definitive medical evidence, it is

commonly thought that these abrupt drops in estrogen and progesterone are connected to the mood swings characteristic of postpartum blues (see page 141).

Menstruation. The nonnursing mother can expect to have a period six to eight weeks after the birth. The nursing mother, because she maintains high levels of prolactin, may not have a period for six months to a year. Prolactin tends to suppress the action of the ovaries, but this is *not a reliable form of birth control!*

The uterus. Once the baby is born, the uterus begins its dramatic transformation from a 2-pound organ back to a 2-ounce organ. This change takes place over a six-week period. The reduction of the uterus to its prepregnant size— *involution*—occurs in a couple of ways. The muscles contract to clamp down on the open blood vessels where the placenta had been attached to the uterine wall. These contractions, or afterpains, prevent hemorrhaging and are strengthened if you breast-feed. The baby's sucking stimulates the production of oxytocin, which triggers the let-down reflex as well as these uterine contractions. Involution also occurs through the shrinking of the uterine muscle cells as protein within them is metabolized and sloughed off through the urine.

The lochia. This vaginal discharge, a combination of blood, mucus, and uterine tissue, will continue for three to four weeks after birth. The lochia starts out a bright red. After three or four days it begins to change color, becoming a paler pink, then yellowish or white. In the first day or two after delivery, you may experience a gush of discharge as you stand up. This is normal.

Though hemorrhaging is rare, it is life threatening. Any of the following symptoms should be reported immediately to your doctor: a temperature above 100°F; excessive bleeding that fully saturates more than one sanitary pad an hour for more than a couple of hours; large clots in the lochia; a foul odor to the discharge, which may mean infection; bright red bleeding after the fourth day (as opposed to a blood-tinged discharge, which is normal).

Urine function. Irregularity in urine function is common in the first twenty-four hours after birth. One reason is that you may have been allowed little to drink during labor. The hospital staff will monitor you carefully to make sure that you void within eight hours after birth. If you do not, you risk a urinary tract infection. If you are unable to urinate, you may have to be catheterized. Try to avoid this by taking an extra long walk to the bathroom, having a big drink of water, turning on the faucet, sitting down on the toilet with one or both legs elevated on a stool (this position puts pressure on the bladder), and spraying your perineal area with warm water. Once you get past these early efforts, you will find that you probably have to urinate frequently as your body relieves itself of excess fluids, including the 30-percent increases in your pregnancy blood supply. Regardless of whether or not you

are nursing, drink plenty of fluids to purge your body of wastes and toxins. Once at home, if urinating is painful or difficult in any way, or if you are running a low-grade temperature, you may have a urinary tract infection and should be in touch with your doctor.

Bowel function. After childbirth, it is normal for your bowels to be sluggish. If you had an enema before birth and little to eat afterwards, there's not much to move. The abdominal muscles that assist bowel movements can be weakened and stretched from the strain of childbirth. To add insult to injury, you may have hemorrhoids that hurt when you push. Concern about tearing your stitches is probably the most inhibiting fear, and it is hard to believe that it is unfounded. *But it is.* It also doesn't help that moving your bowels requires spending "forever" in the hospital bathroom, which someone else may need for the same purpose. Drinking lots of fluids will help, and so will eating lots of fresh and dried fruits (especially prunes and raisins), raw vegetables, and whole grains, including a little bran added to your cereal. If you are really desperate, ask for a stool softener.

The perineal area. The network of muscles surrounding the vagina, anus, and urethra will be tender, swollen, and stretched after birth, whether or not you had an episiotomy. The Kegel exercise (see The Episiotomy; Care of Stitches, p. 135), a warm sitz bath, hot compresses, ice packs, or chilled witch hazel on a sterile wipe or gauze pad should offer some relief.

The cervix. It will be about four weeks before the cervix, stretched open by the baby's head, closes. Until it does, the uterus is vulnerable to infection. This is why intercourse and the use of tampons, douches, and vaginal sprays are forbidden until after the postpartum checkup.

The breasts. Whether you plan to nurse or not, your milk will come in two to four days after

your baby's birth. The hard, hot, painful swelling that you experience in your breasts is caused by a combination of increased blood circulation, the swelling of the tissues, and the pressure of the milk. If you are nursing, frequent feedings, warm compresses, and a well-fitting bra will help. If you are not planning to nurse, your doctor may prescribe hormones to dry up the milk. A growing number of doctors, however, believe that it is better for milk production to decline naturally. They suggest a mild pain reliever to help ease the discomfort. In any case, the worst should be over in a day or two. Many women wonder if nursing will change the shape or size of their breasts. The fact is, any permanent changes are the result of pregnancy, not nursing.

Hair. During pregnancy hair grows faster than normal because of your increased level of hormones. It also doesn't shed as fast. Some women end up losing a good deal of hair four to six months after the baby is born. This loss can be alarming, but it is perfectly normal—the hair had an extra long life and was overdue to be shed. The losses should stop within a month or so.

Skin changes. Some women develop a brown line from the navel to the pubic bone and/or darkened areoli during pregnancy. On others, dark patches will appear around the cheeks, forehead, and nose. This "mask of pregnancy" should disappear within a month or two after the birth. Sun will exaggerate the discoloration, so be sure to wear a sunscreen containing PABA. There is also some evidence that these patches may be caused by a folic acid deficiency, in which case your doctor may recommend a supplement, available in capsule form. Rare is the woman who escapes stretch marks on her abdomen or her breasts. After several months these will fade to white and shrink, but they will never totally disappear. Rubbing your skin with lanolin, vita-

The Episiotomy: Care of Stitches

Most women have an episiotomy with their first vaginal delivery. It consists of a small cut between the vaginal and anal openings to enlarge the birth ring and prevent it from tearing. While some women experience the healing as a mild discomfort and inconvenience, others describe their stitches, especially if accompanied by hemorrhoids, as among the least pleasant aspects of childbirth. They wonder if they will ever be able to walk, sit comfortably, or make love again. But the stitches will feel better with each passing day, and within about two weeks, most new mothers find themselves forgetting to sit down gingerly. In the meantime you can minimize the discomfort in several ways:

- Always wash your hands before you use the bathroom.
- Change sanitary napkins often. When you do so, be careful not to pull the pad from back to front, bringing germs from the rectum toward the vagina.
- To avoid infection, it's important to rinse the perineum with plain water or an antiseptic solution recommended by your doctor after urinating or having a bowel movement. Most hospitals provide new mothers with a simple plastic squirt bottle. When you are done, pat yourself dry, again being careful not to work from back to front. Continue to use this procedure when you go home.
- Heat is also an excellent treatment because it helps relax the muscles and stimulate circulation. A simple reading lamp will work, but a sitz bath may be more relaxing. Fill the tub with a few inches of warm water. Elevate your legs over the side for twenty minutes, two or three times a day. Or take hot showers with the spray directed on the perineum.
- If you have hemorrhoids as well, don't use the heat lamp, but the warm-water treatments mentioned above will help, and so will cold witch hazel compresses.
- The Kegel exercise will help strengthen the stretched pelvic floor and increase circulation to help repair tissue. This exercise may be familiar to you from childbirth preparation classes. To locate the right muscles, spread your legs apart while you are urinating, and try to stop and start the flow. Your ability to do so is an indication of your muscle tone, which after a vaginal birth may be minimal. Tense and relax these muscles a few times to the count of five on the first day, and build up gradually to as many as you like.

min E oil, or vegetable oil may help to smooth and soften them, but beyond this nothing helps save a good suntan.

Varicose veins. If you suffer from these during pregnancy, you will find that they will usually shrink, then disappear after birth. Walking and performing a few toe-pointing movements whenever you have a chance to sit down will help. So will elevating your legs a couple of times a day.

Perspiration. *Diaphoresis,* or profuse sweating, is another of the body's ways to eliminate excess fluids after childbirth. It may continue for as long as a week or two. Be sure to drink plenty of liquids to assist this process. Monitor your temperature if you keep sweating heavily once you are home, and call the doctor if it goes above normal.

A Plug for Walking

Walking is an excellent way to get back into shape. The benefits are immediate: It improves body tone; helps take off weight, and reduces tension, anxiety, and blood pressure—all of which make us feel more positive. Take the baby along in a stroller or a Snugli. She will be soothed by the motion and gently stimulated by the fresh air and the new sights and sounds. Try to find another mother with a baby to walk with to make your outings even more enjoyable.

Postpartum Exercises and a Pep Talk

We all know the important role that exercise plays in getting back into shape, but let's face it, most of us find it rather difficult to get motivated. What mother swamped with the pressing demands of a newborn has time to think about herself? The truth, however, is that your muscles will never be quite the same unless you do some exercises. Back problems caused by weakened abdominal muscles during pregnancy only increase after delivery and grow progressively worse as you bend and lift a baby who grows heavier and more active with every passing day. Just as important, exercise affects your mental health. Motherhood means giving of the self to another human being. But to do that, you have to replenish yourself. If you think of exercise as something you deserve to give yourself, maybe it won't seem like one more thing you *have* to do. Following are some routines that are safe to do before your postpartum checkup. Many will be familiar if you participated in childbirth-preparation classes.

The Kegel exercise. This exercise, in which you contract and release the muscles of the pelvic floor (see The Episiotomy; Care of Stitches, page 135), will continue to benefit you for the rest of your life. It can be done in almost any position—reclining, sitting, or standing—so it is easy to make it part of your daily routine.

The pelvic tilt. Lie on your back with knees bent, feet on the floor, and hands at your sides. Press the small of your back against the floor and hold this position to the count of five. Work up to doing ten of these.

Knee to chest. Lie on your back, clasp one knee with both hands, and pull the leg toward your chest, stretching the other leg out. Hold to the count of five. Release the leg, then repeat with the other leg. Work your way up to ten on each side.

Double knee to chest. Lie on your back, grasp both bent legs, and pull them down to your chest as you raise your head toward your knees. Work up to ten times.

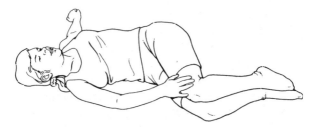

Knee drop or trunk rotation. Lie on your back with knees bent and both feet on the floor. Drop both bent knees to the right and press the left leg down with your right hand, keeping your left arm on the floor at a right angle to your body. Hold the position for several seconds. Return to the original position, then repeat in the other direction. Work up to ten times, alternating on each side.

Lower back stretch. Stand with your feet shoulder-width apart and knees slightly bent. In a rolling motion, bend forward and down, stretching your hands toward the floor. Hold the position for several seconds, being careful not to "bounce." Do this twice.

Weight Loss After Childbirth

The moment you have been waiting for has finally arrived! You've met your baby and examined her from head to toe. You've nursed, diapered, and held her as she fell asleep in your arms. Now she's safely tucked away in the newborn nursery as you await your first visitors. There is time to steal a moment and head down the hall for the scale near the nurse's station. After what you have been through, you are confident that you have surely lost a lot. Even if you still do look five months pregnant, you feel like a sylph compared to the way you felt a few days ago. You find the scale, climb on, and begin to move the weights. Up and up they slide. How could it possibly be? Only 10 pounds! Something is the matter with the scale. This should be taken care of immediately! Where is the head nurse? Here is what you can expect to lose and when.

7 pounds	The "average" baby	
1½ pounds	Placenta	in the delivery room
1½ pounds	Amniotic fluid	
2 pounds	Other fluids and blood	one week postpartum
3 pounds	Surplus fluids	
2 pounds	As the uterus shrinks	six weeks postpartum

17 pounds total
The rest is fat stored for nursing.

Now what? If you gained only 20 or 25 pounds, you are well on your way to sylphdom by six weeks postpartum. But if you gained 35 or 40 pounds, which shows up as a thickened waistline and larger buttocks and thighs, you can feel pretty discouraged. Despite what some books would have you believe, and despite the fact that breast-feeding consumes around 500 calories a day, losing weight isn't easy for everyone.

It used to annoy me to read about new mothers who bounced right back into shape after giving birth because I certainly didn't. I wanted to be thin again, but it wasn't that simple. For one, I was nursing and had a ravenous appetite. I was also very tired and strung out. I used to look great when I went to work. But now, who was I? It was as if the baby was gobbling me up. I felt like I was giving all the time. I think what happened was that eating became a way to take care of myself.

Question: *What is the best way to lose the weight gained in pregnancy?*
Answer: Slowly and sensibly, concentrating on high-energy, high-nutrient foods and avoiding those with empty calories like sweets and junk foods. The breast-feeding mother's body has adapted in such a way that she conserves iron and absorbs calcium with maximum efficiency. The nonnursing mother, however, must make a special effort to pay attention to these nutritional needs after delivery and should ask her doctor about taking an iron as well as a calcium supplement. Exercise, which speeds your metabolism, will not only help speed weight loss but will also make you feel more energetic and optimistic (see page 136).

Tips for Preventing Back Problems

She weighed only 8 pounds at the time. I was kneeling and leaning over and twisted to pick her up when something happened to my back. I'd suffered from backaches during pregnancy and assumed that this was normal. I didn't do any postpartum exercises because, realistically, who has the time or energy? I hardly had time to take a bath, no less exercise. To make a long and painful story short, I was literally flat on my back for eight days, and on medication to reduce the horrible pain. I had to find someone to take care of both of us because my husband had to go to work. I felt so vulnerable and aware that I couldn't afford to be helpless now that I am a mother.

Bend at the knees when picking up baby

Suggestions

• Pay attention to the way you move. Go through bend-and-lift routines such as putting the baby into the car seat, or lifting him out of the high chair, in slow motion in order to analyze the motion and correct it if necessary.

• Never bend from the waist without bending at the knees. Avoid any position in which your back is arched.

• Carry the baby high and close to your chest rather than on your hip.

• Never twist your body to lift or lower an object or the baby. Face it squarely. This is hard to do when you are putting the baby in the car seat or bathtub, but try!

• When you are seated, it is generally restful for your back if your knees are higher than your hips and your lower back is firmly supported. If you are standing for a long time, while cooking for instance, you can give your back a partial rest by placing one foot up on a low stool. You'll also find a rocking chair restful because the back-and-forth motion gently stimulates and realigns the group of muscles in your lower back.

Correct position: Carry baby high, close to your chest

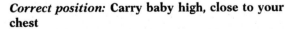

Incorrect position: Do not carry baby on your hip

Side bends. Stand with feet shoulder-width apart and both arms at your sides, facing forward. Bend slowly to one side, hold for a few seconds, then straighten. Repeat on the other side. Raise your arms over your head with hands clasped and repeat. Work your way up to ten times, alternating each side.

Curls. Lie on your back with knees bent and both feet on the floor. Cross your arms over your chest and, while exhaling, lift your head and shoulders until the bottoms of both shoulder blades nearly clear the floor. Inhale as you slowly drop back to the floor, then lift again, exhaling as you come up. Work up to ten curls.

Your Childbirth Story— Telling It Over and Over

Childbirth is one of the most significant passages in a woman's life. With it we enter a new era. During those brief but intense hours, as one mother puts it, "We literally change species." Each woman emerges from childbirth not only with a baby but with a jumble of feelings—from pride, self-confidence, and sheer joy to exhaustion bordering on confusion, a sense of letdown, or even outright disappointment. It takes time to assimilate the events and the emotions, to put them into perspective, and then move on. One way women do this is to tell their birthing stories over and over, to practically anyone who will listen. Talking is useful and important, but consider writing your story as well. The benefit of writing your tale when it is still fresh in your memory is that you will have a permanent record that both you and your child will cherish. On each birthday in our family I find myself reflecting on that child's birth, when our shared life together began. In the back of this book you will find a space for your childbirth story (see page 274). If you don't like to write, consider tape re-

cording your story as you tell it to someone else. Then transcribe the tape. If you wish, use the following questions as guidelines:

• Where were you, and what time was it, when labor began? How did you recognize what was happening?
• How long did the labor last?
• Who was there during the labor, and were they helpful?
• Did you have a sense of what your needs were, and were you able to communicate them?
• How did you manage the labor? What techniques worked best? Were you given medication, and how effective was it?
• What was the actual moment of birth like? What did the baby look like, and how did it feel to meet him?

Cesarean Postpartum

The cesarean mother is experiencing all the normal postpartum feelings and adjustments as well as those resulting from having undergone major abdominal surgery. The rate of recovery varies from woman to woman and depends partly on the type of anesthetic used. If you had a spinal block, you will have to lie flat on your back for eight to twelve hours and will probably have a headache. An epidural will wear off in less time, but if you have had general anesthesia, you may be in a fog and remember very little about the first twenty-four hours postpartum. No matter what kind of anesthesia you've had, when it wears off, your incision will hurt. You will be given painkillers, which will pass into your breast milk in amounts too small to harm your baby. There is no need to be a martyr and refuse this medication.

The cesarean mother will be asked to cough

and blow into a bottle to help expand her lungs and keep them clear of fluid. A pillow on the abdomen will help minimize any discomfort during this procedure. An IV and catheter are standard, and the hospital will carefully monitor fluid intake and output, along with blood pressure, temperature, and pulse. Trapped gas can cause considerable pain, and until your bowels show signs of awakening, you won't be allowed to eat. After twenty-four hours, some liquids are permitted. By two or three days postpartum a new mother has usually made a full transition to a regular diet. Constipation is also normal. Raw vegetables, fresh and dried fruits, whole grains, bran, and fluids will help.

Although it may seem impossible at first, some women—depending on their progress and the hospital's policy—are encouraged to get up and walk within eight hours of delivery. In case you feel weak or become dizzy, a nurse will help you, first to sit up and then to get to your feet. It will be hard to stand up straight, and as you walk bent over in painfully slow, "baby" steps, you may envy the speed and agility of the women who gave birth vaginally. But don't despair. By the time you leave the hospital, within four to seven days, you will be moving easily.

You may also have some psychological discomforts. Childbirth classes have taken some of the mystery out of the cesarean delivery, and hospital aftercare is more supportive than it used to be, but a cesarean can nevertheless be a shock and a letdown to a woman who imagined a different kind of birth. Other new mothers, high on their triumphant deliveries, may inadvertently underscore her disappointment with their blow-by-blow labor tales. It is important for the cesarean mother not to deny any feelings of loss she may have. But she must also remember that her delivery is no less of an achievement than anyone else's. She, too, is a heroine.

There can be other subtle conflicts. After a cesarean, a mother needs care and must depend on others for help. Dependency can be uncomfortable, though, when your expectation is to be a competent and giving nurturer to your baby. For example, a cesarean mother may question whether her need and desire to sleep at night mean that she is self-centered or lacking in "maternal instinct." The challenge here, as with all of motherhood, is to know that taking good care of yourself does not mean that you're neglecting your baby.

On the positive side, a cesarean can provide the new father with an opportunity to become much more involved with the baby than he might otherwise have been. If he can spend time in the hospital room, he can help with many things the mother will not be up to at first. He can bring the baby to and from the nursery, diaper, hold, and cuddle him, give him a bath, offer the bottle, and burp him. If his wife is nursing, his extra hands can help position the baby on her breast. A father who is a competent and confident true partner in his child's care from the very beginning is likely to remain one in the future.

Once home, the new mother needs to devote all of her energy to recovering and to caring for her baby. Help with cooking and housework during the first week will allow her to do this. There is no need to lie prone in bed all day, but you can simplify the logistics of caring for the baby by camping out in one room. You can feed, diaper, and put the baby to sleep on your bed. Use a small crib pad or towel for a changing surface. Keep diapers, wipes, or a small bowl and container of water nearby. Have healthy, high-energy snacks and drinks and a telephone at the bedside, and don't say no to offers of help.

All New Mothers Need Rest, But . . .

The new mother is told, "Be sure to get the rest you need!" but this well-meaning advice can seem like a bad joke. How are you supposed to do it? The demands of motherhood, unlike those of most other jobs, don't end after an eight- or even a ten-hour day. They continue for twenty-four hours a day, seven days a week. A more useful and realistic approach might be to understand exactly how loss of sleep affects us. That way we can temporarily put aside some of the more unrealistic expectations we may have of ourselves and be more accepting of our limitations. This is half the battle. The other half is believing that you won't be this tired forever. It just feels that way!

Question: What are the effects of sleep loss?
Answer: If you don't feel like your old self and can't quite seem to organize your day, untangle your bank statement or find anyone's jokes very funny, you may be suffering from sleep deprivation. Researchers have proven what we might already know: Sleep deprivation can make people irritable, humorless, paranoid, and sporadically enraged. It affects spontaneity, originality, and the ability to deal with unfamiliar situations, and causes us to become more rigid in our thinking. Instead of developing creative solutions to problems, we tend to stick to known ways of doing things. Perhaps most difficult of all, sleep deprivation affects REM or dream sleep cycles, which are crucial for processing information and feelings that barrage us when we're awake. Our dreams help repair the psyche from the wear and tear of consciousness, and we rarely need this rebuilding more than when we are new mothers. At what other time in our lives are we bombarded with more new information, about

which we have very complicated feelings, than at childbirth?

Question: *How can I squeeze more "rest-time" into my day?*
Answers:

• Enlist the help of your husband and other volunteers to care for the baby. Don't think that you have to do it all. Baby care is learned, not instinctive. Newborns will accept comfort from others. The only reason mothers become so skilled is that they get so much practice.

• Take the phone off the hook, and nap whenever you can. Lost sleep does not have to be made up measure for measure. When research subjects are deprived of REM or dream sleep, their naps consist of more REM sleep and have far more restorative value than comparable periods of regular sleep.

• If you have trouble falling asleep, try a snack such as milk, cheese, poultry, peanut butter, or oatmeal, all of which contain L-tryptophan. When this essential amino acid enters the brain, it changes into serotonin, a natural tranquilizer. Warning: Do not take L-tryptophan in pill or capsule form. It has caused severe side effects in some people.

• Don't obsess about being too organized or efficient. You may know other women with babies who strike you as having it all together. Assuming they really do—appearances can be deceiving—they have probably had several months of practice.

• During the postpartum period, rely on conveniences you might otherwise consider luxuries—disposable diapers, paper plates, take-out food, etc.

• It may be hard to believe, but babies grow and change. There *will* be a time when you are no longer so tired. The dizzying fatigue you may feel now is like the pain of childbirth; at some point you'll hardly remember it.

Coping with Postpartum Blues

Many women experience some kind of mild depression shortly after birth. Typically the "blues" manifest themselves as sudden bouts of crying or sadness, anger or irritability, a general frenziedness, sometimes even a mild paranoia or an irrational feeling that no one, but no one, cares.

These feelings generally last about two days and disappear as mysteriously as they come. It has always been thought that the "blues" had some connection to the tremendous drops in estrogen and progesterone and the triggering of the milk let-down reflex by yet another set of hormones that follow delivery. Studies have shown, however, that adoptive mothers and even some fathers experience postpartum blues. The hormonal upheaval is probably only one of many contributors to the emotional volatility a new mother feels. Among the others are the anticipation of labor, the fatigue after childbirth, lack of privacy in the hospital, the continued interruption of sleep, and the growing awareness of the unrelenting responsibilities of parenthood.

Because the birth of a baby is generally considered a joyful event, especially when it is much wanted and planned, these "negative" feelings can be quite unsettling. It is bad enough to feel a little blue or down in the first place but even worse to be hard on yourself for feeling this way. The best way to deal with the blues is to allow for them and to express your feelings without embarrassment or guilt.

Mothers Describe the Blues

I'd been perfectly fine, happy, and all until the second day, when they brought my dinner to me in the hospital. I lifted up the little dome that keeps the main course warm. My food was covered with ice crystals. They'd forgotten to microwave it. I burst into tears. I, of course, took this personally.

• • •

I was so high after the birth that I couldn't sleep the first night. I couldn't stop holding my baby and admiring her, and talked incessantly about her birth to anyone who would listen. Two days later when I was at home I got on the scale, then looked in our full-length mirror. I was really depressed. I looked about six months pregnant. My back hurt and I was still in my nightgown at 2:30 in the afternoon. But the worst was that I looked at Eleanor, who had finally fallen asleep on our unmade bed. She already had dirty fingernails and white pimples on her cheeks! She was a mess. I was a mess. I started to cry.

• • •

I cried a good deal on and off for the first few weeks. It wasn't always sadness, though. I cried because it felt good to let go of all the feelings I was having—of joy and love and gratitude. Every time I thought of my own mother I also cried. I think I wanted her to be with me, even though Bill was at home and being very helpful.

• • •

I felt very mortal, very fragile, yet also somehow part of the continuum of it all. On the one hand, I wanted to survive because I was strong and had to take care of this tiny, helpless baby, but I also knew she would go on living after David and I. This didn't depress me so much as it moved me and unsettled me.

• • •

I was filled with what they call "free-floating anxiety." You know, something awful is going to happen.

• • •

I was bone-tired and frayed. I heard a funny joke, and laughed and laughed and laughed. Then I suddenly burst into tears.

• • •

I felt bad about my irritability at Fred. He was being so incredibly wonderful and helpful, cooking, cleaning, taking over, so I could sleep. He went to Bloomingdales to get me a nursing bra, and I yelled at him when it didn't fit.

• • •

I was in a fog. I couldn't seem to plan how to get from here to there and when. Should I take her out now to the library, in the carriage or the Snugli or wait until the afternoon, but what if she was sleeping then? Is it okay to wake her? What if she cries outside and people think I'm neglecting her? And on and on. Everything seemed like a big, big deal.

How to Recognize
True Postpartum Depression

On rare occasions we hear news stories about women who have attempted to kill their newborns and/or themselves as well. Three to ten days after birth they may have manifested some of the symptoms of the blues as well as delusions, hallucinations, either extreme depression or mania, and/or a tendency toward violent behavior. Such women are suffering from a severe form of postpartum depression called *puerperal psychosis* and need immediate psychiatric care.

Most postpartum depression is not characterized by such dramatic symptoms. It often comes on slowly and insidiously as a general depression, sometimes during the second part of the first year. A mother may feel sad, lonely, and hopeless, or as if very little matters. She may also have bursts of anger and a loss of interest in anything pleasurable, including sex. Also common are feelings of inferiority and severe guilt or

anxiety over just about anything that goes wrong. These bleak feelings can be accompanied by such physical symptoms as head-, stomach-, or backaches, decreased appetite, diarrhea, constipation, nausea, panic attacks, insomnia, low self-esteem, even periods of forgetfulness or mild confusion. The mother may also find herself escaping into alcohol, drugs, or excessive eating.

Most women experience some of these feelings in response to the chronic stress of new parenthood (see next chapter). It is only when a group of these complaints come together that the disorder is given the name *adjustment reaction*. Unfortunately, most new mothers do not get help for an adjustment reaction. They don't know that life doesn't have to feel this way. They may also feel ashamed of their overriding "negative" feelings and embarrassed to acknowledge them. But depression, a disorder particularly common among women, can be treated with a high degree of success.

Depression is like looking though a darkened veil. It colors your entire world view and robs you of the true pleasures that exist. A new mother's depression is not an isolated phenomenon. It is also her baby's loss. Depression dulls that subtle, finely tuned responsiveness a mother needs to have toward her baby in order to read his cues properly and meet his needs. Her responsiveness contributes to the baby's perception of himself as a worthwhile and lovable human being. We need to keep that healthy and optimistic mother alive, not only for ourselves but for our children. Each baby carries a bit of us inside of him for the rest of his life. We want that part to be strong and positive.

Question: When does a new mother need help?
Answer: When a depressed mood *does not alter or lift,* or begins to interfere with a mother's ability to take care of herself and her child, she

Useful Books

Boston Women's Health Book Collective, Inc. *The New Our Bodies, Ourselves* (New York: Simon & Schuster, 1985)

Boston Women's Health Book Collective, Inc., *Ourselves and Our Children: A Book by and for Parents* (New York: Random House, 1978)

Burns, David, *Feeling Good: The New Mood Therapy* (New York: New American Library, 1981)

Eagen, Andrea B., *Newborn Mother: Stages of Her Growth* (Boston, MA: Little, Brown & Co., 1985)

Gold, Mark S., *The Good News about Depression: Cures and Treatments in the New Age of Psychiatry* (New York: Random House, 1987)

Hirschmann, Jane R., and Hunter, Carol H., *Overcoming Overeating: Living Free in a World of Food* (New York: Fawcett, 1989)

needs help. It is widely available. Your obstetrician, childbirth instructor, the social services department of the hospital where you delivered, or your family doctor can refer you to counseling services. Or you can get in touch with your local health clinic or family service organization, such as Jewish Family Service or United Way. The National Organization for Women (NOW) or Planned Parenthood can also make referrals, as can your local mental health association. If money is a problem, there are mental-health clinics where counselors see people on a sliding-fee scale.

• CHAPTER 11 •

The Transition into Motherhood

People will tell you before you have your baby that your life will change radically. They are right. What they really mean is that not only will your life change but also, and more significantly, so will you. The difficulty is that these changes are part of a continual process that is so deep, far-reaching, complex, and mysterious, that it is hard to grasp, no less communicate. Then, too, most people assume that the changes wrought by a tiny baby are unique to themselves. You know the syndrome: "If something as common and universally accepted and approved of as motherhood is this hard for me, then it's got to be *my* fault."

We have largely abandoned the myth that marriage consists of living happily ever after, but the myth still persists to some degree that mothering is, or should be, a self-fulfilling and joyous duty. This is not always so, especially in the beginning. The birth of our first baby pushes us to make the greatest maturational leap of our lifetimes. Within the hours it takes to push that baby out of ourselves into the world, we are transformed from being someone's daughter into being some-

one else's mother. There is nothing in our lives that can quite prepare us for that.

What does it mean to be a mother? It means giving in ways that we have never been asked to give before—truly putting someone else's needs ahead of our own. We must constantly extend ourselves—with our bodies, our minds, and our hearts—to be tuned and responsive, to interpret and fulfill the baby's needs for feeding, comforting, and contact, regardless of how we may feel. It means making a million small decisions that involve the heart as well as reason. Not just "Do I put this undershirt on the baby?" but "Can I possibly leave her in the care of a person who neither knows her as well nor loves her as much as I do?" It also means conquering many logistical problems, from getting to the grocery store and back before the baby falls apart to arranging care for a sick baby when you have to be at work. Becoming a parent means becoming an expert on and advocate for your baby, because nobody else is going to know or care in quite the same way you do.

As if this isn't enough, you may discover that

the supports you have formerly relied on and taken for granted can all change radically or even disappear: a marriage that functioned smoothly; perhaps a job that provided satisfaction, self-esteem, and monetary returns; a circle of friends and/or relatives who share interests and offer moral support; mobility, the freedom to come and go without thinking; and time—so much time—to think, to do what you want to do, to take care of yourself.

As women, we have far more choices today about our own lives and destinies than our mothers or our grandmothers had. We are the women who have the possibility of "having it all," both the love and work that Freud saw as the keys to mental and emotional well-being. While this broadened definition of womanhood feels full and rich, it also raises questions that create conflict and stress. The issue of work outside the home, be it a matter of choice or financial necessity, is central for many of us. If we go to work and leave the baby in someone else's care, will this harm the baby? And will it hurt us, too? If we work outside the home, a part of us mourns the loss of what we may be missing when we aren't there. A working mother also wonders if she is giving her job and her family the time, the thought, and the care that each needs and deserves, and can feel a low-level sense of dissatisfaction, guilt, or inadequacy on both fronts.

The woman who stays at home, either giving up a job or career or temporarily taking a break, can also feel a sense of loss. Will her job be there if and when she returns? Will her skills have diminished, and will she be able to perform competently and confidently? If she doesn't return, can she count on motherhood to feed her imagination, her creativity, and her sense of self-esteem? The mother at home sometimes feels that she has to be a supermom, and do "it" all perfectly to justify her position. She makes tremendous efforts to make use of every bit of free time productively, and may give herself no peace. If she stays at home, there may be a million projects she wants to tackle, but she may not be able to feel a sense of accomplishment when what she starts is seldom completed as quickly as she wishes it were. And then, what if anything does a "project" have to do with the rest of the world?

Being a mother can shake your confidence. It can mean wondering if you are still an interesting person. Whether you work or not, you may question your ability to be a "good mother." Being a mother can also be very lonely when you discover that the rest of the world doesn't necessarily value your choice and give you the recognition you deserve.

The rewards are so many. It's just that they are not quite as tangible as the sacrifices and are harder to articulate. The apparent limitations on freedom, for example, are part of a profound growth process that can expand your horizons more than anything else ever has. I've yet to meet anyone who doesn't feel she has grown, expanded, and matured through becoming a par-

ent. In terms of what you may have come to expect of your life, parenting is a high-risk undertaking. But any venture that promises great rewards must be risky. Though few of us slide easily into motherhood, we would never choose *not* to be that baby's mother.

Question: *What have the hard parts of motherhood been?*
Answer: *Mom can't write a note to get you out of this one!*

A: *I've changed. I used to be happy, playful, and full of life. I was like a little girl at thirty-one. Now I am a woman of thirty-one.*

A: *The responsibility is frightening. I am* totally *responsible for her welfare. She's* totally *dependent on me for all of life's necessities—for how long I don't yet know.*

A: *Everyone told me how wonderful I'd feel being a mother, but I didn't feel it for the first couple of months, and because of that I felt very guilty.*

A: *I've lost my mother-in-law's friendship. She keeps insisting we're spoiling the baby, that we hold her too much, feed her too often, and that we never let her cry. I have to bite my tongue. I do feel, though, that I have more of a common bond with my mother now and that we are more able to share our feelings.*

A: *I've realized how fair weather my so-called friends were. This is the first time I've ever been truly lonely.*

A: *When I did sleep at all I had nightmares that something was happening to Andrea like she was smothering, or someone had stolen her, or that*

she had fallen out of her crib. These really scared me.

A: *Having a baby is such a huge decision. It's a privilege to have the choice. But in some ways it makes it even harder. You postpone pregnancy; you don't think you're ready yet, because you're still trying to find out who you are. Another year goes by and another. You think about it a lot. You finally decide to go ahead, and make this rational choice to have a baby. During pregnancy you're a star. Life goes on as usual. You're well-fed, well-rested, well-exercised, and well-read. When you enter the delivery room, maybe you're even in control and on top of it. Then it's over. Suddenly you have no more choices, and you're out of control. There's no time to think about your identity. There's hardly time to brush your teeth!*

A: *The most difficult adjustment for me was becoming relatively inactive after working for nine years. I missed the stimulation I received from other adults while teaching. But basically I was in such a state of euphoria after his birth that I only started feeling these things after the first six months when life had become more routine. I also still find getting up at 5:30 frustrating. Who can ever accept that?*

A: *I never realized how incredibly difficult it would be to leave Ann with a sitter—as tired as I felt and as crazy as I was to get out. I haven't yet found one whom I feel 100 percent confident about.*

A: *Sometimes I feel a day is lost. Paul will come home from work and ask me what I've done today. Well, I haven't done anything except the usual. Sometimes I feel like nothing is happening. There are so few events in my life. It takes such discipline to create them!*

A: The biggest adjustment for me was not being told that I was doing a good job all the time.

A: I don't have time to think about my appearance. I take a shower every other day now. I do nothing to my hair.

A: Strangely enough, I have found the constant interference of strangers, or a loss of privacy, the most difficult adjustment. ("Is she too cold?" "Where are her mittens?" "Should she be out today?" etc.) People feel they have the right to criticize, comment, compare ("Isn't she walking yet?") when it comes to babies, whereas they wouldn't dream of doing this in any other situation.

A: The time adjustment is hardest for me. I know that I'm grabbing for time for myself so much that this sometimes destroys my pleasure in being with the baby. I wish I could let go, let her in more instead of being so afraid that she will engulf me.

A: I so much miss my own mother, who died two-and-a-half years ago, and wish she was here to talk to.

A: My self-esteem plummeted. I felt less competent all the way around. I used to run a department with twenty people in it. Now I don't know how I did it. I did have an interesting discussion with another woman, though. She felt that baby care was a right-hemisphere kind of experience (feelings, emotions, intuition), in battle with the other hemisphere (the exercise of logic, reason, etc.). When you have a baby, you're tuned in on a different level. Your hearing changes, your sense of touch changes, you sense things about a baby; a cry can affect your whole body—definitely left-hemisphere stuff. Your brain just simply isn't functioning quite the same way as before. And

maybe this is what has shaken my confidence. The part of me that had gotten tremendous satisfaction from being able to think problems through to completion is totally boggled.

Why Does Everyone Pretend It Is So Easy to Be a Mother?

I got pregnant by a man with whom I had no hope of a lasting commitment and continued the pregnancy mainly to please myself and my curiosity about this aspect of my femininity. I devoured anything and everything written about childbirth and geared my life around the moment that another life would emerge from my body.

Unfortunately, I paid zero attention to what I would do with that life once she came. The 2 A.M. feeding came as quite a shock, particularly since it followed on the heels of the 10 P.M. and the midnight feeding. Then we had similar get-togethers at 4 and 6 A.M. Bottle-feeding meant warming and preparing these feasts to the accompaniment of angry hunger cries.

In moments of exhaustion and despair I thought of giving her up for adoption. It was just too hard for me, and I was so alone. No matter what I was going through, there was little empathy for me. I felt that my family and friends were just waiting for me to fall on my face, and so I kept the pain to myself.

The pain at the thought of giving up my daughter far outweighed the pain of her constant care, and so I persevered. The first six weeks were the longest in my life, spent behind closed venetian blinds in a run-down low-income studio apartment. Somewhere around the third month I began to be able to distinguish day from night again. I opened the blinds and knew I'd made it.

Never again did I look at mothers the same way. I'd see a woman with three kids and be in awe as I wondered how she had gotten through the awful period of ceaseless crying and night wakings—three times. I'd look at friends who had older children and wonder why they hadn't told me that it was going to be so hard. Why did everyone pretend it was so easy to be a mother?

Being a mother enhanced my previously hideous self-image. After the early days of my daughter's life, I found myself reaching out to the world and accomplishing in her name and on her behalf. I joined whatever single-parent support groups I could find, returned to school and obtained my B.A., and I imagined all the while that people were saying, "Look at all she does while raising a child alone!" I pride myself on how far I have come since my initiation into motherhood.

A: I am not what I would describe as bored staying home with Timothy, but I am afraid that I am becoming a boring person.

A: The most difficult adjustment for me was to learn to accept imperfection and my own limita-

Advice to New Mothers on What New Fathers Need and Don't Need

Here are some important *don'ts*:

Don't belittle your husband's ability or his concerns about being a good father. Don't grab the baby away from him. Don't ever refuse to let him hold the baby because you're feeling angry or irritable with him. Don't oblige him to take care of the baby because you're angry with him. Don't ever talk to the baby about angry feelings toward your husband.

Don't undercut him. Don't make fun of him. Don't attack his insecurity. Don't carp. Don't do as you would not like to have done unto you by hospital staff, your mother, your mother-in-law. In this regard, do not use guilt as a weapon. For example, suppose your husband is with the child while you're out. If you come home and find your child with a runny nose, probably coming down with a cold, don't blame your husband. It's essential that you acknowledge whatever guilt you may feel for leaving the baby.

On the other hand, here are some important *do*s:

Do be understanding. Do be patient. Do compliment. Do encourage. Do try to keep your sense of humor and ability to laugh at yourself. Do attempt to point out those obvious positive aspects of the bond between your husband and the baby. Do attempt to make him aware of exciting changes as the baby grows and develops. Point out the unique ways in which the child looks like him. Indicate how good you feel about him and his involvement with the baby. Encourage him to play with her, to hold her and smile at her, to fondle and cuddle her. Encourage him to talk and sing to her and even to dance with her. Encourage him to have a special song to sing to her. Encourage him to participate in the baby's visits to the doctor with you. Encourage him to take walks with the baby. Emphasize how important his care of her is to you, how it gives you not only relief but much pleasure to see him enjoying her.

Remember that in encouraging your husband to care for the baby, you are like a teacher. This requires a great deal of energy, patience, and resourcefulness, as well as the crucial ingredient— humor.

—Martin H. Greenberg,
The Birth of a Father

tions: that is, to realize that I can't do it all myself as well as I would like to do it and to accept this about other people as well.

A: Lack of mobility was the biggest shock. A short trip eight minutes away to the grocery store requires real planning. I suppose this is temporary, and someday I'll have all the time I need. But when?

A: It's clear to me that along with the birth of your first child comes the implied dismissal of the child in you. Who's going to take care of you? The biggest adjustment for me was actually believing that I was a parent. Isn't that what it's really about for all of us?

Question: What are some of the rewards of having a baby?

Answer: The biggest reward has been that I have become a more flexible person. It has taken me a full eight months to learn to change my priorities and learn to be this way. I am now finally able to enjoy Lindsay and play with her without worrying about housework, cooking, etc.

A: I never really thought about my own values until I had a child. Then what is important in this life came into focus. For me it's my relationship with God and a clear perception of my own strengths and weaknesses.

A: I'm much more open now that I have Addie. I think she has given me a sense of purpose. Now I don't know how I got along without her.

A: I could not possibly have imagined the flow of love that keeps you going.

A: My baby has taught me more patience. I am more patient with myself and everyone else.

A: I always knew it was worth it, but the day Andrew and I had our first private joke confirmed it. I had just mopped up an unbelievably messy bowel movement—the fourth of the day. I don't usually let him go diaperless in cold weather, but I was sitting there in a state of despair on his bedroom floor, and he crawled away, pulled himself up to stand at the end of his dresser—then he peed. As I was thinking, "Oh, Andrew, how can you do this to me," he let out a scream of delight. He was so thrilled by the spectacle of his huge stream of pee going across the room and the sound it made when it hit the floor. He looked at me. He was waiting for a reaction. I started laughing. Then he started laughing, then he got down and crawled over to me, pulled himself up on my shoulder, and gave me a huge hug. I will always remember this as being the first time when I knew that he knew that I was okay. He was really communicating. This is the direct feedback that we all need, and when it finally does happen, what in the world is comparable? It's enough to make me cry.

A: Sara has given me a sense of fulfillment, a broadening. I am more assertive, more confident, feel more of an adult now that I have someone to protect, someone who depends on me.

A: There is no doubt that the birth of my son has cramped my freedom. But he has brought out that aspect of my character that is more sharing and patient and understanding.

A: I think having Eliot has sort of shaped me up a bit, made me more aware of responsibilities. Having someone depending on me for everything is a very sobering experience.

A: I feel that the baby has provided me with a sense of direction in that my day is pretty well planned out for me. If nothing else, it has taxed my sense of organization and my own creativity to think up interesting things for us both to do. I do see how important it is, though, to keep up my own interests.

A: I felt so powerful when I pushed Lauren out. I felt that that was my purpose on earth and that I couldn't do anything more important. My husband and I cried. She lay on my chest, looking at me. She seemed to know me and looked very calm and curious.

A: I think more of my mother and wonder how she raised ten children and still kept her sanity. With one baby I sometimes wonder how I will get by one more day.

A: I no longer have the "me-first" attitude. My child comes first.

A: I am a more physical person now that I have a baby—quicker to love and hug everyone. I'm also much more easygoing now. I enjoy singing and dancing, since I did so much of it with the baby.

A: I think I can understand much more about human survival just watching Dana as he struggles to master each new physical feat. He practices—and gets frustrated—and repeats something over and over again, until he can do it. One can't help but be impressed and inspired by that kind of determination, that energy and curiosity.

A: I am much more tender. I am easily and deeply moved by stories about any form of child neglect or abuse—though I'm clearer now on where that anger comes from.

A: I've learned to let go a little, which includes letting go of the baby a little each day as she becomes more and more of a person.

A: Having Natalie has made me more political, more in touch with my community. You do not have to be a card-carrying feminist to have your blood boil at the lack of good child-care resources in a city of eight million people. I've become a joiner after having been a loner for most of my life.

A: I have many new friends. We've actually met two couples with babies whom we like to spend time with.

A: You wouldn't believe how close I now feel to my own mother. She just strikes me now as being this truly great woman. I say to her "Mom, how did you do it? How did you raise five children without going bananas? How did you make each of us feel as if we were your favorite one?"

A: Having her really helped me learn the value of my own time and my own work. I don't waste my time now. I either do something or simply try to enjoy myself the way she does—wholeheartedly.

A: I feel like my own parents finally consider that I am an adult. They treat me differently now that I'm a mother.

A: I was happy to stay home after eight years at my job. I accomplished every goal set and then some. I was ready to shift my life in a different direction because I knew what I was capable of doing.

A: I love seeing this nurturing side of me. I didn't know it was there.

A: Ashley was our surprise package! I have four other children ranging from nine to sixteen. When I discovered that I was pregnant, to be honest, I was upset. I'm forty-two and had decided to go back to school in accounting and looked forward to reentering the work world. I knew that would have to go on hold, and I was disappointed. But what a gift she has turned out to be! I take my time with her very slowly and take none of it for granted. I know how quickly it passes. I hold her a lot. I study her perfection and appreciate the true miracle that she is. I say to myself, "I can't believe that this person grew inside of me"—as if I were a young mother for the very first time. One of the loveliest things, though, that has happened to our entire family in this brief six weeks that she has been a part of us, is that we have all created a much gentler place. There is less fighting and more tenderness. My older son said to me yesterday, "Thank you so much for having Ashley."

A: Rewards? It's obvious. The birth of your own baby is nothing short of a miracle. Loving and nurturing a child is an extraordinary experience!

Books and Resources on Fatherhood

The Fatherhood Project
Bank Street College of Education
610 West 112 Street
New York, NY 10025

The goal of this project is to "encourage the development of new options for male involvement in childrearing." Write for more information.

Greenburg, Martin, *The Birth of a Father* (New York: Avon, 1986)

Greene, Bob, *Good Morning, Merry Sunshine: A Father's Personal Journal of His Child's First Year* (New York: Penguin, 1985)

Sullivan, S. Adams, *Fathers Almanac* (New York: Doubleday, 1980)

Worth, Cecilia, *Birth of a Father: New Fathers Talk About Pregnancy, Childbirth and the First Three Months* (New York: McGraw-Hill, 1988)

Books on Mothering

Burck, Frances Wells, *Mothers Talking: Sharing the Secret* (New York: St. Martin's Press, Inc., 1987)

Heffner, Elaine, *Mothering: The Emotional Experience of Motherhood after Freud and Feminism* (Garden City, NY: Doubleday, 1980)

Kelly, Marguerite, and Parsons, Ella, *The Mother's Almanac* (New York: Doubleday, 1975)

Rich, Adrienne, *Of Woman Born: Motherhood As Experience and Institution* (New York: Norton, 1986)

· CHAPTER 12 ·

Babies, Sex, Power, and Marriage

Let's get something perfectly clear. A baby can wreak havoc on a marriage. Like all of life's significant passages, the transition into parenthood presents danger as well as opportunity. If you have a good marriage and nurture it with the love, care, caution, and concern that you do your baby, the relationship can grow and deepen in a way that it might never otherwise. But the opposite is equally true. A baby cannot save a bad marriage, because babies shake up, strain, and complicate matters, even under the best of circumstances.

Parents can become so invested in the joy the baby is supposed to bring to their lives that they fail to be realistic about the normal upheaval that follows. With the birth of a child, the couple must get to know each other in new ways, not only as husband and wife but also as the parents of that baby. Each partner is wrestling with many changes, both external and internal, that offer a tremendous opportunity for growth and intimacy but can also create emotional distance and upset along the way.

Babies almost always change a couple's division of labor, responsibility, and power—inside as well as outside the home. The marriage usually becomes more "traditional" and territorial in feeling. As equalized as male and female roles are becoming, women still tend to take on more care of the baby and home, while the man may feel more pressure to provide economically for his family, especially if his wife has stopped working. The loss of a second income can mean concrete sacrifices that cause stress. What money stands for may have to be reevaluated, too. If the couple can afford it, and the woman is home by choice, she may find motherhood rewarding in many ways but may still have to grapple with all sorts of feelings—from economic powerlessness, dependency, and loneliness to loss of self-esteem—that are new to her and will affect her marriage.

A new mother who works is also subject to stress. It may seem unfair, but she is probably suffering from the almost universal working mother's guilt while the father doesn't seem to worry at all about the effect on the baby of his working. The responsibility of finding and maintaining a satisfactory child-care arrangement usually falls on the woman. She most likely ends up staying home with a sick baby or giving up opportunities to assume more career responsibilities if it means being away from the baby more than she already is.

Most obvious of all, when a couple has a baby they have little time left over to work on their relationship, much less have fun. They may spend evening after evening at home together as a family—he cutting her meat as she nurses and eats a late dinner one-handed—and this may in many ways feel good and appropriate at this point in their lives. But there are fewer opportunities to be relaxed and spontaneous when it comes to affection and romance. And even if the opportunity does arise, who has the energy to pursue it? If you've had no more than three uninterrupted hours of peace for weeks on end, sleep usually outweighs passion.

Couples can also feel out of touch with the friends who were once a large part of their lives. The time may not be there. Just as likely, if the friends don't have babies or young children, you may discover—even if only temporarily—that you have little in common with them. Or they may conclude that you aren't available any more and, even if you are, you have changed to rather boring, baby-centered people.

The relationship with in-laws can alter as well. Now that they are grandparents, they may be more involved in the couple's life. This *can* be positive. Many new parents report a new closeness with and respect for these elders, whose love and support they see from a totally new perspective. But as parents, we may also see the negatives in our parents and in-laws more clearly. Rivalries may develop that never existed before between a new mother and her mother-in-law. This can put additional strains on a marriage.

Few of us, moreover, are aware of the power a baby wields to unearth a complex maze of deeply buried feelings from our own childhoods. Old longings, losses, and anger can surface. For a woman, childbirth can reawaken her own desires to be nurtured, touched, held, and taken care of, and in some cases to make up through the new relationship with her own baby for some lost part of the self that her own mother never provided. Falling in love with her baby is a powerful experience and may satisfy a woman's needs for intimacy in a simple, direct way that can be at odds with an adult erotic relationship, with its struggles to create an equal give-and-take between the man and woman.

A man may perceive his wife's intense emotional involvement with the baby as a rebuff. And he, too, may be experiencing deeply buried feelings from his childhood. Her nurturing of their baby can reawaken his old longings to be dependent and to be taken care of by his mother. No matter how mature, self-aware, and responsible he may be in his "real" adult life, it is normal for him to have jealous feelings toward the baby and to feel the loss of his wife's love and attention.

One part of us is apt to blame the baby for causing all of these stresses. Another part knows that such blame is unacceptable—you can't hold a tiny, helpless baby responsible for creating this new situation. So, when we don't understand the true source of anger and confusion, we tend to blame people we can hold accountable—like our spouses—for causing the problems. If she is deeply immersed in the baby, why shouldn't he immerse himself elsewhere? Some men do just that, either literally or psychologically. They bury themselves in their work, which society approves of now that they must be serious providers, or they retreat to a hobby, sports, exercise, after-hours get-togethers with male friends, alcohol or drugs, or even into the arms of another, seemingly more available and nurturing, woman.

Does this sound bleak? It need not be if couples are aware of these stresses, work at communicating their own feelings, and at the same time make an effort to really see what parenthood looks like through each other's eyes. If we can state our views without blame, we can solve problems objectively and make changes. If a woman feels that she is doing the lion's share of the baby care and making all the sacrifices, for example, she may well feel angry—angry at the baby, at her spouse, and at society for reinforcing rigid sex roles. Rather than blame anything as powerless as a tiny baby or as huge as an entire society, the most likely and convenient target is her spouse. Though it is easy to say and hard to do, instead of alienating him with her anger she might enlist him in a positive way as a problem solver. How can she find some free time for activities that nurture her, so that she does not feel so depleted? If he feels estranged from the mother-baby duo, can he acknowledge this consciously without feeling "childish"? Can she empathize with those feelings? Together, can they come up with one fun activity that they can share?

Question: What adjustments have you had to make in your marriage since the birth of your baby? And do you have any advice to offer others?

Answer: Dennis and I hardly make love anymore. I'm asleep by 9:30. Now sex is a big deal. Having it is a big deal, and not having it is a big deal. It doesn't feel normal or natural anymore. I have no advice other than to get the facts and the feelings out on the table. Then you can either fight about it or joke about it, but I don't know what you do about it—the sex, that is. There just isn't time.

A: We are broke. That's been really hard. Without my job, we have nothing extra. On the other hand, we have this beautiful baby who we adore and dote upon, and who we made together and share. She has his eyes and my father's hands and my ears, we think. That's worth a lot.

A: I am very saddened by the distance the baby has caused between my mother-in-law and me. Apparently she feels I am deliberately defying her by not following her suggestions. Her need to control has really surfaced. Now she won't even come and visit us. My husband is caught in the middle.

A: The baby intensified my rivalry with my mother-in-law a bit, but clearly I have won out, and we now know our places. We needed time.

A: We are more in love, not only because of Benjamin but because of the individual growth the child has awakened in us.

A: I don't get as much attention from my wife as I used to. There is nothing I can do about it.

A: The problem in our marriage is that I expected my husband to be more helpful. Oh, he plays with her and changes her diapers, but he won't bathe or feed her when I'm busy. His excuse? "I don't know how!" I didn't know how either, but I'm doing it. Then he comes home and wants to know what I've done all day and can't understand why housework or other domestic chores aren't done. I tell him it's because I've had to hold the baby all day. But when he's there, she's happy to see him and is on stage for him.

A: I recently had a wonderful experience. Bob gave me the day off. Yes, a day off! He got up with the baby, saw that he ate, bathed him, played with

Getting Back to Sex

Are you wondering if there is sex after childbirth? You are not alone. Perhaps you've been for your postpartum checkup. The doctor has told you that you can "resume normal sexual relations," yet somehow you haven't. There isn't time, or you're tired, or don't feel very sexy when you're 20 pounds overweight, or intercourse feels uncomfortable. The fact is that all new parents experience a change in their sex lives. For some it's a short hiatus that ends in a matter of weeks, depending on when the new mother's episiotomy is healed, breast-feeding is established, the baby's crying diminishes, and how much rest the couple has been able to get. But for others it may take much, much longer to re-establish sexual intimacy.

• When Masters and Johnson studied women during the first three months postpartum, they found that nearly half had little or no interest in sex. Fatigue is the main physical reason a new mother's sex drive may be low, but hormonal imbalance can also contribute. Severe drops in estrogen and progesterone leave the vagina dry and sensitive to pain. The breast-feeding mother will experience even more vaginal dryness because she has high levels of prolactin, the milk-making hormone. Though a water-soluble jelly such as K-Y may alleviate the condition, the woman may not experience the same pleasure as she would when lubrication occurs naturally.

• With no comparable physical problems, the man is more likely to have normal sexual desires. According to a study at the University of Maryland School of Nursing, the level of desire for new mothers and fathers differed not only at four months, which we might expect, but even at twelve months.

• A woman's body image and sense of confidence and competence can be shaken by motherhood. Further eroding her self-esteem, society doesn't recognize and celebrate the importance of mothers. Even mild depression can put a damper on the libido. Sometimes friends or a mother-infant support group (see page 153) are exactly what a mother needs to feel better about herself. Men, however, often don't make these same supportive connections with each other. Don't hesitate to get professional help if your lack of sexual desire gets to the point where it endangers your marriage. Counseling for sexual dysfunction is widely available and often very short-term.

him, and fixed our dinner. I went and got a perm—I've been wanting one for months—and spent the afternoon repotting all of my plants. Bob had no idea before what it is like to spend a day with a baby. He says he now realizes how lonely

it can get and what a production it is to feed a five-month-old three times every day.

A: Larry has become much more concerned with our financial stability. He feels the whole "head of the household burden of responsibility" on his shoulders. I tell him that we share it but, emotionally, he can't seem to shake the feeling that it is all his.

A: The major adjustment has to do with my husband's and my sex life. I wasn't interested while nursing (dry vagina), but then I got a prescription from my gynecologist that helped. I left my job not because I wasn't doing it adequately or doing fine with the baby, but because my husband and I were strangers.

A: We fight more, and this frightens Lindsey, who actually shakes.

A: Our relationship has suffered, and we are now making an effort to go out on a date once a month.

A: My biggest peeve is that the baby belongs to both of us, but 90 percent of the care falls on me, on top of the 90 percent of the housework and the shopping. It's not fair. He's more like a roommate now than a husband. I sometimes resent his freedom. I've got a lot of anger pent up because I've been through so much; I'm different now! I've got gray hairs and wrinkles! He hasn't changed like I have, though of course he says that he has changed.

A: Something has happened to both of us. We seem like two super-serious, middle-aged people, weighted down by the burden of our responsibilities. We don't have any fun! All we talk about, think about, and plan for is the baby. There's a fountain in front of the law firm where I work. I said to my wife, "We need to do something crazy, like cut loose, go downtown, and jump in the fountain."

Resources for Couples

Curran, Delores, *Traits of a Healthy Family: Fifteen Traits Commonly Found in Healthy Families by Those Who Work with Them* (New York: Harper & Row, 1984)
Greenspan, Stanley, and Greenspan, Nancy T., *The Essential Partnership: How Parents and Children Can Meet the Challenges of Childhood* (New York: Penguin, 1989)
Helmering, Doris Wild, *Happily Ever After: A Therapist's Guide to Taking the Fight Out and Putting the Fun Back into Your Marriage* (New York: Warner Books, 1987)
Klagsbrun, Francine, *Married People: Staying Together in the Age of Divorce* (New York: Bantam, 1985)

Public Affairs Pamphlets
381 Park Avenue South
New York, NY 10016
This organization publishes a number of pamphlets on marriage, family, parenting, and more. Write for their list.

A: We're kind of stuck with each other because we don't have time for friends anymore. Our old friends do things like call us up at eight o'clock on a Tuesday night and say, "Why don't you meet us at Joe's for a beer and a pizza?" They have no idea. We rent a movie instead, and then within fifteen minutes we fall asleep together watching it. Romantic, isn't it?

A: Even if we get divorced, we will always be linked by our love and commitment to this child. That's powerful.

Helpful Organizations for Couples

Parents Anonymous
(Child Abuse Prevention)
6733 Sepulveda Boulevard
Suite 270
Los Angeles, CA 90045
(800) 421-0353

Family Service America
11700 West Lake Park Drive
Milwaukee, WI 53224
(414) 359-2111, or consult your local directory

Catholic Charities, USA
1319 F. Street, N.W.
Washington, D.C.
(202) 639-8400, or consult your local directory

National Military Family Association
2666 Military Road
Washington, VA 22207
(703) 841-0462

A: Having Elizabeth really was the beginning of our marriage, even though she came four years after the ceremony. Until her birth, Carl and I had functioned more or less autonomously in our different jobs and interests. We spent many evenings apart because he was involved in politics and I in the theater. We've had lots of fun together, but we've never worked together, and had so much joy together, the way one does with a baby.

• CHAPTER 13 •

Parent Information and Support Groups

I wish, in addition to preparing for natural childbirth together, that Bill and I could have prepared for the difficulties of adjusting our life to a new baby. I don't mean how to give them baths, hold them, mix up formula, or sterilize bottles, but how to understand them and deal with some of the very real logistical and psychological problems that new parents face.

Life with a baby can be less lonely and much more pleasant if you know people who share your feelings and experiences—people who have many of the same questions and concerns that aren't always the pediatrician's bailiwick.

The remainder of this chapter describes a parent information and support group for mothers and their babies by Phyllis Silverman, a group leader trained in early childhood development. At the end are suggestions about where to find a group for yourself or how to start one, as well as a progress report on how Phyllis's group is doing.

• • •

*When I began to lead new-parent groups, I wanted to share the information on child develop-*ment and infancy I have access to as a professional. I felt the newest research and theories on infancy would be of interest to parents in understanding babies, their growth and development, as well as their highly individual differences and personalities, and what this means in terms of parenting.

For instance, parents have found it helpful to know that all children under the age of three go through many alternating cycles of dependence and independence. Understanding the deep attachment of the six-month-old and how this relates to the often rather sudden clinging at that age can help a parent to deal with the very practical necessity of finding appropriate and consistent caretakers. Or the "refueling" behavior of the newly mobile eight-month-old may make more sense if a parent knows how important this "touching base" or holding on is for the baby to recharge before going off on another independent jaunt. This kind of behavior can be mistakenly interpreted, and parents may wonder whether all their love, concern, and attention suddenly added up to spoiling the baby.

Parents may also wonder and worry about an eight- or nine-month-old who appears to be going on a hunger strike. So strong are some babies' drives for autonomy that they may stop eating until Mom surrenders the spoon and introduces finger foods. They may also wonder why the baby won't sleep very much anymore. I don't pretend to be an expert on sleep (frankly, I don't think anyone is), but I can think of many reasons a baby might fight sleep. A new walker, for instance, is often so exhilarated with this new world suddenly available that he literally fights leaving it for quiet restfulness. The baby is not spiting or fighting parents, but rather voting in favor of something else. Sharing this kind of information and talking about it in a group can give perspective as well as some solutions for the day-in, day-out care of a baby.

An informal group that meets in a comfortable, safe space is also a place for parents simply to observe how other parents and their babies act together. If the babies have mastered crawling, I've found it helpful to have someone else on hand, skilled with infants, to care for them in an adjoining room. The door is left open, so the babies can crawl back and forth as they wish. Par-

ents enjoy hearing what their babies have been up to from someone else, and we are all continuously amazed to see how well the babies relate to the others—how they "talk," touch, play, and imitate each other—refuting the theory that socialization does not occur until children are at least two or three years old. The babies I have worked with for the most part come to recognize each other through this weekly contact and genuinely seem to enjoy each other.

As I gather experience running groups, I've found that having information per se on child development and providing the infants with pleasant, stimulating social experiences are only two of the benefits for parents and babies. The groups have many other functions. The often-isolated new mother, who lives away from her family or doesn't relate well to them, can meet other new mothers. A woman with her first child, often out of the nine-to-five job market for the first time and without an accessible or necessarily sympathetic community of friends or much experience structuring her time, can meet new people. In every group some participants have developed friendships.

The groups are also a forum for sharing basic how-to information on many of the daily aspects of baby care: preparing your own baby food; where to buy equipment or find baby-sitters; and so on. But just as important, a group can give feedback that corrects distorted perceptions or information ("All babies sleep through the night by the time they are three months old" or "Weaning from breast to bottle is a simple matter of just doing it"). Talking together confirms that the way a new mother can feel—inadequate, anxious, frustrated, tired, or even angry—is not unusual.

The women in one of my groups, for instance, spent many weeks discussing the lack of support for mothering and how it has affected their own self-esteem. While a mother alone at home is likely to blame herself for not being better organized, more energetic, and "content" and feel guilty for having negative fantasies or thoughts about her baby, mothers together discover that this is normal.

It is much healthier for parents to express their feelings honestly and to work toward solutions openly than to feel angry toward their young children and guilty for feeling this way, which is so often the case. The approach of questioning and looking at problems and finding solutions that a group offers is very helpful for parents to use on their own when the group ends.

Where to Find Your Own Group

New-parent groups are beginning all the time. Many are advertised in community newspapers. Some are offered through local Ys, school boards, wellness programs in hospitals, and child-development departments of colleges and universities. I offered mine through Elizabeth Bing, a pioneer in the prepared-childbirth movement. She has access to many new parents through her prepared-childbirth classes. She felt, as I and many others do, that parents need support through pregnancy and birth as well as during the actuality of living with a baby.

If there doesn't seem to be anything going on in your area, you might take the initiative and approach the chairperson of the child-development department in a local college or ask about resource people at a local counseling agency or the hospital where you gave birth. You can rotate from house to house or find a free space. Schools, libraries, religious organizations, medical groups, and hospitals are often interested in supporting efforts that serve new parents.

If you are looking for other new parents to be in your group, your prepared-childbirth instructor or your pediatrician can be helpful. If you ask your pediatrician, be sure to stress that you are looking for parents with normal questions, fears, and problems. Some pediatricians feel that such groups are only for parents with extreme problems, and that is certainly not the case. Remember that not all pediatricians are amenable to such groups, preferring to do all the problem solving themselves.

The emphasis in any group will, of course, depend on the leader as well as the participants. If you are in a position to choose a leader, I think a firm grounding in child development is necessary if the group is going to have an "educational" focus. It is important, though, that any leader, regardless of his or her focus, be an objective person who is accepting of many life-styles.

Parent-Led Groups

You may, on the other hand, wish to have a parent-led group, which can still offer a great deal of support and an opportunity to share feelings and practical information. A few cautions: Try to choose one topic per meeting. Watch out if discussions begin to turn into psychotherapy sessions. Without a skilled leader trained in dealing with intimate feelings in a group setting, members can be burdened rather than nurtured by the group. Another problem can arise when one or two people dominate the discussion. A tactful way to deal with this before the problem arises is to set a time limit for each person to speak and appoint someone as official timekeeper.

Though this group will provide less of a developmental structure from which parents can make decisions, one way to extend your experience and knowledge is by reading together and/or inviting guest speakers from various fields—child psychology, nutrition, day care, and so on—to the group. Here, again, it is important to hear people with

Joining an Existing Organization

Parent information and support groups exist throughout the country. Rather than start a group from scratch, some parents prefer to form a new branch, adopting the philosophy and format of the umbrella organization.

MELD (Minnesota Early Learning Design)
123 North Third Street
Minneapolis, MN 55401
(612) 332–7563
This is a nationwide organization that helps parents start groups under the auspices of local institutions.

The Family Resource Coalition
Department P
230 North Michigan Avenue
Room 1625
Chicago, IL 60601
(312) 726–4750)
Write for information about local support groups.

Mothers' Center Development Project
129 Jackson Street
Hempstead, NY 11550

This group will help you organize your own support program.

GIFT (Gathering International Families Together)
c/o Spence-Chapin Services to Families and Children
6 East 94th Street
New York, NY 10128
(212) 369–0300
GIFT offers support to families who have adopted children from other countries.

Bananas
6501 Telegraph Avenue
Oakland, CA 94609
A child-care information and referral service that offers a variety of low-cost handouts and pamphlets on how to start a parent group and more.

How to Grow a Parent Group
D. Mason, G. Jensen, and C. Rjyzewicz
CDG Enterprises
P.O. Box 97
Western Springs, IL 60558

---

various points of view who are flexible enough to tell both sides of the story, particularly if you are dealing with relatively "controversial" subjects: working, day care for infants, weaning, etc.

One final word: Our groups ranged in size from five to eight. Fathers were welcome but rarely came because we met in the late morning, during business hours. While I feel that women have a great deal to share with each other, fathers need support, too. If the group agrees to it, one evening meeting every four or five weeks may be sub-stituted for a day meeting so that fathers can attend.

We really are a society in which the roles of parents are undergoing the stress of change—a society that has given lip service to the importance of the mother and the family but has not provided the structural supports that will strengthen them. As a leader of parent workshops, I have had doubts about the way I wanted to try to lead them, but I've never doubted for a moment their importance to the parents who have participated.

Two Mothers Talk About the Benefits of Support Groups

It was so difficult to adjust to staying home after having had a career. I suffered from the "super-mom" syndrome. I felt that because I wasn't earning money, I couldn't be satisfied unless my house and meals were perfect. I feel many mothers suffer from this as well. Then it dawned on me that I was so busy cleaning my house that I wasn't fully enjoying my baby. I think it's so important to

Dear Phyllis,

We wanted you to know how much we missed you at our lunch. We had a wonderful time. Five of us were able to get there, which we considered quite a feat—five baby-sitters, five lunches, five naps, and we don't know how many dollars to pay for it. But it was certainly worth it because we knew that we couldn't have managed seven months ago to all meet sans *babies at one time and in one place. And, of course, we hardly knew each other then.*

There we were in our "real" clothes, having lunch in a restaurant, the sort with candles on the table and numerous dark corners where one suspects lovers might meet. The nicest part was that after two hours, we realized we hadn't mentioned our babies yet because there was so much else to talk about. We are all so interesting.

April is teaching dance therapy six hours a week as an assistant and has been asked to take over the course next semester. Marilyn is taking a course one night a week in filmmaking, and Barbara, who joined the group after it moved to my house, somehow convinced Chase Manhattan Bank to give her back her old job on a half-time basis for exactly half-pay with benefits. Hooray for Barbara (and the bank!). Her husband is taking care of Elizabeth in the afternoons, and she reports that he promptly found himself some relief child care.

Margie is planning a trip with her husband to some not-yet-determined warm climate. The big question is whether to take the baby or leave her with her grandmother, who will do it but doesn't seem thrilled by the prospect of taking care of an almost-walking eleven-month-old for a week. The baby apparently cries whenever her grandmother comes near her.

Cheryl, who couldn't come, was traveling in Israel with her husband and Anna. And Florence, who also couldn't come, is fine. I ran into her a few weeks ago at the Museum of Natural History . . . under the whale. Paul, who is now walking, was climbing the steps with his father—up and down, and up and down—so we had a few moments to chat. She's doing some secretarial work at home for a lawyer and is contemplating returning to school. She reports that Paul has a better social life than she does now that she and some friends have organized a playgroup.

Marilyn did want me to tell you that Andrew has turned out to be "a totally delightful child, even though he still doesn't sleep much." He and the two other downtown babies are in a playgroup. April added that "Samantha is walking and talking. She's not a baby anymore. Oh God! It was so hard! It seems to have taken so long to get where we are. Yet it was over so quickly. I'm a little sad!" Between trips back and forth to nursery school, I, as usual, am slaving away on this book, convinced as always that people are much better than books. But what do you do until you find them?

But the purpose of this letter is mainly to thank you from all of us—for listening and watching, for helping us to interpret and understand, but mainly to talk about our babies and ourselves.

Best wishes,
Frances

remember we're staying at home to be mothers, not maids. *I used to rationalize and say, "I'm doing this work for my husband," but the truth is that he doesn't care if we have a gourmet meal or a T.V. dinner. All he wants is a happy family.*

I now follow the advice I received from your book. I'm in a mothers' group where eight new mothers get together once a week. I also joined a baby-sitting coop and see friends from Lamaze class. It's great. Laurie enjoys interacting with the other babies, and we're hardly ever at home long enough for the house to get dirty anyway! I can't stress enough how much their support has made my mothering a happy, exciting experience.

• • •

When Sarah was four months old, I was going crazy with her nonexistent sleep schedule. Out of desperation I wrote a letter to five other mothers of infants and preschoolers to see if they would be interested in organizing a support group, as you suggested in your book. I photocopied that chapter and included it with my letter. In our small Montana community, it is nearly impossible to draw on professional resource people, but our group has evolved very nicely as an informal monthly get-together. We decide upon a topic for the next meeting, and each of us brings as much helpful material, experiences, and ideas on that subject as we can find. For instance, we've focused on sleep, anger, and discipline. We meet at a church and hire a baby-sitter. The kids who want to go into the playroom can go, and the less secure ones who want to stay with the moms do. Some of the kids go back and forth. We now have anywhere from four to ten women each month. We always take time to discuss the joys as well as the problems. And of course, we call each other in between meetings as needed for information and support. What a blessing these women are to me! I highly recommend such a group!

· CHAPTER 14 ·

Getting Control of Your Time and Your Life

After Julianna was born, for the first time in my life, I found myself secretly poring over articles in women's magazines with titles like "Ten Ways to Save Hours Every Day and Still be Fresh, Thin, Healthy, Beautiful, Interesting, a Fun Supermom, and Sexy Too." I had become part of a huge audience for self-help literature—the harried housewife, the harassed mother—but I had to get control of my time and my life somehow. I didn't know where to begin.

Before you have a baby, people who know will tell you that the scarcest commodities in your life will be sleep and time. There isn't too much you can do about the sleep, but you can try to get control of your time. The first step is acceptance. You are not incompetent, crazy, or lazy if you find yourself still in your nightgown at ten in the morning, even though you've been up since five. If you feel somewhat out of touch with current events, and have not read a newspaper in weeks or a book in months, you're not unusual either.

If you are relaxed and easygoing and have been able to rid your life of many of its "shoulds," so much the better. You are one step ahead of most of us and *should* skip this section. If your baby is under six months, you may also skip this section. It's too soon to worry about being organized.

A Self-Help Exercise

A terrifically useful exercise is to keep track of how you spend a day. In the back of this book (pages 280–295) is a note-taking section. Try marking off the hours in 15-minute segments; carry the chart around with you and make notes about what you are doing, *including your feelings* (pleased, harassed, tired, happy, angry, delighted, proud, guilty, grateful, etc.). Later, when you have time, fill in the notes in more detail and expand upon your feelings. Put an *A* next to any entry that has caused you anxiety, even if it is something as intangible as the weather. Put the whole thing away for a few days, then come back to it.

A number of things will become clear. The most strikingly obvious will be the extent to which your time is fragmented. You will also be amazed at the tremendous number of decisions you make in a day and the amount of physical work you are doing. You should feel good about this! A pattern will emerge around the *A*s. Some of them, as in my case, will have to do with concrete, practical matters—a snowsuit that is difficult to get on and off the baby, or cats that need to be fed, or 150 trips up and down the steps. But just as many of the *A*s will have to do with attitudes. I discovered, for example, that I spent considerable time worrying over trivial matters and that I was overly critical of myself as a housewife and mother. I was pretty resentful that I had no time to pursue my work or other interests, even though I was still quite unclear what those interests were in the first place. I did not want a job so much as a balance to mothering. I was not allowing myself enough time to derive any satisfaction from the small amount of editorial work I was doing in an effort to create that balance.

Then what do you do? Attack those things that are bothering you, *but not all at once*. Group the practical *A*s into one list and the attitudinal *A*s into another list. Establish priorities. The two groups are interrelated, so do not fall into the trap of dealing only with the practical *A*s. The attitudinal *A*s are even more important and take the most time and effort to change. They are deeply ingrained in all of us.

Be sure to put this record of your day away in a safe place. It is a precious record, just as valuable as any photograph of yourself and your baby, and belongs in your family archives.

A Day With an Eight-Month-Old

Following is my minute-by-minute account of a day with my first eight-month-old, Caitlin. I kept track of several days in search of the "typical" one, which I never did find. This was the grimmest day, and I must confess that I chose it on purpose. Anyone reading this has got to feel more efficient and organized than I. The details exist because I carried around a tape recorder, thinking that I would write an article on saving time when you have a baby. The exercise was extremely useful for me. I was able to make some changes that improved the quality of my day-to-day existence. You don't know what else a close examination of your time, thoughts, and feelings in the course of one day will bring. I decided not to write an article but to write this book instead, which has changed the course of my life.

6:35 A.M.: Hear Caitlin crying but am determined to leave her in crib until at least 7:00 because she woke twice last night. I reason she must be tired. Hope she'll become interested in some of the toys I dumped in crib at 2 A.M.

6:40 A.M.: Can't stand crying, so get up to look in her room. It's my morning on while Charlie sleeps. Toys on floor. Caitlin tangled in blanket and trying to stand up. Has hiccups. Bring cup of water because I'm trying to get her to use it. She chokes and splutters with first sip. Give up. Change her, wondering if it is those iron drops

that are making her constipated. Carry her to phone to call pediatrician, but look at clock realizing that his call-in hour does not begin until 7:00.

6:50 A.M.: Take her downstairs and put her in playpen with some toys. Warm up a bottle because house is freezing. Worry about dumping her into playpen, but floors still cold, not to mention dirty.

6:55 A.M.: Hand her bottle, which she can hold herself. Worry if I should do this. Maybe she needs to be held. Wonder if I should ask pediatrician about this. But don't have time to hold her because I have to make pureed apples and pears from scratch to go with cereal. We're out of bananas. Put kettle on for coffee.

7:00 A.M.: Call pediatrician to tell him I think iron drops are making her constipated. He recommends more water, and fruit. Decide not to ask about holding her own bottle, feeling he might think it a foolish question—knowing he would suggest the cup, which he is big on.

7:10 A.M.: Finish straining fruit. Then feed her breakfast on my lap. High-chair tray still encrusted with last night's dinner. Bad housewife! Take it off and soak in sink. She keeps sliding down in it anyway.

7:25 A.M.: Carry her upstairs to dress her. Look for sweater but realize it is still in dryer two flights down. Decide to dress her in two undershirts plus polo shirt. She wiggles, rolls over, and almost falls off changing table. Blow on her stomach. She laughs. Put on her white booties, which are gray on the bottom. Feel bad again about dirty kitchen floor.

7:30 A.M.: Pick her up, go back downstairs, and put her on kitchen floor so that I can finish making coffee. She pulls herself up to stand by counter, edges over to stool, and pulls it down on herself with a crash. Her head goes "crack" on the floor. She screams. Pick her up to comfort her.

7:35 A.M.: Realize I've let coffee boil over on stove. Put her down on floor. Dump out coffee and start over. Baby has found a penny on the floor and put it in her mouth. "No!" I scream, prying open her mouth to retrieve penny. "No mouth!" When I put her down, she whines to be held.

7:40 A.M.: Carry her back upstairs to tell Charlie to get up. Think about getting dressed myself but realize new batch of coffee is probably boiling on the stove. Leave baby on bedroom floor for father, who is just waking up, to watch. Run down and turn off coffee.

7:45 A.M.: Get dressed myself while Caitlin plays on floor with my shoes. "No mouth!" I scream, watching the shoe. Ask Charlie if he'd keep an eye on her while he does his exercises, so I can finish making breakfast and get laundry out of dryer. He says fine.

8:05 A.M.: Discover washer is not working and panic. Call Charlie down, feeling very unliberated. "Where is baby?" I ask. "In living room" (which is right next to laundry room). "Did you put love seat in front of the stairs?" I ask. "No," he says as I run out just as she is about to mount the first step. Grab her. Push love seat across stairway. Put her back on floor and return to adjoining laundry-room door. Washer is not broken. The hose is bent so it wasn't filling with water. Charlie is irritated, though, because broken antique desk is in the way, and the furnace is drying out wood. We argue. Desk wouldn't be here if he would fix it as promised. Argument curtailed because of crash in living room. Rush out. Phone on floor. Baby trying to dial. Grab her. Replace phone. Search through toy basket for her plastic phone. Give it to her. No interest.

8:15 A.M.: Leave baby with Charlie and go upstairs to finish making our breakfast. Charlie calls me to see Caitlin doing exercises on mat with him. We laugh. He's doing push-ups and she is too, sort of. Hear on radio that it will snow by noon and realize I've put baby's snowsuit in washer. No possibility of going out for next two hours.

8:20 A.M.: Sit down alone with cup of coffee, pencil, and paper to make a to-do list, so I won't panic about what I will do all day.

8:25 A.M.: Cats meowing to get fed, so get up and feed them. Start to clean up kitchen and scrub high-chair tray.

8:40 A.M.: Charlie brings Caitlin upstairs, reporting she had great fun standing and looking in bathroom mirror as he took shower; pats it, babbles at it. I hold her and she feels damp all over from steam. Wonder if I should change her clothes, but decide to let it go. House is warm now. She jumps up and down in my lap, smiles, then sneezes. What if she's catching a cold?

8:50 A.M.: Put her in Jolly Jumper in kitchen doorway. She twirls around and makes pass at cat's tail as he goes by. Look for iron drops, which I'd forgotten to give her at breakfast. Water plants. One is dead.

8:55 A.M.: Warm up coffee and sit down with Charlie to eat. We both talk to baby as she bounces happily in doorway. Wonder if all this

bouncing is good for her legs. Should ask pediatrician but don't want to know it's not good for her. She loves it so much.

9:05 A.M.: Charlie leaves. I swear I hear her say "bye-bye"! Continue to work on to-do list, which reads: pay bills, shop for dinner, cleaners, library for new card, pick up cat medicine, ask for rent from tenant, mail it to bank, find mail deposit slips, work on friend's book manuscript. Desperately need my broken desk fixed, so I can put all this stuff in one place.

9:10 A.M.: Baby has hiccups and is fussy. Take her out of jumper. Give her iron drops, which she spits out on white shirt. She cries and rubs eyes. But don't want to put her to sleep until she has iron drops, or I'll forget again. Dryer buzzing.

9:15 A.M.: Carry her down to dryer and get stuff out. Bring it to living room to sort. Move love seat to block stairs. Get her a cup of water for hiccups. She splutters and chokes. Throws cup at love seat. Carry her back upstairs to get bottle of juice, which stops hiccups. Go back down to continue sorting laundry.

9:25 A.M.: Baby starts to cry, so pick her up to take her to bed, but phone rings. Answer it. It's friend asking me how I am doing on her manuscript. Say I haven't gotten to it yet but definitely will. Just haven't had time. Baby crying, can't talk now.

9:30 A.M.: Take her up to her room. Change her and put her down for her nap. Put rattle and small stuffed animals in crib for her to play with. Run down to get iron drops. But by the time I get back with them, the baby is sound asleep.

9:45 A.M.: Sit down with the manuscript. Phone rings. It's Charlie. Report that baby said "bye-bye"—maybe. We agree she's a genius. Charlie reminds me to pay mortgage. It's on my list.

9:50 A.M.: Sit down to start proofreading again. Can't spell any better than author and feel depressed. Why am I doing this? Not good at it and don't like it.

9:55 A.M.: Get up to look for dictionary. Remember it's in baby's room, which used to be my study.

10:00 A.M.: Back to friend's manuscript.

10:45 A.M.: Snow has started falling heavily. Go up to see if baby is awake. She is. Bring her downstairs. With great difficulty, put her in snowsuit, which has zippers running down the insides of both legs. Put on a pair of socks, two pairs of booties, but wonder if that is enough. Put her in playpen and run upstairs to get pair of Charlie's socks. She cries as I leave. Come back and put big black socks on her. She looks absurd. Am all ready to go. Then decide to call drugstore just to make sure cat medicine is ready. Put baby on floor. She makes beeline for cat. Drugstore line busy.

11:10 A.M.: Finally out door.

12:00 noon: Get home, but without cat medicine. Vet hadn't called in prescription. Library won't give card unless I show proof of address, which I didn't have with me. Typical New York attitude!

12:10 P.M.: Put baby in high chair. Give her chicken and sweet potatoes. Rubs them in her hair and keeps sliding down in high chair. Take her out and hold her in my lap.

12:20 P.M.: Put her on floor so I can unpack groceries. She knocks over the cat food, which I forgot to elevate. She samples it. "No!" I scream.

12:30 P.M.: Carry her downstairs to help sort laundry on love seat, which I've moved to block stairs again. She pulls pile of towels down and laughs. So much for folded towels. She crawls away, heading for the rubber tree. Pick her up and place her in front of toy basket, which interests her until I finish folding laundry and put it in basket.

12:50 P.M.: Look at book and women's magazine with her. Notice she likes pictures of babies in Pampers' ad. Laughs at them. Also keeps looking out the window at the snow. Points at it. We stand at window and talk. The snow is already three inches deep. I wonder how I'm going to get back out to drugstore on foot for the cat medicine.

1:05 P.M.: Take her upstairs and change her. Put her in crib and start out the door. She's standing up, crying and banging on the crib. Go back, lay her down. Wind up musical mobile, cover her up, and start out door. She's standing up and crying and banging on the crib again. Go back, lay her down, pat her on back, and rock crib back and forth. Wind up mobile and start out door again. She cries. Go back, wind up mobile, give her a kiss. Go toward door, this time closing it behind me. Go downstairs. Turn on water in kitchen, so I can't hear her. Wash her lunch dish and eat remaining tablespoon of potatoes and chicken and drink a cup of coffee. Baby is quiet.

1:20 P.M.: Go back to friend's manuscript.

2:15 P.M.: Hear her crying. Am determined to leave her there just a few more minutes, hoping she's playing with the toys in crib.

2:20 P.M.: Can't stand crying. Go upstairs and get her out of bed. Put her on bedroom floor and make phone call to new acquaintance with baby. Ask her if she knows how to keep baby from sliding down in high chair. She suggests a piece of foam for traction. Tell her about editorial work. She says, "Oh, can't take full-time motherhood?" I grow defensive and explain that I only do it while she naps and at night. Baby has crawled under bed and bumps head. Cries. Put down phone to reach under and get her. Hold her on lap and talk. Acquaintance wants to know how I plan to get any work done during naps and at night. She's too tired to do anything. Plans to return to work part-time when her baby is in nursery school. Explain that I plan to find some child care so I have time. She says this will require all the money I make and adds that eight months is a terrible time to introduce baby-sitters due to separation anxiety. Grow even more defensive. Explain that I plan to find a wonderful person and introduce her gradually. "Good luck!" she says. Baby starts to cry and use this as excuse to hang up. Cross acquaintance off list of possible new friends.

2:30 P.M.: Take baby downstairs and put her in Jolly Jumper while I look for bills and checkbook. Talk to her while I write checks. Call vet about missing cat medicine prescription. Says he did too call it in in the morning.

2:55 P.M.: Call drugstore to make sure. They have it done now.

3:00 P.M.: Put on her snowsuit. Find stamps for bills. Look out window. Snow now six inches deep. Decide I can't use stroller and will have to carry her. Pick her up to go out, but realize she's had bowel movement all over overalls and snowsuit because disposable diaper tape has come un-

done. Plan to write furious letter to Procter and Gamble! They've ruined my afternoon!

3:05 P.M.: Carry baby upstairs. Take all her clothes off and wash her in sink. Re-dress her in three layers of clothing because snowsuit needs washing.

3:25 P.M.: Finally go out door carrying her wrapped in blanket, under my cape. She loves the snow and puts her hand out to feel it on the railing. "Cold!" I tell her.

4:00 P.M.: Return with cat medicine. Had to wait for prescription to be filled. Decide to take business elsewhere. Undress baby and put her on floor while I catch sick cat. Try to get medicine down his throat, but he throws up. Decide to wait until Charlie gets home, so he can help hold cat. Baby edging toward radiator. Grab her. Say, "Hot!"

4:15 P.M.: Give her half a bottle, which she drinks in playpen while I feed cats. Sit down to think about dinner. Phone rings. It's Charlie telling me he's bringing Herb home because snow has gotten too bad for Herb to make forty-mile drive up Palisades Parkway, which has probably closed by now anyway. "Can't Herb stay in a hotel?" Too late for that because Charlie already invited him. "What about the dirty floors and messy house?" "Herb doesn't care," Charlie says. "I do," I say. Charlie says he will cook. I say okay. He then asks about sidewalk. Has it been shoveled, apologizing immediately for asking such a ridiculous question, but tenant has a right not to kill himself. It's in the lease. At least sprinkle with rock salt.

4:30 P.M.: Take baby to laundry room to look for rock salt. Find it, and wrap her in blanket and stuff her under my cape. Go out and throw salt on sidewalk and steps. Let baby throw some too. She loves this and squeals with delight as the salt hits the ground. We stop and talk to a neighbor, and baby buries her head on my shoulder, refusing to look at her.

5:00 P.M.: Put her back on kitchen floor. Feed cats, but she won't let them eat. Keeps grabbing their tails, even though cats are up on counter. Put cats and dinner out in entryway. Slam door. Baby cries. Pick her up to comfort her.

5:15 P.M.: Warm up her dinner. Give her pots and pans to play with on floor while I search for spaghetti for our dinner.

5:30 P.M.: Take her upstairs and undress her for bath. Turn on shower to warm up bathroom. Undress her for bath, which she loves. She sits and splashes, drinks water out of measuring spoons, and I wonder if bath water is harmful to drink. Too tired to argue. Tries to stand up holding onto soap dish. "No!" I say. I bend her legs at the knees to sit her down. "You'll slip." She stands up again. I sit her down. She tries again, laughing. Finally I distract her by turning on the water. She's interested in measuring spoons, so I clean the toilet while she plays. Face the fact that her hair needs washing. A terrible scene follows.

6:10 P.M.: Take her out of tub into her room to put on her pajamas, which I forgot to bring to bathroom. She shivers. Feel guilty. While dressing her, phone rings. Carry her to our room. She sneezes. It's Sears Roebuck about the dryer warranty. The baby is naked and crawling across our bed to the edge. I ask Sears how they have the nerve to call at such an hour. I slam phone down, feeling better than I've felt all day.

6:15 P.M.: Finish dressing her in pajamas. Phone rings again. It's Charlie saying he's halfway home, but subways are running slow. Thinks he and Herb will walk the rest of the way. "No, please," I beg. "That will take hours, and I want you home! Stick with subway." He says okay, but not to put Caitlin to bed. Herb has to meet her. Tells me to just relax.

6:20 P.M.: Take his advice. Turn on T.V. and watch the news with baby on bed. Play peek-a-boo with pillows. Give her old *T.V. Guide,* which she tears up while I start to put laundry away. Why am I doing this? I stop putting laundry away and get back on bed with baby. We play hide-the-toy-under-the-pillow. We play airplane. I hold her hands while she jumps up and down. She's laughing. I jump up and down with her.

6:55 P.M.: Hear door downstairs opening. "Daddy's home!" Visible delight on Caitlin's part. Carry her down and hand her to Charlie. Remember that I have to find snow shovel. Go down to utility room to look.

7:05 P.M.: Come up with shovel. Charlie and Caitlin are looking out the window at the snow. Suggest that I shovel snow while Charlie and Herb put baby to bed. They agree. I go outside, happy to be alone in the dark and the snow. "Don't forget her iron drops. They are right by her crib," I tell Charlie.

7:45 P.M.: Come back inside, noting that the light in her room is off. She must be asleep. My "real" work is over, for today, at least.

In Retrospect . . .

As you can see, babies keep their mothers busy. Along with the work, however, there were many opportunities during this day to interact, to teach, to learn, to play, and to express affection, leaving me with no doubts that my baby was happy and stimulated. What I needed to do, though, was to make life easier for myself. I was able to make several changes, not all at once, but over a period of months. Here is what they were:

1. I decided to give the cats to my parents-in-law, who live in the country. The cats weren't getting the attention they used to get, and they felt like one more responsibility that I didn't need to think about. I also lent my in-laws the rubber tree, which flourished under my mother-in-law's green thumb.

2. Because I lived in New York City and did not drive a car, and took the baby wherever I had to go on foot, it was imperative that she be protected from the cold. I borrowed a snowsuit from a friend with an older child. This snowsuit was easier to get on and off. It had zippers on the outside of the legs, and it had feet attached to it. I kept the other suit in case of "accidents."

3. I found a new drugstore that delivers. I also found that my grocery store would deliver, too. I had never thought to ask before.

4. I decided to spend an evening every two weeks making enough baby food to last that long and freeze it. I also decided that I would keep some commercial baby food on hand, just in case I decided I didn't feel like making baby food at all.

5. We baby-proofed the entire house and installed safety gates, which we had resisted doing because we knew we were moving into our tenant's apartment in a few months. It was worth it, even for that short period of time.

6. I realized that I hadn't eaten anything but breakfast all day and had had several cups of caffeinated coffee. No wonder I was tired. I immediately went out and bought a bottle of wheat germ and a box of herb tea, and felt healthier just looking at them.

7. I decided to make some plans for the rest of the winter so that I didn't feel so isolated. This meant overcoming shyness and calling some of the mothers I hardly knew in my community and inviting them over. I also decided to look into the programs that the library and the Y sponsored for mothers and infants. By the following fall I'd found four compatible mothers with whom I started a playgroup.

8. The housework, particularly the laundry and dirty floors, was making me feel like a bad housewife. I vowed that when we moved upstairs, we would have the washer and dryer as close to the bedroom as possible and that I'd do the laundry in the evenings. Charlie agreed to wash the kitchen floor, but only when he felt like it and as long as I didn't nag him. The floors are still often dirty, but I keep telling myself I'm a nice person anyway, even if I'm not the greatest housekeeper.

9. Since I was destined to live in a multistory townhouse, I cut down on some of the stair climbing by leaving diapers and extra clothes on each floor.

10. We decided we had to get our morning act together. We tried getting organized the night before. We also abandoned our system of one person getting up with the baby while the other stayed in bed, except on weekends. We decided it was more important for Charlie to get to work early and come home early, when I was desper-

ate for adult companionship, than to take care of the baby in the morning and leave later. We're still working on our morning act. It's far from perfect, but we *try* not to fight *then*, at least.

11. I realized that I didn't have the right kind of support system for working at home. I started by buying a phone-answering machine and an intercom, so that I was sure to hear her when she woke up. I also needed a space for my books and materials. I paid to have my desk fixed by a professional, and when we moved to our tenant's apartment, I reclaimed a room of my own to work in.

12. I was still frustrated and eventually admitted that if I was going to write anything, I needed longer blocks of time during the day. I was too tired at night. When I looked at my day, I could see that I had every reason to be tired. In fact, just reading about it was exhausting! I needed some child care. After much searching and some trial and error, I found two good people, who have worked for us since. I treat them like gold. I still struggle with some guilt about working, be it for the six hours a week when I started writing *Babysense* or the fifty a week that I needed in order to finish.

13. I also decided that I needed some time to have fun alone with Charlie. We decided to make more of an effort to go out together and aimed for at least twice a month.

14. I finally read *How to Get Control of Your Time and Your Life*, by Alan Lakein (New York: NAL, 1974), a book as useful to a new mother as

Resources for Getting Organized and More

Lakein, Alan, *How to Get Control of Your Time and Your Life* (New York: New American Library, 1974)

McCullough, Bonnie, *Totally Organized* (New York: St. Martin's Press, Inc., 1986)

Winston, Stephanie, *Getting Organized: The Easy Way to Put Your Life in Order* (New York: Norton, 1978)

Young, Pam, and Jones, Peggy, *The Sidetracked Home Executives* (New York: Warner Books, 1981)

Sher, Barbara, and Gottlieb, Annie, *Wishcraft: How to Get What You Really Want* (New York: Ballantine Books, 1979)

Dr. Spock. I actually did the exercises in it, which have to do with establishing priorities. I realized that the first place to start was my "to-do" list. I found that I tended to put the most important tasks last, like my work. I stuffed the exercises into the back of the book and looked them over a year later, and I was surprised at how many more things I was doing and how much better I felt. Of course by that point I was an "experienced" mother, which also accounted for my progress.

• PART FIVE •

Child Care

· CHAPTER 15 ·

Separation

You Deserve a Break: A Pep Talk

One of the hardest things about being a parent is allowing yourself to get away from your child and accepting the idea that it's all right to take some time off. Deep within, you secretly wonder whether the baby will survive in the care of someone else who neither knows him as well or loves him quite as much as you do.

In some ways making the break is easiest if you *must* leave the baby regularly, for example, if you work. It can be harder for a full-time "non-working" mother to find a balance between time with the baby and time away. Some women don't feel they can justify the expense of child care unless they have something "pressing" to do. Such mothers may find it easier to take advantage of free child-care solutions, such as enlisting their husbands, trading off with another mother, participating in a baby-sitting cooperative, or seeking the help of a close friend or relative.

In any case, you need and deserve a break purely for your own enjoyment, even if you do nothing but sit in a coffee shop alone and read a magazine. You are truly entitled to time to yourself, because baby care and all the backup work that goes into it is a physically and emotionally demanding job. Once you're actually able to do it—that is, find someone to take care of the baby, and return to find the baby *still alive*—you will find it easier to do so each succeeding time. It does take practice, but eventually you'll wonder how you ever functioned without some time off, and you will be amazed at how good you feel and how delightful your baby is.

How to Make Separation Easier for the Mother

How comfortable you feel about leaving the baby in someone else's care depends most of all on the person you leave her with. You must trust the caretaker, because it simply isn't worth leaving if you don't. And you must be able to communicate with the person about the baby's needs, your needs, and those of the caretaker. Naturally, communication is easier with a grandmother or a close friend, but most of us don't live near our families and can enlist the help of friends only up to a point. Eventually we must rely on strangers.

Genuine trust and clear communication do not occur instantly but over a period of time. This is why it is natural to have some ambivalent feelings about separating from your baby at first. It takes practice on everybody's part, and the best way to practice is through a series of small separations that allow everyone a chance to get to know everyone else. If this approach sounds overprotective, believe me—it's an investment that will save you considerable time and worry in the future.

How to Make Separation Easier for the Baby

There is much to be said for getting some practice at separating in the early months of the baby's life. She will still be amenable to meeting new people. Later, she may begin to experience separation anxiety, which usually peaks in the middle of the second year, begins to decline gradually, and *may* end by the time the child is three.

There is no simple explanation for separation anxiety. It seems to be related to the baby's newfound mobility, which fills her with both a sense of power *(Whoopee, I can crawl away from you, Mom!)* as well as a sense of fear *(Will you be there when I come back because there is no one more important to me than you, and I need you to hold onto, so that I can "recharge" and be off again?).*

Separation anxiety is also related to the baby's growing ability to remember, or to hold an abstract concept in her head. By six months she is beginning to be able to remember something when it is out of sight. She will look for an object hidden under a blanket and will become visibly upset if she can't find it. She is not quite able to deal with the discrepancy between her memory of the object and its absence. Previously, she'd lose interest in finding the object because everything "out of sight" was literally "out of mind"— including mother.

The same worry overtakes her when, for example, her mother puts her coat on. Now the baby can connect that act to her past experience of watching Mom leave. What she cannot yet remember is that Mom will come back. Anticipating separation, she becomes upset. Fortunately, she is apt to forget in a short time that her mother has left. A baby doesn't dwell on such events for very long, particularly if the caretaker is familiar and sensitive, understands what is happening, and distracts her.

Handling Separation with Love

Separation has to be handled with some care and tact, whether you are using a familiar caretaker or not.

• The anxiety connected with separation gets easier to handle with experience, especially when both parent and baby know and trust the caretaker. Start gradually. Introduce your child to a new caretaker for short periods of time on one or two occasions when you are there. Build up to longer absences.

• Try to minimize unnecessary separations during the period of the most intense anxiety. If your baby has had a cold, or is teething, or has just mastered a new feat such as pulling himself up to stand or crawling, he may find separating from you more difficult than usual. This too will pass. Be patient, let him cling, and be as attentive as you possibly can.

• When you are working around the house you will have more freedom and flexibility if you try to make sure that your baby can keep an eye on you. Several studies have shown that babies are able to tolerate physical separation from their mothers and continue playing with toys if the door is left open and she remains in view.

• Encourage the use of a transitional object—a special blanket, cloth diaper, stuffed animal, etc.—early on in your baby's life, so that when you are away, your baby's "lovey" will offer comfort.

Separation is an emotionally charged issue for adults as well as babies. As parents we need to recognize our own feelings, because our attitudes influence our children. If you are resisting finding a sitter, or if after a lengthy and thorough search no one meets your standards, or you consistently have trouble trusting someone who appears to be trustworthy, you might want to think about whether you have had unpleasant separation experiences yourself. The clearer you can be about your own feelings, the more helpful you can be to your child. We don't need to unknowingly pass on behavior, fears, or attitudes that aren't useful to our children.

Objects That Comfort Babies When We Are Away

A transitional object can help ease the stress of separation. A special blanket, a soft and worn cloth diaper, a favorite stuffed animal—these often become endowed after repeated use with a type of magical significance, or the warm and nurturing qualities of the loving parent.

The term *transitional object* comes from the notion of the baby moving from one perception of himself—as being fused to a comforting parent—to a new image of himself as a more independent person. As the baby cuddles and strokes this loved object, he is using his own imagination to "tune out" the external world and tune into a comforting place within himself just the way he did when Mom held, rocked, and nursed him. The beauty of the transitional object is that the baby can find comfort on his own when he needs to lessen his stress or anxiety. Using his imagination to comfort himself can be seen as the baby's first creative act—one more example of the complexity of the human infant! Although the transitional object provides security and comfort and is a type of substitute for the loving parent, it does not develop this significance to the baby because his mother is inadequate. On the contrary, in order to invest an object with supportive and loving qualities, the infant must first have experienced the actual support and love of his parents.

Good Advice on Separation from Experts

Anxiety over being away from you and being with people who are neither you nor known friends, are real fears. Like other fears they will die down most quickly in babies who are given least cause to feel them. At present your baby is too newly in love with you to take you for granted. But if you can ride him through this period of intense and anxious attachment on a wave of securely returned and protective adoration, he will come to take your love and your safety for granted in the end. Only when he has had a full measure of you will he be ready for other adults and for other children. Only a ground-base of confidence in his home relationships will make him free and ready to turn his attention outwards as he gets older.

—Penelope Leach
Your Baby and Child: From Birth to Age Five

. . . Peek-a-boo and all the variations of this game will occupy the baby interminably. He will play the game by pulling a diaper or his bib over his face, then pull it off with cries of delight. He will play hiding games with any cooperative adult, watching them disappear with a solemn expression on his face, greeting their return with joyful screams. He can keep up such games much longer than you can.

What is the pleasure in these games? If the disappearance and return of loved persons is such a problem to him, why should the baby turn all this into a boisterous game? The game serves several purposes. First, by repeating disappearance and return under conditions that he can control (the missing person can always be discovered again with brief waiting), he is helping himself to overcome his anxiety in connection with this problem. Second, the game allows him to turn a situation that would, in reality, be painful, into a pleasurable experience.

—Selma Fraiberg
The Magic Years: Understanding and Handling the Problems of Early Childhood

Who Will Take Care of the Baby?

"Oh, just go out and get a baby-sitter!" It sounds so simple, but it's not. Finding and evaluating child care, whether for two hours a week or sixty, is one of the hardest aspects of being a parent. Good caretakers are hard to find. And once you locate a person or a program, there is no guarantee that either will remain available for as long as you will need them. Child care does not pay well, and it is not nearly as respected as it ought to be. Good people often leave for other work. The field of choice can be narrow, and parents may be forced to compromise on the quality of care they provide for their baby.

Putting the issue of continuity aside for a moment, let's focus on a few points many of us have found useful when looking for child care. The most important: You cannot possibly duplicate yourself, so don't try to. You are the baby's parent, and there is no one like you who will have the same significance in your baby's life. You are not really looking for the much-touted "mother substitute." Instead you are looking for mother complements—a few consistent people whom your baby comes to know and trust. Different people have different positive qualities and experiences to offer a baby. This is what our lives are all about—the richness and variety of relationships and experiences.

What we are looking for are warm and trustworthy people whom we can talk to, who have good common sense, a positive view of the world, some knowledge of infant development, and a realistic view of what babies need in order to flourish. Keep in mind that no one is going to be perfect. If the caretaker spends only a few hours a week with your baby, you may be able to overlook a quality that would be impossible to ignore if that person were to be in charge forty to sixty hours a week.

You can ask a potential caregiver many questions, but do not dismiss your gut feelings. Babies are such totally vulnerable beings. Stories of neglectful or abusive care cannot help but instill a degree of fear and anxiety that colors our search for child care. Rather than try to ignore these fears, we can harness them to sharpen our perceptions so that we recognize what is good and what is harmful. When those vague, funny feelings that "something is not quite right" well up from your subconscious, trust them. Almost every mother who has relied on child care for a number of years has at least one unsettling story to tell that might have been avoided had she really listened to her deepest self. Once you hire someone, it can be even harder to hear your inner voice. One of the reasons is guilt—you know, "How could I have possibly chosen someone who wasn't right for this most important responsibility?" It's painful to think about, and so we block it out. Another reason for suppressing your doubts about a caretaker is the thought of having to let go of that person and face yet another child-care search.

To avoid this, put the time in up front. Interview several people. You'll become more practiced as you go along. This way you will also be building a list of candidates whom you may well need to call upon at some future time.

The following chapter contains general suggestions from parents on evaluating caretakers, along with lists of specific questions you can ask as well as more details on the options for different child-care arrangements. If you are working, be sure to read chapter 17, "Working and Babies" (page 181).

CHAPTER 16

Filling the Need for Child Care

Choices in Child Care

Every family has its own child-care needs, from an extra pair of arms in the late afternoon so that you can work freely in the kitchen to the full-time live-in housekeeper who is available day and night. Whatever kind of arrangement you choose, remember that it is a partnership and will require a certain amount of give-and-take on both sides. No matter how many hours a week someone works for you or how much experience they have, they are not entitled to dictate the terms of your child's upbringing. On the other hand, it is up to you to be receptive to what the caretaker sees and feels. Anyone who spends time with your baby can enrich his life by offering new experiences, sensitivities, and perspectives. Here are just a few of the many choices, with some of the pros and cons of each.

Young Teenager

I needed my sanity at the end of the day. I worked out an arrangement with a friend who has a thirteen-year-old daughter. My friend works full-time and doesn't get home until six. Felicity, her daughter, has after-school activities three days a week. On the other two days she is more than welcome to come here and even bring a friend. She doesn't have to play with the baby, but she always seems to want to, and she is wonderful with her. Young teenagers are sometimes better than the older ones. They can be super conscientious and are still children themselves. They are not self-conscious about being playful. (See the description of Safe Sitter Programs on page 180.)

College Student

I use a college student one afternoon a week so I can go out and do whatever I want. I started when Melissa was about six months old. The first student I got left after a month, just when we were beginning to settle in. She took a waitressing job instead. Then I got another student who quit during exams. Now I have another one, but summer vacation is coming up. They've all been nice with the baby, but none of them has stayed. Now I'm so used to my afternoon that I couldn't possibly give it up.

Live-in College Student

Lisa has lived with us for almost six months now, and the baby loves her. I've learned a lot from trial and error about how to make it work. First, remember that, like it or not, you will be dependent on a person who is a cross between an adolescent and an adult, so you need to adjust your expectations accordingly. Lisa was homesick at first and missed her own family quite a bit. I found myself mothering her a great deal, which was more than I needed as a new mother myself—because I felt that I needed some mothering too. Also, be very specific about the duties. The student employment office recommended that we limit hours to between ten and fifteen a week so that she'd have time for schoolwork and fun. We put everything in writing, including when we would eat together, use of the phone, the car, visitors, etc. We sit down every week to talk. I find this necessary because she is somewhat shy about speaking up when something is bothering her. I also recommend a trial period of at least a week.

Solution: If you are open to a live-in arrangement, you may want to consider an *au pair*, a foreign helper between the ages of eighteen and twenty-five. The two good referral sources below will handle placement, provide social activities and counseling to relieve you of that burden, and will mediate disputes. For more information write or call:

AuPair Homestay USA
1522 K Street, N.W.
Suite 1100
Washington, D.C. 20005
(202) 628–7134

AuPair in America
100 Greenwich Avenue
Greenwich, CT 06830
(203) 869–9090

Daddy

My husband has recently started out as a self-employed dental technician and can keep his own hours. When Elizabeth was eight months old, I had to go back to work part-time, so my husband takes care of her in the afternoons. He is terrific with her, just as competent as I am. In fact she often looks to him instead of me for comfort. I have to confess that I then feel a pang. I'm happy she wants him, but a part of me wishes it was me who she turned to. As soon as I make some more money, we're going to hire someone for at least one of those afternoons so that he has a break. It's hard right now. He has to work at night and on weekends to make up for his baby-sitting time. He's exhausted by then. But it's really an eye-opener for him.

Relatives

I take David to my mother-in-law's. She's okay with him, but a little nervous, and we don't see eye to eye on everything—some things that I wouldn't tolerate with a paid baby-sitter. Like what? Well, like breast-feeding and nutrition. She thinks he's not getting enough to eat and that he's too old to nurse now. She gives him ice cream. He's ten months old. I don't want him to have ice cream. She thinks he needs a haircut. I don't. She thinks he ought to be wearing shoes. I don't. She can't stand the "raggedy old clothes" I dress him in. Should I go on? My husband tells me to be tolerant and not look a gift horse in the mouth. So that is what I try to do. I know she loves him, and that's what's important. But now she's on me about having another baby, a sister for David. Give me a break!

Trading Off

I met a househusband—yes, that rare breed—in the park. John lives in the same student housing complex that we do. We trade off with each other once a week. It's a little tiring taking care of two babies, but all I can say is that it's worth it when it's my turn to be off. We also have an informal evening arrangement. His wife baby-sits for us about once every other week, and my husband for them about once every other week.

Sharing a Baby-Sitter

I'm going to school two mornings a week. I have a friend with a baby near Mariah's age (thirteen months). I wanted someone who was really good with toddlers and who would stick with me if possible for the two years it would take me to finish my degree. I was able to pay quite a bit, but it was hard to find such a person for part-time

work. Here is a solution which worked perfectly for me. I share Lila, who is an ex-nursery school teacher, with a friend who has a fifteen-month-old boy. She works for me two-and-a-half days a week and for Rosalie the other two-and-a-half days. We live near each other. Once or twice a week, she gets the two babies together. It's great fun for everyone. Of course, Lila is a very flexible person. Some people wouldn't be willing to work under these circumstances.

Full-time Baby-Sitter in the Home

Nelly started coming to my house when Abigail was only four months old and has worked for me for almost three years. I feel blessed to have her because she loves my child as if she were her own. Her children are all big now, and she happens to love little ones. We consider her almost a part of our family, and I do whatever I can for her when she needs help, just as she does what she can for me when I am in need. For instance, she's stayed here overnight when I've had to go away on business, and I've given her time off for personal business when she needs it. She is Spanish, and we have many cultural differences, which have not been a problem. If anything we have become too close. We know all about each other. Our lives feel very entangled at this point. But that is the way I am. I can't help but get involved.

The most convenient child-care arrangement is to have a caretaker come into your own home. The baby is already familiar with the environment, and it is set up and child-proofed according to his level of agility and curiosity. All his toys, clothing, and equipment are there, which means that parents don't have to carry the baby plus his paraphernalia back and forth, rain or shine, which adds to stress. There are fewer complications if the baby has a cold, and certainly less exposure to germs from other children. Someone who comes to your home may also be willing to vary her hours. She might stay late or come early if necessary. A full-time caretaker's job may also include some light housekeeping responsibilities, which will make it possible for working parents to spend more time with the baby when they are home.

There are drawbacks, too. Having a full-time baby-sitter in your home tends to be expensive. You should be able to pay for benefits, including vacations, health insurance, and social security—the things that parents expect from their own employers. Even then there is no guarantee that the person will stay. Being solely dependent on another person's physical and mental well-being, goodwill, and humor is a tricky business, especially in the beginning. Until you've developed a trusting working relationship, you have no way of knowing what goes on when you are away, and if difficulties arise in communication, you and the care giver are on your own.

Another potential problem is that a care giver can feel just as socially isolated as a mother, because she may not live in the community where she works. Unless she is outgoing—and unless there are places for her to go—she may become discontented with the job, and your baby may miss out on valuable social experiences that grow increasingly important as he gets older.

Your relationship with a child-care provider can be complicated. Keeping boundaries constructive and healthy is a challenge, requiring maturity and a willingness to face your true feelings. Watch out for the following:

• The working mother may begin to feel heavily dependent on a full-time sitter to care for her child, to keep the household running smoothly, and to give approval. It's not uncommon for the baby-sitter to begin treating a new working

---

Paying for Child Care: On the Books or Off?

The way you handle the "business side" of your child-care arrangement is just as important as the personal aspects of the relationship. Many working parents have some conflict about paying care givers less than they make themselves to love and care for their child. We can attempt to make up for this by treating them with the same consideration that our employers give us by having a yearly review, offering raises, and giving Christmas bonuses as well as paid yearly vacations of at least a week if not two.

Question: Is it better to pay on the books or off?
Answer: Many families decide that they will pay their care givers off the books. Paying them "legally" requires extra time and red tape. In fact, employees also often request to be paid off the books because they do not want money withheld from their salaries, and they do not have to report this income.

Before you agree to this, you should know what your legal obligations are. If you are taking tax deductions for your child-care costs, either on your tax return or through your employer's flexible benefit plan, you will have to submit your care giver's name, address, and Social Security number. While not every state makes you pay for unemployment and disability compensation, federal law requires that you must pay half of the Social Security for anyone to whom you pay $50 or more a year. In doing so, you are helping your worker to have something for retirement. Sometimes care givers and cleaning people retire and discover that they are not eligible for these benefits because their employers have never paid into the system. They have the right to report you to the IRS. If they do, you are liable not only for the payments but also for a penalty of up to 50 percent of the total, plus interest.

For assistance, look at a copy of Internal Revenue Service Publication 503, "Child and Dependent Care Credit, and Employment Taxes for Household Employers." This should be available at your local library or local IRS office, or you can call this toll-free number: 1-800-424-1040.

---

mother like a daughter, especially if the sitter is older and more experienced with child care. Without necessarily knowing it, hidden resentments and competitive feelings can surface and challenge the relationship. Some women find themselves intimidated, afraid to make demands lest the sitter leave. They give away their authority, which undoubtedly makes them very angry, even if they don't consciously realize it.

• It is also possible to go in the opposite direction and become overly critical of the baby-sitter, focusing on every small difference between you. Some differences may indeed need to be resolved, but it's just as likely that you may be feel-

Suggestions for Sitters

- Spend some time showing the sitter how the baby likes to be held for a feeding, how to diaper the baby, where the clothes are, and what the bedtime ritual is.
- Make a photocopy of Essential Information for Your Babysitter (at right) and post it where it can be easily seen.
- Be sure to specify where you can be reached each time you are away. Also review how the stove, thermostat, locks, burglar alarms, etc. work.
- Review baby-proofing tools and tactics, and make the sitter aware of your baby's latest developmental feats.
- Go over policies on visitors, use of television, phone, and stereo, and what food can be eaten.
- Leave written instructions if any medicines need to be given to the baby.

ing jealous. Know that some degree of jealousy is perfectly normal—you're afraid your place of importance will be taken away from you. Working mothers are prime candidates because they are so susceptible to feeling guilty about leaving their babies. Some working parents eliminate any possibility of being jealous without knowing it by making compromises on the quality of care. Doing so reassures them that they are the superior ones when it comes to taking care of their baby.

- Try to be open with yourself about your feelings, whatever they may be. Then consider the following: We know that babies are capable of forming attachments to more than one caring adult and that there is no evidence that this will diminish your baby's attachment to you. Give yourself some credit. Your baby's attachment to his caretaker is positive and is a tribute to you. Babies do not make those kinds of attachments if they are not loved and secure. It's a gift of love on your part to encourage and accept the baby's attachment to another, because it serves him well. He is a totally vulnerable little person and needs to know that someone else cares and will meet his needs when you are not there.

- Try to look at your care giver as a partner, not a rival. If she does indeed seem to know more than you in some areas, try not to view her competence as a threat but instead as an opportunity to learn. Set aside a time each week (paid time for her) when you can sit down and talk about the baby as a mutual concern. And make sure that you haven't given the sitter all the fun parts of baby care and left yourself with the drudgery. This cannot help but make you feel resentful, especially if you're feeling guilty.

- Keep in mind that the baby-sitter may have her own hidden agendas that you might not be able to spot in an interview or even during a trial work period. She may want to put you into a daughterly role, especially if she is older and has children of her own. Or she may subtly try to undermine you because on some level she believes that mothers should not work outside the home. If she undervalues herself, she might become jealous of the power she perceives that you have in the work world.

- You can't change her. But you *can* recognize certain attitudes so that you don't have to fall victim to them. Beyond that, you can be very clear about how much you value what she does—not only with words and small acts of consideration, but also by paying her as much as you can afford to. The irony is that we pay care givers less for a "priceless" service than we pay parking-lot attendants.

Essential Information for Your Baby-sitter

_____
(Our Name)

_____
(This Address)

_____
(Directions to Get Here)

_____
(Telephone)

Child's Name   Birthdate

_____   _____

_____   _____

Father's Work Number _____

Mother's Work Number _____

In Case of Emergency: _____

Doctor's Name _____

Doctor's Phone _____

Address _____

Police _____

Fire _____

Neighbor _____

Poison Control _____

Hospital _____

Ambulance _____

Special house rules _____

_____

Mealtime or Bedtime Notes _____

_____

Medical Release Form

Child's name _____ Home Phone _____

Mother's name _____ Business phone _____

Father's name _____ Business phone _____

Names of friends or relatives to call if you cannot be reached.

1. _____ phone(s) _____

2. _____ phone(s) _____

Physician to be called in an emergency

_____ (phone) _____

I authorize _____ to take whatever emergency medical measures are deemed necessary for the protection of my child, _____, while (s)he is in her care. I understand that this authorization includes calling the physician named above, implementing his instructions, and transporting my child to a hospital or clinic without consulting me.

Subscribed and Sworn to before me this _____ day of _____, 199___

_____

(Adapted from *The Parents' Guide to Day Care*, by Joanne Miller and Susan Weissman, New York: Bantam, 1986.)

_____ _____
(date)   (parent's signature)

Family Day Care

Mrs. Glenn is an institution in the neighborhood. She knows a great deal about children and has five of her own, three of whom are teenagers. She cares for one crib-age baby and one two-and-a-half-year-old every day for a woman on the next street. Her rates are low. One of her teenage daughters helps out with a five-year-old and a seven-year-old who come after school. What I like most about her is that she includes Bryan in her activities, the way I do when I take care of him. She takes the two little ones to the grocery store if she has to go. She reads them a book while she's waiting for the coffee to get made. The two-and-a-half-year-old, Nora, who is there every day, likes to pretend that Bryan is her baby brother. I'm happy with this arrangement. Bryan is part of a normal family setting where life goes on as usual. Yet he is special there.

Many of us use a family day-care provider without giving her that name. The term simply means someone who takes care of your baby in her own home, either alone or with a small group of other children. Some parents use relatives, friends, neighbors, people who have put advertisements in the paper or notices on community bulletin boards, or programs sponsored by their corporation. The only general truth about family day care is that it defies generalization. *Usually,* however, a family day-care giver is a mother herself—young or old or somewhere in between—who has gained her experience with infants and young children through on-the-job training. She may also have gained additional knowledge of child development through a sponsoring agency or a corporation. The quality of family day care obviously has a great deal to do with the mother—her enthusiasm for her work, energy, imagination, patience, and understanding of babies and young children; her connection with the resources in her community; and her work load.

There are advantages to this kind of child-care arrangement. Good family day care is small and personalized, offering babies the warmth and flexibility of a family and providing playmates and "older siblings"—perhaps a seven-year-old who arrives home from school in the afternoon or a grandmother who lives next door and comes to visit. The flexible rhythm of home-based care—ringing phones, a neighbor dropping by, trips to the bank, the park, etc.—can provide just the right amount and variety of stimulation a baby needs. The American home, assuming that it is safe, is a very stimulating place for a baby to be. It is full of educational "toys"—pots and pans, lids and strainers, a sink for water play, cupboards to open and close, pillows to snuggle among, and blankets to hide under—as well as quiet sleeping places removed from the bustle of household activity.

Family day care is also often the most affordable solution. The overhead for small groups in a home is much lower than in a day-care center that incurs additional expenses for rent, staff, etc.

But be aware of potential risks. You are relying on the health and well-being of one person who may not have a backup system if she gets sick or goes on vacation. If your baby becomes ill, you will have to have a backup arrangement or miss work. Most family day care is not licensed, leaving parents totally on their own to judge it. Even if a home is licensed, it may only meet minimal mandated safety standards.

We have all heard horror stories about bad family day care: too many children propped in front of the TV or stuck in cribs; junk food; and harassed mothers. Just as often we hear of warm, loving women who provide good custodial care but few educational or other enriching experi-

ences. Many of these women want further training and support but do not qualify for it because their homes do not meet the often outlandishly rigorous licensing standards in their state.

One positive development is the growth of networks of family day-care homes chosen and supervised by social-service agencies, corporations, schools, or day-care centers. Besides being licensed, providers receive training in child development. Studies have shown that care givers who have some training in child development provide more stimulating and developmentally appropriate care for babies and young children than those who don't. Members of such family day-care networks can also call upon the supervising agency for educational materials or problem-solving help. Professional recognition and support don't compensate for the low wages a care giver usually makes and the long hours she works, but it helps care givers to value their work. This in turn helps to ensure the continuity of care that babies need.

Question: *Does licensing make a difference in the quality of a family day-care home?*

Answer: Only some 25 percent of family day-care homes are licensed, but that does not necessarily mean that those homes are the best. The quality of a licensed home depends upon where you live. Requirements vary greatly from state to state. In California, for instance, workers are investigated for child abuse and other criminal offenses. Their homes are also inspected for fire and other safety hazards. Unlicensed homes, however, can also prove to be just what a parent is looking for. A nationwide study sponsored by the Child Care Action Campaign on the quality of family day care found that in many unregulated homes there were often fewer than three children enrolled. And because these programs were frequently run by a friend, neighbor, or relative,

parents considered the care giver trustworthy.

The same study also found that unlicensed care givers tended to stress a social atmosphere while regulated care givers offered more educational activities. The regulated care giver may also consider child care more of a chosen profession than the unlicensed provider. Licensed or not, the providers who have been in the business at least a year tend to stay in business. (See Evaluating Family- and Center-Based Day Care, page 177.)

Baby-sitting Cooperatives

A baby-sitting pool or cooperative is a good solution for parents in need of experienced free child care. No money changes hands—only time represented by points or the like. A coop offers other fringe benefits as well. Members get to know other neighborhood parents with whom they can share experiences, toys, clothing, and medical and educational information. The group is also a source of playmates, who will become increasingly important as your baby gets older.

The disadvantages of a large coop are that parents probably won't have the same one or two sitters all the time. That can be hard on a baby who is still learning to separate. But if you start your own coop and keep it quite small, your baby can come to know all the parent-sitters. Keep in mind that good coops have written rules or bylaws that clearly explain all procedures—how to join, how to engage a sitter's services, the payment system, complaint procedures, member obligations, etc. You may not immediately see the need for a complaint procedure, but even among friends it is best to have one established before trouble arises. The following bylaws of the East Village Baby-Sitting Cooperative in New York City could serve as a model for starting your own coop.

The East Village Baby-Sitting Cooperative: Rules and Regulations

1. The group will determine the geographical boundaries of the coop, the number of members, policies on day-time and evening sits, how to deal with cancellations and illness, as well as a philosophy about discipline, toilet training, etc.

2. A secretary will act as the record keeper for the cooperative. Each month the duties of the secretary will revolve in the order of the roster of the members. The secretary will arrange the "sits" and keep track of points earned and spent in a ledger with an accounting page for each member. Anyone needing a sitter will phone the secretary and place an order indicating date, time, and number of children to be left. The secretary will call whichever members are most in need of earning points until she finds someone to take the sit.

3. The accepting sitter will then call the family who put in the request to confirm the time and discuss any special needs. At the end of the job, the sitter calls the secretary to report the number of points she has earned.

4. The secretary adds that number to the sitter's account and subtracts that number from the account of the mother whose kids have been "sat." At the end of each month the secretary takes 5 points from each member's account in exchange for the time she has spent arranging the sits and keeping the ledger. At the end of the month, she reports points to each member, then passes the ledger on to the next secretary.

5. A chairperson may be appointed every four months. The chairperson's main responsibility is to arbitrate disputes, run quarterly meetings, and oversee new membership. The chairperson will receive 2 points at the end of her term from each member. The chair is also responsible for making sure that every member has an up-to-date list of home, work, and emergency numbers for each family.

6. The rates for sitting are: 4 points per hour for one child, 6 points per hour for two children, 8 points per hour for three.

7. Time will be rounded off to the half hour if a member returns after the quarter hour.

8. You are under no obligation to accept a sit.

9. The sitter will sit in his/her own home by day. At night the sitter will go to the member in need of services to sit.

10. A family should not incur a debit greater than 60 points and will be warned at that time. A debit of 80 points means that you will automatically be asked to leave the coop.

Infant Day-Care Programs

Rachel is in an excellent day-care program in the teaching college where I work three days a week. I have no reservations at all about the quality of care she is getting. The staff, who are hired by the parents, are really great. The group she's in is small, with six children ranging from five months to twenty months. There are two care givers per group. The center is located right in the college, and the rooms are set up to be like a home—cozy chairs and couches to sit on and lots of toys and books. There are separate sleeping, diapering, and eating areas as well.

The program is very small, with a long waiting list. It costs more than many people can afford to pay, but there is no way around this. We have to pay the teachers decent salaries for this kind of work. If you have a program that is really going to reflect the needs of babies and working parents, you have to hire very special people who are willing to work with the parents as well as the babies.

Our program is still relatively new. There is a lot of parent participation, which I think is important for the well-being of the program, the babies, and the parents. We are still working out some of the policies. This is time-consuming, and I sometimes resent it. I gripe a lot but, as I said, Rachel's really happy. Her language development is quite advanced compared to some of the other babies I have observed in the park. She seems fairly at ease with new people and places. I can visit her for lunch, pick her up early if I want to, and bring her in any time before ten in the morning and stay with her for as long as I want while she settles in. The only problem is germs. We have to have elaborate backup arrangements if she is sick, or Doug, my husband, who is an artist, usually has to give up a day of work.

Your chances of finding an infant day-care program in a center that accepts children under a year are slim. If you do find one, however, it will offer you some advantages over in-home care or family day care. Programs do not shut down if one staff member is ill or on vacation. They are licensed by the state to meet minimum safety standards and, because they are more accessible to the public, it can be easier to drop in and keep tabs on what is going on. A good center will encourage parents to observe and comment, and perhaps to be involved in some sort of parent education. Policies tend to be explicit, and if a parent does have an objection or a complaint, there is usually a procedure for dealing with it. Center spaces can also be designed especially for infants and toddlers, and many of the dangers in a home can be eliminated. A safe outdoor space may also exist, with enough staff on hand to ensure that babies get out every day in good weather.

One of the biggest advantages is that a good center can provide continuity of care. It will respond to the baby's preferences for a particular caretaker and "assign" one, but if this person is sick or on vacation, other caring adults known to the baby will be there in a familiar setting. Well-trained staff will also take pains to ensure that separations are made gradually and with sensitivity over a period of time. It's not easy for a parent to leave a baby in someone else's care, and it's reassuring to find a sensitive staff that has worked with many parents and has training and experience.

On the downside, center-based infant care may sometimes be too structured for the highly individual needs and temperaments of infants and inflexible in accommodating parents' work schedules. It may not be close to your home, and you will need a backup plan if the baby is sick.

Center-based care is usually more expensive than family day care.

Center-based care for infants and toddlers is still a relatively new and rather controversial option in the United States. Like all other child-care choices, types of programs and quality vary. Some centers are part of a large profit-making chain, where quality can be compromised. There are also smaller operations known as "mom-and-pop" centers. Some of these are very good; some aren't. Employer-sponsored programs run by corporations, hospitals, and unions are usually the best. These groups strive to do a good job because their programs are highly visible. A superior day-care program is an excellent way to attract and keep valued employees. Businesses are also concerned about liability, choose and train staff carefully, and provide spaces that are safe and stimulating. Some corporations subsidize costs or offer flexible benefit packages in order to keep fees low and serve the needs of all their employees. (See Evaluating Family- and Center Based Day Care, opposite.)

Evaluating Caretakers

Question: *What qualities were you looking for in a caretaker?*

Answer: *It is hard in an interview to know how well a person will take care of the baby. The baby should be awake and be present, though. I found one good ploy was to leave the room for a few minutes to get a pencil. If there's no action between the sitter and the baby, this is a very good clue. Does she talk to the baby and let him come to her? I had one marvelous English woman who couldn't get a work permit, whose husband was a foreign student. She walked right in, greeted me and the baby. She was at ease. Somehow she included the baby in the conversation. She looked at*

him as she talked to me. She asked me almost as many questions as I asked her. She even asked the baby questions! I felt very good about her. She was warm and demonstrative. She was a mature person who felt good about herself and, I sensed, the world. Come to think of it, this is the heart of it.

Suggestion: More than one mother who answered my questionnaire suggested that if possible you conduct a second interview with potential caretakers in *her* home, which will offer many clues about her.

A: *Never underestimate your baby's likes and dislikes. Harry is quiet and is slow and cautious when it comes to warming up to people. Simone, who came highly recommended and in whom I had great confidence as a trustworthy person, is a warm and effusive woman. But she comes on too strong for Harry. She scared him with her enthusiasm. He was so overwhelmed that he cried for the entire evening we were out. Every time she tried to comfort him, she only made it worse.*

A: *Some people love the tiny baby stage but have trouble once the baby becomes more active and assertive. A four-month-old baby is not the same as a busy fourteen-month-old toddler who pulls the books out of the bookcase, wants to open the oven door, and doesn't want to eat her dinner. If you are looking for someone who will stay with you, you better ask what babies need at different ages—what about limit-setting and toilet training and mess making, etc.? Ask this question of her references as well.*

A: *I interviewed one wonderful candidate who supplied me with three beautiful reference letters. She knew I had never hired a sitter before and said, "You must always check the references with a phone call. You would be surprised how few* parents actually do this." I thanked her and did. I then hired her after meeting two other candidates, one of whose references wrote a nice letter but who had some very negative things to say about her when I spoke with her on the phone.

A: Force yourself to ask all those "what if" questions that are bound to make you uncomfortable. What if the baby rolls off the changing table and bumps his head and is lying unconscious on the floor? Or what if the baby gets a button stuck in her throat and is still breathing? Do you know the right answers yourself?

Suggestion: Mothers and caretakers can both benefit from taking a course in infant CPR and first aid. You can find out about these through your local hospital or Red Cross chapter.

A: I think you should ask a general question about the person such as, "Can you tell me a little bit about yourself?" It's important to know where she grew up and, if she is from another country, whether she has a green card, which allows her to work legally on the books. Is she married and does she have children? How does her family feel about her work? etc. You want to get a sense about whether this person has a full life or not. You are the parent, and you don't want someone who is competing with you. Also, if she doesn't have a full life, your baby may end up fulfilling her emotional needs for closeness, which is not healthy.

A: Does the person come on time for the interview? Is she neatly dressed? Does she ask you some questions about the job? These sorts of things reflect whether or not a person has good self-esteem.

A: I eliminated one candidate because she wasn't willing to work for a trial period in which

I could observe her. Her attitude was "you either trust me or you don't." I am a teacher, and the only way you can judge teaching is to watch the person in action. I want to see how someone acts with my baby. Does she play games with lots of talking? If the caretaker isn't a talker, this can impair language development. Does she: name objects—"Look at the bird!"; point out cause and effect—"Let's turn on the light"; and comment on what the baby is doing—"You're picking up the ball!" In other words, does this person seize that teachable moment?

A: I learned through experience that right off the bat you should talk with a potential sitter about how you would handle differences of opinion, because it's inevitable that they will come up. They start out as little issues which you think aren't worth mentioning. It's a beautiful day outside. The sun is shining. You return home to find the baby has been in all day. You let it pass because you can't always get out yourself either. Some other small thing happens. You come home and the baby's in the playpen. You don't want him to be in the playpen passively drinking a bottle when you are paying someone to amuse him. You let it pass. Before you know it, you're really angry.

A: It is often suggested that you talk about your child-rearing philosophy with a baby-sitter. Well, I didn't have one yet. What I found useful was to try to establish whether or not the person is rigid or flexible. If she's flexible, and you're flexible, you can accommodate each other. If you're rigid and she's flexible, it can still work. If you're both rigid, forget it. How would she handle a time when the baby didn't want to take a nap, or eat her lunch? What would she do when the baby cried when you went out the door? Is she clean, clean, clean?

Some people want that. It's important to get a good fit.

A: Ask if the person smokes.

Evaluating Family- and Center-Based Day Care: A Checklist

In their excellent book *The Parents' Guide to Day Care* (New York: Bantam, 1986), Joanne Miller and Susan Weissman recommend that you visit a day-care home or center-based program at least twice, once with your baby and once without, at two different times during the day. The simplest yet most crucial questions you can ask yourself when you observe are: "Is this the kind of place where I would like to spend time myself?" Are the care givers attentive to the children? Do they participate in verbal exchanges, or are they unresponsive or simply ignoring the kids?

Following are thirteen more good questions to ask. You can use these to devise your own checklist. Don't be shy. We parents must be our children's strongest advocates when it comes to choosing the best child care. Though choosing child care is partially an emotional matter, you can be businesslike and objective in making your decision. Take your checklist with you, and make notes as you go. If you are evaluating several programs or family day-care homes, you will find that you can get programs mixed up unless you keep track. A clear record of each visit is invaluable.

1. Group size. How many children and how many care givers are there in my child's age group? Look for no more than three children to one adult. Babies flourish with individualized attention—highly personalized relationships with a few caring adults who are sensitized or "tuned"

to them and willing and able to take the time to decipher their nonverbal cues. A center may serve a large group of infants as long as they are cared for in small groups of no more than two or three babies or toddlers per adult.

Good group care of any sort, be it center- or home-based, must be small for other reasons. Tiny babies have a protective screening device with which they can block out such unpleasant stimulation as loud noises and physical commotion, but the older they get the less able they are to use it. If there are too many people, toys, activities, and noise, they become cranky, irritable, tired, lost, withdrawn, or overwhelmed.

If you are using family day care, be sure to ask about the maximum number of children who attend on a given day. If four elementary-school-age children arrive for after-school care at three o'clock every day, this might be too overstimulating for a baby.

2. Philosophy. What is the philosophy of the program? Answers will vary tremendously, but what one hopes to hear is some emphasis on responding to the individual differences in temperament and development of each child in a warm yet stimulating way. You might ask, "How do you deal with a cranky baby or a baby who doesn't want to take a nap?" A low care giver-to-baby ratio is also important for providing the flexibility that babies need. By nature they are not conformists. They don't necessarily nap, eat, play, or feel sociable at the same time. They have unique needs for individual attention—holding, cuddling, or time in which to play, make messes, explore, and interact with one another.

3. Qualifications. What are the qualifications of the care givers? You are looking for experience, maturity, stability, and ideally some knowledge of child development. Ask for references: other parents who are currently using the person, and "graduates" from the day-care home or center. *Check the references.* (See How to Check a Reference, page 180.)

4. A typical day. Can they tell you about a typical day? You are hoping that there is a plan—a balance of quiet, individualized time with some group time, some order to the timing of meals, snacks, and naps. Is there a separate, quiet place for naps and enough flexibility and time for the caretaker to devote to sleep-time rituals?

5. Physical activity. How much physical activity will my child have? Here you are hoping that there is a baby-proofed space where your child can move freely to play and explore. Ask to see outdoor spaces as well. You are looking for child-scaled furniture and equipment and, in a center-based program, staff members actually down on the floor, on the level of the children.

6. Meals and nutrition. What food is served? Do *you* (the parent) provide snacks and meals or does the day-care giver or program? Is there a meal plan, and who does the preparation? Is the baby held and fed on demand? Are high chairs and kitchens scrubbed clean?

7. Illness. What happens if a child gets sick? Germs are the biggest problem with group care. A fairly strict policy that prohibits sick children from attending will help protect your child.

8. Care giver's health. What happens if the day-care provider is sick or goes on vacation? Does she have a backup system?

9. Health, safety, and emergencies. What are the health and safety precautions? Is the space carefully baby-proofed, and is there a plan in case of fire? For instance, what do you do if a child has an accident? If she had to go to an emergency room, which one would she go to, how would she get there, and who would take care of the other children when she was gone?

(See sample authorization form on **page 173**.) Also, ask about car safety. Are infants transported in approved safety restraints?

Group care means germs! A study conducted by the American Academy of Pediatrics confirms what common sense tells us: Children in group care have more bouts with illnesses, from colds to gastrointestinal upsets, than children being reared at home. Take these preventive measures: Make sure your child is immunized before going into group care. Ask how diapering is handled. Is the changing table disinfected after each use, and do workers wash their own hands as well as the baby's after a diaper change? How are diapers disposed of? Ideally, they should be sealed in a plastic bag and disposed of in closed containers. Are toys that are mouthed washed in soap and water, and are floors kept clean and disinfected?

10. Separations and adjusting to the program. How does the center help children adjust? You want a policy of introducing the baby to the program gradually and flexibly. If the baby is over six months, you will be listening for references to separation anxiety and suggestions on how to deal with it, including the use of transitional objects such as a special blanket or stuffed animal. Ask about sleeping arrangements and rituals.

11. The staff. Do they have any helpers, and if so, are they people you feel comfortable leaving your child with? If a teenage daughter helps out after school, you want to know that, and you want to meet her as well. For day-care centers, ask how long each staff member has been there. How many part-time staff are there? If a center has a policy of employing large numbers of unqualified part-time staff, watch out. This is a way to save money, and the quality of the program will reflect this. Also ask what kind of background checks are made on all staff, including kitchen and janitorial help.

12. Licensing. If a program is licensed, ask if the record shows violations. If it does, have they been corrected?

13. Parents' responsibilities. What is expected of you as a parent? This ranges from payment policies (How often do you pay? Do you pay for sick days? etc.) to limits on your arrival and departure times.

If it is a center-based program, be sure to ask about parent involvement. Center-based care should be personal. Parents should not feel that they are handing their babies over to a group of know-it-alls. They must feel included. Is there time, for instance, to stop at the end of the day and talk to the care givers about the kind of day the baby has had? Are there discussion groups for working parents? A working mother often doesn't have the time a nonworking mother does to find and establish a community of friends whose support can make the job of parenting easier, less lonely, and more fun. Parents who share a day-care center can form that peer group, in which they share information and discuss problems and concerns unique to their situations.

Finding Child Care

Once you have some idea what your child-care needs will be, including the qualities that you want to find in a care giver, the next step is to find that person or program. Following are some suggestions about where to look.

• Word of mouth is one of the best ways to find someone. Talk to friends, neighbors, local tradespeople, and members of the clergy. If you work, ask your co-workers. Don't forget your pediatri-

cian. The office might have a bulletin board just for this purpose.

• Check bulletin boards in your local supermarket, community center, preschool, day-care center, Y, church, or library. Post your own notices at the same time.

• Read ads in local community papers or place an ad yourself.

• If you live near a college, university, or school of education or nursing, list your name and number with the student employment office as well as with the foreign students' center and the married students' housing office, if there is one.

• Call "60 Plus" if your city has one, or visit the senior citizens' center if there is one. Many elderly or retired people who are separated from their own grandchildren would love to be involved with your baby.

• Check with your local state employment service. They often have a household branch and do some preliminary screening. They charge no fees to the employer.

• For family day care and day-care programs, check with the Department of Social Services or your local community zoning board. These agencies are often the licensing agents for day care.

• Many communities throughout the country now have networks known as Resource and Referral Services or R & Rs, most of which are run by nonprofit agencies. R & Rs provide parents with lists of day-care centers and family day-care providers in their areas.

Contact the National Association of Child Care Resource and Referral Agencies (NACCRRA), 2116 Campus Drive, Rochester, MN 55904 or call (507) 287-2220 to find out the name and phone number of your local R & R.

• Check under "Day Care" in the yellow pages. Most programs do not serve infants, but your

How to Run an Ad for Child Care

When you run an ad or post a notice for a care giver, the following should be useful.

• Women who perform child-care services usually consider the work part-time. Post your ad in the part-time help-wanted section of the Sunday edition of the largest local newspaper. Try to make sure the ad starts with a word beginning with the letter *A* since most newspapers alphabetize their want ads, and job seekers begin at the top of the listings.

• Be straightforward with your wording. You can skip phrases such as "caring," "warm," "loving," etc. and go right to the point. "Able woman wanted for child care, housework . . ." etc., followed by pay, location, proximity to public transportation (if that is an asset), and telephone number.

• If someone calls who is inquiring for a friend about the job, this probably means that the candidate can't speak English very well. You can ask for references over the phone and check them before you interview.

phone calls may lead you to a source that does.

• Ask your employer or union about child care. Many companies have hired Resource and Referral agencies as consultants. Others have established day-care centers alone or in cooperation with nearby companies or unions. Still others provide training to family day-care providers, who may belong to a network that pro-

How to Check a Reference

Never rely on a written reference alone. Call each reference to find out what that person *really* thinks. Some people write glowing letters because they feel sorry for or guilty about letting a caretaker go. In a person-to-person conversation it is difficult to act enthusiastic when you aren't. When you call, tell the reference that you will be brief, and then be brief! Be organized and have your questions ready. You might cover the following:

• Make sure that this person is not a friend of the reference but another mother for whom the caretaker has actually worked.
• You might ask: What were her responsibilities? How long did she work for you? Did her personal life get in the way of her work? Why did she leave? Would you hire her again? How did you communicate, and did she have any difficulties accepting direction or criticism? Did you have any basic philosophic differences in areas such as comforting a crying baby, feeding, bedtime, use of a playpen, toilet training, etc.?
• If the reference is totally glowing, your last question might be something like, "Jane sounds too perfect. Surely there must be *one small thing* about her that was hard for you to deal with?" There might well have been, and this can be fine, too.

vides training in child development and offers shared resources.

• Post a notice where Safe Sitter Programs are offered. Growing numbers of hospitals, day-care centers, Ys, and other community groups are offering young teenagers Safe Sitter Programs. Two intensive, six-hour sessions provide practical training in hands-on care that enables a baby-sitter to meet an emergency: training in rescue breathing for infants and toddlers, and instruction on everything from how to tend to bee stings and bumps on the head to how to deal with a crank phone call. This program is endorsed by the American Academy of Pediatrics. For more information write to:

Dr. Patricia Keener
Community Hospital of Indianapolis
1500 North Ritter
Indianapolis, IN 46219

• Consult the State Child Care Fact Book, which should be available in your local library. If not, write to:

The Children's Defense Fund
122 C. Street, N.W.
Washington, D.C., 20001

Inquire about price as well as other CDF publications that may be of interest.

• CHAPTER 17 •

Working and Babies

To work or not to work? When your child is still a baby, this is a decision no mother makes without considerable thought, anxiety, and a fair measure of guilt. Finding a balance between your personal needs—financial and/or psychological—and the needs of your baby is an issue that growing numbers of women face. The dilemma is complex. Even though more than half of the women with children in this country work, and a startling 50 percent of those working mothers have children under the age of one year, the notion still prevails that the best and only place for the baby or young child is at home with his mother.

These double messages, coupled with a mother's own questions and doubts, can leave her feeling confused and guilty. She wonders if her baby will suffer if she is away for many hours every day. Can she make up for her absence in terms of the quality of time she spends with her child? When is the best time to go back to work? How will she balance the logistics of work and family? She worries also about shortchanging not only her child but also her work, her marriage, and not least of all herself.

There will be advantages and disadvantages to any decision you make about work. The mother who works full-time has to accept that she will not be involved 100 percent with either her job or her child. The woman who stays at home usually has to sacrifice money and power. Part-time work, which can be the most comfortable solution for babies and parents, still isn't as available as it should be.

Whatever you decide, you don't have to defend your position or your feelings about it to anyone else, even though you will probably have many opportunities to do so. If you work, some people will undoubtedly, if they aren't being overtly judgmental, act as if they feel sorry for you and your baby. If you don't work, others will insinuate that you ought to have your head examined for making such a "limiting" choice.

Fortunately, as more and more mothers enter the work force, we are all finding that we can make decisions about work and family with much clearer heads than we could a decade ago. When mothers were still pioneers in the workplace, they had to prove that they could do it all, and do it perfectly, in order to justify their choices. Back then the working mother could not afford to show any ambivalence about her decision either to work or to stay home. In fact, at some jobs it was best not to mention that she even had a child. That was when we also used to hear the phrase "quality time," which presumed that superwoman could dispel her guilt for being away all day by coming home from her job and participating in stimulating one-on-one activities with her children.

Fortunately we have become more realistic, tolerant, and flexible. We are willing to acknowledge that our babies change us. Whether we remain in the workplace or not, motherhood makes us richer and fuller than we were before. Women are also realizing that there are times a job may be more or less important and that they can find many solutions for combining work and family. The traditional male path to success is not the only way to advance. If we take a break from a job or career and don't advance quite as quickly as we might have, we needn't stagnate. We can grow and change in other ways that add to our value as human beings.

Question: *Are there long-term dangers in leaving infants under one year in day care (defined as the use of child care for more than twenty hours a week)?*

Answer: Researchers generally think that high-quality child care for children beyond the age of a year can be a positive experience. Until recently, however, they have not looked at the effects on younger children. Many people worry that early day care will cause infants to be less securely attached to their mothers. Attachment develops over time with the contact involved in the day-in, day-out care, thought, and effort that parents make to meet their baby's needs. The parent's growing sensitivity to the baby's cues—which become clearer with time—enable her to know him and figure out what he wants. Each time she feeds him when he is hungry, or holds him when he is lonely or in pain, or wraps him up when he is cold, he is learning that he can count on her. This is the foundation for basic trust. The degree of trust the infant feels for the mother affects the quality of all future relationships in the child's life.

The research on how day care affects infants has not yielded conclusive results. Measuring the strength of attachment between infant and mother is a crude and subjective process at best. Experts disagree on both the methods used and the significance of the findings. Some research suggests that a small percentage of infants in day care are insecurely attached to their mothers. These studies, however, did not look at family background or the quality of day care.

More and more mothers of babies are working. If that is what you choose, it doesn't help to focus on whether it is harmful, especially in the absence of conclusive evidence that it is. Instead, figure out how you can make going to work the most positive and least stressful experience for each family member. This means having realistic expectations of yourself as a parent and as a worker. It also means finding the very best child-care arrangement you can afford.

Babies are capable of forming attachments to more than one person. We can see that they attach to their fathers and their siblings. In many cultures where the extended, rather than nuclear, family is the norm, infants willingly receive care and comfort from many people. If you ask yourself how it could possibly be negative to have other significant, loving people in your baby's life, you can see complementary care not as a loss but as the enrichment that it truly can be. Read on!

Question: *What practical suggestions can you give on making it easier to work and care for a baby?*

Answer: *My family day-care giver has limited space for each child's supplies, so I can't leave much there. Instead, I keep my car trunk stocked with extra diapers, wipes, bottles, pacifiers, and clothing so that I can replenish whatever is needed on the spot.*

A: *With twins I have become very organized. I often don't have enough time to sit down every day with my sitter and catch up on the small things that have happened. What I have done to keep the communication going is buy a special notebook, which I call The Child-Care Log. My baby-sitter, Ruthie, and I write down certain bits of pertinent information every day. For instance, if Jenny has a very short nap, or Paul hardly eats any lunch, or one of them waved bye-bye for the first time, Ruthie makes a note. If I'd like her to throw in an extra load of laundry, or to watch the rash on Jenny's bottom, I jot that down. This way not too much slips by at the end of a hectic day. I recommend a log for all working mothers. There are no little pieces of paper to lose, and as the notebook fills up, Ruthie and I kind of pat ourselves on the back as we see just how many small but important observations and decisions go into baby care.*

A: *Streamline your exit! In the morning as I rushed out with Ben in my arms, I'd find that I'd sometimes forget to lock the door because my keys were buried in the bottom of my bag. Something as simple as installing a snap lock not only saved precious minutes but spared me a lot of aggravation. Then I could enjoy the car ride with Ben to the day-care center.*

A: *I'm too tired to cook at night. We keep it simple. On the weekend I wash a lot of salad greens for the two or three salads to go along with the main dish. One night it's a crockpot dinner; another it's eggs or grilled cheese; Wednesday is pasta or rice; Thursday a roast chicken that the baby-sitter starts; Friday, when we're really pooped, it's frozen or canned convenience food, or take-out pizza, or Chinese.*

A: *Divide and conquer. When both parents work it's only fair to share the "babywork" in the morning. My husband thought he couldn't do it all and get out in time, so I made him a checklist that is posted by the door. What to take to the sitter's, etc. He's become a whiz.*

A: *We do absolutely everything we can the night before. I make the baby's lunch and our lunches, pack his diaper bag, and lay out his clothes and my own, no matter how tired we are. We bought a coffeepot that makes the coffee ahead.*

A: *We get up forty-five minutes earlier than we used to. It's still dark, but it's peaceful! We have breakfast together and read the paper before Hilary wakes up.*

A: *I am a single parent on a very small budget, but I do give myself one luxury service a week. I pay my teenage neighbor who just got her driver's license to run errands for me on Tuesdays after school. For a very small fee, she picks up the dry cleaning, goes by the post office or the library, etc. That way I'm free to be with Sarah.*

A: *It was rush, rush, rush, all day. Then the minute I'd walk in the door, with a tired baby under my arm, the phone started ringing and my head started filling with all the things I needed to do to the house. At the end of the day it's hard to change gears. You can't expect to be able to cool out, but you can simplify things by setting one or two hard-and-fast rules to live by. For instance, I leave the answering machine on and don't make or take any calls until he is in bed.*

A: *I work a fifty-hour week and have since Lucy was seven months old. I take it day by day, trying to remember that each day is a new beginning. If yesterday wasn't so great, that doesn't mean that tomorrow won't be just fine. My goal is to enjoy my child, not feel her as a burden. My mother always worked, and I think she was a wonderful mother. She cross-stitched a sampler for me that hangs in my kitchen. It's become my mantra. It says:*

> *Quiet down, cobwebs*
> *Dust, go to sleep*
> *I'm rocking my baby*
> *And babies don't keep.*

To Work or Not to Work: One Mother Thinks It Through

Before: *Right now I'm trying to decide whether to return to work. My six-month leave will be up in two months, and yesterday the woman I work under called to remind me that my job won't be*

To Get Organized,
Here's a
Helpful Book:

The Sidetracked Home Executives, by Pam Young and Peggy Jones (New York: Warner Books, 1981).

---

there unless I make a decision soon. The possibility of part-time is an option, but I have some doubts about whether or not it will be worth it.

After Caroline was born, I was certain I would go back to the magazine after my postpartum checkup. Those first weeks were very rough on us because she had colic, wasn't sleeping, and we were still renovating the house to make a room for her. In the midst of the plaster dust, the mounting carpentry bills, her crying, and our bickering over my resentment about the full responsibility for the baby and the supervision of the workmen as Bill went out to work in his nice, neat suit every day, my job was my ace in the hole if the going got too rough. I was, of course, ashamed to admit this and was too busy and exhausted to look for a housekeeper then.

As the weeks went on the colic disappeared, Caroline started sleeping through the night, and now at four months she is a delightful, smiling, cooing baby. I'm really enjoying her. The carpentry is done, and Bill and I have stopped arguing—most of the time, at least. I'm trying to make the decision about work more rationally.

I have discovered in the course of searching for a housekeeper that I have many more opinions

---

about the kind of care I think our baby needs than I previously thought. I know I am a perfectionist and am quite critical of people who don't do things exactly the way I want them to be done. I have interviewed several women for the position. One woman was very nice and gentle, but she didn't talk. Another was so aggressive and opinionated that she literally pushed me aside when I was trying to pick up my baby. Another woman was terrific, but it turned out that she was pregnant herself and wasn't sure what she would do with her baby when it was born. Bill, who is much more flexible (and I think more easily satisfied) than I am, points out that no one will seem good enough and that maybe I don't want a job after all.

We could always use the money. But financially I will be making a great deal less if I work part-time and pay for a housekeeper as well. So I then try to evaluate what the job offers me personally. I've been there for six years and get tremendous satisfaction from the responsibility, the prestige, and the challenge, but of course every job has its negatives, too. Journalism does mean working late hours sometimes, and as a part-time worker I wonder if I will be taken seriously. Will I be given good assignments or stuck with the routine ones? And now that we have a baby, will the job provide me with the independence I enjoyed?

But more to the point, I wonder why we decided to have a baby if the mere thought of leaving her with someone else makes me feel so guilty. How will I feel when I actually do it? How will the baby feel? Will she flourish the way she seems to be flourishing now? Can anyone else take care of her quite as well as I do even if I do make mistakes? But if I stay at home all the time, will I feel engulfed and trapped? Will I stagnate and turn into a hausfrau? Will I be able to reenter the job market in a couple of years? I'm thirty-four now.

You asked me how I was thinking through the

question of going back to my job, and I'm afraid I haven't answered the question very well. For me, at least, it's very complicated. I do know one thing, though: If I do decide to go back, I am determined to regard it as an experiment.

After: *We were in touch when Caroline was four months old. She is now a year, and I wanted to let you know what has happened. In the first place, I'm a lot calmer now and far less of a perfectionist than I used to be. I did decide to go back to my old job on a part-time basis. I now work three days a week and one late night instead of five days. I waited until Caroline was nine months old. It turned out that my employers were more flexible than I thought, once I explained that I needed more time with the baby, more time to find a good person to take care of her, and some time for us all to settle in.*

I found a wonderful woman to come into our home. It may be useful to others to know that it does take a couple of months for everything to begin to work smoothly. After some trial and error, we have worked out what Mrs. Brown's role is. We've both had to make some minor concessions in terms of the way we do things, but we do agree on the basics.

Her first responsibility is to take care of the baby and to have fun with her. Caroline is now walking and is busy exploring. There isn't much time for Mrs. Brown to do anything but keep up with her, do a little of her laundry, and keep her room clean. The house is not as clean as I would like it to be. We can't afford cleaning help on top of child care, but I feel it's worth trading the sticky floors and cracker crumbs for the peace of mind I have knowing that Mrs. Brown really loves Caroline. Somehow Bill and I share the cleaning when it gets unbearable.

I had been very worried about not spending much time with the baby on work days, but she put herself onto her own crazy schedule, and it works well for all of us. She's up until nine-thirty or ten at night, then sleeps to nine in the morning. This isn't as exhausting as it may sound. Now that she walks, she's quite good at entertaining herself, and of course her father is home in the evenings to help out. Bill and I don't have that much time together in the evenings because of her late bedtime, but we're surviving.

We live even more simply than we did after Caroline was born. Bill does all of the grocery shopping once a week. We used to shop daily, a New York City syndrome, I think. For each meal I cook, I often make a double portion and freeze the remainder. We very rarely entertain and, when we do, it's very simple. We never go out on weeknights. I also try to do errands during my lunch hour near the office. For instance, I've found a dry cleaner and a shoemaker near work. If I have to get my hair cut, or go to the dentist, I also do this during lunch. I make it a point to get home at a set time every day to relieve Mrs. Brown. By a quarter to six, she's had it. This is the hardest part of the day. There's no time to wind down. I'm in the door and Caroline's in my arms or pulling on my shirt as I try to make her dinner.

As for the guilt, probably my biggest concern before I went back to work, I'm still a victim, but not nearly as great a one as I had thought I would be. Some mornings when I leave her crying with her nose pressed against the window, and I'm late anyway, and the house is a disaster, and the roof is leaking and the roofer hasn't arrived as he said he would, and the heel of my shoe is falling off, and my skirt is wrinkled, I wonder why I'm doing this. The first month was hell. I fell into bed at ten o'clock every night. But my imagined guilt was far more severe than the real guilt. I have simply to look at Caroline, myself, and Bill and see that though we're all a little crazy the way we live, we are pretty happy.

As for the job, I am doing my old job in three days instead of five, for less pay, of course. I had feared that I would not be taken seriously as a part-time worker, but in my case, at least, this isn't true. After three months back, I have actually gotten a promotion in terms of responsibility. I'm so efficient! Working mothers have to be that way, you know. The pay raise is yet to come, but it's been promised.

Timing Your Return to Work

There is no magic formula for knowing the best time to go back to work. Each age presents different challenges to parents as well as babies. The decision rests on factors as wide-ranging and unpredictable as your baby's age and particular temperament, his sleeping and eating habits, and your physical and emotional adjustment after childbirth, as well as on more concrete issues—your financial situation, the length of your maternity leave, your job security, and the availability of good child care. Mothers elaborate:

I run a small publishing company at home and have had a delightful baby boy at the late age of thirty-eight! However, I would advise all mothers who are self-employed and work at home to stay away from work as long as possible. I had only two weeks, and it was a mistake—even though I work from home. Babies are tiny for such a short time. I had no idea I would treasure those first months so much. I was worried while pregnant that I would somehow not want to be with the baby, that the magic "bonding" would not occur, that I was cool and independent and might not be that interested in the baby (boring, I thought). Well, mother nature, hormones, whatever takes care of this—the magic worked. You'll want to be with the baby, and work will, for a while, seem secondary, even though you struggle between them.

• • •

I had to go back after a six-week maternity leave. It was hard because Aaron was colicky, not sleeping through the night, and I was a zombie. I felt guilty and deprived—as if I just hadn't had enough of the baby—yet a part of me just wanted to run away from the whole situation. But once I was at work I felt as if I couldn't give my very best because all I did was think about the baby. My pediatrician was very helpful. She, too, had had to go back to work when her baby was a newborn. She said, "You are a good mother, but you don't have to act as if everything is just perfect when it isn't. You'd rather be home right now, but you can't be. Whatever you do, don't deny your feelings of longing and grief. They are appropriate, and they will pass. You'll get through it." And we did. My life is coming back together now. Aaron is almost five months old and is flourishing, and I'm proud of all that I've been able to handle.

• • •

I "eased" back into part-time work when Jesse was three months old. I started my search for child care then, thinking it would take time to find a good person and that I'd go back when he was five months old. But I couldn't pass up Elena, the woman I found to watch him. There was a long overlap period when I was around holding him, nursing him, and playing with him. Elena didn't have that much to do. In retrospect I can admit that I felt jealous of her. It was to her credit that she seemed to understand how important it was to me to be the most important person in Jesse's life. Every week I added a few hours to my schedule, so that by the time I was back full-time I was feeling more comfortable about everything.

• • •

Four-and-a-half months after giving birth, I'd say returning to work has been a fairly smooth adjust-

---

Having a Voice about Child Care

Did you know that if you lived in France you would be eligible for sixteen weeks of maternity leave, with pay, after the birth of your first and second child? Should you have a third child, you would get twenty-six paid weeks off. This government policy guarantees that your job will be there when you return.

Until it hits you personally, you may never have wondered why such family-centered policies—paid maternity leave, flexible work hours, training and standards for child-care providers, and more—are so lacking in the world's richest society when other, less affluent, countries have them. Many parents have no choice but to leave their babies before they feel ready, and many must leave them in inadequate, if not dangerous and neglectful, care. The price of this neglect is immeasurable for each one of those children and for our society as a whole.

As parents, we have an increased stake in and commitment to the world we live in. The only way we can make our communities, our employers, and our government more responsive to the needs of children and families is to assert our considerable power. We cannot do that if we remain isolated, left alone to struggle with our individual child-care dilemmas.

What can you do? Join Parent Action, a grass-roots organization whose goal is to promote the concerns of families. Among these: improving child-care choices; working for laws and policies, such as nationwide parental leave, that help families balance work and home life; and making health-care services more accessible to families. Parent Action is also developing a nationwide information and referral network for its members. For further information write to:

Parent Action
230 North Michigan
Suite 1625
Chicago, IL 60601
Membership dues are $5.00.

---

ment. Curtis has been sleeping and eating on a regular schedule for the past couple of weeks. It's hard, though, to tear myself away. He is so delicious! He'll watch me as I move around the room doing chores. Then he'll start making his little spluttering/cooing noise. I'll say, "Look, I've got to put the laundry away!" But before I know it I'm down on the floor playing with him instead. He kicks and wriggles in delight as if his whole body is smiling. My life is so hectic, and I can't get

anything done! But my attitude is, so what! The house is a shambles, but he'll only be this age once. The woman who watches him in her home for us says that when she takes him to the grocery store, he's such a smiley that a whole crowd gathers around him. I'm sad about missing that but grateful that she seems to love him and be almost as proud of him as I am.

• • •

Annie was six months old the day after I returned to my job five weeks ago. I bring her to the day-care center my company sponsors. The center is small. There are only three babies there, and I like the staff. I feel very good about the care she receives, but it is hard to leave her crying every morning. Marsha, her care giver, assures me that Annie stops by the time I've reached the parking lot. I go and nurse her at lunchtime and feed her her solids. Then she cries when I leave again. She does this at home too when I leave the room. I know it's a phase, but talk about feeling hard-hearted!

• • •

I took a writing assignment when Georgie was eight-and-a-half months old and at her clingiest, crawling after me wherever I went, pulling on my leg until I picked her up. I had a lovely baby-sitter who had been coming for three or four months and whom she loved. The problem was that when the baby would hear my typewriter going, she'd start to cry. It would constantly remind her that I wasn't there. I felt so torn. We worked out a solution: The sitter agreed to take her to her house instead of coming to ours.

• • •

I had planned to return when Daisy was a year, but by the time she was ten months I felt ready and felt she was ready, too. Through the company I found a very good woman who does family day care. That took a couple of weeks to work out. Then Daisy got her first tooth and first ear infection and took her first step all in one week. I had started to wean her but felt we had to slow down. She was clingier than she had ever been. To make a long story short, I returned three days before her first birthday. I advise that parents allow themselves plenty of time to get organized, and if you can, be flexible, because babies aren't very predictable.

How to Get Your Employer Involved

The philosophy at most offices is that you should leave your personal life at home, but this is unrealistic when you have a baby who is the center of your life and is on your mind a great deal of the time. I'd be a better worker if the workplace were more supportive of me and acknowledged some of the real issues I face as a worker and a parent.

Good child care is vital not only to our babies and ourselves but also to our economy as a whole. A growing body of research confirms what working parents already know: Productivity suffers, absenteeism and tardiness increase, and workers are more stressed when families compromise on the quality of their children's care. Some workers are even forced to quit their jobs because of inadequate child care. A study on child care and productivity by the Bank Street College of Education estimates that one out of two workers with children is currently trying to cope with some kind of child care–related difficulty. Most parents must deal with these issues from work by calling their homes and/or child-care providers. Of course, this takes time and energy away from the job.

Employers *are* responding. Growing numbers are providing on-site day care, pooling their resources with other companies to fund new centers, or training and monitoring family day-care providers in their communities. Other businesses provide resource and referral services that offer information on the types of care available in the community. Some companies offer direct financial assistance for child care or flexible "cafeteria-style" benefits. Job sharing, flextime, and longer parental leaves are also on the rise.

But it remains up to parents to make their needs known to their employers. A surprising

Useful Books for Working Mothers

Balaban, Nancy, *Learning to Say Goodbye: Starting School and Other Childhood Separations* (New York: New American Library, 1987)

Berg, Barbara J., *The Crisis of the Working Mother: Resolving the Conflict Between Family and Work* (New York: Summit Books, 1987)

Buhler, Danalee, *The Very Best Childcare and How to Find It* (Rocklin, Calif.: Prima Publishing & Communication, 1989)

Held, Julius, and Shreve, Anita, *Remaking Motherhood* (New York: Simon & Schuster, 1987)

Hochschild, Arlie, and Machung, Anne, *Second Shift: Inside the Two-Job Marriage* (New York: Penguin, 1989)

Johnson & Johnson Baby Products, "Guide for the First-Time Babysitter" (Grandview Road, Skillman, NJ 08558: Consumer and Professional Services, Johnson & Johnson Baby Products)

Norris, Gloria, and Miller, JoAnn, *The Working Mother's Complete Handbook* (New York: New American Library, 1984)

Sanger, Sirgay, and Kelly, John, *The Woman Who Works, the Parent Who Cares: A Revolutionary Program for Raising Your Child* (Boston: Little, Brown & Co., 1987)

number of employers do not have a realistic view of the American family in the 1990s. When Harvard University polled executives about what percentage of their employees were traditional breadwinners whose wives stayed home to care for the kids, estimates ranged from 40 to 70 percent. The reality: Only about *19 percent* of American households now fit that description.

If you are interested in becoming a child-care advocate at your job, be sure to remember the bottom line: defining the issues in terms of corporate self-interest. Connect these issues to long-term, broad-based corporate goals such as job recruitment during the coming labor shortages and reduction of the absenteeism and tardiness, which hurt productivity. Also be sure to focus on the needs of both men *and* women. In the past we have assumed that child-care problems are primarily "women's turf," but this is not true. They affect men as well. If you are interested in knowing what employers can do for families, write to:

The Conference Board
845 Third Avenue
New York, NY 10022

Ask for *Family-Supportive Policies: The Corporate Decision-Making Process,* an in-depth guide for corporations that want to help employees with child care.

Employers and Child Care: Benefitting Work
**   and Family**
The Women's Bureau
U.S. Dept. of Labor
Washington, D.C. 20210

The Child Care Action Campaign
99 Hudson Street
Suite 1233
New York, NY 10013

This group publishes more than thirty fact sheets on such subjects as sick child care and speaking with your employer about child-care assistance.

Helpful Organizations for Working Mothers

National Association of Child-Care Resources
    and Referral Agencies (NACCRA)
2116 Campus Drive S.E.
Rochester, MN 55904
(507) 287–2020

The Woman's Bureau
Work and Family Clearinghouse
    (800) 827–5335
This bureau provides information to employers interested in sponsoring child-care programs.

· PART SIX ·

Practical Matters

· CHAPTER 18 ·

The Portable Baby

The following notes for this book and its revision a decade later reflect the difference in the way I felt about getting out with my first baby versus my third baby.

I was quite nervous about taking her out the first time, but I knew I had to do it. For two days I planned a trip to the store, which was only two blocks from my house. I had fed her but was still afraid she'd get hungry at the store. As we walked along, I worried over how I was going to breast-feed her as I waited at the meat counter, especially since I'd worn a dress that zipped up the back. What would people think of me subjecting my new two-week-old baby to the 95° heat, the air pollution, and the germs in the city? What would happen when I took her into the air-conditioned store? Maybe I should have brought a hat for her. And even worse, what if we both got hit by a bus on the way home? What would Charlie do without us?

• • •

With Caity it seemed like getting out and about was something of an ordeal, but I realized by the third baby that all of those anxieties were in my head. I'd learned to go with the flow. I had to go out to take care of business. Because I had other children who needed to go places, I was out all the time. I also knew how much more difficult this would be once the baby was a wild and woolly toddler. If I forgot something, I simply made do. If Georgie missed her nap, it wasn't the end of the world. If she cried, I did my best to comfort her without worrying whether I was disturbing other people. That's life. Babies cry. So my advice is go out with the baby as much as you can. Have fun. Go to lunch with friends, go to museums, go shopping, because you sure can't do any of those things once you have a toddler. By then you can't even have a conversation with another human being. Remember, too, that being mobile with a baby is like any other aspect of baby care. It takes practice.

• • •

If nature had designed us for living in the modern world, we would be like kangaroos with handy pouches for our babies. We'd pop them in, and all those basic needs for food, warmth, cuddling, and love would be met as we went about the business of our lives. But life with a real baby is not quite so simple. Though we have the equipment to enhance mobility—baby carriers, strollers, car seats, etc.—the logistics involved in getting yourself and the baby out the door to make use of these conveniences can be positively daunting. By the time you've gotten the baby fed and dressed, zipped and buttoned, found your keys and your coat, the baby has had an "accident," which has gotten all over his clothes, or the weather has changed, or the sun has set, or you've misplaced the one and only pacifier he likes, or you both have simply grown too tired to go out anyway.

You may wonder, "Is it worth it?" Although it sometimes seems easier to stay home, the answer is a definite "yes" and "yes" again! Getting out is key to a mother's sanity. If it helps to make an outing a day more possible, then put it on your to-do list. It is all too easy to become a shut-in when you have a baby. The needs of infants are immediate, pressing, and genuinely wearing. But that does not mean that you have to focus all of your time, thoughts, and energy on the baby. This isn't good for either of you. When you are constantly giving, you need to have something coming back to yourself, be it as simple as the stimulation of a walk down the street. When you are out with the baby, time passes differently than when you are at home. An outing leaves you feeling renewed. If nothing else happens in the course of your day—and it's hard to complete tasks when you have a baby—at least you can say you've been out. Check it off your list of accomplishments.

It's good for the baby to get out, too. If we followed Dr. Spock religiously, our babies would be aired winter and summer for at least two hours a day. No matter how long you can be out, motion, a change of perspective, new people, sights, sounds, and smells are interesting to babies, who learn in myriad ways about how the world functions on those trips to the bank and the grocery store. And if the baby is fussy and has been fed, burped, bathed, held, rocked, and sung to, maybe he'll forget his woes once he's out in the world.

An Expert Answers Common Questions About Taking the Baby Out

Question: *When can I take the baby out?*
Answer: *If you've brought the baby home from the hospital, you've already taken him out. Next question.*

Question: *Is air conditioning all right for the baby?*
Answer: *Chances are, the hospital nursery in which the child spent the first days was air-conditioned. The mother's room, however, may not have been so equipped, and the baby was moved back and forth without any ill effects.*

Question: *When is the weather too bad for the baby to go out?*
Answer: *It is never too cold, too rainy, too snowy, too sleety, or too windy for the baby to go*

out *(even though* you *may prefer not to go out), since the child will be properly dressed and will thus be adequately protected from the elements. It may, however, be too hot and humid outdoors.*

Question: *What is too hot and humid?*
Answer: *If it is hot and humid enough outside for you to be decidedly uncomfortable, it is too hot for an infant; you will both be better off indoors, in the presence of air conditioning, or at least a fan to draw off perspiration.*
  —Virginia E. Pomeranz, M.D.,
   with Dodi Schultz
   *The First Five Years: The Relaxed
   Approach to Child Care*

Planning Is Everything

You truly can go almost anywhere with a baby. The single most important factor in a successful outing, be it a stroll around the block or a lengthy world tour, is advance planning. The outcome has everything to do with the thought and preparation you put into it before you leave. Parents advise . . .

Going out with a baby is like going to Europe. You practically need a suitcase and itinerary. First you size up the state of the baby. Is he in a good mood today? How long will he sit in the stroller—moving or stationary? Is it worth waiting at the bank or better to send in the deposit by mail? I got pretty good at planning the route—before rush hour, making the most important stops first, where to go to avoid revolving doors with the stroller, which department stores had a ladies' room with a changing table and chair where I could sit to nurse if we didn't make it back home in time.

• • •

We took Allison everywhere. And yes, our circle of friends did narrow. We felt most comfortable

with other couples with young children. They understood we might have to leave early if things got bad. Barbara and I always made an agreement beforehand about who would take care of her. She'd be "on" for part of the time, then it was my turn. That way neither of us was always stuck walking her back and forth when everyone else was eating dessert.

• • •

Sam and I couldn't handle taking Joanne to social gatherings like a lot of our friends did. Even if she slept, I found I was always aware of her, wondering when she'd wake up and whether she would feel strange in someone else's house when she did. What if she needed something that I'd forgotten? In retrospect, I think it was me who wasn't very flexible, much more than the baby, but I have to respect that too.

• • •

Jake was born in June, and we went to all sorts of outdoor events, picnics, and concerts. This seemed to work better than being in an inside environment, but maybe we felt freer ourselves outside and he picked up on this.

• • •

I delayed getting the work done on my teeth because I didn't know what to do with Vanessa. I didn't want to leave her with a sitter because she was still nursing every two hours. I had all of these complicated solutions worked out—like asking a friend to come along to hold her, or having my husband meet us there at lunch hour. As I was explaining my plans to the receptionist, she suggested that I bring Vanessa whenever it was best for me. I never would have thought to ask, but she said entertaining babies was one of the best, though rarest, parts of her job. It worked out really well. They had a fish tank in the waiting room, and she loved the lights and bubbles. We went every single week for sixteen weeks. By the time I had finished the treatment, she was crawl-

ing, and the waiting room was completely baby-proofed. Don't be daunted. Always ask. You never know.

Useful Equipment for the Portable Baby

There is a tremendous amount of equipment on the market for making a baby portable. But it's important to remember that everything costs, has to be kept relatively clean, and takes up storage space. Some items are more useful than others because they are multifunctional or have longer lives. What you buy or even borrow obviously depends on your own needs and the way you live.

When you shop for some items that have to be worn, such as back, front, or sling baby carriers, it's a good idea to take the entire family along. See just how easy it is to get the carrier on and off without assistance. If more than one parent will be using the carrier, make sure it fits both of you. And, of course, make sure the baby seems comfortable.

Don't buy any kind of equipment that does not have clear assembly and how-to-use instructions. If you are borrowing, remember that you are not a fool if you don't understand exactly how to use something. So ask! (With great difficulty and little satisfaction, I wore a borrowed Snugli backward for a month and couldn't understand why everyone thought it was such a great product!) You are not an ingrate to inquire whether anything is missing, not functioning, or is dangerous in any way either in terms of its design or the way it is used.

Infant Seats

Molded infant seats as well as wire-framed fabric seats or bounce chairs can provide the baby with

---

What to Carry: Staging Your Exit

If you plan to take the baby out, be sure to carry a waterproof hand or shoulder bag containing:

- A changing surface (a small blanket, towel, or cloth diaper will do)
- Diapers plus plastic bags to contain used cloth or disposable diapers
- Premoistened towels, or a washcloth and small container of water
- Plastic bottles and nipple covers, or a thermos and cup containing something to drink
- Special straws to fit into the standard nipple and ring for the baby who can sit up and hold his own bottle (The 8-ounce size can be cut in half to fit a 4-ounce bottle.)
- A nonmessy snack (which might make the difference between being able to wait in line or not)
- A "busy" toy that delights and entertains
- Sunscreen if the baby is over six months of age; otherwise, a wide-brimmed hat when it's hot and sunny and a snug cap when it's cold (Heads are the prime area for body heat loss.)

In cold weather, put a dab of petroleum jelly on cheeks and chin and above the upper lip if the baby has a runny nose. This will prevent chapping.

Question: Is there any such thing as a quick exit with a baby?
Answer: It all depends. The following should help:

- One staging area—even a hook or shelf—near the door for the baby's bag, shoes, snowsuit, mittens, hat, pacifier, etc. (These items are small and easy to misplace.)
- A safe place to put the mobile baby while you get organized yourself (This is the primary function that a playpen often serves.)
- Leave extra diapers, clothing, bottles, and pacifiers in the car, carriage, or stroller.
- The last thing you do is dress the baby. Then you go out the door and let the telephone ring if it's ringing.

---

a welcome change of perspective and a larger view of the world from the newborn period to four or five months, or until the baby becomes too wiggly to tolerate confinement. The seats have multiple uses. Some parents also use lightweight plastic models to help bathe their newborns in the sink or tub. That way they don't have to hold onto the slippery baby. After a feeding, the semiupright position can aid the baby's digestion. Rocking models may also help soothe or stimulate a baby. The smaller models can fit easily into the main basket of a grocery shopping cart, the only safe place for it. You can skip this purchase if your baby's car seat doubles as an

Shopping with a Baby Along: Mothers Share Tips

I am an emergency-room nurse and would like to warn parents that every year several babies and young children end up in our ER with concussions, fractured skulls, lacerations, etc., when they fall out of shopping carts. I use a special Velcro belt, which I bought at my baby-products store. It fits around Jink's waist, then through the wire opening in the cart. If you can't find one of these, a harness, used for babies who sit up in their carriages, will also work.

• • •

When I grocery shop I carry my eleven-week-old into the store right in his bucket car seat. It fits neatly into the bottom of the shopping cart. There isn't too much room in the cart, so I carry one of those little baskets in addition.

• • •

Remember that stores often have help available on request to wheel a cart to the parking lot. I notice that mothers of infants and young children seldom take advantage of that service when they could.

• • •

In winter I see lots of babies sweating away in snowsuits at the supermarket. This isn't comfortable or healthy. Before I take Lucy to the store, I dress her in layers. I can then peel off the windbreaker but leave a warm sweater on underneath. This is a lot easier than dealing with an entire snowsuit.

infant seat. These have convenient handles for carrying the baby from place to place.

Buying Suggestions

The very lightweight models are quite tippy. When you shop for an infant seat, choose one whose base and rear support systems are wider than the seat. If the rear support system consists of the carrying handle in a flipped-back position, make sure that the latch is strong. Press down on the seat, then shake it to see how easy it is to tip over. Look for a base with a nonskid surface. If the baby wiggles and kicks, you don't want a seat that moves with her. Also, a good but easy-to-operate safety belt is essential. Cleanability is another important factor. Vinyl upholstery or washable fabric seat covers are a plus.

Safe Usage

• Never use an infant seat to replace an approved car seat. Beside the fact that they are not made to be anchored to the car, they are not designed to withstand the impact of a collision.
• According to Consumer's Union there have been thousands of accidents involving infant seats. Most occur when they fall off tables and counters or other high places either because the baby moves or startles suddenly or because the metal support wires give way. *Always belt the baby in.* Even a newborn can startle and lurch forward and out. A vibrating surface such as the top of a washing machine or dryer can cause the seat to "walk" off the edge. Whenever possible, place the seat on the ground. If you do put the seat on a table or countertop, get in the habit of keeping one hand on the seat if you must turn away.

Front (Soft) Pack Carriers

One of the oldest, most comfortable, and most convenient ways to transport a baby is by carrying her on your front, hip, or back. In any of these positions, a small baby can nap or observe the passing scene as you go about your work with both hands free. The motion and your familiar warmth, breathing, and heartbeat can also be soothing to a fussy baby. And if you must get out on foot, rain or shine, there is no better way to travel in bad weather. You can both fit under the umbrella.

There are three types of soft carriers, each with various advantages and disadvantages. In general, manufacturers state that these are useful until the child is between 30 and 35 pounds, which means the child will be well over two. While a strong parent might be able to carry a child that large, most babies, by the time they are a year old, or walking, will tolerate the confinement for only short periods of time.

Pouch Carriers

These are designed to hold the baby against your front in a zippered pouch made out of a variety of fabrics, from corduroy to lightweight seersucker. The Snugli, a superior product, was the first of these to come on the market. Inside the pouch there is an adjustable fabric seat that can be raised as your baby grows, and changeable bibs for the baby's face to rest against. This design offers the newborn good head support. It also holds the baby very closely and securely, leaving a parent's hands free. Look for well-padded shoulder straps and easy-to-operate zippers and snaps. The pouch carrier is one of the few baby products that is really worth the money. Though these carriers are somewhat expensive,

The *Rebozo*

If you are traveling, consider bringing along a *rebozo,* the Spanish word for "shawl." Take any three-yard piece of nonstretch fabric. When not in use the fabric can serve as a cover or diaper-changing surface (see illustration). Follow the directions, which sound more complicated than they are.

  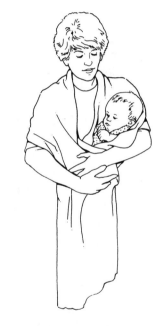 

1. Drape the shawl or *rebozo* to its full width across your shoulders. Leave it shorter on the side where you will place the baby.

2. Fold both edges of this short side over the baby, leaving his feet hanging uncovered. The bottom edge of the shawl may hang free or may be wrapped around the baby.

3. Lift up the long end, holding it away from your body, then lay it over the baby. Bring this end around under the baby as far as it will go and pull it up between the baby and your chest.

4. What is left of the long end will now be inside and top side of the baby. This can be tucked around the baby on the side away from your body.

they are far superior in design to the less expensive, more open, strap-on versions described below.

Open Soft Carriers

A second type of carrier is more open in feeling. It consists simply of a fabric seat that holds the baby up like a pair of pants. These usually come with headrests to give the newborn head support. Though these carriers are considerably less expensive than the pouch carriers, they are not really the bargain that they may seem. They are usually difficult to put on without another person to help with the straps while you hold on to the baby. Another drawback is that they are so open on the sides that the baby can tip if not almost slide out. A parent instinctively puts a hand on the baby's back to provide a more secure feeling. You are then, in effect, operating with one hand, and little sense of security, which cancels out many of the advantages of a baby carrier.

Hip Carriers

These carriers balance the baby on your hip, which is not everyone's style. Though they provide a secure feeling, not everyone finds these comfortable for walking.

Back (Frame) Pack Carriers

A backpack is useful for the "older" baby who sits up well and can withstand the bouncing motions of riding this way. By this time she's probably getting a little heavy to carry comfortably on your front or your hip without putting strain on your back. She'll also appreciate a better view and more freedom to move her head and arms than soft packs permit. Lots of fathers enjoy carrying their babies this way. Most packs now

---

Car Travel Alert

WARNING! Never substitute wearing the baby in a front pack carrier in the car for using an approved safety restraint system. In a collision the baby could be crushed between you and the dashboard or you and the back seat, even though you may be wearing your safety belt. Also, never bicycle with the baby in any type of carrier other than an approved bike seat.

---

come with built-in loading stands, which make loading by yourself easier. Whatever type you choose, it's a good idea to practice and build up your carrying time over a period of days when you first start out. If you don't use your backpack for a number of weeks, you also may have to build up your carrying time again.

Buying Suggestions

• Definitely try this out before you buy; it may not be your style.
• A pack must have an easy-to-operate, reliable safety belt so that the baby can't climb up and out.
• The seat in the carrier should be located midway down your back. This is important for two reasons: This is the most stable position, and it places the weight on your back rather than on your shoulders.
• Check to make sure there is plenty of room for the baby's legs to rest in a normal position, out to the front rather than squeezed to the sides. Make sure leg openings are not restraining.
• Make sure that the shoulder straps at the top

are adjustable and well padded. If they are not, the pack can be excruciatingly uncomfortable.
• Look for a pack anchored to the frame at the top as well as the bottom. The shifting of the baby's weight in a pack that is not well anchored can be bothersome and uncomfortable.
• Make sure that all metal parts that come in contact with the baby are padded.
• If you choose a pack with a loading stand, make sure the locking device is strong and won't trap fingers.
• Remember to bend from the knees when you bend down while wearing the baby on your back. Otherwise the baby may spill out.

Strollers

Nothing has improved the mobility of parents and babies quite as much as the advent of the lightweight, foldable stroller and stroller/carriage. There are numerous styles on the market, from the featherweight umbrella models with fabric sling seats that can be "worn" on the arm and easily fitted into a hall closet or trunk of a car, to the bulkier deluxe models offering cushioned reclining seats, shock absorbers, and dual brake systems.

What you choose will depend on your budget, available storage space, how often you will use the stroller, and the baby's age. In general the soft sling seats are not good for newborns because they force the baby into a slumping position. A firm-back model that flattens almost completely and has either a frame or fabric siding to keep the baby from rolling out is better. Do take your baby with you when you shop for a stroller. Put him in the stroller and wheel it around, keeping in mind that the needs of newborns and toddlers are quite different. A tiny baby, for instance, may need to sleep comfortably. A toddler, on the other hand, needs a foot-

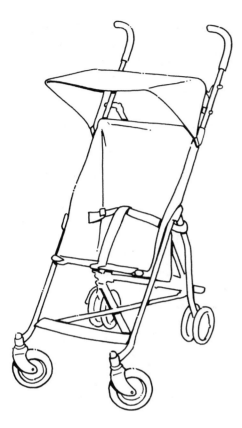

Umbrella-type stroller

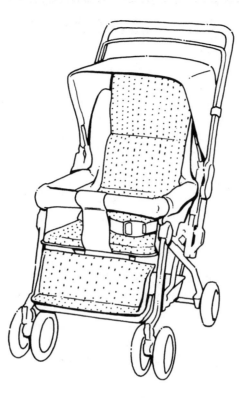

Firm-back stroller

rest that adjusts to the length of his legs, so his feet have support and don't dangle.

Buying Suggestions

• Try out the seat belt. It should make positive contact all the way around the front of your child's waist as well as provide crotch restraint to keep the child from slipping down and out or climbing out. Squeeze-type buckles are easier to operate than those that must be double threaded like a conventional belt.

• Are the brakes good, and are they easy to operate by hand or by foot? There are two kinds of brake systems: those that apply pressure to the tires and those that lock one or both of the rear wheels in place. Dual rear wheel brakes are preferable.

• Does the stroller ride, steer, and turn well? The wheels are what make a difference. Generally the larger the wheels, the easier it is to steer. Some strollers have double sets of wheels. All of them should make contact with the floor or the stroller will not steer straight. Test this by push-ing it across the floor with one hand. Some models offer swivel front wheels that can also be locked into a forward facing position, which make a stroller easier to manipulate on bumpy surfaces. This is a useful option for parents who have to negotiate a variety of terrains. Check the shock-absorbing system. Pads or springs on all four wheels generally provide a smoother ride.

• Is it stable? The wider, lower, and longer the wheel base, the sturdier the stroller. Try tipping it backward. Parcels hung on the handles make a stroller very tippy. Consider those with optional baskets for packages that fit low between the wheels. If you choose a model that reclines, make sure it won't tip with a child lying down in it.

• Foldability is another consideration. Is it easily folded? When you fold it, keep your baby or toddler away from it because the moving parts can trap small hands and fingers. Are there any small parts that can come off? For instance, some handles have plastic caps that could be removed and swallowed by a toddler. And how cumbersome is it in that position? Will it fit into your car trunk or closet? Occasionally a stroller in use will collapse into its folded position, causing the baby to be hurt. Besides having a locking mechanism to keep the stroller unfolded, it should have a backup lock as well to prevent accidental collapse.

• If you buy a stroller with options or extras, such as wind or rain shields, hoods, etc., make sure these attachments are simple to operate.

• Is the stroller easy to clean? A newborn isn't eating graham crackers and spilling juice yet, but a toddler will. Though a mild solution of baking soda and water will remove many spills from fabric, vinyl is easier to clean.

• Finally, think about your own comfort. Are the handlebars high enough for both parents not to have to lean over? Is the stroller lightweight enough to carry, to manipulate up and down curbs, etc.?

Safe Usage

- Never leave a baby or young child unattended in a stroller or carriage.
- Always use the seat belt.
- Keep the baby away when folding or unfolding the stroller.
- Don't let your child play with the stroller.
- Remember when crossing streets that the stroller is out in traffic ahead of you. Drivers may not notice it because it is low to the ground.

Bicycle Seats

Bicycling with a baby can be lots of fun if you are a good cyclist, but don't attempt this until the baby can sit up well. Otherwise, his back muscles will not be strong enough for the upright position and his neck will not be strong enough to cope comfortably with the joggling, bumpy motions of cycling. Keep the rides short.

There are two kinds of bike seats: front-mounted and rear-mounted. Though the front-mounted seats make it easier for parents to be in touch with the baby, there are many disadvantages to them. Besides making it awkward for a parent to mount and dismount, they make steering and handling the bike difficult. It's something of a risk to bicycle with a baby in the first place, and it doesn't seem worth it to make it even more dangerous with a front-mounted seat. Instead, choose a rear-mounted seat.

What to Look For

- Look for a seat that provides foolproof protection for the baby's feet as they straddle the

wheel. A foot caught in the spokes can be seriously injured.
- Make sure installation instructions are clear and simple.
- Look for a high back to offer good support.
- A strong and reliable safety belt is a must.
- Put a helmet on the baby! This can make the difference between a few cuts and bruises and a serious head injury should you fall. Look for a lightweight helmet made of thick, molded styrofoam, with a lining that can be added for a secure fit; snug-fitting straps; and good ventilation. Choose yellow or white for the best visibility.

All About Car Safety Restraints

An infant car restraint will be one of the most important items you own. Make sure you buy this item *before* your baby is born so that he or she can ride home from the hospital in it. Even though all states now have laws requiring babies and young children to be restrained while traveling by car, there are still more than 1,000 children under the age of five who die in car accidents every year. In addition, more than 100,000 children in the same age group are injured each year, often because of improper use of the seat. It is crucial, therefore, not only to have the right seat but also to have it correctly installed and to use it properly every single time.

A great deal of information follows. Though it may seem tedious to read, try to be patient and take the time to do so. This is one item where you really should know what you are looking for and why before you go to the store to buy. Your friends might have useful recommendations or hand-me-downs to offer, but remember, if your car is different from theirs their advice or their car seat may be of little use to you.

Is Your Car As Safe As It Can Be?

- Did you know that most car accidents occur at low speeds close to home, and that ejection from a vehicle increases the chance of dying by twenty-five times? Locked doors and restraints keep passengers from being thrown from the car.
- Is your car equipped with a first-aid kit along with working safety flares, change for a phone call, and a flashlight?

If the Expense of a Car Seat Is a Problem . . .

Call your county health department, local Red Cross chapter, hospital, childbirth education association or your automobile insurance company. Many of these organizations sponsor low-cost rental or loaner programs. Some hospitals, for instance, will lend you a seat for three to five months. You pay a deposit, and when you return the seat you receive half to two-thirds of it back. This is also a good option for families who aren't sure what seat to buy or are in the process of buying a new car.

Types of Car Safety Restraints

The first decision you will be faced with when choosing a child restraint system is whether to use a rear-facing model designed for babies weighing less than 20 pounds or a convertible model that can be used during the early months in a rear-facing position and then converted to a front-facing position when the baby is older and lasting until he weighs about 40 pounds.

The reason the young baby must face backward in a semireclining position is that in the event of an accident, the forces are spread as evenly and gently as possible across his back, which is the strongest part of his body.

The "two-for-one" design is clearly more economical than the rear-facing model. But it is also bulkier and generally more complicated to install. The rear-facing-only seats have the advantage of being more portable and can double as infant seats in the house, on airplanes, in grocery carts, etc.

In any case, once your baby weighs more than 20 pounds or is between eight and twelve months, you will need to choose a forward-facing restraint from an overwhelming array of products.

Question: *How do I choose the right seat?*

Answer: Research is important in order to choose the right seat for your car. But it is just as important to be realistic about how you will use the seat. In your wish to be the most conscientious parent on earth, you may choose the top-rated seat for safety. However, this may not be the easiest for you to install or use correctly *every single time.* Physicians for Automotive Safety have found that three out of four child safety seats are being used incorrectly, which of course nullifies their lifesaving benefits. If the belting

and buckling mechanism strikes you as too time-consuming or awkward to handle, choose a different model. If placing a permanent bolt in your car to hold a tether strap is something that you might not get around to, don't buy a seat that requires it. Besides considering seat height, width, and upholstery, you will also want to evaluate such things as the ease of adjusting straps to fit and of operating buckles and reclining mechanisms.

Before you do anything, look in your car owner's manual for instructions on how to install a child restraint properly. Don't buy or borrow a seat that requires a top tether strap unless your car has been designed for mounting the anchor for the strap. Also, remember that most foreign cars' lap/shoulder safety-belt combinations allow belt movement after the buckle has been fastened. The safety belt may then loosen, allowing the car seat to slide around. Something called a *locking clip*, which will be mentioned in the instructions that come with the car seat and in the owner's manual, will remedy this. You may also need seat-belt extenders.

Question: *If I need a locking clip or seat-belt extender, where do I buy these?*

Answer: These are generally available through auto supply stores, car dealers, and some baby-product stores. Locking clips can be purchased through the mail for $2.00 from the National Child Passenger Safety Association, Suite 300, 1705 De Sales Street N.W., Washington, D.C. 20036.

Car Seat Designs

There are many variations on each of the designs described below. Before you make your final decision, take the opportunity, whenever possible,

to talk to parents about what they have chosen. A supermarket parking lot is a very good place to do this kind of research.

- **The five-point harness model.** This model has one strap per shoulder, one for each side of the baby's lap, and a crotch strap between the legs; all of these straps converge and fasten together into a single buckle. The advantage of this design is that it is adjustable as your child grows and, when properly adjusted, holds onto the child's strongest bony structures—the shoulders and hips. Some of these designs have play trays and armrests that have no safety function. The disadvantages are that parents sometimes forget to adjust these for a tight fit, or rush and don't buckle the harness at all.

- **The harness/partial shield model.** This comes with front shields that fit against the child, taking the place of the lap part of the five-point harness. The shield looks a little like a tray. Though these appear bulky and cumbersome compared to the five-point harness system, they are actually simpler to operate because the straps stay flat.

- **The retracting-shield model.** This is the newest design. It features a chest shield with a narrow stalk that buckles into the seat between the child's legs. The advantage to this design is that a baby can be safely installed in the seat with one pull-down-and-lock operation that can be performed singlehandedly. However, in crash tests, it appears that some of the forces are directed to the center of the child's pelvis rather than to the sides, which are stronger. There is no documented evidence that such a change in force distribution has caused any harm to a child.

- **Tether straps.** Some seats are designed to be held in place with a tether strap. When this is properly installed it restricts the upward and

Warning about Used Car Seats

Don't buy a seat manufactured before January 1981. This date should appear on the back of the seat. If you inherit a seat, check it carefully to make sure that safety straps are not frayed, or metal parts rusted, and that the buckles work smoothly. Instructions for installation and positioning should be permanently affixed to the seat. If they are missing for some reason, contact your car dealer or seat manufacturer.

Car Seats for Premature Babies

Some car seats are not safe for premies because the straps and harness system do not fit snugly. Seats with lap pads or shields are unsafe because the shields can hit the baby in the neck or face. Choose a seat with multiple harness locations. Pick one that is no greater than 5½ inches from seat back to crotch strap. Even so, you may have to wedge a blanket between the baby and the strap. Place rolled blankets on either side of the baby to support the head.

side-to-side movement of the restraint during a collision and minimizes neck and back injuries. If you do not install the tether strap correctly, the seat will lose its lifesaving benefits, so consider carefully before you buy one. While some cars come with brackets already in place, others require that you install them yourself. Installation means bolting the strap bracket to the shelf between the back seat of the car and the rear window. The shelf must be made of strong metal.

Question: How do you install a seat in a recreation vehicle or a seatless van?
Answer: Write for instructions to the University of North Carolina Highway Safety Research Center, Chapel Hill, NC 27599.

Question: My baby hates the car seat. What can I do?
Another parent concurs: I am not a mother who would ever consider leaving my baby to cry himself to sleep at night. My problem is that he hates the car seat and screams every time we put him in it. I would almost risk his coming to physical harm rather than the psychological damage I know is being done when I ignore his panicked cries to be released. Even though it is against the law, when it gets really bad, I sit in the back seat with him cradled in my arms.

Answer: There are times when a parent's best intentions can be lethal. You simply cannot protect a baby by holding him in your arms in a moving car. Researchers at the University of Michigan set up a test to demonstrate the powerful forces at work in low-speed collisions. Volunteers, wearing seat belts, held 17-pound baby dummies in tests simulating 15- and 30-mile-per-hour crashes. Warned when the impact would occur, they were told to hold on to the dummies with all their strength. Not a single volunteer,

male or female, was able to keep hold of the baby. A low-speed collision or even a sudden braking can wrench your child from your arms with a tremendous force, thrusting him forward at the speed the car was traveling—until the baby hits something and stops. An unrestrained baby involved in a 30-mile-per-hour crash is hurled against the dashboard with a force of 300 pounds, the equivalent to the impact of falling from a third-story window. If an unbelted adult is holding the baby in lap or arms, his weight hits the baby with between one and two tons of force.

Tips and Tricks for Car Travel

Most tiny babies hardly notice they're in the car. The steady churn of the motor and the soothing motion put them right to sleep. But as the baby get older and more physically active and curious, sitting in a safety restraint for more than a magical amount of time can become sheer torture for everyone.

We soon learn what the limit is, and it grows ever shorter. A quick trip is tolerable because the end is in sight, but on a longer ride a "bag of tricks" is a necessity. The following suggestions, gleaned from thousands of miles of travel, are geared for driving under the worst possible conditions: alone in 95°F weather, when you *have* to get there.

• Always, always, always buckle your baby into the restraint correctly. This is important for safety reasons, and it is an important habit or ritual for your baby to become familiar with. Babies are compliant; toddlers aren't necessarily.

• Although the safest location for your child's safety restraint is in the middle of the back seat, consider moving the restraint to the front seat if you must travel a long distance alone. If someone else is driving, get in the back seat with the baby.

- Remove *all* loose objects from the car, be they on the back window ledge or back seat. Groceries and suitcases should be in the trunk. Flying objects are very dangerous in the event of a crash.
- In summer dress the baby in comfortable loose clothing, and take off her shoes if it is hot. Use overnight diapers for the best absorbency. In winter use a legged snowsuit and extra socks rather than shoes for comfort. If you are traveling a long distance, don't use the snowsuit. Use layers instead, which can be removed as the car warms up.
- In hot weather line the restraint with a cloth cover, which you can buy where you got the seat. When you leave the car, cover the restraint with a blanket or towel to keep the metal parts from getting hot.
- Use big looseleaf-type rings rather than string or elastic to secure a toy or two to the restraint so that the baby can't drop them. It is frustrating to the baby to have toys drop to the floor, and dangerous for the driver, should a toy roll under the foot pedals.
- Music is a wonderful distraction—the car radio, tapes, or your own voice.
- Bring soft finger foods that are easy for the baby to chew and swallow. If appearances are important, cover the baby with a large bib, and bring along a damp washcloth in a plastic bag or packaged towelettes, to clean up the baby.
- Don't push the limits. Decide before you leave when and where you're going to stop. You'll be less tempted to take a howling, furious baby out of the restraint if there is a concrete goal in sight.

• • •

We just about gave up long car trips when our children were young. When we had to make them, *we took turns driving and sitting in the back seat to sooth and cajole, feed, and entertain Sally.*

• • •

We found the car seat is entirely tolerable if used in combination with a pacifier. But lose that pacifier at the Dairy Queen and you're in for it! I suggest you be sure to bring a couple of them along.

• • •

We drive at night. It's the only way to cover a decent distance without having to stop.

• • •

Howie and I used to drive as many miles as we could with the fewest stops. When we had Harry, we had to change our style, because we sure couldn't change Harry. He was good for about an hour at a stretch. Then it was as if he was being tortured. You can't drive safely under those circumstances. Our goal is no longer simply to get there, but to get there in a sane way. We stop often. We start again when we feel the baby is ready. We see a lot more on the way. We feel this is a plus.

Flying with a Baby

Flying with a baby certainly is preferable to driving thousands of miles to get where you are going. The tradeoff is that flying is a "public" event. It takes planning, a little extra time, a good dose of humor, and a bit of courage to pull it off.

In 1989, the *Wall Street Journal* ran an article by Cathy Trost entitled "Pampered Travelers (of the Tiny Kind) Take Over Airlines." The article is reprinted here; which side are you on?

"Try flying on any plane with a baby," author Nora Ephron once wrote, *"if you want a sense of what it must have been like to be a leper in the fourteenth century."*

These days the airplane kid wars are escalating

Useful Resources

The National Child Passenger Safety Association
Suite 300
1707 De Sales Street
Washington, D.C. 20036
(202) 429–0515
A nonprofit organization for parents and professionals that can answer any questions on automobile safety.

The National Highway Traffic Safety Administration
400 Seventh Street S.W.
Washington, D.C. 20590
Auto Safety Hotline
(800) 424–9393. In Washington, D.C. (202) 426–0123
A nonprofit organization that provides information on safety belts, child safety restraints, and more. You can also report defects in car safety restraints to this group.

as rapidly as the fare wars. The friendly skies are filled with tiny travelers who have given the term pampered passengers *a new depth of meaning.*

"I had to change a really smelly diaper once next to this businessman," Dana Carr, a Vienna, Virginia, teacher, says of a flight she took with her baby daughter. "There's no place to be discreet, but I had to lay her across the seat and go to it. I knew he [the businessman] was ready to throw up."

Jet Setters in Snugglies

Many travelers do seem inured to it all. Their attitude seems to be that there, but for the grace of a baby-sitter, go I. But others are ready to ground the tots.

"I have been thrown up on, had dinners spilled all over my business suit, and had my seat kicked for hours," Janet Hanson, a Californian, complained in a letter to Condé Nast Traveler magazine.

"I log at least 75,000 miles per year, many of them plagued by kicking children and incessantly crying infants," wrote Charles Jeffrey Weiss, a traveler from Connecticut.

The conflict is heating up as more kids take to the air. Airlines don't keep track of child passengers, but most agree their numbers are growing. Many are children of the tribe of baby boomers, whose nomadic traditions encourage children on pleasure and sometimes even business trips. "This particular generation of parents is very affluent and very well traveled," says Janet Tice, president of a New York travel agency for families.

Crew's Little Helper

Airlines diplomatically say they receive few formal complaints about little ones. But some crew members grumble about being flying nannies. "Babies are in fact not welcomed by flight attendants," an attendant for an unidentified "major carrier" wrote to the Washington Post last year. "Babies and lap children provide no revenue for airlines but do provide grief to crews and passengers."

Ann Hood, a novelist, says that as a Trans World Airlines flight attendant for seven years, she saw many strange things. There was, for example, the passenger who wet-nursed her cat. But children and their parents, Ms. Hood says, were among the worst. On a flight from Boston to Los Angeles, a little girl repeatedly canvassed passengers for drink orders that she relayed to exhausted crew members who were "ready to kill her," Ms. Hood says.

"Somebody should get a leash for this kid!" Ms. Hood finally griped to a passenger, who turned out to be the child's father.

"Every parent thinks their kid is the cutest," she says. "They forget what it's like to be stuck on a widebody plane with a screaming baby, and you have to climb over five people to escape it." Even worse, "people would put dirty diapers in the seat pockets," she says. "We were warned early on never to jam your hand in there."

Parents, for their part, complain that flight attendants are often insensitive to their needs, lavishing attention instead on the more lucrative and generally tamer adult and business crowd.

Sally Jackson, a Washington, D.C., travel agent, recalls a "nightmare" trip home from Paris with her daughter, Gabrielle, who was two months old. At feeding time, she says, the TWA attendant "would not open the formula for me. They said it was against federal rules to have a can opener on board." A businessman refused to make an easy seat change so the family could sit together. The baby was fussy and cried.

The final indignity occurred, Ms. Jackson says, when a woman chastised her at the end of the trip for "not being a better mother."

Ms. Carr, the Virginia teacher and a mother of three, says her worst experience came last holiday season when her three-year-old daughter announced that she had "to go poop" as their American Airlines flight from Dallas was taking off for San Diego. The flight attendant was "quite annoyed" and said she had "to hold it," according to Ms. Carr, who snapped back: "This child has to go. [She'll] either poop in the seat or in the bathroom, it's your choice."

The attendant finally allowed the child to go to the lavatory but, Ms. Carr says, "she was put out and kind of abrupt to me the rest of the trip."

The airlines say their crews must enforce safety and other rules. Child-weary business travelers want them to go further. Some even call for a ban on children on airplanes. Others urge that they at least be barred from first and business class or segregated into children-only sections. Many parents who travel with children say they would prefer to sit in a section dedicated to kids.

These ideas don't yet fly with airline officials. "We've not gotten to the point of suggesting segregated cabins," says Joyce Coleman, vice-president of in-flight services for TWA, "though it isn't as farfetched as it sounds." George Mueller, vice-president of customer services for American Airlines, says segregating cabins "isn't practical."

Instead, some airlines are trying to engage the traveling tykes with entertainment. American Airlines, which says it pays special attention to routes that are heavily traveled by children at certain times of the year, is installing a children's channel on its international-flight audio system and introducing a new activity book.

Pan American World Airways has actively marketed to families with a kids-fly-free (when accompanied by a paying adult) promotion; the airline notes, too, that its sensitivity to children has grown as more of its flight attendants become mothers.

"I think actually some smart airline will start saying we are very good with families," says Harold Evans, editor-in-chief of Condé Nast's Traveler magazine, who frequently flies with his three-year-old son, George. Mr. Evans envisions a crib-class section with its own bathroom, video gallery, and storage, partitioned from other passengers, with warnings posted for those bothered by children.

Most airlines, however, say they are satisfied with current services. "We've not seen any trends developing that denote anything other than a very positive experience," says a spokesman for Delta

Air Lines, which offers kids a "Fantastic Flyer" magazine and other materials.

In fact, many parents report smooth flying, often with the help of genuinely attentive attendants. Stephanie Havenstein, a Bethesda, Maryland, mother pregnant with her fourth child, had no problems when she made a recent trip on Piedmont Airlines with her children aged five, two, and one. But she says she flew at off-hours to avoid "running into a bunch of men with business suits." The stewardesses helped her get settled and took the children to meet the pilot.

Many adult passengers take the small fliers in stride, too, says Lena Zezulin, a partner in the Washington, D.C., law firm of Thomas Hart & Associates. Her two-year-old son has traveled so much that he has a frequent-flier number. In these travels, she reports, she has seen "very crotchety old men be basically nice and not get upset when potato chips get spilled on their trousers."

(A response to the Wall St. Journal, published here in Babysense for the first time.)

Dear Ms. Trost,

Thank you for the long-overdue article on flying with babies and young children. I consider myself a veteran, having traveled alone with three children under six during heavy business traffic hours. I can attest that one does feel like a fourteenth-century leper. I was burdened with a stroller containing the three-year-old, a front-pack carrier with the newborn, a diaper bag, as well as an additional bag of food and distractions. With my free hand, I held on to the six-year-old. No one offered to help, and I felt those looks of contempt from the flight attendants and the businessmen and women. To my credit, I have overcome the guilt I once suffered when the baby howled. Let my fellow flyers suffer! This is real life

that I present them with. It is I who deserve a medal for taking on this brave mission. And should I ever travel alone—with free hands—I vow to assist anyone in need who is traveling with young children. I won't ever forget how it feels.

Sincerely,
Frances Wells Burck

Tips and Tricks for Airplane Travel

Knowing how your fellow passengers will feel when they lay eyes on you and your baby, it's best to prepare with the utmost thought and care. The first thing you can do is consider leaving half of what you think is necessary behind. Until "people movers" are standard equipment at airports, you may find yourself walking more than a mile to get to your seat, an exhausting prospect, especially if you're juggling a baby, coat, pocketbook, diaper bag, stroller, and possibly a car seat as well. Consolidate the diaper bag and pocketbook. If you must wear a coat, make it a lightweight one (you'll be sweating as it is), and whatever you do, don't wear high-heeled shoes! Opt for the less fashionable but infinitely more comfortable walking or jogging shoe or plain sneaker. Wear plain, washable clothing, too. And leave that great novel that you haven't had a chance to read since you became a parent at home on your bedside table. You won't have a moment to read it anyway. Before you get on the plane, make use of changing tables in the airport ladies' rooms, and make sure you get to the departure gate early enough to take advantage of one of the few privileges parents with children are awarded—getting on board first.

During takeoffs and landings have the baby sucking on a bottle, a pacifier, or your breast. Swallowing helps to clear the ear passages, which become blocked when the air pressure in

the cabin changes as the plane changes altitude. But if the baby won't drink or suck, and cries, don't be too upset. Crying helps clear the ears, too.

Some parents ask their pediatricians for something to help the baby sleep during the flight. If you do this, however, be sure to try it out in advance. Drugs affect everyone differently, and sometimes they actually make a baby more active. If you have a free seat next to you and your baby sits up well, pull down the tray. The tray is good for playing on, banging on, and eating from—at least for a little while.

What to Bring in Your Carry-on Bag

Pack one carry-on bag, preferably one with a shoulder strap and enough room in it to put your entire pocketbook, or some of its contents. This will give you free hands to carry the baby and the following:

- Appropriate change for tipping, phone calls, etc.
- Disposable diapers and plastic bags to wrap them in (Count on using about one diaper an hour.)
- Premoistened towelettes
- Diaper-rash ointment, or A and D Ointment, in case the baby has to sit in a dirty diaper longer than normal
- One or two complete changes of clothing for the baby, including a sweater and bib
- Blanket or towel as a changing surface
- Pacifier plus two extras in case of loss. Pack the third in your suitcase
- Juice or formula kept chilled with an ice pack—or a premixed sealed bottle, or powder plus sterile water or bottled water (Don't give a baby airline water.)
- On a long international flight, you might

How to Make an Airline Reservation

- Explain that you will be traveling with an infant. Ask which flights are likely not to be crowded and whether it would be possible to be placed next to an empty seat.
- By law, infants must be protected with a safety restraint in an automobile. Yet curiously enough, on an airplane there is no such protection for babies. The National Highway Traffic Safety Administration has conducted extensive tests on the use of car restraints in airplanes and recommends using them in the seat next to yours secured by the safety belt. Many parents who are concerned, and who can afford to buy an extra seat, do bring along their car safety restraints. This can be useful at their destination, not only in the car but also as an alternative to an infant seat.

    If you want to use your car seat, ask if the airline allows it, and if so what the cost will be. Not all airlines allow car seats. Also, for a seat to be used on a plane, it must be approved by the FAA. All seats manufactured after February 26, 1985, have a label approving use.
- Ask if you can make seating arrangements when you call rather than at the airport. If so, request the bulkhead seat. There is more legroom there and a small space to put the baby on the floor. Some airlines have bassinets that attach to the bulkhead wall or hang from above, or that can be placed at your feet. You must order this in advance as well.
- Ask if the airline requires that you check through your stroller or if can you carry it on. You can also ask if the airline provides strollers. Some do. If strollers are available, and you will need one, must it be reserved, and where exactly do you pick it up?
- Ask if they will warm a bottle or a jar of baby food, and whether they carry diapers. Some international flights do. Do they open cans of formula? Or is it necessary for you to bring along your own can opener?

want to bring extra clothing for yourself, or an apron or smock, in case you get urinated or vomited upon.

- A nose suction bulb if the baby has a cold
- A few tried-and-true toys with high distractibility value (Everything in the seat pocket should be of interest to the baby, momentarily at least.)
- Soft, easy-to-chew snacks for the baby and a snack for yourself, too (You might not have time to eat!)

Bus and Train Travel

Everything that applies to airline travel also applies to bus or train travel. Prepare in advance as much as you can, travel light, and then endure! Child safety restraints are allowed for use on board buses and trains; however, you will have to pay a child's fare in both cases. Neither conveyance has passenger safety belts, so securing your restraint will not be possible. If you face it rearward, it will be safer than if facing forward.

Taking Care of Health Needs
Away from Home

What are you going to do without the pediatrician's call-in hour at seven in the morning? Who but your own doctor knows whether or not cork is digestible, how many bowel movements qualify as diarrhea, what the strange crust is on the baby's eye, or if the blotches on his back are prickly heat or roseola? A sick baby is so helpless. Caring for one is nerve-racking no matter where you are. Should the baby get sick, though, you will probably find your intuition and common sense sharpened when the doctor is a hundred or a thousand miles away.

If you haven't traveled with your baby before, you might want to schedule a visit or phone call to your pediatrician or clinic at least a week before you leave. You will be assured that the baby is in good health and will have a chance to go over any concerns you might have. If the baby needs shots, the reaction (if any) will be over by the time you leave. You will also be able to find out if there is anything you need to take along.

If the baby is prone to ear infections or stomach upsets and has been treated regularly for these before, you might consult your doctor about taking the proper drugs along, particularly for travel outside of the country, or about getting a prescription that can be filled once you get there. (Check the country or state's regulations because they may not honor the prescription of an out-of-town doctor.)

Miracle potions to soothe the baby on the airplane or in the car should always come from your doctor. Don't rely on anyone else's advice or anything you have in the medicine cabinet for adults. Also, if you are still sterilizing bottles and your baby is more than three months old, ask your doctor if it's still necessary. If it isn't there will be one less thing to think about. Be careful with the water you offer your baby, however. Don't offer airplane, bus, or train water. Use bottled water instead.

Traveling with Medicines

• Make sure old medicine will still be good by the end of the trip.

• If a medicine's label says "keep refrigerated," find out if this is truly necessary. Many medicines retain their potency for up to a week when kept at room temperature. They should never, however, be kept in a hot place, such as in the glove compartment of a car.

• If medicine is not already in a plastic bottle with a good child-proof cap, have your druggist transfer it along with directions.

• Before leaving, ask your baby's doctor, especially if you are going abroad, to prescribe something for diarrhea and a decongestant for a bad cold. Bring a thermometer, acetaminophen (Tempra, Tylenol, Panadol, etc.) to lower a fever, your favorite health-information book, vitamins, a quick-drying sunshield if your baby is older than six months, and diaper-rash medication. (New foods, changes in weather and water, as well as fewer diaper changes in transit, can bring on diaper rash.) Also bring your doctor's phone number and your medical insurance card and numbers.

• Remember that you can always go to the emergency room of the nearest hospital or to one of the growing number of drop-in medical practices all over the country if your baby gets sick. If traveling abroad, consider joining the International Association for Medical Assistance to Travelers. IAMAT is an extensive network of English-speaking doctors in more than 120 countries and 450 cities around the world. Member-

ship is free and includes a sheaf of health tips for travelers. Write to:

IAMAT
736 Center Street
Lewiston, NY 14092
(716) 754–4883

Tips from Parents on Making Any Trip More Pleasant

We actually found ourselves looking for parks for Anna to play in instead of visiting museums. Next time I think we would make traveling in Europe more informal. Maybe we would go camping where we would meet other people with young children. Then we wouldn't have to worry about eating in restaurants so often.

• • •

If you have a mobile baby who can get into everything, be sure to warn host and hostess to child-proof their house. In fact, you might want to photocopy that particular chapter in Babysense. *I also brought a portable safety gate with me to my mother's house as well as a roll of strapping tape to tape kitchen cupboards closed, and a bag full of blank outlet plugs.*

• • •

I've been in Los Angeles with Jessica for a week, and she's holding up really well. I'm not. Meals are a real struggle. What a drag it is to hold a wiggly ten-month-old baby in my lap three times a day. If we weren't coming home tomorrow, I would beg, borrow, or steal a high chair.

• • •

We wish we hadn't loaded up the car with so much stuff—a high chair, play pen, and walker. We could have made do with less. If you're in a big city, consider renting a high chair or a crib. Look in the Yellow Pages under "Baby Rentals" or "Rentals."

• • •

My babies don't eat as much away from home, and they have all survived. I offer only one kind of food per meal from the jars. Sam has fruit for breakfast, meat for lunch, and a vegetable for dinner. I give him the whole jar. I throw out any leftovers. I also use one of those totally plastic molded bibs. Then I rinse it in the sink.

• • •

When we travel, I carry a garlic press in my pocketbook. I use it to grind up small portions of food from my plate for the baby's meal.

• • •

When I pack to travel with my eight-month-old twins, I make a list of everything I put into their suitcase. I tape the list on the inside top. Then I check off every item when it is time to pack. Otherwise there is no way of knowing whether or not I've picked up all those small odds and ends.

Eating in Restaurants

It was six o'clock and Caitlin was really hungry by the time we pulled into a restaurant called the Chicken Stop. A huge plastic chicken overhead made us think it was a fast-food place. Well, it wasn't. All the guests were dressed up on their way to a concert. We waited twenty minutes for a table. She'd already had her bottle in the car and was delighted with the mints fed to her by the cashier. When we were finally seated, I took one look at the high chair and knew we were in trouble. It had no strap, which was fine for a while. She sat quietly, shredding up the paper napkins, opening the cellophane packages of oyster crackers, stuffing them in her mouth, and blowing them out at us. Then she ate a few ice cubes, but when I turned to cut up the chicken, which finally came, she stood up, lunged for the ice water and knocked it over. The waitress slipped and almost fell with her tray. By that time Caitlin's only interest in the chicken and mashed potatoes was rubbing them into her hair. We asked for the check, left a huge tip, and ran.

If you have never taken the baby to a restaurant and know you will have to do so when traveling, screw up your courage and try. If you haven't been to one in a couple of months, try again before you start traveling. Things change. The baby who is still happy in an infant seat can be a wonderful dinner companion. Even an eight-month-old can be a perfect guest, babbling and playing enthusiastically with a spoon. But an eleven-month-old can be an absolute horror!

For the best results, choose an appropriate restaurant. Go early, armed with healthy snacks and a few good toys or books. Bring a harness if you are unsure about the high chairs, and request a table out of the main traffic flow.

Clothing Tips for Travel

When you are traveling, proximity to a washer and dryer really helps. Following are some suggestions from parents who've logged thousands of miles with babies. Also consider that dark clothing looks cleaner longer than light clothing.

• • •

The only way Betsey is happy in the car is if I feed her crackers, which she of course mushes up and makes into paste. I carry a "smock"—a long-sleeved oversized shirt—for her and a big waterproof bib. She wears one or the other. Otherwise I'd have to do laundry every day.

• • •

Here is my mother's theory. There are four ways to wear a shirt: the right way; backwards; inside-out frontwards; and inside-out backwards.

• • •

Baby Etiquette and More

Dear Frances,
My husband Bill and I have developed a ritual of taking our nine-month-old daughter, Clarissa, out to brunch every Sunday. She makes a terrible mess at the table and all around her on the floor. Are we expected to clean up after her or not?
Answer: *Big tips don't make up for big messes. Cleaning up after a baby or young child is beyond the call of duty for any restaurant employee. Always travel to restaurants with a good wad of paper toweling—if not a small damp sponge—in your diaper bag and a plastic bag in which to dispose of it discreetly. Do the best you can, and apologize for the rest. A good tip will also help.*

• • •

By the third baby, I finally figured out that breakfast is the most successful meal to eat out when you're traveling. The baby is still relatively fresh and hungry, and breakfast foods—French toast, scrambled eggs, and juice—are all perfect for babies. For lunch we usually stop for a picnic by the road if the weather is nice, and for dinner, I feed Ben a jar of baby food in the motel room, while the others go out to eat. Then I go out, happily, alone.

• • •

When Brandon was a newborn, I ordered a special baby folding mirror from Johnson and Johnson. From the time he could sit in a high chair, he has enjoyed seeing the baby make faces and talk back to him. We have never had a problem in a restaurant, and I credit it all to this wonderful toy. We save this "special toy" for restaurant outings only.

When we traveled in Europe I brought lightweight clothing rather than denim or corduroy. It was easy to pack and dried quickly when I washed it out by hand at night.

• • •

Have your travel agent check which countries have disposable diapers for you. We lugged a ton of them on the plane with us, when we could have bought them right there.

• • •

Sleeping away from home gets harder for a baby the older the baby gets. Expect to spend more time getting the baby to sleep. It helps to bring the special blanket or stuffed animal, the familiar music

box or tape and tape recorder. I also bring my own flannel crib sheets.

• • •

Don't wean the baby before you go away. Old, familiar comforts are really important in new places.

• • •

My mother warned me! She said she didn't have a real vacation until my sister and I went to camp at ages ten and twelve. Do you think we'll have to wait that long?

Yes, alas, I do!

• CHAPTER 19 •

Safety

The Baby-Safe House

For your baby's safety and well-being and for your sanity, take your first safety tour of the house *before* he learns to crawl. At this point you can still move faster than he can (you often can't with a toddler) and can calmly remove many of the dangers for the baby and frustrations for yourself. A newly mobile baby has no discrimination or "taste" when it comes to sampling furniture polish, lighter fluid, aspirin, or the contents of your button box. What he lacks in taste, he makes up for in imagination. "Water play" in the toilet bowl, teething on the frayed toaster cord, testing paper clips in the electrical outlets, and tasting beautiful bits of sparkling glass from the garbage—all have infinite appeal and can be lethal for the curious baby.

It is both discouraging and alarming to consider that approximately 22 million children are involved in accidents annually. Most of these occur at home, and nine out of ten of them could have been prevented had parents been truly committed to making their homes child oriented. Child-proofed environments are necessary not only for our children's physical safety but also for their psychological well-being. Children suffer emotional damage when their parents are continuously anxious, annoyed, and even angry at the risks they take as they are driven to explore anything and everything that captures their interest. What is the point of being annoyed at someone who doesn't know any better—when what parents and babies really want and need is to enjoy each other?

Changing Our Ways

In the early years of our children's lives, we do have to give up some things. One of them is a completely adult environment. Try to make it easy for yourself and the baby. Put away the dangerous furniture; eliminate the temptations rather than waste your energy fighting over them. Change the location of the kitchen trash can by putting it out of sight or up high. Feed the dog when the baby's not around. Block off the stairs.

We can also learn from our baby's curiosity. Rather than seeing it as a reckless annoyance, regard it as an opportunity to provide him with safe alternatives. For instance, if he is fascinated by opening and closing a heavy door whose hinges can pinch him, give him his own "safe" cupboard, with nonbreakable plastic containers. His interest in the dog's water dish or the toilet may be quelled by some extra playtime in the bathtub.

It is also important to be realistic about your own limits. Pay attention to yourself. If you are stressed, tired, distracted, or not feeling well and you have to make dinner, and the baby is into everything, this will only add to your tension. At this point the fairest thing to do is to make it easier for yourself. Use the playpen or the walker for a short period of time and give yourself a break.

Parents Share Their Fantasies and Fears About Safety

The baby-proofed house has washable padding that covers the floors and runs up the wall for about three feet. The furniture is low, made of washable foam, and nailed to the floor. An adult-

elbow-height shelf runs around every room for precious or dangerous objects. And, of course, there is a professional vacuuming service on call twenty-four hours a day.

• • •

My fear is that I'll never be able to be careful enough. When Jason was tiny, we came home one night and discovered that the baby-sitter had put the pacifier on a string around his neck. I was horrified. When he learned to crawl, the mouth battle began. No matter how clean I thought the floors were, he could find the nastiest, rustiest old carpet tack and put it in his mouth. Then he learned to stand and kept slipping on the hardwood floors. I was sure he would be permanently brain damaged from all the falls. Two weeks ago it seemed preposterous that some parents actually remove the knobs from their gas stoves. Not so now. . . . On bad days I sometimes wonder how the human race has survived.

• • •

I fantasize that if John and I had been younger when Nelia was born—I was forty-one—it wouldn't be quite so nerve-racking and exhausting to keep up with her. A newly walking eleven-and-a-half-month-old can literally trash an entire apartment in fifteen minutes. I fall into bed at night, dead, comatose. John feels basic training for the Marine Corps was easier.

• • •

When Sara was eleven months old and not even walking yet, my absolute worst fear was realized. She somehow climbed up on a low bookcase under our bedroom window, which won't open more than six inches in damp weather, and got out onto the fire escape. She is still alive to tell the tale, but I hardly am. Since I couldn't fit out the window, I had to coax her back in. Words can't describe my panic or my guilt.

Sage Advice About Babies and Safety

Nothing is more fundamental to solid educational development than pure, uncontained curiosity.
—Burton L. White
The First Three Years of Life

• • •

Parents cannot prevent all accidents. If they were careful enough to try, they would only make their child timid and dependent.
—Benjamin M. Spock and
Michael B. Rothenberg
Dr. Spock's Baby and Child Care

• • •

Somehow, as parents, you have to find ways of staying on the same side as your baby, making the most of the good bits of each day and laughing at the misfortunes. An absolute determination to enjoy yourselves is what makes this possible. Find pleasure in being clever enough to guide him without his noticing, distract him before there is a clash, and save him before there is an accident. Teach yourself to look at life from his point of view as well as your own. Be intent, above all, on loving him and enjoying his passionate love for you. The last thing he wants is to displease you. You are his Gods. But it will be a long time yet before he can understand what does please you. Your pleasures are not the same as his. You don't like gravy on the floor . . .
—Penelope Leach
*Your Baby and Child:
From Birth to Age Five*

• • •

We read in a baby-care book that we should get down on our hands and knees and make a tour of the house. So we did it. Like fools we slithered around on our bellies for a good hour. Besides ending up filthy dirty we found a treasure trove of matches, coins, perfume bottle lids, toothpaste caps, straight pins, paper clips, exposed nails, springs, ant traps, lost earrings, tie studs, collar stays, bus tokens, vitamin pills, batteries, cigarette lighters, pipe cleaners, and metallic candy wrappers. Besides knocking over a lamp and the cat's water dish, we also received scrapes from the rough underside of tables and the piano stool. My husband banged his head on the corner of the glass coffee table. I tipped over the wobbly telephone stand. We got rid of both.

Question: *When are accidents most likely to occur?*
Answer:

• When any hazard—a sharp knife, a busy street, a bottle of aspirin, etc.—is too accessible or too attractive for a child to resist
• When a baby and/or parent is hungry or tired. More accidents occur between 3 and 6 P.M. than at any other time. Also, as the week progresses more accidents occur, beginning on Thursday and reaching a peak by Saturday
• When families are rushed, and when routines are not consistent
• When a mother is ill, pregnant, or about to menstruate, or when other family members are ill or are the center of the mother's attention
• When the relationship between parents is tense, or when there are other family conflicts such as divorce, illness, or death
• When a child is not carefully supervised
• When a child has no safe place to play
• When parents or caretakers lack understanding of which new activities to expect at each stage of a child's development
• When a child is in the care of an unfamiliar person or a brother or sister too young to be responsible
• When a child is in a new environment—on vacation, for example, or in a new day-care situation

Useful Safety Devices

The market is flooded with safety devices and gadgets designed to protect your child. The choices can be both confusing and overwhelming. Some are helpful and some either so complicated or so poorly made that they are useless. The child-safety sample kits seem like a good idea, but be aware that you may be paying for items that will not necessarily be of use to you. Following are a sampling of products to suggest the range of choices rather than specific brands.

When you make your household safety tour, take a pad of paper, a pencil, and a tape measure with you. On page 301 you will find a space where you can make safety notes and include sketches and dimensions where needed. Keep in mind that even the best of these safety devices are no substitute for your careful eye.

Appliance latches. These are specifically designed to lock microwave oven, conventional oven, and refrigerator doors. Generally, appliances with good gasket seals are difficult for babies to open, so these are optional.

Stove knob covers. A curious toddler can reach the burner knobs if they are on the front of the stove. Stove knob covers prevent burner knobs from turning. Some parents simply remove the knobs.

Stovetop guard. This suction-based, hinged railing is designed to raise the stove front and sides so that young children cannot pull pots over. Generally it is a good idea to cook on back burners with pot handles turned away from the front of the stove.

Drawer and cabinet safety latches. These safety latches consist of long, flexible, plastic hooks that fit into catches. A drawer can be opened enough for an adult to slip two fingers in, press down, and release the hook from the catch. Other drawer protectors are battery operated. A

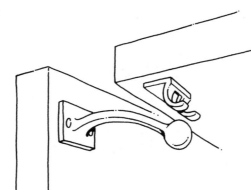

light-sensitive alarm goes off when the drawer is opened.

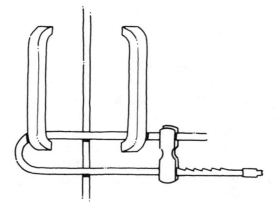

Cupboard U-bar latches. These are useful for cupboards with handles generally no more than 10 inches apart. Adult dexterity is required to slide the latch bar while pressing down on a release button. As a useful alternative, at home or in someone else's home, securely tie handles together or use strong strapping tape to keep cupboards stocked with dangerous items out of bounds.

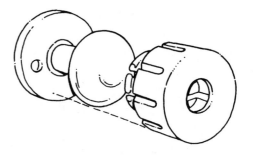

Doorknob covers. These will make it quite difficult for a baby or toddler to open a door—for a while. A hook-and-eye lock placed at adult eye level is much more effective for high-risk rooms such as the kitchen, bathroom, laundry room, and basement.

Door slam guards. These brace doors before they close to prevent slamming on small hands and fingers. Or you can install a pneumatic or hydraulic door closer that comes with a pressure adjustment to slow down the door in the last few seconds prior to closing.

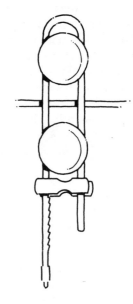

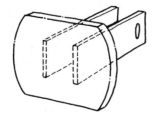

Blank electrical outlet plugs. These cover outlets that are not in use. They are difficult for both adults and babies to remove. However, they are small and do pose a choking hazard if you take them out, casually put them down while you are using the outlet, and then forget to replace them.

Electrical outlet covers. These devices are screwed in over the entire wall plate. They not only protect unused outlets but also prevent a baby from pulling an electrical cord out of the outlet. These are useful for outlets that are permanently used by a television, stereo, or lamp—rather than, say, the vacuum cleaner—because they must be permanently affixed with screws.

Cord shorteners. These are used to coil and shorten electrical cords so that they cannot be pulled. A garbage-bag tie is just as effective. Roll up excess cord and secure with ties.

Cord guards. These fasten onto a table edge to hold an electric cord in place and will prevent your baby from pulling objects off surfaces by the cord. These are particularly useful for table-lamp cords.

Toilet latches. Children can drown in toilet bowls. These latches keep the toilet lid closed. Most toddlers can eventually master this latch. Again, a more effective alternative is to mount a simple hook-and-eye lock on the outside of the bathroom door and other high-risk areas such as the kitchen and utility room.

Bathtub spigot guard. This is a cushioned plastic guard to prevent injury if your baby should fall against the spigot. The deluxe models also measure water temperature.

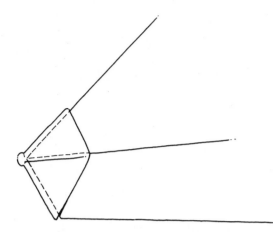

Corner guards and edge tape. These guards pad sharp corners on furniture. However, unless corners are perfectly square, the guards may not attach properly. You should also be aware that, ironically, some models are small enough to pose a choking hazard! The adhesive or suction devices can also wear out, so check periodically to make sure they are still adhering correctly. The life of edging tape, packaged by the roll, tends to be short because the adhesive wears out. If this tape becomes loose in one place, a curious baby can pull it off, and a long piece could present a strangulation risk.

All About Safety Gates

Safety gates can be useful for closing off high-risk areas where you simply don't want the baby to be. Unfortunately, they can provide a false sense of security, because none of the models on the market is truly safe—be it the portable pressure-mounted gate or the hardware-mounted gate in accordion, mesh, or vertical-slat style.

In general the hardware-mounted gates, though not conveniently portable, are safer because a child cannot dislodge them. Even these

---

Fighting Fire

Did you know that a fire burning in a house for one minute grows to three times its original size? In four minutes, it grows to eleven times its size, and in just six minutes, it reaches fifty times its original size. Don't be ill prepared to handle an emergency fire. After you read the following points, go over them with anyone caring for your baby, either in your home or in theirs.

- According to the International Association of Fire Chiefs, the presence of properly cleaned and maintained smoke detectors can cut your risk of dying in a fire by half. Have at least one alarm per floor; check the batteries monthly and replace them each year (use the Safety Notes section on page 301 to help remember dates). Show baby-sitters the location of all smoke alarms.
- Keep a fire extinguisher and a box of baking soda handy in the kitchen. Show baby-sitters where these are located.
- Make sure that all heating equipment (such as space heaters) is placed at least three feet away from any object that can burn.
- Check rooms for matches, cigarette lighters, and ashtrays within the baby's reach. Never smoke in bed!
- Do you have an escape plan? Are there two ways out of each room—a door and a window, for instance? Be sure to decide on one meeting place outside the house, where you can regroup. If you live in an apartment, are you familiar with the location of fire exits? Again, note this information in the Safety Notes section on page 301.
- If you use child care either in your home or in someone else's, make sure that you have gone over what to do in the event of a fire. This is particularly important if you are using family day care where one adult is responsible for more than one infant or young child.

---

gates are considered a risk at the top of a flight of stairs. Whatever gate you choose, check all hardware and mesh for sharp edges. Look for small parts that could break off and choke a baby or small child. If you use the pressure-mounted model, make sure the pressure bar is on the *opposite* side from the area accessible to your child. Keep large toys that a child could use to help climb over the gate away. Follow the manufacturer's instructions for installation and use.

Once the gate is three-quarters of your child's height—that is, when your child is 36 inches tall or weighs 30 pounds—get rid of it.

Accordion-style gates. In the past these gates, which open up to form diamond-shaped spaces with wide Vs on the top, have entrapped the heads or necks of several children, causing death by strangulation. Although the most dangerous aspects of these gates have been modified by manufacturers (the diamonds are smaller), many old-style gates are still in use as hand-me-downs or as yard-sale items. Avoid newer models

Household Pollutants

It seems that almost every day we hear about some new danger to our health and our children's health—be it in the food we eat, the clothes we wear, the water we drink, or the air that we breathe in our own homes. Rather than attempt to cover everything that could be of danger to your baby, I refer you to Debra L. Dadd's *The Nontoxic Home: Protecting Yourself and Your Family from Everyday Toxins and Health Hazards* (Los Angeles, CA: Jeremy P. Tarcher, Inc., 1986). In addition to this I suggest that, if you live in an old house and there is any possibility that your drinking water contains dangerous levels of lead because it flows through lead pipes, you contact your health department immediately for information on getting it tested. In the meantime, to lower possible lead content, let water run for three minutes before drinking it, and never use hot tap water for mixing any of your baby's formula or food. For further information, send a postcard with your name and address to: Lead and Your Drinking Water, Environmental Protection Agency, 401 M Street S.W., Washington, D.C. 20460 or call the EPA Safe Drinking Water Hotline: 800–426–4791. In Washington, D.C., call (202) 382–5533.

Can You Answer These Two Safety Questions?

Question: Do you know where your pocketbook and/or briefcase are and exactly what is inside that would be of interest to a baby or toddler?

Possible Answers: Loose change, cosmetics, perfume, medicines, hard candies, cigarette lighters, tobacco, pens or pencils, nail clippers, sharp keys, pen knife. If you don't already have a special hook for your purse and/or briefcase well above toddler level, install one now.

Question: What do you do about safety if your baby is being taken care of in someone else's home?

Answer: It can be very touchy to insist that you take a safety tour of someone else's home. Perhaps you could suggest that they read this section of the book first to get an idea of common hazards and preventive measures. Then you might ask if there is anything you can do to help eliminate the obvious dangers. For instance, you might offer to share the cost of a needed safety gate if finances are a consideration.

Watch Out for Tiny Button Batteries!

These minute batteries are becoming more and more common in watches, toys, computer games, and musical cards. If your baby swallows one, it may pass undigested through his system without causing any harm. If he's not so lucky, it may become lodged in his esophagus. Don't let the baby play with button battery–powered toys designed for older children. Keep all replacement batteries locked away, and dispose of discards immediately. If you suspect your baby has ingested a button battery, immediately call your poison-control center or the 24-hour National Button Battery Ingestion Hot Line: (202-625-3333).

that have wooden tabs at the top that could catch a child's sweater and cause entrapment or strangulation.

Vertical-slat gates. Some vertical-slat gates swing open, an appealing convenience for parents. But beware! Federal regulations control the spacing between bars on cribs but have nothing to say about the spacing of bars on these gates. Some not only exceed the 2⅜-inch spacing acceptable in cribs but also have rather flexible bars, making them even more dangerous. Be sure to check measurements very carefully.

Mesh gates. A highly active toddler can climb over one of these gates if the mesh is widely spaced enough to allow a good toehold. The mesh can also trap fingers, toes, arms, and legs. Buttons and buckles can get caught in the mesh. In addition, there are also opportunities for entrapment of extremities or limbs in between the hinged joints and sliding panels of some models.

Alternatives to gates. You can make a gate by installing wood channels on either side of the door frame and cutting a piece of plywood to fit. You can slide this in and out as needed. Or you might consider installing a screen door, which will give you visibility, or a half-door, with the lock out of your child's reach. Unquestionably, installing custom-made gates and doors requires more thought, time, effort, and possibly expense on your part, than simply buying a few safety gates. However, consider it an investment that will be useful for at least two-and-a-half to three years. If you are considering having another child, you will get even more use out of these.

Taking a Safety Tour of Your House

As you make your safety tour from room to room, making notes in the back of this book (see page 301), don't forget to check all of your windows. Do they lock securely and are they open only at the top? Do not rely on screens to protect your baby. Instead, install special window guards, choosing those that will not cause any sort of entrapment. As you proceed, move any furniture that could offer a step up to a window. Shorten or remove all cords that could cause strangulation from blinds and drapes.

As you go from room to room, mark large glass doors and plate-glass windows with decals at baby and toddler height to prevent your baby from running into them without seeing them. Check balconies and outdoor stairs for spaces more than 2⅜ inches between bars.

Finally, make all fans and space heaters inaccessible to your baby.

Living Room, Dining Room, and Bedrooms

• Whenever you enter these rooms, check for small objects on the floor or on tables and beds that the baby could choke on.

• Remove spindly or tippy furniture that is not stable enough for a baby to pull herself up on to a standing position.

• Be careful of swinging doors and door hinges in general.

• Make sure that you have adequate smoke-alarm protection in all these rooms.

• Don't smoke near the baby. Remove accessible tobacco, matches, and ashtrays. Cigarette lighters, especially the bright and colorful plastic kind, are easy to operate.

• Make sure that liquor, including wine in a wine rack, is stored up high or locked away.

• Check that fireplaces and wood-burning stoves are adequately screened and that splintery wood is covered or removed.

• Wedge books and records tightly in their shelves and elevate or store all breakables.

• Watch out for tablecloths; they are ideal for pulling.

• Watch out for rocking chairs, recliners, and hideaway beds that can pinch small hands and feet.

• Move furniture in front of outlets or cap them with plugs or other safety devices.

• Secure all cords on table lamps within a baby or toddler's reach.

• In bedrooms especially, lock up or elevate all shoe-shining equipment, perfume, and jewelry. Hang neckties, scarves, and belts well out of your child's reach. Dispose of all plastic wrapping from the dry cleaner immediately.

• Cut loop cords open on blinds and draperies.

The Kitchen

The kitchen is the most dangerous room in your house. It may also be the room that you and your child spend the most time in together—when your attention is most divided. Some safety experts go so far as to suggest that you simply keep babies and young children out of the kitchen. For most parents this suggestion is totally unrealistic. Instead, do your *very* best and remain attentive. Periodically go over the kitchen with the following checklist.

• Whenever you enter the kitchen, check the floor for small objects, bottle caps, paper clips, coins, etc.

• Consolidate all poisonous household cleaners and make them completely inaccessible, either in a latched or locked cupboard or in a cupboard high above a young child's reach.

• Remove all ant, roach, mouse, or rat poison. It's too dangerous. Boric acid, a primary ingredient in many commercial ant and roach powders, is highly toxic and can be lethal.

• Pull out on all drawers to make sure that they catch and do not fall on the floor.

• Consolidate all dangerous knives and pointed cooking utensils and place them in a drawer with a safety latch. Move glass items to high shelves and leave unbreakables in low cupboards.

• Stacked drawers can be locked in a closed position by inserting a long wooden dowel through drawer handles.

• Make matches inaccessible.

• Move heavy canned goods, appliances, cooking pots, and pans up and out of reach.

• Elevate garbage or "lock" it under the sink. Get rid of your trash compactor. A small child can fit in it.

• Pick up broken glass with a wet paper towel or vacuum.

• Make sure your convection and microwave oven doors have good gaskets to keep them closed and adequate insulation to keep the doors from getting too hot.

• Cook with large pots on back burners. Turn all pot handles facing away from the front of the stove.

• If necessary, remove stove knobs or purchase a stove-knob cover (see page 209).

• Keep an eye on your hot cup of coffee or tea. Get in the habit of placing these on high surfaces and not near the edges of tables or counters. Don't carry your baby and hot beverages at the same time.

• Have a working fire extinguisher in the kitchen. Also keep baking soda handy to snuff out a small fire.

• Never fill the dishwasher cup with detergent when the baby is nearby. The swinging cup is appealing to a baby. The detergent is a powerful disfiguring chemical that can burn mouths and throats.

• Don't allow appliance cords to hang down from coffee makers, blenders, toaster ovens, etc. Either coil wires, or fasten them along the wall with insulated staples.

• Keep pails of hot, soapy water off the floor.

• Make sure there is nothing dangerous in your refrigerator such as batteries, film, medicines, or alcohol.

• Lock up plastic wraps and bags that could cause suffocation.

• Do you have a long dangling phone cord on your kitchen phone? If so, install a high hook or peg to drape it over when not in use.

These could cause strangulation.

• Remove slippery scatter rugs.

Stairs

• Block stairs at top and bottom and make sure they are well lit.

• Don't wax stairs and, if they are carpeted, make sure tacks are firmly in place. Check for objects on the stairs.

• Put railings and banisters on open stairs. Make sure that existing banisters are no more than 2⅜ inches apart.

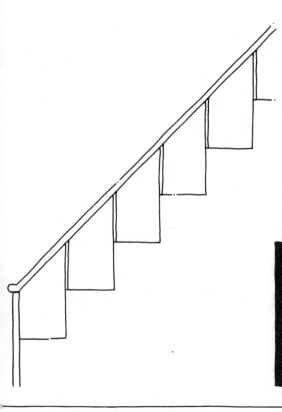

Bathrooms

The bathroom is probably the second most dangerous room in your house, following the kitchen.

• Bathrooms should be off-limits without adult supervision. Either lock them from the outside with a simple hook-and-eye lock, or use a doorknob cover (but regard this as a deterrent, not a foolproof solution). You can also hang a cluster of jingle bells on a hook high on the bathroom door as a warning.

• During these early years you simply can't be too careful about drugs, cosmetics, and cleaning agents. Lock up *all* of them or elevate them far beyond a small child's reach. Request child-proof caps on all prescription drugs as a matter of course, but keep in mind that these are not totally reliable. Some children can open them.

• Dispose of razor blades carefully.

• Never leave electric appliances plugged in near water. Keep such items as hair dryers, hot curlers, and curling irons in the bedroom. A baby can be electrocuted if these devices accidentally fall into the sink or tub while he is bathing or if the curious baby decides to plunge one into the toilet.

Rooms Off-Limits

• Make laundry areas, utility rooms, basements, and garages off-limits. If you have to have a mobile baby with you, set up the playpen near you and put her in it.

• Never leave a young child alone in the bathtub. If the phone or doorbell rings, either ignore it or take the baby with you. Do not count on bath seats, which help a baby to sit up in the tub, for safety. These seats provide a false sense of security and should not be used for that reason alone.

• Get in the habit of turning off hot water first because hot tap water can cause a severe burn. Babies are notoriously interested in faucets. Keep water temperature below 130°F or 55°C. Note the fact that as the temperature rises, severe burns occur more quickly. At 124°F what is called a *full-thickness burn* can occur in three minutes. But at 140°F it takes only five seconds. At 158°F and up only a second is required.

• Put nonslip stickers in the bathtub.

• Get in the habit of keeping the toilet lid down.

• Install a spout cover to cushion accidental falls.

Outdoors

• Fence play yards, swimming pools, wells, cisterns, and storm drains.

• Cover window wells around the house foundation.

• Cover woodpiles, and lock away yard and garden tools, including the lawn mower and gasoline can. Don't forget to lock up insecticides, pesticides, fertilizers, and seeds.

• Cover outdoor electrical outlets with safety caps, and remember to unplug and then put away outdoor extension cords immediately after use.

• Know which outdoor plants are poisonous, and check often for mushrooms and fungi that could harm a young child if ingested.

• It's impossible to keep a yard totally clear of small ingestible objects on the ground. Never leave a baby or young child unsupervised outdoors, even in an enclosed yard.

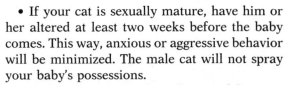

Babies and Pets

Most babies love action, and for this reason a pet can have great entertainment value. For safety's sake, never leave your dog or cat alone with a new baby. Even a friendly animal can accidentally scratch or bite or inadvertently suffocate a newborn. Following are a few reminders to help keep your baby safe from your pet.

• Be sure to pay attention to your pet the way you did before the baby arrived, just the way you would an older sibling. Otherwise the animal truly will suffer emotional damage and could even become untrustworthy around your baby. Some experts recommend that you tape record a baby's cries and play them for the animal ahead of time, so that he can get used to the sound.

• If your cat is sexually mature, have him or her altered at least two weeks before the baby comes. This way, anxious or aggressive behavior will be minimized. The male cat will not spray your baby's possessions.

• Dogs and cats can carry all sorts of diseases, including rabies, ringworm, toxoplasmosis, and strep. If your animal has not had a regular checkup recently, make an appointment with the vet before your baby comes home from the hospital. Shots should be up to date. Also, check your animals regularly for fleas, mites, and ticks.

• Hygiene is important. Wash your hands and your baby's after handling your pet. Keep litter boxes clean and out of reach. Also, keep your pet's food dishes and water bowls out of reach and clean.

Poisonous Plants

Many common house and garden plants are dangerous and can cause various injuries. The numbers that follow plant names are keyed to the four different reactions listed below.

1. skin irritation
2. mouth- and throat-lining irritation

3. stomach and intestinal irritation and
4. poisoning of the system

Houseplants

Angel's Trumpet	4
Caladium	2,3
Castor Bean	3,4
Dieffenbachia	1,2
Elephant's ear	1,2
Mistletoe	3,4
Philodendron	1,2
Poinsettia	1

Ornamental

Bleeding Heart	1,4
Daphne	1,2,3
English Ivy	3
Mountain Laurel	4
Oleander	4
Rhododendron	4
Wisteria	3
Yew	3

Forest Growth

Baneberry	3,4
Bittersweet	3,4
Bloodroot	3,4
Deadly Amanita	4

Fly Agaric Mushroom	4
Jack-in-the-Pulpit	2,3
Mayapple	3
Moonseed	4
Poison Ivy	1
Poison Oak	1
Rosary Pea	4
Snakeroot	3,4
Yellow Jessamine	4

Flower Garden

Autumn Crocus	4
Belladonna Lily	3,4
Christmas Rose	1,3
Daffodil	3
Four O'Clock	3
Foxglove	4
Hyacinth	3
Hydrangea	3,4
Iris	3
Larkspur	4
Lily of the Valley	4
Monkshood	4
Morning Glory	4
Narcissus	3

Snowdrop	3
Sweet Pea	3

Vegetable Garden

Asparagus (unripe shoots)	4
Flax	4
Potato (eyes, stems, spoiled parts)	4
Rhubarb	4
Tomato (leaves)	3,4

Field Plants

Buttercup	2,3
Death Camas	4
False Hellebore	4
Lupine	4
Milkweed	4
Nettle	1
Nightshade	4
Poison Hemlock	4
Poison Ivy	1
Pokeweed (Inkberry)	3,4
Snow on the Mountain	1
Sour Dock	4
Tobacco	4

Trees

Apple	4
Black Locust	3,4
Box	3,4
Cherry	4
Chinaberry	3
Elderberry	4
English Holly	3
Fig	1,2
Golden Chain	3,4
Horse Chestnut	3,4
Lantana	3,4
Oak	3,4
Osage Orange	1
Peach	4
Privet	3

Marsh

Cowslip	3
Lady's Slipper	1
Skunk Cabbage	2,3
Sneezeweed	4
Water Hemlock	4

Lead Poisoning

The severe consequences of acute or chronic lead poisoning have been known for many years; they are anemia, mental retardation, blindness, convulsions, and death. Now researchers have also linked low-level lead ingestion to less visible but still insidious effects. These include hyperactivity, retardation of brain growth, slow learning, and increased susceptibility to viral disease.

Lead poisoning is not a disease peculiar to the inner-city poor. According to findings of a recent four-year survey conducted by the Department of Health and Human Services, approximately 675,000 American children between the ages of six months and five years have dangerously high blood lead levels. The survey results also indicate that children of all geographic and socioeconomic groups are at risk. The major source of lead exposure is lead-based paint, despite the fact that the lead content in house paint and paint used in children's furniture and toys has been limited since 1977. Some 27 million households in this country are still contaminated by paint produced before these controls became effective. Prior to that time, lead content in paint could be as high as 50 percent.

If you have a hand-me-down crib, playpen, or other furniture from the 1950s or early '60s that a baby is likely to chew on, and you suspect they were painted with lead paint, sand them down and repaint them with lead-free paint. Take a special tour around your house and look for and remove peeling paint, especially on windowsills and old radiators. Check the outside of your house as well and the ground around the house.

Also, don't let the baby play with or chew on the colored sections of your newspaper: the funnies, advertisements, and the magazine sections. They contain lead-based inks.

Poison Prevention

To prevent poisoning:

- Get in the habit of reading labels when you buy household cleaners.
- Keep all medicines and household cleaners on a high shelf, out of sight, or locked up. After use, recap and relock immediately.
- Keep all medicines and cleaners away from food.
- Keep all medicines, drugs, and cleaners in their original containers. Many deaths have occurred when the last bit of turpentine or bleach was stored away in a Coke bottle and then was mistaken for a drink.
- Periodically clean out the medicine cabinet. Throw out all drugs from past illnesses. Don't forget to put away vitamins. If they are old, throw them out.
- Be aware of common house plants that can be dangerous. (See Poisonous Plants on page 217.) If you don't already know the names of plants you have, take a piece of each one to your local botanical society, plant store, or nursery for identification. Label each plant with the correct botanical name and the reaction, if any, it can cause. Place dangerous plants out of reach of your baby.
- Have on hand a ½-ounce bottle of syrup of ipecac as well as one can of activated charcoal. Note: According to a study published in *Pediatrics*, the journal of the American Academy of Pediatrics, even if ipecac is older than its expiration date, it remains effective for up to four years.

Poisoning: What to Do If Your Child Ingests a Poisonous Substance

1. If breathing has stopped, start CPR immediately (see page 82, step 6, for instructions).

2. Call the poison-control center. Be prepared to tell them:
- Age and weight of your child
- What was ingested (Bring the container, the berry, etc., to the telephone with you, so that you can describe it.)
- When it was ingested
- How much was ingested
- How the child is feeling or acting right now
- Your name and telephone number

3. If instructed to do so by the experts at the poison-control center, give the child a glass (or bottle) of water or milk.

4. If directed to induce vomiting, use syrup of ipecac:
- Small child: give ½ ounce (15 milliliters) with 8 ounces (250 milliliters) of water as marked on the bottle.
- Repeat after twenty minutes if vomiting has not occurred and you are advised to repeat the dose.

5. Never induce vomiting unless instructed to do so by experts at the poison-control center. Never induce vomiting unless the child is conscious. Some substances can burn the tissue inside the throat and lungs when vomited. Do not induce vomiting if:
- The child is unconscious
- You see burns around the mouth or on the hands
- You smell gasoline
- The child is having seizures or is exhausted

6. Do not follow the antidotes on labels of poisonous substances, as they can be outdated or inaccurate. Call the poison-control center instead.

—Elena Bosque, R.N., and Sheila Watson, R.N.
Safe and Sound: How to Prevent and Treat the Most Common Childhood Emergencies

Baby Safety Lessons

- There is *nothing* you can do to prevent your baby from putting anything and everything in sight into his mouth. Be low-key about it and try not to call a great deal of attention to it. Distraction is very useful. Substitute a safe plastic toy for the toothpaste cap, for example. Besides removing dangerous temptations (see Play and Learning, page 247) by checking the floor every time you enter a room, try to teach your baby to say "ahh." An "ahh" will give you the chance to see what's in the baby's mouth and grab it.

- Teach the baby the meaning of the word "hot." One supervised experience with a radiator or oven door is often all it takes.

- You probably won't need to teach your baby how to climb *up* the stairs, but do teach her to climb down backward. If you can, mount a safety gate a few steps up, put a pillow below, and let her practice.

- The administration of medicine and vitamins should be low-key and rather serious. Don't let a baby or young child see you taking medicines at all.

- An easy way to release something from baby's tight grasp is to stroke the back of his hand lightly.

- Don't put your baby to bed with stuffed animals that contain cassettes or batteries. Unraveled cassettes could cause strangulation. Small batteries can be swallowed.

Postscript

By providing maximum access to the safe home, you have also gone a long way toward making possible the preservation of a balance of interest. Just think for a moment of the contrasting situation where, to avoid danger, the extra work, the stress, and so forth, you routinely prevent your child from moving about the home by using a playpen. You may in the short run have an easier time of it, but in the long run the negative effects of such confinement on a child's curiosity and on the growth of his capacity to play alone far outweigh the short-term returns.

—Burton L. White
The First Three Years of Life

Safety Resources

Bosque, Elena, and Watson, Sheila, *Safe and Sound: How to Prevent and Treat the Most Common Childhood Emergencies* (New York: St. Martin's Press, Inc., 1988)

Chemical Referral Center
800–CMA–8200 (9 A.M. to 6 P.M. EST, weekdays except holidays) A nonemergency referral to manufacturers of industrial household chemicals or to the EPA for information about health effects and safety of chemicals. For *emergency* information on chemicals, dial (800)-424-9300.

Gerber Products Company
445 State Street
Freemont, MI 49412
Attn: Medical Marketing Service
Send for "A Handbook of Child Safety"

Green, Martin I., *A Sigh of Relief: First-Aid Handbook for Childhood Emergencies* (New York: Bantam, 1984)

Metropolitan Life Insurance Co.
One Madison Ave.
New York, NY 10010
Send self-addressed stamped envelope for "Fire Safety," "Planning for Safety," and "First Aid for the Family."

Video on Fire Safety
"Plan to Get Out Alive"
Send $9.95 to McDonalds
c/o Mediatech
110 W. Hubbard Street
Chicago, IL 60610

Check Out Equipment for Safety

The following can be useful to determine if specific brands of new or used baby equipment are safe.

Sandy Jones with Werner Freitag and the Editors of Consumer Reports Books, *Guide to Baby Products* (New York: Consumer Reports Books, 1988)

If you or your child has been injured by a consumer product, or you have found a product that is defective or unsafe, contact
Consumer Product Safety Commission (CPSC)
Washington, D.C. 20207
800–492-CPSC
800–492-8363 (Maryland)
800–638-8333 (Alaska, Hawaii, Puerto Rico, Virgin Islands)

If you have questions or complaints about the safety of food, drugs, cosmetics, or medical devices, contact:
Food and Drug Administration (FDA)
5600 Fishers Lane
HFE 88
Rockville, MD 20857
(301) 443–3170

Emergency Information

Photocopy the following emergency information box and post it by all of your phones. If you work, take a copy with you to the office. Make sure your child-care provider is aware of this list.

Doctor _____

Hospital (including address and instructions for getting there from your house) _____

Poison-Control Center _____

Druggist _____

Parents' Work Numbers _____

_____

Neighbor's Name _____

Neighbor's Phone _____

Neighbor's Address _____

Fire Department _____

Police _____

Ambulance Service _____

Taxi Service _____

Parents' Full Names _____

Child's Full Name _____

Address of house (including the nearest cross streets) _____

_____

Periodically update the following information on a separate dated card, and keep near the phone
Age of your child _____

Weight of your child _____

• CHAPTER 20 •

Health Care for Your Baby

It's a good idea to decide on a health-care provider for your baby well before his or her arrival. The relationship you form with your child's health-care provider is among the most important that you will have during your child's first year. Not only will you meet regularly for well-baby visits, but also there may be periods of time when you talk on the phone daily. There is enough newness to deal with when you have a baby without having to shop around for a doctor, be it during a crisis or simply when you are in need of reassurance or advice. This is why it's so important to meet in advance.

Excellent medical credentials are only the minimum to expect from the health-care provider you choose for your baby. The right person, or the right team of people, must make you feel comfortable, not only in the role of someone in need of information and health services, but also in the role of the parent/expert on your baby. Good listening skills are crucial. This person should also be a willing explainer and sharer of information. Even though you may be lacking medical credentials, you should never be made to feel foolish for asking questions.

What Are Your Health-Care Choices?

When we think of finding health care for our baby, a pediatrician, a doctor trained specifically to care for infants and children, usually comes to mind. Following are some other medical specialists who can be involved in your baby's health care.

Family Physician

Before you settle on a pediatrician, you might want to consider finding a family physician who can take care of the entire family's health needs. Although the title may remind you of *general practitioner,* a family physician differs from a GP in that s/he is actually a specialist. S/he is required to train in a three-year residency program in family care, which covers everything from pediatrics to alcohol abuse to exercise hazards. This training equips these doctors to handle most illnesses and to know when further specialization is required. To find a family physician in your area, you can write to the American Acad-emy of Family Physicians, 1740 West 92nd Street, Kansas City, MO 64114.

Physician's Assistant (PA)

These medical professionals have completed a two-year training program and have usually graduated from college as well. They are qualified to take medical histories, give physical exams, and order lab tests. They work alongside the doctor and in some states may also develop treatment plans and prescribe medication.

Nurse Practitioner (NP)

Nurse Practitioners are a growing breed of registered nurses who have completed a special program at a university or hospital. Most NPs also hold a masters' degree. NPs work in conjunction with a physician and are qualified to perform a well-baby exam, take medical histories, and diagnose routine childhood illnesses.

Clinics

You may have seen references to well-baby clinics. This is a collective term for any clinic treating infants from birth to one or two-and-a-half years of age. Most are operated in connection with a hospital or social-services agency and never seem to be listed in the phonebook under "well-baby." To find out about clinics, you can call the hospital in your area as well as the Department of Health or Social Services, or the country medical society.

A clinic can provide good medical care at less expense than a private doctor. Fees are often based on a sliding scale adjusted to income. While qualities like warmth, smallness, and lack of bureaucracy don't necessarily influence the quality of medical care a clinic offers, these things can make a tremendous difference in the baby-parent-clinic rapport.

If you live in a large metropolitan area and are in a position to choose, it is worthwhile to call a couple of clinics in advance and get a feeling for how they operate. Following are some questions you can ask on the phone.

- Does the clinic accept all babies? Some require a referral by a hospital-affiliated doctor. Others require that the baby be born in their hospital. Still others will treat only children who live within a certain geographical area.
- What kinds of services does the clinic provide? Do they see only well babies? If so, who sees a sick baby? Is there a way of dealing with routine questions over the phone?
- Are there walk-in services, or do they require that you make an appointment?
- What are the fee scales? What proof of income, if any, is required?
- Will you see any one of a number of staff doctors, or is an effort made to assign the same doctor to you each time you visit?

How to Make the Final Decision for Health Care

Use the Telephone for an Initial Screening

Once you have assembled a few names and addresses, use the telephone to evaluate your health-care candidates further. Have a piece of paper and a pencil handy, along with your list of questions, so that you can find out several bits of pertinent information from either the doctor or his or her nurse. You can ask about training and hospital affiliations as well as fees and the cost of the immunization program during the first year. This is usually an additional cost that can come as a surprise if you aren't prepared for it. You can also ask whether he or she thinks it's a good idea to meet with you in advance. If the doctor doesn't feel this is necessary, you might at least ask why before you consider going elsewhere. You may or may not have to pay for an advance visit but, if you do, it is well worth the cost.

Meet with the Doctor

If it's at all practical, both parents can benefit from meeting the pediatrician in advance. Two opinions are always better than one. More important, though, a father who has met the doctor has established some sort of relationship with him or her and may be more comfortable when calling with questions or taking the baby for a visit in the future.

An advance visit should be as important to the doctor as it is to you. The better sense he or she has about what kind of people you are, your his-

Where to Find Health-Care Professionals

- The best way to find a doctor is through people who use them the most: other parents, preferably those who know you as well as the doctor. Comments like "a little crisp or efficient," "rather rushed," or "not specific enough or too vague" can be useful clues. Friends are also likely to know the real truth about how the office runs, how available the doctor is to take phone calls, and how well he gets along with older children, not just infants, etc.
- Your obstetrician can be a good source for a referral.
- You can inquire at the nearest accredited (preferably teaching) hospital or medical school. Request a list of pediatricians on the staff as attending physicians, and choose a few to talk with who are conveniently located. One pediatrician whom I interviewed recommended calling the chief resident in pediatrics at the nearest hospital and asking him or her for a referral.
- The Directory of Medical Specialists, found in the medical sciences section of the library, or at the county medical society, lists pediatricians. The Visiting Nurse Association will also provide a list of qualified doctors in your area.
- If you are looking for a clinic, call the hospital where you will deliver, or check with the Visiting Nurse Association.

tory, and your particular concerns, the easier it will be for him or her to interpret your needs and put you at ease.

While you are waiting in the office, you can also get a feeling for how it runs—perhaps what the nurse's role is, or how incoming phone calls are handled.

Ask Questions!

Some of the suggested topics cover areas in which you might not yet have opinions. But the purpose of asking the questions is not just to get the answers; it is to see how the doctor goes about answering them.

• If the doctor is in solo practice, who covers for him when he is not available? If he is part of a group, how large is it? The advantage of a large group can be a diversity of medical expertise. The disadvantage can be the difficulty in establishing a relationship with one doctor. Is it possible to see the same doctor regularly, at least for well visits?

• What system does the doctor have for answering routine questions? For instance, is there a special call-in hour, or does the office accept routine calls all day, then have the doctor get back at his convenience? How do you reach the doctor in an emergency? Who takes his calls and how are messages relayed to him?

• Ask about the role of the doctor's nurses, PAs, or receptionists. Some act as intermediaries between you and the doctor. For instance, they may take calls, ask and answer questions, weigh and measure the baby, and make suggestions. Not surprisingly, at least one study has shown that parents working through a nurse or nurse-practitioner feel more comfortable asking questions, and that the nurses in question spend more

---

All Those Silly Questions!
Rx: Reread This Good Advice from an Expert

Dr. Spock offered this excellent advice several years ago in *Redbook* magazine. It still holds true.

If I were a parent expecting my first child, I would confess to the physician that I was an anxious type (even if that wasn't true) and that I imagined I would raise lots of questions in the early weeks of my baby's life. Then I would watch his reaction. Did he tighten up at the prospect of a thousand trivial, time-wasting questions? Or did he laugh reassuringly and say that he expected a barrage of questions at first? I want to make a point of "silly questions" because they are an uncomfortable issue for most parents in the first two or three months of the first baby's life. It's no exaggeration to say that half the questions you'll ever want to raise will come up in that period—and you are entitled to the answers. If you've been persuaded that this will make you a nuisance, you'll spend half your time in a stew—needing information or reassurance but afraid of irritating the doctor. It shouldn't be that way.

My advice, then, is to sound out a prospective doctor on this subject. If he shows traces of impatience, drop him before you get started. If you have already started, then you should try to work things out. Summon the courage to say that you have the impression your questions bother him. If he's any good, he'll apologize and encourage you to ask away. If, on the other hand, he implies that you do *have too many questions, I'd leave him and find another doctor. (Redbook, November 1983)*

---

time providing answers than do the doctors they work for.

• How does the doctor feel about circumcision? (See To Circumcise or Not, page 226.)

• How does the doctor feel about breast-feeding? Does she consider problems with breast-feeding her province, or will she refer you to your obstetrician? Some pediatricians have nurses who are trained as lactation consultants to help nursing mothers. You might also ask when the doctor suggests introducing solid food and why. If it is before four months, then this

doctor probably isn't very knowledgeable about breast-feeding.

• If you work, inquire about how the doctor feels about this, particularly if he is an older male. You need someone who will be supportive of your choice as well as available. Inquire about evening or weekend well-baby visits.

• If you have any particular philosophies or medical problems, or a life-style that may raise differences or require specialized information or services from your doctor, this first interview is the time to talk. If you are a vegetarian, for exam-

To Circumcise or Not

Circumcision has been a controversial and emotional issue ever since its ancient beginnings some 3,500 years ago. The American Academy of Pediatrics has gone back and forth on the advisability of circumcising baby boys. In 1989 the AAP reversed its negative stance. Though there is a small risk of postprocedure infection or other complications, the AAP takes the position that circumcision "has potential medical benefits and advantages." This change of mind is based largely on studies by Thomas Wiswell, a pediatrician who found that uncircumcised male infants suffer eleven times as many urinary tract infections as those who have been circumcised. It is suspected that bacteria trapped under the foreskin spreads up to the urethra to the kidneys. Besides reducing urinary infections, circumcision virtually eliminates the possibility of cancer of the penis and may also reduce the possibility of contracting sexually transmitted diseases. Many choose circumcision for religious reasons or because of the "locker-room syndrome"! They don't want their sons to feel different from their fathers, brothers, and friends.

By no means do all pediatricians agree with the AAP's position. Like many parents, some pediatricians oppose the procedure because it seems unnecessary and unnatural and is painful. If you do decide to circumcise your baby, don't have it done immediately in the delivery room. Wait at least twelve hours after the baby's birth, so that he has a chance to accustom himself to life outside the womb. The usual hospital procedure takes between fifteen and thirty minutes. The baby is strapped to a "bodyboard"; then, using a clamp, the physician makes several incisions. To counteract the pain, the AAP states that a dorsal penile nerve block may be given, but only by an experienced member of a surgical team, not a resident or junior member.

Another alternative, which may be less stressful, is to use a *mohel,* a Jewish ritual circumciser. The *mohel* makes one incision while the baby is held by a family member. The procedure takes a mere fifteen to thirty seconds.

Circumcision is a subject you might want to bring up when you are interviewing a prospective pediatrician. See How to Make the Final Decision for Health Care, page 224.

---

ple, and want to rear your child as a vegetarian, ask the doctor how he or she feels about this. If you have a family history of allergies or if you are against having your baby immunized, mention these things, too.

Well-Baby Visits

Monthly well-baby visits during the first year are extremely important for the baby's sake and your own. These visits ensure that your child has several thorough physical examinations, all the routine tests, and those very important immunizations. They also provide parents with the opportunity to ask questions, get answers, learn a little bit about medicine, and, not least important, receive the much-needed reassurance that their baby is progressing well.

Don't be shy about asking your health practitioner questions. You can keep a running list in the back of this book (see Health Notes, page 300). My babies' pediatrician, Dr. Irwin Rappaport, was kind enough to elaborate on what goes into a well-baby examination.

Question: What are you looking for in a well-baby examination?

Dr. Rappaport: The most important thing in a well-baby examination is not, at first, to touch the baby but rather to look and observe.

First we are looking for growth and development, that is, what the baby is doing and how the baby has changed since the last visit. There are many things to look for, and these vary according to the age of the baby and whether or not the baby is full-term or premature. The lag time between the baby's development and the actual gestational birth are factors. If the baby is truly only eight months when born, it will be a month behind in development as opposed to a baby who has had a nine-month gestational period. The catch-up period occurs during the first year.

Beyond the actual age of the baby, though, growth and development is a very individual matter. There are wide *margins of normalcy. You simply can't expect to compare your baby, with your limited exposure and experience, to your friends' babies and know what is normal and what is not. It's very important that a parent not get uptight about small differences that may appear to be larger.*

Then, again, rather than touching the baby you look at the baby and see, for example, the color of his skin, how he breathes, and how responsive that baby is. Responsiveness is most important. We see this in the interplay between the mother and the baby, or the effectiveness of stimulation between the parent and the infant. If, for instance, you say to the mother, "That's a beautiful baby," does she turn and look at the baby? A vast majority will turn to the baby on that question. You also can get a good idea about whether or not there is emotional interplay—if the baby smiles or starts to respond to visual observations from the mother. In the later months of the first year, we look to see if the interplay includes opportunities for the baby to mimic, because this is most important for learning.

Some mothers are very good at this, and it seems to come naturally. But others are not very expressive. They feel as much love as anyone else for their baby, but they just don't stimulate the baby as much. In this kind of situation, you try to encourage the parent to play more with the baby, to make some extra time available—perhaps to stop during a feeding or a diaper change or take a few extra minutes while giving the baby a bath. You encourage them to take the baby outdoors and get the baby to see the world a little bit.

Question: *Can you really tell during a visit that a parent is not stimulating the baby enough?*

Dr. Rappaport: *You certainly can. You can see clearly if there is good rapport between mother and child. This is extremely important. It's also important to get a father involved because there are two parents. We're really much more concerned about the nonphysical parts of a well-baby examination than anything else.*

Then we're going to want to know about nutrition. This, of course, is a very individual matter. Breast-feeding is great. We encourage it because it is the finest of all feedings. But there can be questions that relate to diet, to food trends. Parents read about natural foods, vitamins, low cholesterol, and so on. There is plenty of room for individual approaches to feeding, but at the same time we want to make sure that the baby is being adequately nourished. I always ask about diet. For instance, I've seen parents who give nothing but 64 ounces of milk a day, so that the child is bloated. A routine blood test for anemia is also standard.

Then we turn to the physical part of the examination. The baby must be completely undressed—no diaper—in order to observe the skin color, activity, and breathing. We take the weight and height and the head and chest circumferences. We're looking for a child who has about one-and-a-half inches difference between head and chest. If the head is too large in proportion to the chest, then we may suspect hydrocephalus; if it's too small, microcephalus.

There should, of course, be a proportion in height and weight gain that is related to that particular baby's body structure. Body structure depends on the baby's genetics. We use percentile charts for height and weight gain as a check. If there is any dropping off in the baby's height percentile, we would look for other clues as to whether or not the baby was developing normally.

Genetics are also extremely important. On the first visit we take a complete family medical history and continue to look for any implied difficulties. Then, after measuring and weighing the baby, we check the eyes. We want to make sure that both eyes are functioning properly, that they move in unison, and that both eyes have a good ability to converge. This will be very important when the child is learning to read. If there are any problems, we want to start right away with corrective measures.

We also watch for symmetry of the ears—of the auricles. They should be quite similar, though not necessarily absolutely identical. We do this because we know that if there is malformation of the ears, this occurs at the same embryologic time as the development of the kidneys. If the baby has a malformed ear, we do a urinalysis and culture to make sure he doesn't have something else going on.

We're also looking for the fontanels—checking to make sure that both are present and open before four months and, after that, that the posterior one is closing. As far as the neck is concerned, we check to make sure it is supple, that it moves well, and that the mouth can open and has an intact palate. Sometimes you have to be careful here and feel with your finger for what is called "skin covering" over an opening in the palate. We also check for any kind of masses in the thyroid area. And we check, on the first visit, to see if the clavicles are intact because these are the bones most frequently fractured at the time of a vaginal birth.

As far as listening with a stethoscope—this is one of the least important things you do. With most babies you can tell about their breathing by observation and by the color of their skin. It should not be blue. You can also tell by the speed of the respirations, the retractions, whether a baby is having difficulty. Then you listen to make sure, to verify your observations. As for heart murmurs—yes, many babies have them. Most of them go away. After checking the heart, you feel the abdomen for any enlargement of the liver and spleen as well as for any masses. You also check for intactness of the spine to make sure that you feel all of the vertebrae and that there is no malformation that could allow the spinal cord to protrude out.

You also check the genitals, male or female, and check for any hip dislocation. If dislocation is present, it is best corrected before three months. We are also looking for neurological abilities—the so-called Moro, or startle, reflex, as well as the ability to suck and to cry. Beyond these, most neurological reflexes are not very important.

Spotting Early Vision and Hearing Problems

At your well-baby visit your doctor will be looking for early vision and hearing problems among other things. However, parents spend the most time with their babies, and if a baby does have any health problems, parents are often the first to note them. The earlier any visual or hearing problems can be detected, the more quickly a child can receive corrective help. Following are a few signals to be aware of.

Some Signs of Poor Vision in Infants*
- The baby is visually very unresponsive.
- He holds things very close to see them.
- He often bumps into large objects.
- He cannot pick up small objects with accuracy.
- He constantly favors one eye when looking at an object.
- One or both eyes turn in or out for noticeable periods of time.
- The baby squints or closes one eye frequently.

Some Signs of Poor Hearing in Infants and Young Children**
- A newborn does not act startled when someone claps sharply from three to six feet away.
- At three months the child does not turn his eyes toward the clapping sound.
- At eight months to one year, the child does not turn toward a whispered voice or the sound of a rattle or a spoon stirring in a cup, when the sound originates within three feet behind him.
- At two years the child cannot identify some object when its name is spoken, cannot repeat a word with a single stimulus, cannot repeat a phrase, and does not use some short phrases while talking.
- The child is not awakened or disturbed by loud sounds, does not respond when called, pays no attention to ordinary crib noises, uses gestures almost exclusively instead of verbalization to establish needs, or watches parents' faces intently.
- The child has a history of upper-respiratory infections and chronic middle-ear trouble.

* Adapted from "Parent's Guide to Children's Vision," Public Affairs Pamphlet No. 339.
** Adapted from "Helping the Child Who Cannot Hear," Public Affairs Pamphlet No. 479.

Question: Do you look for all this every time you see the baby?

Dr. Rappaport: Yes, absolutely. For example, the first time I saw one particular baby, he was crying. On examination, he seemed fine. The next time I saw that same baby a month later, he wasn't crying, and his eyes were open. On that visit I found bilateral cataracts. When a child is crying, it's very difficult to open the lids.

You try, of course, to examine everything as thoroughly as you can without great difficulty or discomfort to the baby, and sometimes you cannot. It takes a lot of practice to tune into a heart examination or a chest examination on a child. Sometimes a pacifier is a way to try to calm the baby. Or I may suggest that the mother hold the baby in her lap. But you must check for each and every thing, hoping that you have not missed something in the past and, if you have, that you will pick it up this time. The repetition of this is not only for the baby's security and the parent's but also for the doctor's. Repetition is necessary in order for a doctor to be as thorough as he possibly can, to eliminate human errors, which you cannot predict in any examination. No one is infallible. And so the only way is to double-check and triple-check and quadruple-check.

Question: That's why regular well-baby visits are so important?

Dr. Rappaport: Exactly.

Immunization

One hundred years ago infant mortality touched almost every family. Old cemeteries are full of tiny headstones that belong to infants who died painfully of sicknesses such as smallpox, diphtheria, whooping cough, tetanus, polio, measles, and meningitis—deadly diseases that have been practically eradicated thanks to early, comprehensive immunization programs.

In recent years, some parents have decided not to immunize their children for various reasons. Some mistakenly think that these diseases have been totally eradicated and that there is no need to submit their infants to a shot. Others are alarmed by reports of potentially serious side effects caused by some vaccines. As a result, according to a report by the National Association of Children's Hospitals and Related Institutions, only 60 percent of children under the age of four in the United States have received the basic series of shots necessary to protect them.

Rather than act out of a false sense of complacency, or out of ignorance or fear, parents need to know how immunizations work in order to weigh the risks against the numerous benefits. They also need to know the occasional side effects of a vaccine and under what circumstances the vaccine should be delayed.

Question: How do vaccines work?

Answer: A vaccine contains a small amount of the virus or bacteria that is related to the disease. When the vaccine enters the bloodstream, the body's immune system responds to this miniature attack by producing specific antibodies to fight that particular disease. Should the body be invaded by the real virus, these antibodies, which have remained in the bloodstream, will recognize the enemy and will be ready to attack and destroy.

Question: Is it possible for a child to contract the disease or suffer from serious side effects from the immunization?

Answer: The chances are very, very slim. Read on.

Question: What about the DPT vaccine?

Answer: The pertussis (whooping cough) vaccine, which is part of the combined DPT immunization, further described below, has received considerable negative publicity. In rare instances the shot has been associated with brain damage and convulsions. Research studies, however, do not support this. When researchers in the Department of Pediatrics at the University of California at Los Angeles compared the rate of adverse rections among children given DPT vaccine and those given only the DT vaccine, they found no difference in the side effects. Another study found that the risk of brain damage from the pertussis vaccine was 1 in 310,000. A Mayo Clinic report cited the risk of death from whooping cough at 1 in 1,000; the chances of brain damage from the vaccine, 1 in 10,000. The Mayo Report reiterated the fact that during the 1970s some 70 percent of the babies in England were not immunized against pertussis. In 1979 and 1980 more than 100,000 cases occurred, with 36 deaths. After a thorough review of the existing research on the efficacy of the pertussis vaccine, the American Academy of Pediatrics recommends that children continue to receive it. They believe that the risk of having a serious adverse reaction is far lower than the risk of an unvaccinated child's becoming seriously ill with pertussis.

The Vital Vaccines

Following are the immunizations for children recommended by the American Academy of Pediatrics. Also included are possible side effects, as well as information on who should and should not receive them. A summary timetable appears on page 231. On page 277 you will find a space for a permanent Immunization Record.

The DPT Vaccine for Diphtheria, Tetanus, and Pertussis

This vaccine protects against three of the most deadly diseases: highly contagious *diphtheria*, which causes a high fever, sore throat, labored breathing, and, in some cases, paralysis and heart failure; *tetanus*, or lockjaw, a noncontagious disease causing painful muscle spasms and possible death (in 40 percent of victims) from complications such as blood clots and pneumonia; and *pertussis*, or whooping cough, a highly contagious disease that produces a cough so violent and persistent that its victims can hardly breathe, eat, drink, or sleep. Complications include pneumonia, convulsions, and permanent brain damage.

DPT vaccine schedule. The DPT vaccine is recommended for children under seven years. Three shots are given the first year, at two, four, and six months. A fourth should be given at fifteen to eighteen months, with boosters given between the ages of four and six. If your baby is even mildly ill, have a discussion with your pediatrician about the pros and cons of delaying the DPT.

DPT vaccine: possible side effects. Common side effects include some redness and swelling at the injection site, some fever, and irritability for up to forty-eight hours after the shot. Rare side effects include loss of muscle tone, shock, constant, inconsolable crying for up to three hours, very high-pitched crying, excessive sleepiness, pale skin, and lack of muscle tone or convulsions within three days of receiving the shot. If your baby experiences any of these symptoms contact your doctor immediately.

When not to give the DPT vaccine. Do not give the DPT vaccine if the infant has experienced any serious side effects from a previous

DPT shot; if the child has a history of convulsions or a confirmed or suspected neurological disease; or if the child is undergoing treatment for such diseases as cancer, leukemia, or lymphoma, which lower the immune system's ability to fight infection. On a case-by-case basis a doctor may recommend eliminating the pertussis part of the DPT and offering the DT instead.

OPV, Oral Polio Vaccine, or IPV, Inactivated Poliovirus Vaccine

OPV is the recommended polio vaccine for infants and young children. Because of OPV, the infectious viral disease of polio is now extremely rare in the United States. When it does strike, symptoms range from a fever coupled with an overall weakness to a paralysis that can cripple and kill.

OPV schedule. The OPV is given at two months, four months, fifteen months, and between four and six years of age.

OPV: possible side effects. Though there are virtually no side effects of OPV, paralytic polio may occur in 1 out of 8.1 million recipients. The risk from the OPV increases for those who suffer from diseases or who take medications that weaken the immune system, and for this reason they should receive the somewhat weaker IPV, which can cause redness and swelling at the injection site. Also, once in every 5 million doses a person in close contact with a recently vaccinated person may develop paralytic polio.

When not to give the OPV. Anyone with cancer or who is taking a drug that affects the immune system, pregnant women, and anyone living with someone who has any of the above conditions should check with their doctor, who may recommend the somewhat weaker IPV as an alternative.

The MMR Vaccine for Measles, Mumps, and Rubella

Believe it or not, measles is considered among the most serious of childhood diseases. Highly contagious, the measles virus causes a red, itchy rash, high fever, cough, and crusted eyes and can cause such serious complications as ear infections, pneumonia, and brain damage. Mumps causes painful swelling in the salivary glands and in some rare and severe cases can lead to permanent hearing loss, sterility in males, and brain damage. Rubella, or German measles, produces a rash, swollen glands, and, in extremely rare instances, brain damage and death. If German measles strikes a pregnant woman, it can cause miscarriage and birth defects in the unborn fetus.

MMR vaccine schedule. The MMR vaccine should be given at age fifteen to eighteen months.

MMR vaccine: possible side effects. One to two weeks after the shot, one out of five children will develop a rash or mild fever for a few days, swollen glands, and occasional joint pain in fingers and toes. Serious side effects, including encephalitis, occur in one out of a million cases.

When not to give the MMR vaccine. Infants who have an allergic reaction to eggs should not receive the MMR vaccine because small amounts of egg may be in the measles and mumps components of the vaccine. Anyone suffering from an illness or taking medication that suppresses the immune system is also ineligible.

PRP-D (Formerly Known as HIB or PRP Vaccine)

PRP-D is a fairly new vaccine and provides immunity to infections caused by the *Hemophilus influenzae* type b bacterium, which includes

---

Moms, Dads, and Child-Care Providers Should Be Up-to-Date with Their Immunizations, Too

- All adults should have a DPT booster every ten years, and those who have never been vaccinated for diphtheria, tetanus, and pertussis should receive three shots, each at one- to two-month intervals.
- All women of childbearing age should have a blood test to check their immunity to rubella. If you are not immune, you need to be vaccinated at least three months before trying to conceive. You cannot be vaccinated if you are pregnant.
- Most adults in the United States are at minimal risk of contracting polio. Unvaccinated adults can be exposed to live polio virus in the feces of vaccinated infants and young children and may want to consider receiving an IPV.

---

meningitis, pneumonia, and epiglottitis, as well as blood, bone, joint, and soft-tissue infections.

PRP-D vaccine schedule. Children should receive this vaccine at eighteen months of age.

PRP-D vaccine: possible side effects. So far the only side effects of this vaccine are occasional redness and swelling at the injection site with the slight risk of mild fever.

Immunization Schedule Recommended by the American Academy of Pediatrics

	DPT	POLIO	MMR	PRP-D	TB (TEST)
2 MONTHS	X	X			
4 MONTHS	X	X			
6 MONTHS	X				
1 YEAR					X
15 MONTHS			X		
18 MONTHS	X	X		X	
4–6 YEARS	X	X			

When not to give the PRP-D vaccine. Anyone who has had a life-threatening reaction to thimerosal, a mercurial preservative, should not receive the vaccine.

How and When to Call Your Health-Care Provider with Questions

Be Prepared Before You Call

New parents have lots of questions about their babies. Before you call, familiarize yourself with some of the special characteristics of the newborn (see pages 13–16). Also, for safety's sake, look over the box entitled Call the Doctor Immediately for the Following Emergencies, page 236. Most of your questions will fall into such categories as baby care and baby health and development. Keep a running list of these questions in the space allotted on page 300. They can be asked in person at a well-baby visit or during a telephone call-in hour. Of course, it takes time to know what is routine and what isn't. Be patient with yourself (see Developing the Art of Diagnosis: Parents Advise, page 232).

When the Baby Is Ill . . .

There is nothing quite so sad as a sick baby—and the worn, concerned parents who belong to it.

Pediatricians Rate Parents

When *Pediatrics* polled pediatricians to find out what they valued most in parents, they discovered that some 38 percent did not particularly care whether mothers were friendly. What they consistently valued were mothers who communicated clearly, understood and followed recommendations, and kept appointments. The mothers who were conscientious about stimulating their infants and using car restraints, and who kept their children's immunizations up to date, also found favor. Interestingly, the study found two significant differences in pediatricians in regard to sex and age: Women pediatricians were more positively influenced by mothers who made efforts to calm a scared child and who comforted a crying infant than were their male counterparts. Older pediatricians of both sexes liked mothers who readily sought out their advice and who gave positive feedback.

The awesome sense of responsibility that we already feel rapidly escalates when faced with the vulnerability and misery of a helpless infant. If it is any comfort at all, the first bout with sickness is surely the worst. From then on, though it's never pleasant, with each cold, fever, or ear infection we gain experience and a calm and confidence that adds to our adult sense of self.

Before you call the doctor, get organized. Have a pencil and paper at the phone, with bits of per-

Developing the Art of Diagnosis: Parents Advise

It takes time to get the right perspective in the beginning. I didn't want to be a pest, so I tried to limit myself to things that I considered life-and-death issues (which was almost everything!). For instance, I knew diarrhea could kill a tiny baby. I once actually arrived at the doctor's office with one of Sean's dirty diapers. The doctor was very nice but said that he would have been willing to trust my descriptive powers over the phone. In the case of a diaper rash, I was so casual that I let it go for two weeks. When I finally did get him to the doctor, he had a very bad fungus infection.

• • •

You do make mistakes. I'd been trying to feed Elissa for two hours. Every time I stuck the bottle in her mouth, she'd suck, then scream frantically. I was frantic myself. I called the doctor and described each of my attempts. I was sure that there was something wrong with her throat that he had missed when he examined her. It turned out that I'd been using a closed nipple.

• • •

I want to put in a plug for good old-fashioned mother's intuition, which is something that I didn't really trust enough until I had my second child. Believe that you know your baby better than anyone else does. From holding him, you know what his body feels like against your own. You know what his eyes look like when he's cheerful and well, and whether or not he's eating in his usual pattern—even if he doesn't have any overt symptoms of illness. All babies are different. My second had no fever and hardly even whimpered when he had a raging ear infection, yet I knew something was wrong because he just wasn't quite himself.

• • •

As a single parent I found the times when Jason was sick the very hardest. The weight of the responsibility felt very, very heavy, but there was also the loneliness of it. There was no one else to say, "Hey, this kid doesn't look like himself. Don't worry though. It will all be okay. We'll call the doctor, and we'll deal with it." It took time to trust myself. It also took time to be able to admit openly. "This is hard! I don't have to love every single minute of it." No one likes it when their kid is sick, if they're alone or not.

tinent information based on observations that you have made (see Observing the Sick Baby Before You Call the Doctor, page 233). Also have the name and number of your drugstore handy. When you actually place the call, if it is an emergency, say so right away. Then give the child's full name, age, and weight. If you do not reach the doctor directly, and must leave a message with an answering service or a nurse at the office, after you hang up stay off the phone so that your line is free. When you get the pediatrician, write down exactly what the doctor says. It's very easy to get rattled and forget numbers, times, and amounts. Repeat it back if necessary.

Two Common Questions

Question: *Is it okay to give a sick baby a bath?*

Answer: Yes. Make sure the water is warm. Make the bath quick, then dry the baby immediately in a towel. Don't overdress the baby if he has a fever.

Question: *Can you take a sick baby outside?*

Answer: Yes, as long as he is dressed appropriately for the weather.

Choosing a Vaporizer or Humidifier

If your baby can't breathe through his nose because of a cold, or can hardly eat or drink his dinner without suffocating, or can't sleep comfortably, your pediatrician may prescribe the use of a steam vaporizer or a cool-mist humidifier to help relieve some of the congestion.

Vaporizers release hot steam and are useful when medicants are prescribed, but the boiling water can cause burns if the vaporizer is accidentally overturned. If you decide on a vaporizer, look for double-wall construction, a low, extra-wide base for stability, and a locking cover.

A *humidifier* that generates a cool mist is a good alternative to a vaporizer, as long as it is meticulously cleaned every day that you use it. Otherwise, germs and molds multiply quickly and are sprayed into the air that your baby breathes. Cleaning tablets are available at most drugstores, or you can scrub the unit with dish detergent, followed by a chlorine bleach–and–water rinse. New ultrasonic models are now available. Although they are somewhat expensive, they are efficient and quiet and present no health hazards if filled with filtered or distilled water.

How to Take a Baby's Temperature

There are two ways to take a baby's temperature: rectally and axillarily (under the arm). The rectal method is preferred because it is much more accurate and it is quicker. When you use the rectal method, you must use a rectal thermometer, be it a battery-controlled digital model or the glass type with a small glass bulb on the end. For the axillary method, either an oral or rectal thermometer will do. An adhesive "fever strip" that you place on a child's forehead is not recommended as a reliable method for taking a temperature. For the most accurate picture, if possible

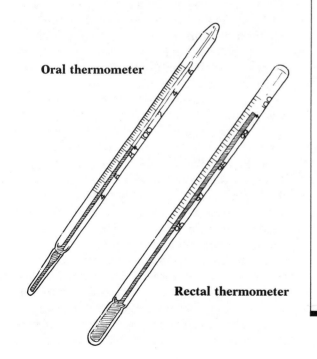

Oral thermometer

Rectal thermometer

General Behavior
Is the baby's behavior in any way unusual? For instance, is he more irritable, or crying or sleeping more or less than normal? Is he drowsy or lethargic? What is his "posture" like—floppier than usual? Is the baby pulling on his ear? Is he trembling or having chills? Are there any motor symptoms? For instance, is he having difficulty moving any of his limbs or his neck?

Skin and Eyes
What is the baby's skin tone like? Is he pale, flushed, or bluish? Does the baby have any sort of rash? If so, where, and how would you characterize it? Are the eyes red, dull, or runny? Do they appear half-lidded or sunken, or do they have dark circles under them? Is there any kind of discharge, and if so, how would you characterize it?

Fever
Before you take the baby's temperature, test with your own touch. Use the back of your hand or your lips on the baby's forehead, as well as on his back between his shoulder blades. Keep in mind that vigorous crying can raise a baby's temperature, and so can an overheated house, as well as warm, insulating clothing such as a blanket sleeper. Note the differences in temperature between a rectal or axillary (armpit) reading, and be sure to mention which method you used to the doctor.

Appetite and Digestion
Is the baby eating more or less than usual? Is the baby vomiting? If so, how often, and is the vomiting forceful or projectile? What does the vomit look like? Is the baby having normal bowel movements? If not, how would you characterize them? Are they more frequent, looser, or smellier than usual? Is the baby urinating more or less than usual, and is the urine a different color than usual, say a darker yellow, or even a pinkish hue?

Breathing, Mouth, Nose, and Throat
Is the baby breathing normally or is his breathing labored and congested? Is he coughing? Is his nose running and, if so, what color is the mucus? If you can see into the baby's mouth, note whether the throat is red or white and whether there are any white patches on the tongue, palate, or gums.

take the temperature twice, with half an hour to an hour in between.

Whichever method you use, first wash the thermometer with soap and cool water, then shake down the thermometer. To do this, take the end opposite the bulb and shake by snapping your wrist quickly two or three times, until the mercury is below the normal body-temperature mark.

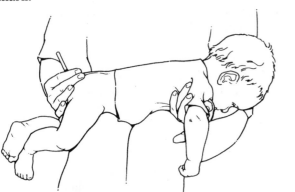

Rectal Method

1. Be sure to lubricate the thermometer with a bit of petroleum jelly, so that it will be easier to insert.

2. Take the baby into a well-lighted room with a chair where you can sit comfortably.

3. Next, speaking in reassuring tones, place the baby over your knees with his legs hanging off. An alternative position is to place the baby facedown with a small pillow under the stomach to elevate his bottom.

4. With one hand gently spread the buttocks apart, so that you can see the anal opening.

5. With the other hand, slip the thermometer about 1 inch into the rectum. The temperature will register in about a minute.

6. Note: Rectal readings are higher than oral or axillary readings. A normal rectal temperature is 99.6°F or 37.6°C.

Axillary Method

1. Use this method if you don't have a rectal thermometer, if your baby has diarrhea, or if she won't tolerate the rectal method.

2. Make sure that the baby's arm and chest are free of clothing. Then, as you talk soothingly to the baby, place the bulb end of the thermometer snugly under her armpit.

3. Hold it there for at least four full minutes. A normal axillary temperature is 97.6°F or 36.7°C.

Reading a Thermometer

You need good lighting to read a thermometer. With your left hand hold the thermometer by the mercury end; hold the glass end with your right hand. Then rotate the thermometer until the numbers and marks are facing you. Continue to rotate it a bit more, until a column of mercury appears just under the numbers. The point at which the column ends is the temperature. Keep a temperature chart, with the time and the reading, either in the back of this book in the Health Notes section (see page 300) or on a piece of paper posted in a place where you can easily find it.

The Facts About Fever

Naturally, a baby with a fever scares us. Perhaps we've heard a horror story about a sick child with a high fever who suffered some kind of permanent damage. We also associate high fevers with febrile seizures or convulsions (see pages 235–36). Or maybe we are simply remembering our own mother's alarm as she tried to cajole us into keeping a thermometer in our mouths. For whatever reasons, many of us have mistakenly come to believe that fever is a disease and therefore bad, and that getting rid of it when it strikes is the appropriate medical treatment.

This isn't always the soundest approach, however. As the ancient healers such as Hippocrates knew, fever actually helps the body marshal its defenses against viral or bacterial illness. When white blood cells turn on "the enemy," they release a substance called *pyrogen*, which instructs the brain to reset the body's thermostat. The body's heating system revs up to fight off the invaders that are making you sick. In fact, a Yale University study found that up to twenty times more of certain antibodies are produced when the body's temperature is boosted just 2 degrees above normal. Knowing this, consider that the casual or too-hasty dose of acetaminophen may actually be doing your feverish child a disservice. Following are some facts to demystify fevers further. (See How to Take a Baby's Temperature, page 233.)

• For the first half year of your baby's life, her temperature-regulating mechanism does not work very efficiently. Infants and small children can go through rapid and extreme temperature rises that have little apparent cause, then return to normal just as quickly. What constitutes a dangerous fever for a child or infant is not the same as for an adult. Some infants and young children seem very comfortable with a temperature of 103°F, whereas the same temperature in an adult would be nearly incapacitating.

• Call the doctor if your baby has had a fever over 102°F that has lasted longer than six hours; your child is two months old and has a fever; your child has a convulsion, has purple spots on the skin, has a stiff neck, experiences difficulty breathing, cries or whimpers inconsolably, or if the fever is higher than 104°F. A fever of 106°F is dangerous and should be treated as an emergency. Take steps to lower the fever (see below) and call the doctor right away.

• Not all rises in body temperature are fever. We tend to get warmer as the day progresses. Physical activity can raise a temperature, as can warm clothing or an overly heated house. Crying also elevates an infant's temperature.

• The child with a fever should be dressed lightly. Take off the sleeping bag or the heavy blanket sleeper with feet.

• To lower a fever: Dress the baby lightly. Offer fluids to replace what the body is losing. Dehydration, indicated by a dry mouth, infrequent urination, and/or a doughy feel to the skin, is dangerous for babies. Also remember that "feed a cold and starve a fever" is bad advice. The feverish body burns calories very rapidly. Offer, but don't push, the breast or bottle as well as easy-to-digest foods. If the baby is hungry, he will

eat. A sponge bath with lukewarm water is also effective in bringing down a high fever. Don't use rubbing alcohol; the fumes can asphyxiate an infant. Don't offer fever-reducing medicines such as acetaminophen to infants under two months without consulting your doctor. Offer acetaminophen to older babies only if you have had prior discussions with your doctor about how to treat a fever (see Getting the Right Dose of Acetaminophen, page 237). Acetaminophen rather than aspirin is recommended. There is some evidence that aspirin given during chicken pox or a viral illness may lead to Reye's Syndrome, a serious disorder that can damage the brain.

What to Do in Case of a Febrile Seizure or Convulsions

Febrile seizures are very frightening, but they are also fairly common, are usually unpreventable (so it's not your fault!), and rarely do damage to the baby. Seizures are most likely to occur when the body temperature rises very quickly from normal to a high level. What happens is that a

---

Stocking the Medicine Cabinet

Have the following things on hand so that you are not out looking for an all-night pharmacy when your baby runs his first fever or has his first cold. Keep all of the following locked away from babies and young children.

• Rectal thermometer
• Petroleum jelly to lubricate the thermometer
• Acetaminophen in liquid form, for reducing fevers (See Getting the Right Dose of Acetaminophen, page 237.)
• A rubber nasal aspirator (This has a small rubber bulb with a plastic tip and works very well for suctioning mucus from a baby's congested nose.)
• Antipoison medications: Syrup of ipecac is given to induce vomiting; activated granulated charcoal mixed with milk is given to a child who has swallowed poison that is extremely caustic and should not be vomited. The charcoal and milk help to neutralize the chemical in the child's stomach.
• Diaper-rash cream (A protective zinc oxide–based cream such as Diaperene or Desitin or a medicated powder such as Caldesine should help.)
• Calamine lotion, for summertime bug bites
• Hydrogen peroxide, or other antiseptic, for painlessly cleaning a wound
• Blunt-ended nail scissors
• Tweezers
• An assortment of bandages, gauze squares, etc.
• Humidifier or vaporizer (optional, but very useful, see page 232.)

sudden fever irritates the brain, which in turn sends incorrect messages to nerves and muscles to contract—first producing rigidity, then jerking, twitching, and grimacing motions. The child's eyes may roll back, and he may froth at the mouth and lose consciousness.

• Don't panic! Stay with the baby, preferably leaving him unrestrained in your arms, on a bed, or on a soft rug. Make sure he won't bump into anything that could injure him.
• Turn the body to one side if vomiting occurs.
• Do not try to pry open the baby's mouth or put anything in the mouth.
• When the seizure has ended, the baby will probably be sleepy. Keep him on his side.
• Call the doctor immediately.
• If the doctor is not available right away, you can begin to cool down the baby by sponging his face, arms, neck, and back with lukewarm water. Keep him lightly covered.

A Word About Medicines

At some point during your child's infancy, you will probably have to administer medicine. The National Council on Patient Information and Education has prepared a list of five questions that all medical consumers should ask either their doctors or their pharmacists before taking (or giving their child) any prescription drug. Get in the habit of asking these five questions. Jot down the answers in the Health Notes section of this book (see page 300) so that you will have a record for now and the future.

1. What is the name of the drug, and what is it supposed to do?
2. How, when, and for how long should the baby take it?

Call the Doctor Immediately for the Following Emergencies

• Any serious accident or injury (For poisoning, call your Poison-Control Center.)
• Bleeding that cannot be stopped
• Unconsciousness
• Severe respiratory problems such as croup, a loud, deep dry cough often coupled with breathing difficulties and characterized by a "crowing" sound.
• Severe diarrhea: frequent loose stools (though this can be hard to determine with the breast-fed baby); watery stools that may smell fishy or worse than usual (With infants under two months consider three or four such stools in one day "frequent.")
• Black or bloody bowel movements
• Convulsions: limbs stiffen and jerk, eyes roll upward, breathing is heavy or labored, baby is unconscious
• Head injury, particularly if there are symptoms of a concussion or skull fracture—bleeding from the nose, mouth, or ears; unconsciousness; an odd, unequal look to the pupils; or vomiting
• Projectile vomiting, particularly in a baby under two months (This is vomiting so forceful that the stomach contents will fly through the air and land a few feet away. This could be indicative of pyloric stenosis, a condition in which the valve leading from the far end of the stomach into the intestine will not open up satisfactorily to let the food through. If pyloric stenosis is diagnosed, immediate surgery is required.)
• A marked change for the worse in a baby who is already sick
• Any kind of fever in a newborn. In an older baby: fever of 104°F (40°C) taken rectally, or 100.5°F (38°C) taken rectally for the older baby who has never been sick before
• Two or three unexplained symptoms, whatever they may be
• Signs of dehydration: prostration or sunken eyes, which may accompany severe intestinal infection (also characterized by very loose or watery stools, pus or blood in the stools, or vomiting and fever)

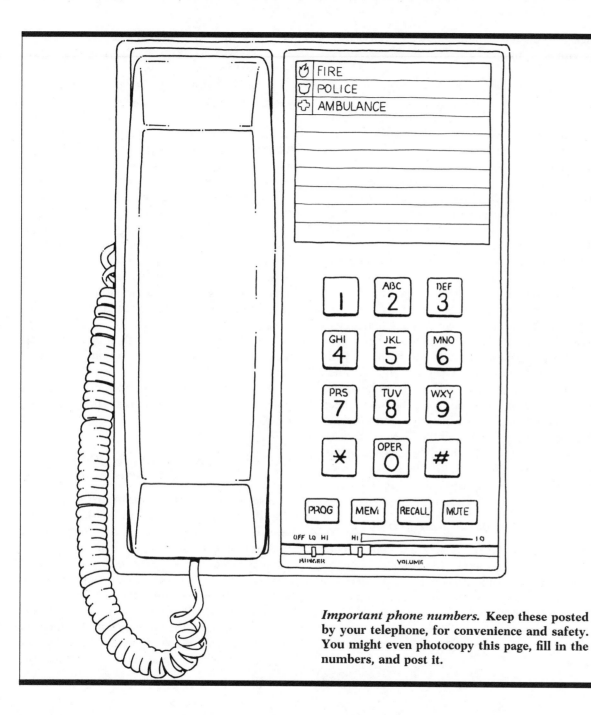

FIRE
POLICE
AMBULANCE

Important phone numbers. Keep these posted by your telephone, for convenience and safety. You might even photocopy this page, fill in the numbers, and post it.

Getting the Right Dose of Acetaminophen

All liquid acetaminophens are not equal, so be sure to read labels carefully. Acetaminophen drops for infants are considerably stronger than acetaminophen elixir for children, and the two are therefore not interchangeable. Dose your children according to their weight rather than their age.

3. What foods, drinks, medicines, or activities should the baby avoid while taking this drug?

4. Are there any side effects, and what should I do if they occur?

5. Is there any written information available about this drug?

A Note about Antibiotics

Antibiotics are substances that are produced by microorganisms and that kill bacteria or prevent their multiplication. Rather than alleviate symptoms directly, these drugs lower the number of bacteria in an infection, so that your own antibodies can handle the remainder and cure you of the infection. Antibiotics are generally ineffective against common viruses but are usually prescribed for ear infections, strep throat, bronchitis, and pneumonia. Sometimes they are given preventively if, say, a child has been exposed to a serious bacterial infection such as meningitis or if a child suffers from chronic ear infections. Remember that:

• The indiscriminate use of antibiotics can result in the propagation of new strains of particularly hearty bacteria resistant to that antibiotic. If an antibiotic is overused, the entire population of nonresistant bacteria within the child can be be killed off. The remaining resistant ones will multiply in the future.

• In order for an antibiotic to work effectively, it must be taken for the *entire* period for which it has been prescribed. If the doctor says ten days, then it's ten days. Sometimes the baby starts feeling better in a few days, and the parent is tempted to stop giving the antibiotic in the mistaken belief that a little medicine is better than a lot. This is wrong. Using a short course of antibiotics may actually make an illness worse. The result can be a partially treated or chronic infection that becomes resistant to the medicine, rendering it ineffective.

• Antibiotics can cause diarrhea. For the baby who is eating solids, yogurt will help. Otherwise, consult your pediatrician.

• Allergic reactions to antibiotics do occur in some children. If your baby breaks out in hives or has swelling around the face and difficulty breathing, call your pediatrician immediately.

• Throw out leftover antibiotics. You won't be tempted to use them inappropriately, or without a visit to the doctor.

The Correct Way to Give Medicine

Maybe Mary Poppins found it easy to make the medicine go down the throats of her little charges, but it's not that way for most of us. Most children, no matter what their age, dislike taking medicine. It's easier to administer if two people are around, one to hold the furious baby and the other to measure accurately and get it in. Four hands are a luxury, however. The following tricks should make giving medicine easier, alone or with a partner.

1. Before you begin, check the expiration date on the bottle, check the dosage, and make sure you have stored the medicine correctly. Never give medicine in the dark. If a baby-sitter is giving it for you, make sure that you leave written instructions. In the back of this book, you will find a space for Health Notes (see page 300). Here you can keep a record of which medications you give your baby, for how long, for which illness, and whether or not there are any side effects.

2. If you are alone, measure the medicine in advance and place it on the table, right by the chair you will sit in (see Just a Teaspoon of Medicine . . . , below).

3. Be relaxed and positive. Assume that all will go well. You will have to move fast and precisely.

4. Hold the baby on your lap, with her head facing away from you. If you are right-handed, use your right arm to hold both of her arms down. Use your left hand to tilt the baby's head back gently and squeeze her cheeks together, so that her mouth opens slightly. Then, with your free right hand (right arm still braced against the baby's arms), go for it! Squirt the syringe, insert the spoon, etc., with dispatch and confidence!

Just a Teaspoon of Medicine . . .

True or false? The teaspoon from your kitchen drawer is just right for dispensing medicine. False! According to the American Academy of Pediatrics, the typical household teaspoon is one of the worst devices for measuring medicine. A teaspoon dose can vary from three cubic centimeters to almost eight. Consider these alternatives:

• Use a measuring-spoon teaspoon for accuracy. Then transfer the medicine to whatever works best for you and your baby.

• A calibrated oral syringe is an inexpensive option available at your local pharmacy. Or premeasure the medicine into a small cup, then use the dropper from an empty liquid vitamin bottle to administer it. Squirt the fluid along the inside of the cheek instead of on the tongue where it's easier for the baby to spit out.

• Try a "flexidose" spoon, a hollow tube with measurements and a spoon on one end. Position this toward the back of the tongue, but not so far back that the baby gags. Then tilt the spoon.

• If the above methods fail, try administering the medicine in the nipple of a bottle. Once the baby swallows the medicine, add a chaser of water from the same nipple to make sure that he has gotten every drop.

• As a final resort, and with your doctor's approval, mix the medicine with a small quantity of tasty solid food.

• If the baby spits out the medicine, don't despair. See Common Questions about Administering Medicine, opposite.

Nose Drops, Ear Drops, Eye Drops, and Suppositories

Nose drops Ask your pharmacist to dispense nose drops in a plastic spray bottle. With one hand you can turn the bottle upside down and dispense, drop-by-drop, to control the dosage.

Ear drops are very simple to administer. They will feel better in the baby's ear if you warm the bottle slightly under hot water.

Eye drops ideally require two people: one to hold the baby and the other to pull down on the lower lid and put the drops in the pocket formed between the eyeball and lower lid. When you release the lid, and the baby blinks, the drops should be right where they are needed.

Suppositories should be kept in the refrigerator and removed about an hour in advance of use. At the risk of sounding silly, check to make sure the foil wrapping, which can look remarkably like the coating on a pill, is totally removed. Dip the suppository in petroleum jelly. Speak gently to the baby, and place him over your knees with his legs hanging off. An alternative position is to place the baby facedown with a small pillow under the stomach to elevate his bottom. Gently spread the buttocks apart and slide the suppository about 1 inch into the rectum. Hold buttocks together for about five minutes.

Common Questions about Administering Medicine

Question: *When the doctor says give the child medicine three or four times a day, does this mean every six or eight hours, or does this mean three or four times during the baby's waking hours?*

Answer: Unless the doctor specifically says so, most medications are meant to be given during the baby's or your waking hours, starting as early in the morning as possible, and ending as late at night as possible.

Question: *What if the baby spits out some of the medicine?*

Answer: The best you can do is estimate how much medicine didn't make it and try to get that amount into the baby. Keep in mind that there is a relatively large safety margin with acetaminophen and antibiotics. Cold, cough, and antiwheezing medications are more toxic. If you find that you are running low on a medication because of so many repeat doses, call the doctor and explain that you need a partial refill.

Question: *What if the baby throws up an indeterminable amount of the medication?*

Answer: If half an hour has passed without the baby throwing up, he has probably absorbed the full dose (another good reason to make sure you note the time you gave the medicine). Medicines are brightly colored for a reason. If none shows up in the vomit, assume that it has been absorbed.

Question: *If you use a dropper from the bottle of liquid acetaminophen, nose drops, or eye drops, do you have to wash it before you put it back in the bottle? And what if you don't?*

Answer: What do the directions say? It does make sense to wash the dropper, just as you would wash a spoon after using it, but few of us think about doing that when we have a sick baby on our hands. There are preservatives in medicines to help keep bacteria from growing. If you have more than one child, however, it is safest for each one to have his own bottle of acetaminophen, nose drops, and eye drops.

Common Health Concerns, Conditions, and Minor Miseries

Cradle Cap

Cradle cap, a yellow, flaky crust on the baby's head, and sometimes behind the ears, is more of an embarrassment than a health hazard. It occurs when the oil glands have been stimulated by the mother's hormones in utero. It can be a persistent problem, returning just when you think you've gotten it under control. If you don't keep on top of it, it can get worse and worse.

To treat cradle cap, you'll need baby oil, a soft brush, a fine-tooth comb, and, for persistent cases, a dandruff shampoo such as Sebulex, Sebucare, Ionil, or DHS.

Start by vigorously scrubbing the baby's head with a soft brush. If the cradle cap is very thick, rub the encrusted spot with warm baby oil and, if you can, wrap the baby's head in a towel for ten or fifteen minutes. Then remove as much of the scaling as you can with the fine-tooth comb. If necessary, as a final step, shampoo with a dandruff shampoo.

Diaper Rash

There isn't a baby bottom in the world that isn't susceptible to diaper rash, no matter how conscientious we are. The chafing diaper—poorly ventilated, moist, and full of germs and irritants from urine and feces—is rugged on a baby's delicate skin. The result is diaper rash. It used to be felt that diaper rashes were the result of specific causes such as teething, something in the diet, or ammonia in the urine. Though these things might well contribute to the rash, experts now believe that irritation is caused primarily by moisture and chafing.

Some diaper rashes come and go within a matter of hours without any medical intervention. A bottom bath, air drying, a fresh diaper, and the application of common-sense diapering tactics (see page 240) do the trick. But if the rash doesn't disappear, it can worsen to the point where painful open sores spread from the bottom up the back, to the abdomen, and down the upper thighs. Bad diaper rashes are more likely to occur in babies who are eating solids; who have frequent stools (especially if the dirty diaper is kept in prolonged contact with the baby); and babies on antibiotics. If the rash does not go

Common-sense Diapering Tactics to Nip Diaper Rash in the Bud

- Change the baby often.
- Eliminate diaper wipes, especially those that contain alcohol, which can dry and irritate the skin. Instead, clean the baby with warm water and a mild soap when you change a dirty diaper. Pat dry carefully, making sure you reach all the creases.
- Expose the baby's naked bottom to air whenever possible. Three twenty-minute airings a day should make a difference. If the weather is warm, and the baby is not yet crawling, place the diaper, and then a waterproof pad, under him.
- Get rid of plastic pants if you use them. They trap moisture. If you are using disposable diapers, poke holes in the plastic casing so that more air can circulate.
- If you wash your own cloth diapers, a residue of soap may be contributing to the baby's rash. Rinse with ½ cup of vinegar, or add a special diaper rinse. (For more suggestions, see Everything You Ever Wanted to Know about Diapers, page 124.)
- Further protect the baby's bottom by applying a coating of ointment containing zinc oxide.

away within two or three days, it's a good idea to phone the doctor. Your baby may be suffering from a tenacious rash that requires a specific treatment.

Rashes Caused by Yeast or Monilia

This type of rash consists of small, bright-red spots that can form entire red areas. Your doctor may wish to prescribe a topical cream over the phone or may prefer to examine the baby to confirm the diagnosis. These rashes can occur if the baby or nursing mother is on an antibiotic. Antibiotics rid the body of friendly bacteria as well as harmful bacteria. Without these friendly bacteria, yeast is more apt to grow.

Impetigo

This rash, characterized by many whiteheads and/or a yellowish crust, is caused by bacteria. The doctor may suggest a nonprescription antibiotic ointment. However, if improvement is not rapid, the baby may need antibiotics by mouth.

Prickly Heat

Prickly heat looks like a fine, pink, pimplelike rash and usually starts on a baby's shoulders and neck, spreading down the front as well as the back. Overheating is the cause, and the overdressed baby in winter is just as susceptible as the overheated baby in summer. Prickly heat doesn't seem to bother babies very much. To treat it, dress the baby in fewer clothes, dust the affected area with cornstarch using a fresh cotton ball or clean cloth, and dab the rash two or three times a day with a solution of baking soda and water—1 teaspoon of soda to 1 cup of water.

Hiccups

Hiccups are common, especially with newborns. They seem to disturb parents far more than they do babies. Try burping the baby. Though a few sips from a bottle of water might help, don't go overboard and fill the baby up, or give the breast-fed baby a reason to get hooked on or confused by the rubber nipple.

Colds

When a baby gets a cold, it's no fun for anyone! Though immunities to some viruses are passed from mother to child, these don't include protection against colds. So, expect your baby to have two, three, and even more colds per year if he is exposed to young children who have been in groups. Don't feel guilty! Regard each cold as collecting interest in the cold immunity bank.

First, diagnose the cold accurately. Colds usually start with a runny nose. The fluid is clear and watery looking and will get slightly thicker over the next few days. The baby's appetite may lessen. She may become crankier, and in some cases she may have a fever. A cold will last from three to ten days. If your baby is under three months, touch base with your doctor with a phone call. Also, keep a careful watch for complications that will require a call, and then a visit, to the doctor. A yellowish, greenish, and/or odorous discharge may signal a bacterial infection in the nose or sinuses. Ear infections can also follow on the heels of a cold. An infant's eustachian tubes, which connect the ears to the nose and throat area, are small and apt to become clogged with mucus, causing an inflammation.

Some babies become noticeably crankier, howl, and pull at their ears when they have an ear infection, letting you know that they are in pain, but others hardly react at all, leaving it to the parents to follow their intuitions. Another possible complication of a cold is a lower-respiratory infection called *bronchiolitis,* signaled by wheezing or labored breathing. Croup, an inflammation of the larynx, is typified by wheezy breathing and a rough barking cough. Following are some suggestions.

• It is no small matter that a baby with a cold can't breathe through his mouth and suck at the same time. We can try to offer relief in a number of ways. If the nose is running rather than clogged, at least he can breathe. To help keep it running, saline nose drops, available at your pharmacy, will help to soften hard mucus. Any other kind of nose drops, sprays, or decongestants should be prescribed by your doctor.

• If you have no success with nose drops, a nasal aspirator may come in handy. (The risk here, however, is that the baby will hate the aspirator, cry, and generate more mucus!)

• Moist air from a humidifier or vaporizer is another alternative, especially at night. As a last resort, many mothers resort to sitting on the closed lid of a toilet seat or the icy edge of a bathtub, feeding the baby amidst a cloud of steam from the hot shower.

• Put your baby to sleep facedown to help ear fluids drain more efficiently through the eustachian tubes.

• Keep up liquid intake to replace fluids lost from runny nose and fever. Continue to breast- and bottle-feed the baby as usual, but if the baby is on solids, cut back on other dairy products, which create additional mucus. Increase foods containing vitamin C in the baby's diet as well as your diet, if you are a nursing mother.

Teething

Teething has a terrible reputation! Unless we are thoughtful, observant, and patient, it can, like breast-feeding, mistakenly become the dumping ground for a host of unexplained behaviors and miseries that might merit a different kind of concern.

First and foremost, teething is a very individual matter. The first tooth (often the lower central incisor, see page 242) usually comes in between the fifth and seventh month. But variations are great. Some babies cut a tooth at three months; others go toothless until after their first birthday. Teething patterns tend to be hereditary, so grandmothers who have kept good baby records may be able to supply helpful information.

Secondly, there is no reason to brace yourself for a continuously miserable experience for the baby (or yourself). It is true that some babies have a difficult time cutting a new tooth, particularly the first one and the molars. They become irritable, uninterested in food, wakeful at night, or all of the above. Others will simply drool, put everything into their mouths, gnaw on tables, and even bite their parents, but they manage to produce all twenty baby teeth without a whimper.

Question: How do you know the baby is teething?

Answer: Teething is not an illness. Though some babies are fussy and irritable when they teethe, cutting a tooth shouldn't make the baby sick, i.e., cause a fever, vomiting, or diarrhea. The first clue that your baby is teething may be a tiny glimmer of white on the gum. Five other common signs are these:

Drooling. Drooling is often associated with teething, but keep in mind that it can begin several months before the baby actually cuts the first tooth. While some babies hardly drool at all, others drip continually for months, so that their chins, clothing, and bedding are constantly wet. Their saliva can irritate the tender skin around their mouths, giving it a red, chapped look. Keep the baby as dry as possible by dabbing his chin with a soft, dry washcloth or cloth diaper. An absorbent terry-cloth bib will protect clothing from moisture. At night you can pin a towel to one end of the crib sheet to help absorb the wetness. If it is cold outside, you might want to help "seal" and protect chapped areas by coating them with a bit of petroleum jelly. The baby may also cough a little bit from all the extra saliva. This is nothing to be concerned about unless he shows signs of having a cold or allergy.

Swollen tender gums. Chances are the baby with tender gums will seek his own relief by chewing on anything and everything he can get into his mouth. The colder the object, the more numbing and soothing it is. Whatever you offer, make sure the baby is in an upright position and monitor the situation carefully, lest the baby gag or choke. (See Mothers Share their Teething Tricks, page 243.) Also, be aware that plaque on the baby's gums can add to irritation. To prevent plaque buildup, keep the baby's mouth as clean as possible by wiping his gums with a soft piece of gauze. Some parents do this after every meal, which is fine if the baby doesn't object. This is also good preventive dentistry.

Loose stools. Loose stools (not diarrhea) may be caused by the baby producing more saliva when teething and then swallowing a great deal of it, diluting the material in the intestines. Offer icy-cold liquids, preferably water, for comfort as well as to replace fluids lost from drooling.

Diaper rash. When a baby is teething, she may also sleep for shorter stretches at night and stir in her sleep enough to wake up and wet herself.

Average Teething Times and Baby's Personal Teething Record

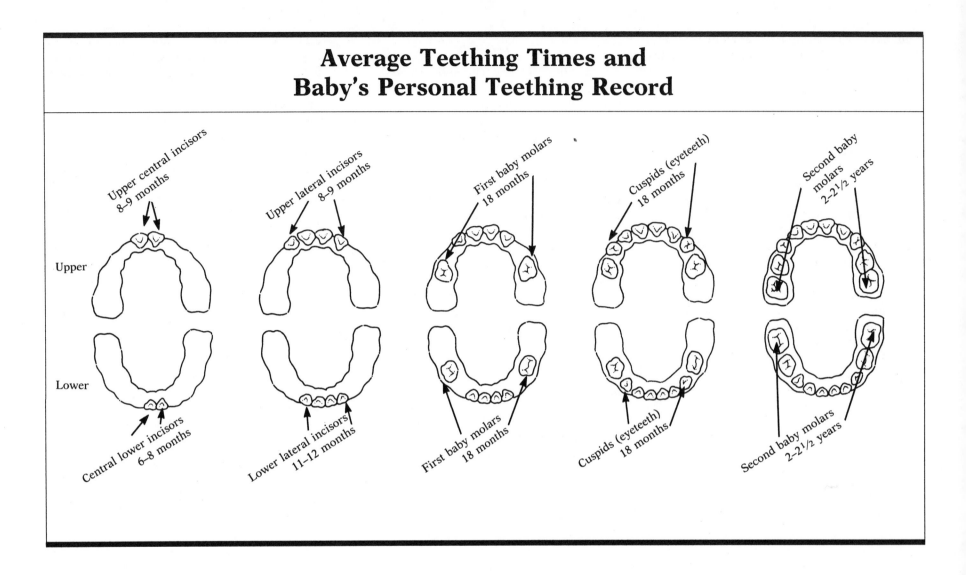

Upper central incisors
8–9 months

Upper lateral incisors
8–9 months

First baby molars
18 months

Cuspids (eyeteeth)
18 months

Second baby molars
2–2½ years

Upper

Lower

Central lower incisors
6–8 months

Lower lateral incisors
11–12 months

First baby molars
18 months

Cuspids (eyeteeth)
18 months

Second baby molars
2–2½ years

Mothers Share Their Teething Tricks

A chilled carrot (with the tip cut off), an ice cube, or a chilled apple slice, wrapped in a handkerchief, knotted with a rubber band, may help.

• • •

Dip your own (clean) finger into ice water, or wrap it in a chilled washcloth and rub the baby's gums.

• • •

My grandmother recommended that I pour a drop of fruit brandy onto my finger, then rub the baby's gums.

• • •

I swear by the old-fashioned bumpy rubber teething rings. If you use a ring filled with nontoxic jellies that you chill in the refrigerator, check the construction often to make sure that it is holding up under the wear and tear of your baby's chomping.

• • •

I buy teething biscuits from the health-food store, and Jessica loves them. But be aware that even so-called healthy foods, high in carbohydrates, especially if consumed over a number of hours, can cause tooth decay.

• • •

I offer Lucas a bottle of formula or juice that has been chilled in the refrigerator. The cold nipple and the cold juice together do the trick.

• • •

Smooth, cold foods like yogurt and pureed fruits helped to sooth Danny's gums.

• • •

Marcie was so irritable that I finally asked the pediatrician if I could give her some Tylenol (acetaminophen, an aspirin substitute). When he determined that there was nothing else going on, he gave me the okay.

(*Note:* Paregoric, an old-fashioned teething remedy, is *not* recommended because it contains barbiturates, which can make the baby drowsy, and can become habit forming.)

The diaper becomes progressively wetter with each waking, and by morning she may have a rash. In this case, put an extra protective layer of petroleum jelly or zinc oxide on her bottom before bed.

Refusal to suck on breast or bottle or take solids. Some teething babies appear to want to nurse or suck on their bottles more than ever, but the moment the nipple makes contact with their mouths, they pull off, screaming in pain and frustration. Before a feeding, try some of the teething tricks (shown at left) to get the baby into a more comfortable state. Most teethers are old enough to try a cup with a small amount of cold liquid. If the baby who is already eating solids seems to lose interest in food, don't be too concerned. If this persists, however, do check with your baby's doctor.

Preventive Dentistry

Many children have cavities by the time they become toddlers with full sets of teeth. This is unfortunate. Even though these are "only baby teeth," their health and well-being are important. Problems with baby teeth create an unhealthy environment for the permanent teeth, which are forming underneath in the jaw. We also tend to forget that some of the baby teeth stay with the child for twelve years. Losing any tooth prematurely can lead to spacing problems when permanent teeth come in. To protect your baby's teeth:

• Practice good nutrition. In most respects the nutritional needs for maintaining healthy teeth and gums are similar to those for maintaining good health in general. Adequate amounts of calcium and phosphorus are necessary for normal tooth and bone development. Vitamins A and D help the body absorb and utilize these minerals. Vitamin C is important for healthy gums and tissues. Fluoride, however, is thought to be the single most important element in relation to dental care. If your water supply is not fluoridated, by all means ask your pediatrician about supplementation.

• Limit the frequency with which your child eats foods that contain sugars and starches, such as teething biscuits and toasts. Remember that fruit juices, even the so-called natural ones, are loaded with sugar. Dilute them with water.

• Wipe your baby's teeth with a gauze pad after each feeding to remove food residues that foster the growth of bacteria.

• If you offer a bedtime bottle, make it water from the very beginning. Milk and juice both contain sugar, the ideal environment for bacteria. If the baby is already hooked on milk or juice at night, dilute the contents with water. Gradually decrease the milk or juice until only water remains.

The Poop on Poop:
A Primer on Bowel Movements

Never before in your life (and one hopes never again!) have you been as involved and at times puzzled by another person's bowel movements—how many, at what intervals, and of what consistency, color, and texture—as you are with your baby's. Naturally, we are concerned because what comes out provides clues to what is going on inside the baby. Keep in mind, though, that what is considered "normal" may be surprising until you get used to it. Also remember that a baby's stools are "individualistic expressions," as it were, and can vary tremendously from movement to movement, day to day, and baby to baby!

Very First Stools

For the first day after birth, the baby's stool consists of *meconium*. This sticky green-black substance made of cast-off cells from the baby's liver, pancreas, and gall bladder is what fills the baby's intestines as he grows in utero. If the baby has passed meconium during labor, which is indicative of fetal distress, his first stools may be what is called *transitional*. Read on.

Transitional Stools

After the meconium has passed, your baby will produce *transitional stools*, loose stools that are greenish-yellow or brown in color, that may contain mucus or be grainy or seedy in texture, and that may occasionally have small streaks of blood, usually caused by the baby swallowing some of his mother's blood during labor. In the bottle-fed baby these tend not to last beyond the third or fourth day. Breast-fed babies, however, may continue to have bowel movements closely resembling these until solids are added.

Stools in the Breast-Fed Baby

Be warned in advance that the stools of breast-fed babies tend to alarm those not familiar with them! Their characteristics and variations call upon our greatest descriptive powers. They can resemble: a mere stain on the diaper, ranging from a delicate yellow to a bright chartreuse; runny scrambled eggs; curdy yellow cottage cheese; Grey Poupon French mustard; bright yellow, "ball park" mustard; or, variously, curds, lumps, seeds, mucus, cream, or even gelatin. As for frequency, almost anything goes. Some breast-fed babies move their bowels after every feeding; others, once or twice a day; and still

others every couple of days. T. Berry Brazelton cites one perfectly healthy nursing baby who was content to move his bowels every twelve days. One thing that is agreed upon is that the stool of the totally breast-fed baby has a yeasty, not unpleasant odor.

Stools in the Bottle-Fed Baby

The bottle-fed baby produces a somewhat firmer and darker stool than the breast-fed baby. The color ranges anywhere from a pale yellow to a greenish-brown. If the baby is taking iron drops or drinking an iron-fortified formula or a whey-as opposed to casein-based formula, the stool will be darker—ranging from a dark greenish-brown to black.

Green Bowel Movements

These are quite a shocking sight but not necessarily cause for concern. As T. Berry Brazelton explains in *Infants and Mothers: Differences in Development* (New York: Dell, 1983):

Stool color is a source of concern to caretakers of babies. The green often seen in them is due to bile from the upper part of the gastrointestinal tract. As it passes through the lower tract, it changes to yellow, orange, and then brown. Greenish-black is also undigested bile. The color, then, reflects the speed with which it comes along this pathway.

Fluid is absorbed from the stool in the large intestine, or colon, and hence a liquid movement also means a rapid movement through it. A loose, wet, and green movement simply implies this rapid transit. Breast milk commonly is laxative in its action on the infant's intestinal tract. Sugars are laxative. New solids are also responsible for loose, greenish stools until the digestive system becomes accustomed to them. Infection and gastrointestinal allergy are the two pathologic conditions to be concerned with. When the stools are frequent (that is, five or more per day for the bottle-fed vs. the breast-fed baby) and are wet, foul-smelling, and green, it is time to consult your physician. With these guidelines in mind, one can distinguish between important and unimportant intestinal upsets. Mild diarrheas occur frequently. When they persist they may be indicative of a more significant intolerance to some aspect of the diet. One need not worry as much about breast-fed babies—human milk is too easily digestible by the human infant.

Black Stools

These can be caused from formula fortified with iron as well as iron supplements, and there is nothing to be concerned about. Contrary to what we might suspect, studies have shown that iron does not cause stomach irritability.

Blood in the Stool

Bright blood accompanying a hard stool most often comes from a crack or fissure around the anus. To treat this, pediatricians usually recommend softening the bowel movement by giving the baby a little prune juice if he's on solids, or a laxative food such as prunes. To protect the fissure, spread petroleum jelly around the anus two or three times a day. If it doesn't heal rapidly, it should be checked by a physician. Darker blood can mean digested blood, which could be coming from higher up in the intestinal tract. This is a sign of difficulty and should be reported to the baby's doctor.

Mucus in the Stool

Mucus in the stool is a sign of intestinal irritation, possibly caused by the introduction of a new food that the baby is not yet able to digest. It is not cause for concern unless it continues. Then you might want to isolate what in the baby's diet is causing the problem. If you get nowhere, by all means discuss this with your pediatrician.

Adding Solids

Once you add solids to your baby's diet, the character of his bowel movements will change. If you breast-feed, gone are those sweet, soft, almost yeasty-smelling, pale-colored stools. Enter a darker, firmer, and smellier product sometimes containing substances whose color and texture look very much like what you shoveled into the baby an hour or two before. Don't be alarmed when pureed carrots and beets color the stool. When the baby begins to self-feed, expect to discover undigested lumps of food, sometimes accompanied by small amounts of mucus. This does not mean that you should go back to feeding the baby pureed food from a spoon. Be assured that the baby is absorbing what he needs. The importance of self-feeding far outweighs the nutritional cost of a few undigested lumps of food.

Health Resources

The Columbia University College of Physicians and Surgeons Complete Home Medical Guide (New York: Crown, 1985)

Harrison, Helen, with Kositsky, Ann, *The Premature Baby Book: A Parents' Guide to Coping and Caring in the First Years* (New York: St. Martin's Press Inc., 1983)

Pomeranz, Virginia, and Schultz, Dodi, *The Mothers' and Fathers' Medical Encyclopedia* (New York: New American Library, 1984)

Spock, Benjamin M., and Rothenberg, Michael B., *Dr. Spock's Baby and Child Care* (New York: Dutton, 1985)

Asthma and Allergy Information Line
1-800-822-ASMA
(Twenty-four hours, seven days a week except holidays)
Provides referrals to local doctors, plus written information on allergies and asthma.

Children in Hospitals, Inc.
31 Wilshire Park
Needham, MA 02192
(617) 482–2915
National Information System for Health-Related Services
(800) 922–1107 (9 A.M. to 5 P.M. EST, weekdays except holidays)

Information about specialized services for children with disabilities or special health-care needs: referrals to parent support groups and diagnostic and treatment centers across the United States.
Parents for Prematures
13613 NW 26th Place
Bellevue, WA 98005
Support for parents of premature babies.

• CHAPTER 21 •

Play and Learning

Stimulating the Baby

A generation or two ago it was considered appropriate, if not essential, to run a tight ship where the baby was concerned. Keep him clean, quiet, and protected from noise, overhandling, and overstimulation. Feed him on a strict schedule, exercise and "sun" him regularly. Otherwise leave him to play quietly alone in the playpen with a few well-scrubbed toys. The object, one guesses, was to foster independence and not spoil the baby. This philosophy suggests that the job of the parent, specifically the mother, was to create or mold the baby into a predictable being who exercised "good habits" and who would not grow up to be an embarrassment to the family.

Nowadays we feel differently. Through the growing amount of research on infancy and, just as important, our own observations, we know that babies thrive on being held, cuddled, and talked and sung to, and that they respond early to the human face and voice. Some of the most fascinating research on language development suggests that babies move synchronously with adult speech as early as the first day after birth.

Videotapes of the baby's movements and gestures form a distinct pattern in response to the speaker's movements, gestures, rhythms, pitch, and stress patterns. This suggests that the baby communicates immediately through body language and is hardly the passive and isolated being he was once considered to be.

We also know that babies thrive in a visually stimulating environment. The pastel baby is passé. The nursery of today may well be the most colorful room in the house, even if it is the least utilized. The baby spends her waking hours moving around the house on a parent's back or at a parent's side, or out in the world. She may take in a few cultural events such as a museum exhibition or concert long before her first birthday. She may also have a social life of her own by the time she is walking, particularly if her mother organizes a playgroup.

All this reflects our understanding of the baby as tough rather than fragile, a highly adaptable, alert, sentient, curious, communicative being. And as parents, we cannot help but marvel at our baby's imagination, curiosity, drive, and determination to practice, discover, master, and control the world around her. In fact, never again, as she strives to reach, turn over, grasp, creep, sit, crawl, stand, and finally walk and talk, will her strides in development be quite as dramatic as they are in the first twelve to sixteen months.

As knowledge about the capacities of the infant grows, more and more attention is being paid to stimulation techniques with a capital S and toys that teach with a capital T. An awareness of what is happening in terms of motor, speech, and social development is both fascinating and useful, but not if it intimidates us. Not surprisingly, when asked, "Are you concerned about stimulating your baby enough?" many parents will answer "yes" a bit nervously. There is no question that we all want "the best" for our children, but sometimes the wish for a "superkid" can grow way out of proportion. Now there are even flash cards and programs that promise to teach infants how to read and do math. Besides being totally unnecessary and boring, such programs can be downright damaging. They turn time that a parent and baby might have spent feeling close and affectionate while having fun, into work.

Americans are constantly being analyzed by

What's Wrong with Superbabies?

What's the harm of early learning programs for infants? David Elkind, author of *Miseducation: Preschoolers at Risk* (New York: Knopf, 1987), writes in *Parents* magazine, October 1987:

In what way does miseducation during the first year of life put infants at long-term risk? To answer this question, it is helpful to distinguish between "warm" and "cold" interactions with an infant. Warm interactions encourage attachment and a sense of trust; cold interactions mar attachment and encourage distrust. By and large, we spontaneously engage in "warm" interactions because of love for, and enjoyment in, our infant. Such interactions are spontaneous and effortless. In contrast, many cold interactions are deliberate and are experienced as effortful.

We engage in warm interactions when, during the course of routine caring activities such as feeding, changing, bathing, and comforting the baby, we accompany our ministrations with talking, cuddling, singing, and playing. We tell the baby in many different ways that we like him or her as a person and really enjoy his or her company. By showing our attachment in a warm, lively way, we encourage attachment and trust on the part of our baby.

In contrast, cold interactions are task rather than child oriented. They involve demands, stern looks, and words, and the threat of punishment or, what is worse, the threat of withdrawal of love. Of course, some cold interactions are inevitable, particularly when the baby does something potentially dangerous, and our harsh words and tones come from our anxiety about the baby's welfare.

However, engaging in unnecessary cold interactions with infants in order to teach them some tricks such as recognizing words, pictures, or numbers from flash cards is miseducation. The child is put at risk for an impaired attachment and sense of mistrust. And because attachment is critical to later learning, the parent who engages an infant in cold interactions with the aim of giving the child an edge in academics may be doing just the opposite. The child may be handicapped because the attachment and trust essential for later learning have been impaired.

experts—pediatricians, psychologists, psychiatrists, educators, sociologists—who tell us how to be parents. The media also play to our deepest fears that we are inadequate and imperiled. We really need not be as self-conscious and intimidated as we sometimes are. Experts, studies, and books notwithstanding, parents who are involved with their own babies hour by hour, day by day, know a *great* deal about stimulating them, precisely because they are there to observe and delight in each step or bit of progress in the baby's development. Without thinking too much about it, we tend to play the games that the baby is "developmentally" ready for without laboring over whether we are encouraging "eye-hand coordination" or "fine motor development."

Most parents know better than to coop their babies up in playpens. They give the baby access to the best possible laboratory for learning—the (baby-proofed) American home. Here the naturally curious baby encounters a variety of objects of different sizes, colors, textures, and weights, objects—or "toys that teach"—that make different sounds when they are patted, squeezed, poked, rattled, banged, rolled, and hurled on the floor. When the baby goes out with us, she learns, on the most basic level, how the world operates. Most parents know—though we may sometimes wish otherwise—that babies seldom play quietly alone for more than a few minutes with expensive toys purchased to enhance learning. It's our warm and loving interaction, encouragement, and reinforcement of the baby's discoveries that help to teach more than any toy can. We talk to the baby, perhaps not consciously to stimulate language or speech development, but because it's fun and satisfying. And it's evident that the baby enjoys this.

What we need to hear a little more often is not how to teach the baby, but how much the baby already knows and how good we are at reinforcing this. We need to hear the simple common-sense advice to relax, to trust our own instincts and to *enjoy the baby.* We also need to remember that comparisons of our baby with the baby down the street—or any of the babies in this book for that matter—are dangerous. Babies are individuals with unique temperaments, who learn and develop at their own rates. We might also take time to marvel at our own development. A baby challenges us in ways that we have never been challenged before and offers us the gift of growth and self-discovery.

Newborns During the First Eight Weeks

Your newborn baby does not need a tremendous amount of stimulation so much as he needs your gentle help organizing his random behavior as he works at adjusting to life outside the womb. His movements are jerky and his breathing can be puzzling. His attention span is limited and he seems to be turned inward into his own world. Be sensitive to his cues. When he averts his gaze, he's probably had enough and will drift into sleep. Though his main occupations are eating, sleeping, and crying, he is an amazingly competent person (see The Amazing Newborn, on this page). Over the weeks his behavior will "smooth out" a bit. His movements will become less jerky. He'll gain more control over his head and will be able to turn it from side to side on the mattress. By the end of one month, when exhausted parents may just about have had it with "unexplained crying," night waking, and erratic feeding schedules, nature comes to the rescue: the baby will smile. His smiles may be fleeting at first, but once smiling becomes a regular phenomenon, you will be hooked.

Question: How do you stimulate your newborn?
Answer: I made brightly colored crib bumpers for Timothy.

A: We taped a "happy face" by the changing table.

A: Jim noticed that Matthew seemed to like to look at his polka-dotted tie when he holds him on his lap.

A: Babies are always dressed, but their bodies are very sensual. Danny lies down and puts the baby on his bare chest, then pulls the covers up to keep him warm. Sometimes we gently massage him with baby oil after his bath. This seems to calm and soothe him.

A: Be sure to hang the mobile to one side over the crib, because babies seldom look directly up.

A: I taped "Rock-a-Bye-Baby" and several other lullabys that we play whenever we put her in her bassinet.

A: I carry Tasha in the Snugli a good deal of the time. This is the only thing that calms her. I had also read that babies who are carried a lot are more alert when awake and fuss less. I'm not so sure that that's true, but I keep trying!

A: Now that Rosey's smiling officially, we spend a good deal of time being spellbound by her. We coo and gurgle a lot at each other.

A: I shake a rattle to one side of Tommy's head, and he turns that way. Then I move it to the other side, and he turns that way.

Babies During the Third and Fourth Months

This is the beginning of a delicious period. Colic is over. Sleeping and eating may not yet have fallen into a schedule, but a sense of order and predictability is beginning to emerge. The baby is definitely engaged with the world. His smiles are regular occurrences, a cheerful background to the chirps, coos, bubbles, and laughs that increasingly characterize his social interaction.

His movements reflect his excitement with being alive and increasingly engaged with the world. He vigorously circles and kicks with his arms and legs while on his back and will eventually turn himself up on one side and at some point flip onto his front (though some babies turn first from front to back). It's time to begin to be more cautious about leaving him in the middle of a bed or on the couch. When he's not

The Amazing Newborn

Did you know that the newborn . . .

- enjoys the sound of the human voice, and when talked to will increase the intensity of his sucking?
- within a few hours after birth can distinguish its mother's voice from that of another woman?
- likes to look at human faces, especially faces that are animated and talking?
- will look longer at her mother's face than that of another woman?
- can single out her mother's distinctive smell and prefers her mother's breast pad to those of another nursing mother?
- can see best when an object is between eight and twelve inches from her eyes and to one side, which is about the distance between a nursing mother's face and her baby?
- prefers patterns in bright colors and high contrast—especially black and white?
- will look longer, and with more interest, at an object when held in an upright position (say against your shoulder) than when lying down?

in his infant seat, a quilt on the floor is safest.

One of the most engaging aspects of babies this age is their growing fascination with their hands. At first he will draw his hands close to his face and study them, as if they are beautiful, fascinating toys. Though he initially does not know that they are "connected" to himself, he is working on this concept as he moves them in and out of view. Until recently his fists have been clenched shut and of little use to him. But now they are open as he reaches with both arms and tentatively bats at an object. If you place the object within his grasp, he will hold it for a while, then drop it in a random fashion. As time goes on he will eventually be able to bring the object to his mouth with more precision. This act involves eye-hand coordination, a sophisticated process that requires looking at something, figuring out how far away it is, then coordinating the arm and the hand to reach and grasp, and eventually bring it toward his mouth. This is a time to begin to use the pacifier with discretion at high-need times so that the baby's mouth is free to explore appropriate objects (see Good Toys for the First Six Months, opposite page).

Question: *What is your three- or four-month-old baby doing, and what games and activities does he enjoy?*

Answer: *At thirteen weeks he laughs out loud and blows raspberries back at me when I blow them at him. He's found his hands and brings them close to his face, so that his eyes cross. We can't help but laugh. He also sleeps with his hand in his mouth and wakes up with it red from sucking.*

A: *Mark now has good control of his head and holds it up well. His father takes him on little house tours to look at the fish tank and out the window. His favorite game is to lie on my lap and push against my stomach with his feet. He also likes to be pulled up by the arms into a sitting position—"pull-ups," we call them. He squeals with delight and says "oooh!"*

A: *It's almost as if Kevin (four months) is talking. He gets very excited and babbles away, and*

then he pauses and looks at me as if to say, "It's your turn now, Mom." Then I'll babble away for a while until it's his turn again. He also talks to our bird, whose cage is near his baby swing.

A: *Jack flipped over this month from back to stomach. Now he is working on getting from his stomach to his back.*

A: *I made a simple toy which our baby loves. I crumpled up some waxed paper and wrapped a red bandanna around it and tied up the loose ends. She can hold this and loves the crinkly sound of the paper inside. When the paper loses its oomph, I change it and wash the bandanna.*

A: *Kevin is almost five months old. He seems frustrated because he can't sit on his own and doesn't like to lie down anymore. The infant seat is too restricting, and he kicks to get out of it. Our biggest success is his bounce chair.*

A: *Harry likes his crib gym. He bats at it with both hands. He'll also kick it.*

A: *I have a mirror by the changing table, and we always play "look at the baby in the mirror," which never fails to interest Curtis.*

Babies During the Fifth and Sixth Months

By now your baby may be beginning to get around a little bit by rolling from back to front or "bellying" across the floor to an object. He'd rather crawl and is working on this by strengthening arm, leg, and back muscles in many ways. His drive is upward toward a vertical position, which allows him to see more and reach more in the world around him. For instance, he now enjoys being pulled up by the arms into a sitting

position and will learn to show you this by reaching his arms out to you in an irresistible gesture. Once sitting he may want to stand. If you support him under his arms, he may even bounce up and down in your lap.

With some practice a baby can now sit in a "tripod" position. Place him squarely on his bottom with his legs spread apart. For balance he will lean forward with both hands on the floor between his legs like a tripod. He will soon tire and list or topple to the side, so place pillows around him. Keep a good eye on him. When he tips over, he may not yet be able to remove his face from the pillow if he lands in an awkward position.

If you are lucky, you may catch him in one of the most charming baby poses of all, "the flying baby"—balanced on his stomach with arms and legs out as he rocks back and forth. This, and the push-ups that babies do with the upper parts of their bodies, so that they look like little seals, are precursors to crawling. It isn't long before he'll get his rear end up at the same time. Some babies rock back and forth in this position, then hurtle themselves forward.

By this age, babies begin to become increasingly adept with their hands. They stroke and pat different surfaces—your face, your hair, your buttons and jewelry, the crib railing, the rug, grass, a towel—and appear interested in exploring textures. Their grasp has also gotten stronger. With cupped fingers some are able to scoop up objects, including food, in order to bring them to their mouths. The baby may also begin to use objects to make an impact on the environment by banging, rattling, shaking, and squeaking.

The baby in the fifth and sixth months is babbling a good deal of the time, either to you or to objects. The sweet, gentle cooing of earlier months is beginning to become interspersed with consonants. You will begin to hear sounds like "ma," "pa," "da," and "ba." Over the months it has become clearer and clearer that you are the light of your baby's life. Now there is no doubt that he is attached. He singles you out with special gestures of delight and may even "call you back" when you leave his sight.

Question: *What is your baby up to in the fifth and sixth months, and what activities and games does he like to play?*

Answer: *Aaron is just five months and loves to be naked on a big quilt outside in the yard, wiggling, rocking, and looking up at the light in the trees.*

A: *She's so much fun now and loves to play "This Little Piggy" and "Trot Trot to Boston," which means bouncing in my lap.*

A: *Alexis loves people more than anything else, especially her two older brothers, who are ten and twelve. She sees them coming and squeals with delight. They pick her up and carry her all around the house. They tickle her and bounce her on the bed. I sometimes worry because they seem so rough, but she loves it.*

A: *Thomas is almost six months, and the bath is the highlight of his day. We still use the kitchen sink. I'm soaking wet by the end! Watch out for the soap at this age. They eat everything.*

A: *Eliza isn't much on moving, but she loves books. I made one out of a small photo album. I put in pictures of cats, dogs, birds, cars, and babies—things she sees all the time. I also made a texture book, with different kinds of fabric, which she likes to explore, not only with her hands but with her mouth—naturally.*

A: *At six-and-a-half months, Casey likes to sit in his high chair and watch me make dinner. I give him small bits of soft food to taste. If you can stand the mess, I recommend pouring some finely textured bread crumbs onto the high-chair tray. He likes to rub his hands in them, but at least they are safe when they go in the mouth.*

A: *At six months Samantha is terrific fun. She's a real ham. Her favorite game is "here are your eyes, here is your nose, etc."*

A: *Brandon is very, very active. He started sitting, crawling, and pulling himself to stand all within a few days of each other. It seems like I've been on the move ever since. I'm only twenty-five, but there are days when I feel fifty!*

Good Toys for the First Six Months

Mobiles. A wind-up mobile that provides motion and music will be of interest to the baby when awake and can become part of a soothing bedtime routine as well. Be sure that you consider how the mobile will look from your baby's horizontal position. Choose bright contrasting colors including black and white, and hang it between eight and fourteen inches above his head, the distance at which he focuses best during the first three months. Studies have shown that infants under three months look to the right most of the time. After three months, alternate the placement from side to side, and move it out of reach once the baby is able to pull himself into a semiupright position. Remember that mobiles are not meant to be touched. Many consist of string and other small swallowable parts that could cause choking or strangling.

Music boxes. A sturdy plastic windup music box that can be attached to a crib or carried

Wind-up musical mobile

about by a little handle is a good investment, not only to amuse the baby but also to take with you as part of a portable sleeping ritual. Try to choose one with a tune that you can live with over and over and over!

Mirrors. Mirrors interest babies from a very early age and can provide a great distraction for the wiggly baby as he has his diaper changed. Any of the well-designed nonbreakable ones for babies and young children that can first be attached to the crib or wall, or stand free, are good investments for your child's early years. At first the baby will not recognize himself but will be attracted by the changes in pattern, of light and dark, from the reflection of his moving body. Later he will think there is another baby in the mirror, but before long he won't be tricked and will know that this is just an illusion.

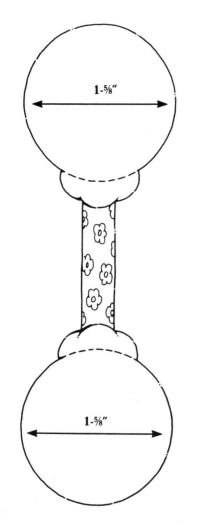

Recommended minimum rattle size set by the Consumer Product Safety Commission

Rattles. Babies love rattles. Besides providing experience with grasping, they teach one of the first lessons of "cause and effect": shake it, and something happens. When the baby makes this connection, it gives him a sense of mastery and control. A dumbbell or telephone shape is easiest for the young baby to grasp. Rubber squeak toys and teething rings are fun, too. Make sure they are safe. Check them against the illustration.

Dolls and stuffed animals. Your baby may receive many stuffed animals, dolls, hand puppets, etc., as baby presents, and one may well become a "lovey" or a favored friend (see the discussion of transitional objects, page 166). But right now, when everything still goes into the baby's mouth, encourage the use of those that are safe, durable, and washable. Choose stuffed toys with embroidered rather than button features. Pompons, yarn hair, long tails, tongues, and even long hair or fur can present a choking or smothering hazard. Remember, too, that when the baby learns to stand, a stuffed animal may provide a step up and out of a crib or playpen.

Toys to Make for Young Babies

Texture Blanket

Materials

• a variety of 4 × 4-inch fabric squares of different colors and textures, such as terry cloth, seersucker, corduroy, wool, velvet, suede or leather, satin, and taffeta
• fabric for backing

Babies learn about the world through their senses. A texture blanket is interesting both to look at and feel. Simply sew the squares together to form one large rectangle or square. Using this as a pattern, cut out a backing. You might want to use soft vinyl on the back so that the blanket can double as a portable changing surface. Pin the wrong sides together and sew along three edges. Be sure to leave an opening large enough so that you can turn the blanket right-side out. Slip-stitch the opening closed.

Happy Face and Happy-Face Puppet

Materials

• white paper plate
• nontoxic markers or crayons
• dowel or tongue depressor
• tape

A newborn baby prefers the human face to any other sight. Draw simple features on the plate. Tape the face to the side or end of the crib or by the changing table. A face in motion is even more interesting. To make a simple puppet, glue two plates together with the undersides facing out. Then cut a wedge-shaped slice large enough for a dowel or tongue depressor to go through. Insert the dowel in the opening and tape the plate to it. Dangle or dance the puppet in front of the baby. You might want to turn on some music. By three months, if you watch carefully, you will notice that the baby is kicking rhythmically.

Simple Rattle

Materials

• a small plastic bottle, checked for safety against the diagram on page 262 to make sure that it will not get lodged in the baby's throat
• permanent glue
• bells, colorful beads, sand, paper clips, etc.

Choose from a variety of fillers, including colored water, then glue the bottle permanently shut.

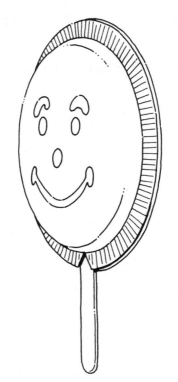

Happy-face puppet

Beanbags

Materials

- brightly colored fabric
- fillers: dried beans; cellophane; tissue paper; bells; etc.

Beanbags are fun and easy for a baby to hold and mouth, but you can also make them interesting to listen to by stuffing them with noisy fillers. Cut out two identical shapes and, with the wrong sides together, sew them back to front, leaving a small opening for the filler. Double-check to make sure your seams are foolproof and that none of the filler can come out. Turn right-side out, fill, and slip-stitch the opening twice for safety.

Babies from
Seven through Nine Months

This is the beginning of an active period that will last for the next couple of years, so rest up while you can! The baby will become proficient at sitting on his own and will be able to reach for and pick up objects in this position. If you sit him down on the floor with toys of different weights and shapes, with holes and textures, he may busy himself for quite a while picking them up, studying them carefully, transferring them from hand to hand, and eventually banging them together like primitive tools or musical instruments. By the end of nine months he will have mastered all of the different choices on his activity boards— the phones to dial, bells to ring, buttons to push, and barrels to spin. He will also delight in emptying and filling containers and would appreciate his own cupboard full of safe items.

This is a period when babies are particularly receptive to music and will show visible delight in favorite songs that you sing or have on records or tapes. They become good mimickers and attentive listeners, and they really seem to understand what you say. If you announce that "Daddy is home!" they will register visible delight and may even say "bye-bye" as a greeting.

When not engaged in these "quiet" activities, your baby will probably be busy moving one way or another. Some babies are crawling with great proficiency by the end of the seventh month, whereas others are still in the practice phase at nine months. Babies have many crawling styles. One will do push-ups, either on all fours, or first on the front and then the rear, lurching forward. Many, however, crawl backwards to begin with. Another will lift his belly off the floor and walk on all fours with a stiff-legged, bearlike gait. And there are babies who never crawl in conventional ways at all but remain in a sitting position and "hitch" sideways across the floor like little crabs.

As he's learning to crawl he may also be pulling himself up to stand and beginning to "cruise," that is, move sideways as he clings to the furniture. He may crow with delight with his trick, until he wants to get down and doesn't yet know how to do so without falling. Even though pediatricians assure us that their still-flexible skulls are designed to take these falls, it is discomforting to hear your baby's head crack on the floor. A carpeted room for practicing is ideal, or you can lay down a quilt or moving pad and secure it with furniture so it won't slide. You can also help him learn to fall safely. Make a game of it. Bend him forward at the waist, then gently guide him down so that he lands squarely on his bottom.

Ironically, all the energy that goes into crawling, standing, and cruising may make the baby want to sleep less than before. He may have trouble settling down to sleep and may begin waking at all hours. Babies of this age are capable of becoming overstimulated by their own passionate engagement with the world. They don't want to give up the action or the people they love. Separating from you is painful, so do take his anguished cries and clinginess seriously. This is a time when consistent sleep rituals, including some extra quiet holding before bedtime, are imperative. One way to settle the busy baby is to spend some time with books. The physical closeness and one-on-one attention are soothing and reassuring (see the chapter on sleep, beginning on page 107, as well as the chapter on separation, beginning on page 165).

With each passing day, you will find that the baby is capable of getting into more and more areas of the house. He will soon learn to open and close cupboards, pull out drawers, and empty the contents of a bookcase in minutes. He is capable of discovering hazards you may never have known existed. Get into the habit of checking the floors every time you enter a room. And remember to hang your pocketbook and/or briefcase on a high hook. His fine-motor skills will be developed enough so that he can pick up the tiniest and most delectable bits of dust, dirt, paper clips, coins, etc., all of which will still go right into the mouth.

These are the same skills he needs for self-feeding, which he will be able to do with greater and greater efficiency from now on. There are babies who insist on self-feeding and refuse to let their mothers feed them with a spoon. Don't despair. This is a great stride forward. Read up on nutrition, page 74, for reassurance and see page 81 for ideas for healthy finger foods. Do not be surprised when he begins to drop a good deal of his food, or anything else—cups, dishes, toys—from his high-chair tray. He has only recently learned to pick up objects with the use of the thumb in apposition to the forefinger, a gesture that has allowed human beings to surpass other species in our inventiveness. Now he is learning to let go of them, which adds to his sense of power. Look at the effect he has on the world when the cup goes crashing down. He's also interested in timing. How long will it take the spoon to reach the floor? He waits attentively. The sound the spoon makes, he soon discovers, is also different from the sound the cup makes.

One toy that young children never seem to tire of is water. Water play—splashing, pouring, filling, drinking, catching bobbing toys—helps the baby feel masterful. Water is also relaxing and may just calm him down enough so that he drops off into blissful sleep at the end of a busy day for both of you. From now on, if they haven't already begun a ritual of getting out by themselves, mothers need to take breaks to recharge. See page 165 for a pep talk if you feel in need of one.

Parents Describe Their Seven-, Eight-, and Nine-Month-Olds

Gabe is seven-and-a-half months old and loves the busy box attached to the side of his crib. He babbles at it when he wakes up at 5:30 in the morning. I hear the little door opening and closing, and the squeaker going, and the bell ringing. It keeps him busy for a little while at least.

• • •

Lauren's favorite toy at eight months is a rather large plastic ball with a bell inside.

• • •

Georgianna isn't as driven to move as her sisters were. At seven-and-a-half months, she sits quietly and observes the action. She has learned that she can get a big laugh out of them when she spits her food out in disgust. They egg her on, and she loves it.

• • •

Danny is eight-and-a-half months. We think he's very musical. He bangs on the high-chair tray to the sound of the radio. Country-and-western is his favorite.

• • •

When Jenny, almost nine months, isn't busy cruising around the coffee table, she loves to drop her big colorful pop beads into a tiny coffee can, then dump them out. She also has a fascination with our golden retriever and anything that belongs to him. Yesterday I discovered her crawling with his toy bone in her mouth!

• • •

My nine-month-old's favorite game is getting his father to let him crawl up the stairs over and over and over.

• • •

Jack loves the baby in the mirror. He kisses him and pats him and "ooohs" and "aaahs" at him. When we go to the park, I notice that he really seems to interact with some of the other "real" babies. He wants to touch their faces.

• • •

My baby shakes his head a lot, so much so that I called the pediatrician to ask him if he was okay. The doctor said that what he was doing was normal—feeling the power of experimenting with different views and perspectives on the world.

• • •

Thomas, who is going to be ten months next week, loves light switches. We can't pass one without a squeak from him. He has to turn it on and off and never seems to tire of it.

• • •

My nine-and-a-half-month-old baby, Matthew, likes books, especially ones I make out of cardboard. He can turn the pages himself.

• • •

I don't know whether to laugh or cry. My baby, who will be ten months old tomorrow, started to walk three days ago. She gets herself up and kind of lunges forward from the couch to the coffee table, then over to the bookcase. She reminds me of a little bumper car, one that is always just about to careen out of control.

Question: *Are playpens bad for babies?*

Answer: It is tempting to use the playpen to contain the curious baby at this age. But be moderate. Use it sparingly, when you must have a safe place to deposit the baby when you're getting ready to go out, or are unloading groceries, or have to run to answer the door and can't take the baby with you. If you go out of his sight momentarily, reassure him that you will be right back.

Babies from Ten Months to One Year

By the baby's tenth month you will be entering a period in which you will have few complete conversations with other adults during your child's waking hours. Those that you do have will be punctuated with "excuse mes" as you race off, heart pounding, to see what the baby is into now. You'll find yourself gasping "no!" when you discover that he's able to reach behind a piece of furniture and get at an electric cord you thought you had carefully concealed. He loves to use his index finger and pokes dexterously at electrical outlets if they are accessible.

He's also becoming even more adept at climbing and may have figured out that he can use the step stool to get up on a kitchen chair and then to a table and counter. He's a good imitator now and may have seen you pushing the buttons on the food processor. Obviously, this is dangerous, and there is no question that you must curtail such activities with a firm "no!" Continue to monitor your house carefully for dangerous places where a baby-size hand can fit.

If it is at all practical, install a safety gate up two or three stairs, so he can practice going up. You'll probably have to show him how to back

Gym and Swim Classes for Babies

Baby exercise and play classes are a growing phenomenon at local Ys and health clubs. Some are also offered through franchised programs with standardized equipment and curricula. There is no question that it can be fun to get out of the house, get down on a mat, and play with your baby in the company of other parents. But it isn't necessary. There is no evidence that such early instruction has lasting benefits. In fact, babies get plenty of exercise on their own. Think of the energy that they expend during one simple diaper change alone! Beware of any exercises or routines that purport to hasten your baby's motor development. These could be dangerous. Each baby is a unique and special person who develops at his own pace and in his own way. Be attentive to your own reactions. There is no need to pressure your baby or to compare him with another. Disappointment in his "progress" can subtly lower his self-esteem.

Swimming classes: As your baby moves out of the newborn stage, his bath may become the highlight of his day. Water feels good and can be a wonderful toy. His comfort in the water may prompt you to think about a swimming class. But before you sign up, check out the program carefully.

Though the goal may be to have fun, there can be some risks involved. Besides the fact that babies chill easily, they run the risk of contracting middle-ear infections from pools. Swallowing water can also cause water intoxication, the symptoms of which range from irritability and lethargy to disorientation, vomiting, and seizures. Mild symptoms often do not show up for several hours, and parents think the baby is simply tired from so much exercise. The water in pools where babies and toddlers who are not toilet trained swim may also be either polluted or heavily chlorinated to kill bacteria.

Do not be lured into an infant swim class on the grounds that teaching your baby to swim is a reflection of how responsible a parent you are. As the parents of young children, our main responsibility is not teaching them how to swim, because that is not what is going to save them from danger in the water at this young age. What is going to protect them is our alert and watchful presence. If you do choose a class, ask the following questions:

- How long is the class? Half an hour should be the maximum.
- Are there any submersions? A baby can hold her breath underwater but then may open her mouth, take in water, and swallow it when she comes to the surface.
- How clean is the water, and how heavily chlorinated is it?
- Babies chill easily. Is the water temperature at least 85°F?
- Last but not least, is there someone with a thorough knowledge of infant CPR on the premises at all times?

down at first. He may also be cruising with a fair amount of agility and at some point may fashion a self-styled walker by pushing a kitchen chair across the smooth floor. Some cruisers let go and stand without support for a few moments at a time or invite parents to hold their hands, so that they can practice walking. This prewalking practice can go on for several months. Though some babies do walk as early as ten months, stiff-legged with arms out for balance, most don't begin until their first birthday or later.

There will continue to be many falls and bumped heads, so make the environment as safe and soft as possible. Then try not to hover fearfully over the baby. Without meaning to, a tense parent sends the message that the world is a fearful and dangerous place. Rather than coop up the baby in a playpen, see if you can thoroughly baby-proof at least one room of the house where you and the baby spend time. Give him his own cupboard stocked with coffee cans, plastic containers, and some paper cups. The latter can be used as simple nesting toys. Show him how they fit inside each other. He may also enjoy dropping small blocks and other safe objects into a coffee can. As he does so, you can observe whether or not he has yet started to use each hand in a different way. For instance, he'll hold a container with his left hand while he fills it with blocks with the right or vice versa, depending on the hand that he is now beginning to favor.

Another somewhat frustrating development can be that your baby, whose idea of bliss might once have been quietly taking in the excitement at the supermarket, no longer wants to be contained in the grocery cart or the stroller. He'll wiggle and squirm, attempt to stand up, and protest in what may sound like an angry tone. There is no doubt that this can be frustrating for parents, but there is really nothing that we can do except leave the baby at home with someone else

or adjust our expectations accordingly, and move quickly to get the shopping done.

Toward the end of the first year the baby's fine-motor skills allow him to self-feed quite well. It is good to encourage this even though parents worry about how little the baby appears to eat (see Self-Feeding, page 80). Experts reassure us that this coincides with a time when the baby's growth has begun to slow and fewer calories are required.

During this time you will also notice that your baby's babbling will sound more and more imitative of adult speech in its tone and inflections. You may swear that he is exclaiming over the weather or asking your husband to pass the salt—just as you yourself did the moment before. Another exciting development is that you may hear his first word. It might be recognizable— "Bye, bye," "Dada," "Hi," or "ball"—or it may not be a "real" word at all. But that doesn't matter. The important thing is that the baby is using language, not just to make a delightful sound but to communicate with you.

As she approaches her first birthday, be prepared for more testing and teasing behavior. For instance, she'll cruise or toddle over to the telephone table, then look at you mischievously as she puts her hand on the receiver. When you say "no telephone," she'll look at you impishly, pick up the receiver, and start to babble or even say "Hi!" You may remove her and turn around for a moment, only to discover that she's back at the phone again, clicking the receiver and trying to get a dial tone—just in case you hadn't noticed. Then she'll grin at you and say "no, no, no." When you distract her with a tantalizing toy, she will probably forget about the phone. But she may not and might have the first of many temper tantrums.

It is important to distinguish between annoying behavior and dangerous behavior. Then you

have to figure out how you are going to deal with the former because there will be a lot of it coming. Finding a balance between setting limits and "giving in" is one of the most difficult and challenging aspects of being a parent. The issue of who is in control will test your maturity and flexibility for many years to follow. Rationally, we know that the best way to get a child to cooperate is not through excessive anger, control, or "training" that may be contrary to his developmental abilities. This style of discipline not only inhibits pleasure and curiosity but also eliminates opportunities to master and feel successful. It's also extremely hard on the parent to intervene and control every moment. All that thought and energy could be more productively directed elsewhere.

Now, as the first year comes to a close and when the issues are still quite simple, is a good time to start observing yourself in situations that require limit setting. The best way to seek cooperation, no matter what age your child is, is to try to understand and appreciate what he is interested in and capable of at the time and gear the environment, the limits you impose, and your expectations accordingly. Sounds easy, doesn't it? Well it's not, especially if this isn't the way you were treated as a child.

There are many excellent books on discipline. You have a whirlwind year ahead! You'll probably be too tired to read very much, so I have listed only a few in the resource section on page 265.

P.S. Once the baby is walking, we tend to think of him as more "grown up" than he really is. Toddlers invite this in other ways, too, especially as they begin to talk and use their imaginations to play more like older children. They enjoy pretending to cook, or to feed a doll or stuffed animal a bottle, or to put on a hat just like Mom or

Dad. But at the same time, this newfound freedom and mobility, coupled with their growing use of imagination, can be a bit frightening and overwhelming. Many new toddlers go through another period of fearfulness, separation anxiety, and night waking. They need our reassurance more than ever. We need to let them know that they can continue to be babies for as long as they want to be.

Parents Describe Their Ten- to Twelve-Month-Olds

Danny is ten-and-a-half months. Give him the stairs, and he is happy. We put the gate on the third step and a pillow at the bottom so that he can practice. He makes a funny little hooting sound as he goes.

• • •

Sammy's favorite activity is to stand up. I now have to change him and dress him that way. Sometimes I do it while he is still in the crib because it's safer. I find that the best way to distract him is to play his favorite game: "Here are you eyes, where is your nose, where is your mouth?" etc. He also has a little nonbreakable mirror. He loves to look at himself. He'll point to his eyes, his nose, etc. He hugs the mirror affectionately, too.

• • •

We think that Jenny is destined for the stage—she is such a ham and a flirt. I have a big pink straw hat with a rose on it. She loves to put on the hat, then pull it down over her eyes and peek out coquettishly as she sings along to her music box, waving her arms, playing to her audience—her adoring parents. We clap and hoot, and then she claps and hoots for herself. Then her father puts on the hat, and we all laugh some more. She really gets the joke. It's much funnier when he puts that hat on than when I put it on.

• • •

Amanda has a big old blue leather jewelry box which my mother gave her. She loves to open and close the box and put her treasures in it and take them out. Her word for box is "boo." Her older sister will say "go get your boo," and she crawls away lickety-split to find it in the toy basket. She talks to the "boo" very sweetly and sometimes will lie down on her quilt and rest her head lovingly on it like a pillow. Her sisters were each attached to a special blanket. We think it very original that she has chosen a box to love!

• • •

Jilian feeds herself entirely now. She also likes to feed me, my husband, and the dog! I'm worried that she doesn't get enough to eat, but the pediatrician says that she is in the 90th percentile of height and weight, and not to worry. You should see the floor after a meal. I recommend that everyone with a baby have a dog.

• • •

Sarah is eleven months old today. She walks while pushing a chair in front of her, or when I hold her hands. She practices her balance by letting go of whatever she is holding onto and standing for as long as she can before thunking to the ground. She crawls upstairs easily and backs down with a bit less confidence. She also says "moo" whenever she sees a cow or when we ask "What does a cow say?" (she also says "moo" for the cat though) but has a "moo-ha" version for horses and is working on a unique noise for the dog. She loves to use a spoon. I put the food on it for her, and she usually gets about half in her mouth. She can drink from a cup with a spout but prefers to dump the milk out and play with it on the high-chair tray. She also loves to play in the toilet bowl!

• • •

Julie loves her baby doll. She pats it, talks to it, burps it, and sings to it, just as I do for her. She also loves her books, especially the photo album

Bedtime: A Pep Talk

If bedtime hasn't been a struggle before, it may become one in the last part of this first year. It's as if the baby, so full of zest for life, not only won't but can't relinquish his hold on the day. He can drive himself so hard that by bedtime, instead of being worn out, he has gotten his second wind. When a parent attempts to put him to bed, he protests to the point where the tired adult is tempted to give in and keep him up.

If he hasn't given up his morning nap, it may help to do so. Somewhere around the first birthday, most babies can manage to stay awake until after an early lunch. The trade-off is a grumpy baby in the late afternoon. But if you can somehow slog through this hard time of the day without giving him a nap, you might have better luck settling him at a reasonable bedtime.

Don't fall into the trap of letting a revved-up baby stay awake past a reasonable hour. It's not good for the baby or for you. You need and deserve a break and some adult time for yourself and for your spouse. If you don't get this, you will, with reason, feel resentful.

that has pictures of herself. Being naked thrills her and so does her bath.

• • •

Aaron likes his own cupboard full of my plastic Tupperware. He uses the containers like blocks. He's begun stacking two or three up, then knocking them down. He has a little wooden truck that

Early Attempts at Talking

The more you talk to your baby, the more stimulating this will be for his language development. You will know when your baby is really starting to talk when he uses the same name for a person or thing consistently. Though this word may not be the right word for the person or object, resist correcting him. Instead, go along with his imaginative choices and show him that you understand. Your pleasure and interest is just the kind of positive reinforcement that spurs him on to continue to make those connections between words and concepts and the things and processes in his life.

There is no reason to try to teach your baby how to talk formally. If you find it enjoyable, however, you can cut out pictures of objects, paste them onto cards, and look at them with the baby, or you can look at books together. Keep in mind that practically from birth, the baby has been attentive to human voices and has come to associate yours in particular with pleasure. Most parents, without thinking, keep up a simple running commentary on the action and objects in their household: "The dog is barking." "Whoops, I dropped the sponge!" "Oh the water is too cold!" "Here are your socks," etc. As you are chatting, the baby may also be touching the dog's soft fur, the moist sponge, the cold water, and the cuddly socks. This process of saying and "feeling" words over and over in their "real," physical context is what encourages language development. And so does the reading of books and talking about the pictures (see page 261 for some good choices).

P.S. Be sure to note what these first words are in the back of this book. Your seven-year-old will not be nearly as interested in knowing when he began to walk as he will be in his own baby talk—especially those wonderful made-up words that were part of his own private language.

---

he pushes across the coffee table while he makes a "souped-up-car" sound. He has two big sisters who never did that as babies.

• • •

At eleven-and-a-half months Jake crawls unbelievably fast, using his mouth to drag a pull toy by the string.

• • •

Becky is a year—walking, babbling, and opening the safety gates! She loves to put her face in the water and to play with a slightly deflated beach ball. She likes her toy telephone and is obsessed with opening and closing all cupboards and doors. She likes books, too, especially ones with raised surfaces that she can feel.

• • •

He has so many bumps and falls. I wish they made crash helmets for babies!

• • •

I have a baby girl, one year exactly. When people tell me that boys are more active than girls, I stand right up and tell them a thing or two!

Toys for Babies
Age Six to Twelve Months

Most of us make the mistake of loading up on too many toys before we realize that there is no single toy that will keep a baby interested for very long. When you do buy for the baby over six months, look for well-made, washable toys that your baby can pick up and manipulate easily with his still-limited motor skills. The best toys are those that illustrate cause and effect, i.e., the baby can make something happen to them by squeezing, shaking, pulling, poking, banging, or dropping them. A good toy will "respond" by moving, making a noise, or by changing shape or appearance.

Keep in mind, too, that your home contains many objects that are just as interesting for your baby to play with as those you buy from the store: pots, pans, and spoons for banging; plastic food storage containers or measuring cups to stack, knock down, fill, nest, or float in water; measuring spoons to jingle and clatter; empty cereal boxes to bat and knock down; juice and coffee cans to fill, dump, and roll; paper cups and cardboard tubes from paper towels; magazines; even paper bags and paper to crumple or tear make great toys. The light switch is a powerful example of cause and effect and offers endless fascination, as does water play. And of course you are the best toy of all when you play "This Little Piggy," or blow soap bubbles, or sing, dance, and act sillier than you've ever before allowed yourself to act.

A Safety Mirror

You may already have a child-safe mirror that attaches to the crib or can stand free on a dresser or changing table. A nonbreakable hand mirror that the baby can grasp himself will provide entertainment and distraction for years to come.

Small Lightweight Blocks

Blocks are versatile and everlasting. The baby will enjoy these for grasping, mouthing, banging, filling, throwing, dropping, and eventually building. The beauty is that these can be incorporated into larger, heavier sets of blocks that children love to work with.

Blocks

Materials

- 2 empty and clean cream cartons for each block
- tape
- brightly colored Con-Tac paper or magazine pictures covered with clear Con-Tac paper

These lightweight blocks will not hurt the baby when she knocks them over on herself, and they are very simple to make. Simply cut the tops off two empty cream cartons. Fit one cream carton inside the other to form a cube. Snip off the pointed corners. Tape the cartons together and cover with Con-Tac paper. If you wish, you can put something that rattles inside before you tape the containers together.

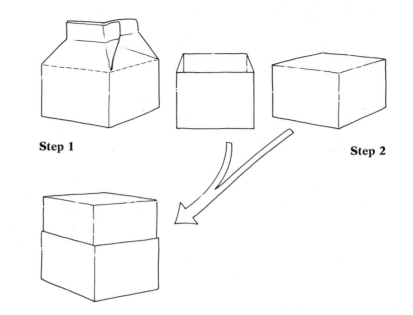

Step 1

Step 2

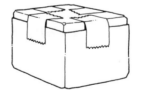

Step 3

Step 4

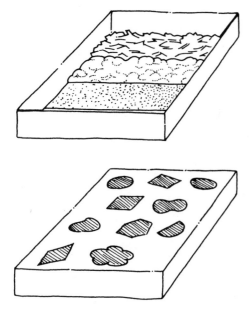

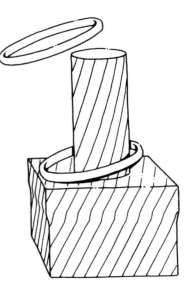

Poke-and-Feel Box

Materials

- a very shallow box, such as a shirt box
- tape
- glue
- a variety of materials of different textures, such as fine-grade sandpaper, cotton, burlap, velvet, or crinkly tissue paper

The life of a poke box may be rather short—the baby will soon want to pull out the materials her curious fingers are poking. Start by measuring the width of the box and drawing lines that divide it into four or five equal sections. Do the same to the outside of the box lid. Cut out four or five strips of different-textured materials, each the size of one of the sections, and glue them onto the bottom of the box. Go back to the lid, and cut two or three holes in each section. The holes

needn't all be round; use your imagination. Tape the lid of the box to the bottom, and give it to the baby. She'll probably figure out what to do with it before you have a chance to show her.

Shoe-Box Game

Materials

- shoe box
- tape
- Con-Tac paper
- assorted objects of different textures, colors, shapes, etc., such as a small sponge, a paper cup, a block, a piece of fabric, or crumpled-up paper

Babies love surprises, and they also love to empty containers. Simply cut a hole large enough for the object to fit through. Tape the top of the box closed and cover it with brightly col-

ored Con-Tac paper. As the baby empties the box, talk about what comes out.

Simple Spindle Toy

Materials

- small cardboard box with a lid, or a shoe box
- paper-towel roll
- assorted wooden curtain rings with screw-eyes removed; or inexpensive plastic bracelets; or rings made from pipe cleaners
- Con-Tac paper
- glue

Decorate the box and the paper-towel roll. Then, using the end of the roll as a pattern, draw a circle on the lid of the box and cut out a round hole. Place glue in the bottom of the box and insert the paper-towel roll. Show the baby how to

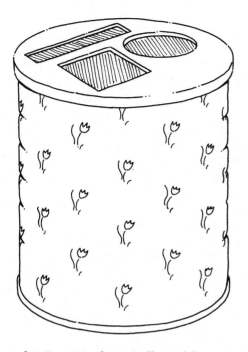

place the rings on the spindle and how to take them off. By about nine or ten months the baby will be able to use the thumb and finger quite well to perform this skilled operation. Large rings made from pipe cleaners are good to start with. When this becomes easy, make the rings smaller.

Coffee-Can Shape Sorter

Materials

- coffee can with plastic lid
- sharp knife or razor blade
- small blocks, jar lids, etc.

You can modify this toy to make it more challenging as the baby gets older. Start by cutting out a simple, largish square in the plastic lid. Show the baby how to drop a block through the square hole. When the baby has mastered this, take another plastic lid and make a slotlike hole for jar lids. Eventually you can work up to more complex shapes and matching holes.

Matchbox Toy

Materials

- a matchbox
- magazine pictures or your own creations
- nontoxic glue
- clear Con-Tac paper

Babies love to slide these open and discover a surprise picture glued inside. If you use a colored magazine picture, be sure to cover it with clear Con-Tac paper because four-color magazine print contains toxic lead dyes.

Oversized Pop Beads Especially for Babies

Toys that can be used in many ways inspire imaginative play. These lemon-sized beads are fun for mouthing, dumping, filling with water, and eventually assembling into crowns, necklaces, or strings or "tails" or "trains" that can be pulled.

Musical Instruments

Maracas, xylophones, tambourines, jingle bells, drums, and of course pots and pans and spoons are all good musical instruments for babies.

Simple Jack-in-the Box and/or Activity Board

The traditional jack-in-the-box with the little handle to turn will be too difficult for a baby right now. Simpler versions in which a series of boxes are "activated" by pushing a button, dialing a phone, or moving a lever provide the baby with multiple opportunities to practice different hand actions, as do activity boards or "busy boxes."

Balls

Balls are wonderful for babies. There are many to choose from—fabric balls, balls with chimes or bells or liquid inside, beach balls, tennis balls, etc. Beware, however, of any ball the size of a Ping-Pong ball or smaller—it is a choking hazard.

The Joy of Books

Your baby will enjoy cuddling up in your lap and looking at a good book. Talking about pictures stimulates language development, and it's fun! The first books should be simple, with brightly colored, familiar objects that are depicted realistically. But don't underestimate a baby's interest in action and love of slapstick humor as well. Nothing is funnier to a baby than a picture of another baby trying to feed herself or an adult falling down or dropping something—catastrophes that are second nature to babies. Here are just a few good books to read with babies in the first year. For more ideas as your baby grows, I recommend *The New York Times Parents' Guide to the Best Books for Children,* by Eden Ross Lipsom (New York: Times Books, 1988).

Anybody at Home?, by H. A. Rey (Boston: Houghton Mifflin, 1942)
The Baby's Bedtime Book, by Kay Chorao (New York: Dutton, 1984)
Finger Rhymes, by Marc Brown (New York: Dutton, 1980)
Goodnight Moon, by Margaret Wise Brown (New York: Harper & Row, 1977)

Toys to Grow On: No-Choke Testing Tube

Small toys are lethal if they are swallowed or become lodged in a baby's mouth and block the airway. This is a device that allows parents to test the size of toys and other objects (see illustration). An object that fits entirely or almost entirely inside the cylinder is dangerous. The No-Choke Testing Tube is available from a toy manufacturer called Toys to Grow On, P.O. Box 17, Long Beach, CA 90801. Telephone for credit-card ordering: 213-603-8890; for questions or problems, call 213-603-8895. The device is free with an order of toys from the company. Otherwise, it costs $1.

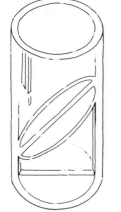

The *No-Choke Test Tube* is used by the toy industry to determine which toys are dangerously small for children under three. It was developed by the Consumer Product Safety Commission based on recommendations by the American Academy of Pediatrics and the Toy Manufacturers of America.

Toy Storage

A few baskets placed strategically around the house are good collection spots for small numbers of toys. Rotate them often. A set of low, sturdy, open shelves is also good for making toys accessible to the mobile baby.

If you are considering a toy chest or box, eliminate those with heavy lids that can fall from an open position and hurt the baby. Look for those with lightweight hinged lids with lid supports and holes that provide ventilation, should a baby or young child accidentally become trapped in the box. Be aware that a toy box can provide a step up for a crawling or walking baby. Don't place it underneath a window or next to another, higher piece of furniture.

Holes and Peeks, by Ann Jonas (New York: Greenwillow, 1984)

How Do I Put It On?, by Shigeo Watanabe (New York: Putnam/Philomel, 1984)

Hush Little Baby, by Jeanette Winter (New York: Pantheon, 1984)

Max's First Word, by Rosemary Wells (New York: Dial, 1979)

Over the Moon: A Book of Nursery Rhymes, by Charlotte Voake (New York: Crown, 1985)

Read-Aloud Rhymes for the Very Young, edited by Jack Prelutsky (New York: Knopf, 1986)

See the Circus, by H. A. Rey (Boston: Houghton Mifflin, 1956)

Where's the Bear?, by Charlotte Pomerantz (New York: Penguin, 1985)

Playgroups

At some point you may want to start a playgroup for two or three of your baby's contemporaries. The babies will make friends—and so will the mothers. When researcher Jacqueline Becker at the University of California at Berkeley studied nine-month-old pairs of babies, she found that they spent more time having positive interactions than negative ones. These included looking and smiling at each other, touching, vocalizing, and even showing a toy to each other. In the ten sessions held in a twenty-day period, the babies became more and more social with each other.

A group that meets once a week for an hour or so can become the basis for deep and supportive friendships and a chance to gain perspective. Who doesn't need to be reassured that you aren't the only frazzled person who wants to talk about teething, night waking, and when to wean the baby from the breast?

Keep the group small and rotate from house to house. This will give all the babies an opportunity to explore different toys and environments. Another added benefit is that your baby will come to know the other mothers. You can then comfortably trade off baby-sitting for each other.

As the babies grow to toddlerhood, you will need enough toys to go around. It's unrealistic to expect toddlers to share, so don't even bother. You may also want to extend your hours and include time for a snack, an outing in the neighborhood, or a dip in the wading pool in hot weather.

Miscellaneous Baby Equipment

Baby Walkers

A baby walker can provide diversion, an upright point of view, and mobility for the baby who can sit up and use his toes and feet to scoot the device about. Like playpens, however, walkers are really for a parent's benefit—to contain or divert the baby, rather than to provide the baby with a "developmentally appropriate" experience. Despite what manufacturers say on the packaging, a walker will not help your baby to walk any faster than he is meant to walk. Walkers actually demand the use of an entirely different set of leg and back movements than those required for crawling or balancing on two feet. When your baby is in a walker, he is not moving freely down on the floor where he can practice his prewalking skills. For this reason alone, walkers should be used in moderation.

Parents should also know that walkers can be dangerous, so much so that the Canadian Pediatric Society has asked for a ban on sales in their country. The Consumer Product Safety Commission reports that more than 24,000 babies are injured each year in these devices, making them among the most hazardous of baby products. They can catch on door sills and tip over; trap, and in some cases even amputate, tiny fingers and hands; careen down stairs; and bump into hot stoves and space heaters.

If you decide to buy a walker, make sure that it is stable. Look for a wide wheel base and a model that carries the label *Certified by the Juvenile Products Manufacturers Association* (JPMA), which means that it has met certain voluntary safety standards. Keep in mind that the spidery-looking X-frame walkers are not as stable as the round ones. If you must have an X-frame design, make sure that the springs and scissorlike X-joints, parts that could pinch, are covered and that locking devices to keep the walker in its upright position are foolproof. The older versions, often found at yard sales or passed on as hand-me-downs, don't have these safety features.

Making Your Own Books

Materials
- sturdy poster board in a variety of bright colors for pages
- pictures, including photos of family members including the baby—sleeping, eating, getting dressed, riding in the car, etc.
- clear Con-Tac paper (to keep pictures intact and ensure that the baby doesn't chew or eat four-color illustrations that contain harmful inks)
- nontoxic glue or paste
- hole puncher
- yarn for tying pages together, or looseleaf rings, or a small looseleaf binder (address-book size is perfect) so that the baby can easily turn the pages himself

How to Make the Book
1. Cut the pages to desired sizes and round the corners.
2. Paste or glue pictures on both sides.
3. Cover with clear Con-Tac paper.
4. Round off page corners.
5. Punch holes.
6. Tie together with yarn or use rings, or place in binder. Change pictures often for variety.

A What's-Inside Book
The baby who likes to play hide-the-toy may enjoy an "envelope" book. Instead of using poster board for the pages, use office-size manila envelopes. Paste a picture on the outside, and cover the picture with clear Con-Tac paper. For the inside, you can make cutouts of objects mounted on poster board and covered with clear Con-Tac paper.

What's on the envelope can correspond with what's inside. For instance, you might have a baby carriage on the envelope and a baby picture inside, a tree on the envelope and an apple inside, a hen and a chick, etc. The baby will enjoy fishing in the envelope to find the picture.

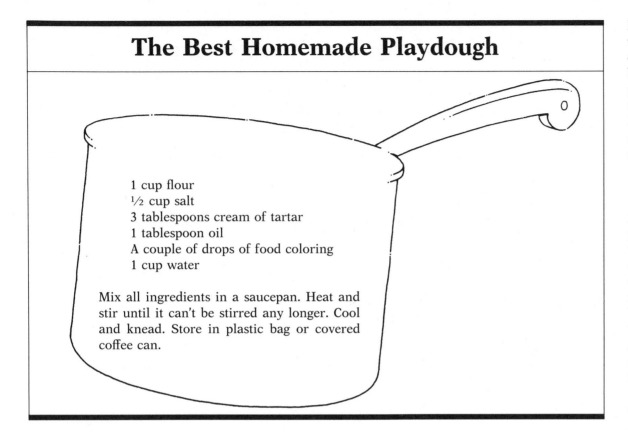

The Best Homemade Playdough

1 cup flour
½ cup salt
3 tablespoons cream of tartar
1 tablespoon oil
A couple of drops of food coloring
1 cup water

Mix all ingredients in a saucepan. Heat and stir until it can't be stirred any longer. Cool and knead. Store in plastic bag or covered coffee can.

If you do use a walker, never leave the baby unattended. Make sure that both of the baby's feet touch the floor and that the baby is strapped in with the restraining device. Don't lift the walker with the baby in it, and of course, make sure that it is never used near stairs or raised door sills.

Jumpers

Baby jumpers are for prewalking babies. They are swinglike devices suspended from springs or rubber cables that clamp like ice tongs to the top of a doorway molding or hang from a hook. The baby sits in a canvas harness or seat, with feet touching the floor, and bounces up and down. Some babies love this—not only the bouncy action but also the opportunity to rotate, and have a 360 degree view. These devices can give parents a chance to cook a meal while their baby plays. Other babies absolutely hate jumpers and don't know what to do once in them. One suspects that they don't like being confined and hung to dangle. Before investing in a jumper, it is wise to borrow one and try it out. Also, keep in mind that accidents do occur with jumpers when babies knock their heads on the sides of narrow doorways. It is awkward to put a baby in or take him out of a jumper. Accidents occur because the baby can be scraped, bumped, or entangled in parts. Some jumpers have been recalled because they had small parts that posed choking hazards. Like walkers, jumpers reinforce leg motions that are totally different from those needed to creep and crawl.

Playpens

Most parents have mixed feelings about playpens. They are useful for containing the baby when you have to find your car keys, put on your coat, and assemble all that baby paraphernalia in order to get out the door. But beyond this we recognize that they are bulky, not useful for terribly long, and confining. As one mother wrote: "We've hit upon the perfect use for the playpen. Julie hates it, so we now keep the stereo, with all its tantalizing knobs, and flashing lights, safely inside of it."

The standard-design mesh playpens with vinyl-covered lightweight aluminum frames, or the more old-fashioned wooden models, appear to be safe places to put a baby. But the Consumer Product Safety Commission estimates that at least 4,000 babies and children suffer from playpen-related injuries every year. The most serious hazard exists in mesh models with drop sides designed so that adults can stoop to get the baby in and out rather than have to perform a back-breaking bend-from-the-waist motion as they lift the baby. What may happen is that the busy parent can easily forget to put the side of the playpen back up. When left down, the side forms a pocket into which a young, still immobile baby can roll and suffocate (see illustration). Some manufacturers have responded to this problem by pro-

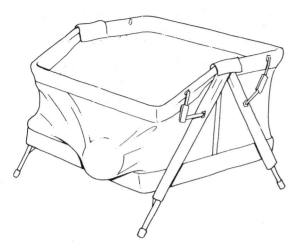

Dangerous playpen position: Baby can inadvertently roll into the side "pocket" and suffocate. Never leave the playpen's side down.

ducing playpens with sides that lower only during the folding-up action. Another design includes a rigid "antipocket" guard around the floorboard.

If you buy a playpen, look once again for the JPMA seal. This means that the product has met voluntary safety standards that require, among other things, that: the mesh be tightly woven so that no small fingers or buttons on baby clothing can become trapped and possibly cause strangulation; the vinyl must be thick and strudy enough so that a baby can't bite a piece off and choke; there are no sharp edges or joints that could cause pinching; there be a locking device to prevent a baby from lowering or folding the playpen side. If you want to buy a wooden playpen, make sure that the spaces between the slats are no more than 2⅜ inches apart. Playpens should be used only for short periods of time, and you should never leave your baby unattended.

Useful Books and Organizations

Books
Elkind, David, *Miseducation: Preschoolers at Risk* (New York: Alfred A. Knopf, 1987)
Fitzpatrick, Jean Grasso, and Rocissano, Lorraine, *Helping Baby Talk: A Pressure-Free Approach to Your Child's First Words from Birth to Three Years* (New York: Avon, 1990)
Roiphe, Ann, and Roiphe, Herman, *Your Child's Mind: The Complete Book of Infant and Child Mental Health Care* (New York: St. Martin's Press, Inc., 1985)
Samalin, Nancy, and Jablow, Martha M., *Loving Your Child Is Not Enough: Positive Discipline That Works* (New York: Viking, 1987)

Organizations
Association for Childhood Education International
3615 Wisconsin Avenue, N.W.
Washington, D.C. 20016
This organization helps teachers, parents, and care givers by publishing materials and an educational journal on childhood education.

The National Center for Clinical Infant Programs
733 15th Street, N.W.
Suite 912
Washington, D.C. 20005
This nonprofit organization aims to improve and support professional initiatives in infant mental health and development.

National Center for Education in Maternal and Child Health
38th and R Streets, N.W.
Washington, D.C. 20057
(202) 625–8400
This organization is a gold mine of up-to-date information on child health and development, and parenting. Call or write for their list of resources.

Dear Frances,

My best friend, who at the time had a four-month-old, gave me your book as a shower gift when I was pregnant. I read it at my leisure, cover to cover. When I was done, I called to thank her. "Did you like it?" she asked. I said, "Yes, I liked it, I guess. I got some ideas about what to buy for the baby." I didn't want to hurt her feelings, but I really thought some of the parents in *Babysense* were making a much bigger deal out of baby care than they need have. So many questions, so many doubts, so many adjustments. Just reading about it all made me feel exhausted. I thought, maybe that's the way it is for them. They aren't very organized or together. But it's not going to be that way for Chris and me.

Now we have Alix, who is seven weeks old. The only reason I have a single moment to write you this letter is that my mother-in-law has taken him out for a car ride, so that we can have a break from his crying. (I think she is worried about our marriage!) Chris is sound asleep on the couch in the den, where he's been camping out for the last month or so—along with the dog, the undone laundry, the unread newspapers and magazines, and a stack of mail that we haven't even opened.

My sister came by tonight to tell me she is pregnant. I said I was thrilled for her. Alix would have a cousin! Then I cut her off mid-sentence and raced up two flights of steps, through three closed doors, to pick up my crying baby. I know what she was thinking. What's happened to my sister?

You know what I'm about to say, don't you? All of you who have been there do. Until you actually live with a baby twenty-four hours a day, every single day, there is no way to understand what that relationship and responsibility really mean. How is it? Why is it? What is it? I'm so attached. He's on my mind and in my heart every second. I've been taken over in a way I never could have imagined. Isn't it hard, and isn't it wonderful and joyful and miraculous all at the same time? Will we make it?

I'm giving my sister a copy of *Babysense* though I'm not sure there's any hope of her "getting it." She'll have to find out for herself. Don't we all?

Best,
Lucinda Garvey, Kansas City, MO

• THE QUESTIONNAIRE •

Dear Parent,

Enclosed is a questionnaire on baby care, a topic on which you are an expert.

I am writing to ask for your help in the revision and expansion of *Babysense: A Practical and Supportive Guide to Baby Care,* by me and 500 parents.

Babysense first came out in 1979 and has sold more than 100,000 copies—a tribute to the diversity of voices and truly practical and supportive advice from parents like yourself. It is now time to update the book with what you know about living with a baby.

Babysense is a celebration of what parents have to offer each other. In the back of the book is a long list of contributors. I would like to add your name to that list.

Many thanks for sharing your Babysense.

Best,

Frances Wells Burck

P.S. I know your time is gold. If you answer only one question and send it back to me, you will be making a real contribution to a book that has proved useful to parents for more than a decade.

Questionnaire for *Babysense: A Practical and Supportive Guide to Baby Care* by Frances Wells Burck and 500 Parents

Return to:

Frances Wells Burck
41 Glen Byron Avenue
South Nyack, NY, 10960
(914) 353-3423

Please answer the questions on a separate sheet of paper. Don't worry about neatness! If you leave plenty of space in between questions, you can go back and add to answers as thoughts come up. Be sure to write down your name and address, so that I can acknowledge your contribution and remain in touch with you. Thanks!

1. I am interested in tips on selecting, saving money on, using, cleaning, storing, etc., any and all types of baby-related items and equipment. What should and shouldn't parents buy (car seats, strollers, carriages, back and front packs and slings, high chairs, cribs, changing tables, playpens, walkers, infant seats, bottles, pacifiers, bath aids, breast pumps, baby clothes, diapers, safety devices—you name it)?

2. Do you breast- or bottle-feed? Does your baby now take solid food? What questions or problems have you had, and what discoveries or solutions have you found that would be useful to other parents?

3. Are you able to figure out why your baby cries? How do you comfort your baby? Have you had to cope with colic? If so, do you have any advice to offer?

4. How does your baby sleep? Do you have questions or suggestions that might be useful to other parents?

5. Do you have any questions or tips on bathing, diapering and dressing a baby, doing the laundry, organizing clothing, etc.? What clothing is useful, and what isn't?

6. Do you have any tips for traveling locally or for long distances with a baby? Have you figured out easy ways to shop with a baby, or travel by car or plane that would be useful for other parents to know about?

7. Are you pleased with the health care you've chosen for your baby? What health and safety questions have you had?

8. During the postpartum period, how did you feel? What went well, and what could have been better?

9. How has motherhood changed you? What are the joys and rewards as well as the challenges and the difficulties?

10. How has parenthood affected your marriage—both positively and negatively?

11. I don't think men read baby-care books, but I'm not giving up! Should I add a chapter for fathers, and if so, what should be in it? Will your husband fill out this questionnaire?

12. How has motherhood affected your relationship with your friends as well as your family of origin?

13. If you are a working mother or a mother who stays at home, what are the rewards and difficulties of each? What questions do you have? What advice do you have for other mothers in your position?

14. How could employers as well as our society in general be more supportive of new parents?

15. I'm interested in what you have to say about all aspects of finding, evaluating, and working with different child-care arrangements, from the use of the occasional sitter to full- or part-time day care.

16. What do you know now about life with a baby that you wish someone had told you before?

17. What haven't I asked you about that you would like to find in a baby-care book? If you are familiar with *Babysense*, what do you like or dislike about it? How can I make it better?

Do you know anyone with a baby to whom I could send this questionnaire? If so, please include names and addresses.

Birth Certificate

Paste a copy of the birth certificate here. It will be important later for establishing your child's right to attend school, to marry, obtain a passport, etc.

(paste here)

Name _____

Date of Birth _____

Time of Birth _____

Place of Birth _____

_____

(city)   (county)   (state)

Height _____

Weight _____

Length _____

picture of newborn baby

(paste here)

Labor and Birth Experience

Use this space to describe the birth.

Record of Growth

AGE	WEIGHT	HEIGHT
birth		
1 month		
2 months		
3 months		
4 months		
5 months		
6 months		
7 months		
8 months		
9 months		
10 months		
11 months		
12 months		
13 months		
14 months		
15 months		
16 months		

Feeding

Interval between feedings as newborn

_____

_____

At three months

_____

_____

Introduction of solids   TYPE OF FOOD   DATE   REACTION (IF ANY)

_____

_____

Full or partial weaning

_____

_____

Fed from cup

_____

_____

Self-feeding with fingers

_____

_____

Self-feeding with spoon

_____

_____

Medical Record

Immunizations   *Dates*

Diphtheria, Pertussis, Tetanus (D.P.T.) _____ _____ _____

Tuberculine Test _____ _____ _____

Measles, Mumps, Rubella _____ _____ _____

Trivalent Oral Polio _____ _____ _____

Well-Baby Visits

Date: _____ *Report:* _____

Questions: _____

Date: _____ *Report:* _____

Questions: _____

Date: _____ *Report:* _____

Questions: _____

Date: _____ *Report:* _____

Questions: _____

Date: _____ *Report:* _____

Questions: _____

Date: _____ *Report:* _____

Questions: _____

Date: _____ *Report:* _____

DEVELOPMENT   Age of Baby   *DEVELOPMENT*

Lifts head briefly _____   Rolls from stomach or side to back _____

Rolls part way to side from back _____   Grabs objects _____

Follows objects with eyes _____   Babbles _____

Smiles! _____   Laughs! _____

Can hold head up for a few minutes _____   Puts objects in mouth _____

Grasps and holds objects if placed in hand ____   Splashes in bath _____

Bats at objects _____   Puts toes in mouth _____

Sleeps through the night! _____   Plays with rattle _____

On stomach holds chest as well as head up ____   Understands name _____

Enjoys being pulled to stand _____

Coos and squeals _____   Vocalizes to get your attention
(interrupts conversations) _____

Explores face, eyes and mouth with hands ____   Rolls from back to stomach _____

Vocalizes when talked to _____   Creeps _____

Rocks like an airplane _____   Sits with some support _____

_____

_____

_____

DEVELOPMENT   Age of Baby   DEVELOPMENT

Transfers object from one hand to other _____   Takes interest in books and pictures _____

Disturbed by strangers _____   Drinks from cup _____

Loves peek-a-boo _____   Climbs on furniture _____

Tries to feed self _____   First words _____

Crawls _____   Points to parts of the body when you name them _____

Pulls self to stand _____   Forms attachment to security object
(a blanket, etc.) _____

Sits alone _____   Puts spoon in mouth _____

Imitates actions _____   Teases parents _____

Looks for hidden toy _____   Walks! _____

Crawls upstairs _____   Points _____

Stands alone briefly _____   Tries to undress self (shoes and socks) _____

Sidesteps or cruises along furniture _____   Gives up morning nap _____

Seems to understand "no"
or a few other simple words _____   Hugs you! _____

Plays pat-a-cake, so-big, waves bye-bye _____

_____

_____

_____

Notes, Observations, Questions, and Feelings During
The First Month

picture

**Notes, Observations, Questions, and Feelings During
The Second Month**

picture

**Notes, Observations, Questions, and Feelings During
The Third Month**

picture

Notes, Observations, Questions, and Feelings During
The Fourth Month

picture

**Notes, Observations, Questions, and Feelings During
The Fifth Month**

picture

**Notes, Observations, Questions, and Feelings During
The Sixth Month**

picture

Notes, Observations, Questions, and Feelings During
The Seventh Month

picture

**Notes, Observations, Questions, and Feelings During
The Eighth Month**

picture

Notes, Observations, Questions, and Feelings During
The Ninth Month

picture

**Notes, Observations, Questions, and Feelings During
The Tenth Month**

picture

**Notes, Observations, Questions, and Feelings During
The Eleventh Month**

_____

_____

_____

_____

_____

_____

_____

_____

_____

picture

_____

_____

_____

_____

_____

_____

290

Notes, Observations, Questions, and Feelings During The Twelfth Month

picture

**Notes, Observations, Questions, and Feelings During
The Thirteenth Month**

picture

**Notes, Observations, Questions, and Feelings During
The Fourteenth Month**

picture

**Notes, Observations, Questions, and Feelings During
The Fifteenth Month**

picture

Notes, Observations, Questions, and Feelings During
The Sixteenth Month

picture

What to Buy for the Baby

Borrowed Items

Notes on Breast- and Bottle-Feeding

Dates: _____

Dates: _____

Dates: _____

Dates: _____

Dates: _____

Dates: _____

Dates: _____

Dates: _____

Dates: _____

Dates: _____

Dates: _____

Dates: _____

Dates: _____

Dates: _____

Dates: _____

Dates: _____

Dates: _____

Dates: _____

Dates: _____

Dates: _____

Dates: _____

Dates: _____

Dates: _____

Dates: _____

Dates: _____

Dates: _____

Dates: _____

Dates: _____

Dates: _____

Dates: _____

Dates: _____

Dates: _____

Dates: _____

Dates: _____

Notes on Adding Solid Foods

Health Notes

Tips to Share with *Babysense* Readers

· ACKNOWLEDGMENTS ·

Arlene Aburemailen
American Academy of
  Pediatrics
American Baby
Alexandra Anderson
Barbara Anderson
Tricia Clark Anderson
Ann Arensberg
John Attardi
Maureen Attardi
Glen Austin
Rosalie Hall Austin
Jonathan Ayres
Baby Talk
Dabney Bankert
Judd Bankert
Ann Banks
Nancy Banks
Basic Trust, Inc.
Jenny Wells Bealke
Lin Bealke
Walter Benoist
Florence Benson
Jay Benson
Joel Berman

Carl Bernstein
Lynn Berry
Isabel Hall Biesterfeld
Elizabeth Bing
Marilyn Bittman
Sam Bittman
Evelyn Blatz
The Blessings Corp.
Rosemarie Bone
Mona Boyer
Marie Brandmaier
Doris Bratton
Larry Bratton
April Kingsberry Brookes
Brooklyn Botanical Gardens
Judy Brown
Michael Dennis Browne
Betty Bufano
Gilbert Burck
Mildred Burck
Robert Burck
Kari Burke
Eslida Buxbaum
Robert Buxbaum
Kathy Caffery

Pat Caffery
Julie Anne Callahan
Kevin Callahan
Cathy Carmany
Dorothy Carpenter
Freida Catton
Peter Center
Sue Center
Jim Charlton
Debra Chase
Mrs. Mead Cherili
Diane Churchill
Tammy E. Clark
Marilyn Clayton
John Clemens
Andrea Connolly
L. K. L. Conrad
Cris Cory
Charlie Clagget
Katie Mullins Clagget
Clarkstown Pediatric
Diane Clawson
Jessie Cochran
Columbia University Institute of
  Human Nutrition

Columbia University School of
  Social Work
Kathleen Cox
Jane Larkin Crain
John Crain
Tracy Strike Crocker
Terese Croft
Brenda Daly
Mary Danko
Debra B. Darvick
Nelly Davila
Jane Dickson
Anna Jo Dubow
Dick Dubow
Robert Duffy
Sara Duffy
Mary Dunne
Tom Dunne
Sue Dzamba
Lynn Eakin
Ann Prewitt Eaton
Barbara Einsig
Jerry Eisner
Marilyn Eisner
Jody Elmer

Carolyn Ennis
Mrs. Dart W. Everett
Dart W. Everett
Linda Fagen
The Family Center at Bank Street College
Penny Feder
Dick Feinberg
Pamela Feinberg
Kathleen M. Fellin
Roz Field
Sheri Field
Alan Finger
Marie Finamore
Karen Finger
Maralyn Fischer
Beth Fitzpatrick
George Fitzpatrick
Mary Foss
Bill Frerichs
Linda Frommer
Ellen Galinsky
Norman Galinsky
Carol Garber
Beverly Garsman
Jay Garsman
George Gill
Joyce Gluck
Ronnie Gluck
Robert Goell
Dawn Goetz
Ethel Perry Good
Fred Good
Good Housekeeping Institute
Charlie Goodrich
Marian Goodrich
Joann Hughes Goodwin
Ridgeway Goodwin
Francine Gordon
Steve Gordon
Margaret Grace

Ann Dinsmore Gralnek
Judy Wells Gray
Diane Grayshan
Bob Greenblatt
Prue Glass Greenblatt
Jean Griffin
Rosaura Griffin
Kate Grimes
Debbie Gross
Dick Grossman
Adrianna Burck Grudem
Michael Gruen
Vanessa Gruen
Inez Grundy
Edith Gwathmy
Jane Hall
Debbie Harding
Judy Hardy
Mike Hardy
Susan Harman
Carol A. Hayter
Harriette Heller
Annette Hollander
Cheryl Holtzman
Pud Houstoun
Harriet Hudson
Maria Huffman
Meredith Hughes
Tom Hughes
Caroline Hull
Renwick Hull
Nancy Ilgenfritz
Bob Ingram
Mary Lightburn Ingram
Katie Isseler
Bram Jelin
Margie Jelin
Lorraine Johnson
Judy Johnston
Virginia Green Jordan
Peggy Jory

Terry Jory
Barbara Joseph
Steve Joseph
Judy Justad
Julaine Kammeath
Barbara Keil
Bonnie Kelly
Chris Kelly
Jean Kelly
Carolyn Kent
Peggy Killmer
Jack King
Paula King
Murray Kiok
Susan Shapiro Kiok
Lisa Kirk
Jill Kneerim
Al Kramer
John Krance
Martha Krance
Doris Kreibich
Robbyn Kreigsman
Patricia Kruska
Bette Lacina
Ivan Lacina
La Leche League
Mary Suzanne Lamont
Jane Lattes
Danny Lauffer
Susan Lauffer
Mel Layton
Adrian Leaf
E. J. Lee
Debra Levin
Mary Levine
Gail Levy
Bob Lewicki
Katie Lewicki
Pricilla Lewis
Janet L'Leurex
Marian Lizzi

Shelia Lowney
Dan Loyd
Lisa Loyd
Ruby Ludwig
Barney Lyles
Wendi Lyles
Joan MacNamara
Eleanor Magid
Pat Main
Manhattan Maternity Center
Lorraine Manz
Randy Manz
Teddi Marsh
Mary Jo Martin
Linda Martinez
Carol Matthews
Becky Wells Mattison
Peter Mattison
Eric Mayer
Rochelle Mayer
Kathleen McAuliffe
Jill McCabe
John McCabe
Jane McCauley
Florence McCormack
Tammy McDaniel
Kathy McGuire
Lorna McKay
Kim McMullin
Lisa Mullins McMullin
Mental Health Association of Rockland County
Carmen Merrell
Elizabeth Metcalfe
James Metcalfe
Joanne Michaels
Swenne Miorca
John Miorca
Jim Morris
Lisa Reitnaur Morris
Ann Morrison

Carol Morse
David Morse
Eve Moser
Mothers Center of Rockland
    County
Pat Murphy
Sylvia Nassar
National Center for Education in
    Maternal and Child Health
National Organization for
    Women
Helen Nelson
New York Hospital
Patty Nickel
Mrs. George Nikolajavich
Una Nilsson
Carol Novick
Mary Roudebush Nowatny
Walter Nowatny
Lois O'Brian
Annette Duffy Odell
Diane O'Donovan
Cathy O'Gara
Joel Oppenheim
Susan Oppenheim
Denise Oswald
David Outerbridge
Lilias Outerbridge
Lila Pais
Esmeralda Party
Lionel Party
Jo Paul
John Paul
Kathy Paul
Yvonne Pearson
Debra Peterson
Physicians for Automotive Safety

Kathy Pike
Pat Pilger
Howard Posner
Janie Posner
Dennis Predovic
Marsha Predovic
Princeton Center on Infancy
Doug Puder
Lynn Putnam
Phillipa Quarrell
Amy Rabino
Maggi Rader
Bobbie Rappaport
Irwin Rappaport
John Ratcliff
Stephanie Ratcliff
Maria Rea
Beverly Red
Joanne Rich
Nelda Summers Richards
Margie Rivas
Virginia Robinson
Wade Robinson
Lorraine Roccissano
Rockland Council on Young
    Children
Jeannie Day Roggio
Nancy Rosenfeld
Shelly Kraut Rosenthal
Alice Rovleau
Pat St. Laurant
St. Louis Parent and Child
    Association
Mary Salsbury
Lucia Saradoff
Misha Saradoff
Judy Savage

Judith Schaefer
Rae Schapp
Rosemary Scharrenbroich
Glenda Schneider
Jason Schneider
Judy Schwartz
Leni Schwartz
Stephanie Schwartz
Keith Scott
Shawn L. Scott
Suzanne Stoessel Seitz
Carolyn Serviss
Tene Setje
Brooke Sheaver
Anita Shreve
Jackie Siewert-Schade
Phyllis Silverman
Judy Simonson
Mike Sitrick
Nancy Sitrick
Arlene Slingerland
Bill Smith
Daniel Smith
Genny Wilson Smith
Lorna Carrier Smith
Patricia Ann Smith
Suzanne Smith-Freeland
Fifi Delacorte Spangler
Special Delivery After Birth Care
Jock Spivy
Jo-Ann Steeves
Jill Marie Stocks
Katherine Stoessel
N. Stoneman-Bell
Derby Wixon Stout
Mary Summerbell
Strobe Talbot

Doris Tallyn
Ingrid Taylor
Janice Taylor
Richard Taylor
Diana Thewlis
Sally Thran
Janet Tingey
Arthur Tobier
Ann Tonetti
Barbara Torney
Eleanor Tracy
Michael Trazov
Nancy Elliot Ulett
Lauren Usher
Kathy Waterbury
Pearl Watler
Sheila Weiss
Fran Weixel
Frances Wells
Carol Wend
Ann Werdel
Leslie Werther
Brenda Will
Suzanna Willingham
Derinda Wines
Richard Wines
Harold Wise
June Wise
Mike Witte
Sally Witte
Bill Zabelsky
Leslie Zabelsky
Anita Zednik
Richard Zednik
Jerry Zeidner
Margie Lewis Zeidner
Karen Zimmerman

• INDEX •

Train travel with baby, 204
Transitional objects, 166, 206
Transitional stools, 244
Traveling with baby, 191–206
   by bus or train, 204
   by car, 198–201
   by plane, 201–204
   equipment for, 193–200
   useful resources for, 201
   what to carry, 193
TRIS, 122n

Ultra-absorbent diapers, 125
Undersupply of milk, 40–42
Urine function, postpartum, 134
Uterus, postpartum, 133–134

Vaccines, 228–231
   schedule of, 231
Vans, installing a car seat in, 200
Vaporizer, 232–233, 241
Varicose veins, postpartum, 135
Vegetarian babies, 73
Vision problems, spotting, 228
Visiting Nurse Association, 8
Vitamin supplements
   baby's need for, 73
   breast-feeding and, 35
Vitamins and minerals in foods, 35, 72–73

Waking a sleepy baby, 27
Walkers, 262–264
Walking, postpartum, 135

Weaning from the breast, 50–53, 84–85, 206
Weight loss after childbirth, 137
Well-baby visits, 226–228
What's-inside book, 263
Windows, safety and, 213
Women's Bureau, The, 187
Working mothers, 181–187
   breast-feeding and, 43–45, 49–50
   organizations for, 187
   transition into motherhood and, 143–144, 149
   See also Childcare

Yeast rashes, 240
Yogurt, 71

Additional copies of **Babysense** or of Frances Burck's **Mothers Talking: Sharing the Secret** may be purchased from most booksellers or by mail using the order form below. Substantial discounts on orders of ten or more books are available. For information, call St. Martin's Press, Special Sales Dept., Toll Free (800) 211-7945. In New York State call (212) 674-5151, ext. 530.

Order Form: Copies   Price

Babysense: A Practical and Supportive
Guide to Baby Care ($15.95)
(050569)   _____   _____

Mothers Talking: Sharing the Secret ($7.95)
(01069-9)   _____   _____

                              Postage ($2.00 for
                              first book, plus $.75
                              for each additional book)   _____
                              Amount enclosed _____   _____

Name _____

Address _____

City/State/Zip _____

Send this form with payment to: Publishers Book & Audio Mailing Service, P.O. Box 120159, Staten Island, NY 10312. Visa, Mastercard, and American Express accepted; call Publishers Book and Audio at (718) 667-6483. Please allow three weeks for delivery.

P.S. Enjoy Your Baby!